Chained to the System

Chained to the System

The History and Politics of Black
Incarceration in America

Arthur H. Garrison

cognella® | PRESS

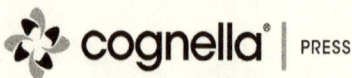

cognella® | PRESS

www.cognella.com   800-200-3908

As the scriptures say, "without Me you can do nothing" and "all things are possible through Christ who strengthens me." I dedicate this book to Him and all who supported me in its writing.

"Let the words of my mouth, and the meditation of my heart, be acceptable in thy sight, O Lord, my strength, and my redeemer."

Thoughts on Race, Crime, and Justice

Open your mouth for the mute, for the rights of all who are destitute. Open your mouth, judge righteously, defend the rights of the poor and needy.

Proverbs 31:8–9

Let this be recorded for a generation to come, so that a people yet to be created may praise the Lord: that he looked down from his holy height; from heaven the Lord looked at the earth, to hear the groans of the prisoners, to set free those who were doomed to die.

Psalms 102:18–20

In the 1950s Black communities were the most civilized communities in America. There were ties of empathy and bonds of sympathy. Unbelievable embrace of others who came in. Out of the seventies, we don't have neighborhoods as much as we got hoods.

Cornel West (2016)

Factories ... used to employ thousands of people ... Then the unions got busted. Workers replaced by cheap labor or robots. They locked us in ghettos and called them projects. The police stopped policing and let the gangs pump our veins with poison. And only then did the police return, in full militarized force to imprison the very addicts and dealers they created in the first place. ... This is what institutions give you. Neglect. Abandonment. Destitution.

TV series *SWAT* "Encore"
Season 2, Episode 13 (1/31/19)

To open the eyes that are blind, to bring out the prisoners from the dungeon, from the prison those who sit in darkness. Seek justice. Defend the oppressed. Take up the cause of the fatherless; plead the case of the widow.

Isaiah 42:6, Isaiah 1:17

The end of Law is ... to preserve and enlarge Freedom. ... [W]here there is no Law, there is no Freedom. For Liberty ... cannot be, where there is no Law.

John Locke, *The Second Treatise of Government* (1689)

Though justice must be tempered with mercy, it can never lose a sense of retribution or it is no longer justice.

TV series *Law and Order* "Kids" Season 4, Episode 15 (2/9/94)

The arc of the moral universe is long, but it bends towards justice.

Theodore Parker (1853) quote later made famous by
Martin Luther King in his Selma speech in 1965

What does the Lord require of you, but to do justice, love mercy, and walk humbly before your God? The Lord does not see as man sees; for man looks at the outward appearance, but the Lord looks at the heart.

Micah 6:8, 1 Samuel 16:7

Contents

Preface

C riminal justice in America is a story, and I wanted to tell that story to give context to why blacks are disproportionately arrested and incarcerated in America. This book grew out of my desire to write a book that incorporated how America developed with how the criminal justice system developed. I wanted to write a book that integrated the story of America's greatness with the truth of the injustice done to blacks and have a book that provides a context for the divisions and disputes on criminal justice policy in America today.

This book assumes the following: America is a great country because she is based on the great principles of the Judeo-Christian faith, the Enlightenment ideals of individual freedom, rule of law, and republican government. These principles are enshrined in the Declaration of Independence and enforced in the Constitution of the United States. Second, great nations are defined by the fact that they are based on great principles. Where white social conservatives and I part company is that I assert a third reason for American greatness: America has never lived up to these principles but is defined by its attempt to do so. While I don't run from the truth that America adopted and operationalized racism more than a century before it adopted the Declaration of Independence and the history of blacks in

America begins with blacks being brought to her shores for the sole purpose of serving whites and that history means something in today's rhetoric about criminal justice; white social conservatives dismiss this part of American history as a footnote to be forgotten.

As I discuss in detail in the book, I use the term white social conservatives to explain a worldview that has had a negative impact on blacks. This worldview formed the basis for states' rights and justification of slavery by southern slave-owning senators and Confederate leaders before the Civil War, southern democrats after reconstruction, segregationists under Jim Crow, tough-on-crime advocates in the 1980s and 1990s, and those who assert that blacks are criminogenic today. It's this worldview that asserts that the history of slavery and Jim Crow are of little to no consequence in today's policy making and political rhetorical landscape. To be clear, white, male, and socially conservative does not mean racism per se. But implicit racism has found a home in white social conservative orthodoxy. As an example of how I approach explaining race and politics and policy in this book, consider the difference between a white male who is socially conservative and the advocate of white social conservative orthodoxy that downgrades the significance of the history of slavery and makes black suffering under Jim Crow racism an almost irrelevant footnote in white American history.

When William Barr became President Donald Trump's attorney general, he gave a speech[1] at the Department of Justice's African American History Month Observation in which the theme was "black migration" to which Barr observed,

> The first Black Migration to this country was forced migration. It was the Middle Passage. Over the course of centuries, millions of Africans were taken in chains, branded with hot irons, and put on small, overcrowded boats for a treacherous journey to this land. That journey could take weeks or even months.
>
> In these conditions, many died before they even reached the shore. In a 1789 speech to Parliament, William

Wilberforce cited an estimate that one in every eight slaves bound for Jamaica died on the Middle Passage, and that one third died soon after arrival.

Slavery was our nation's original sin. James Madison himself recognized as much in a letter he sent decades after he helped draft a Constitution codifying it.

Writing in 1820 to his old friend the Marquis de Lafayette, Madison described the political turmoil that had resulted from the inexcusable tolerance of slavery as "the dreadful fruitfulness of the original sin of the African trade."

It took the bloodiest war in American history and three constitutional amendments to finally end slavery and to give African-Americans the freedom to migrate where they chose.

....

President Lincoln may have signed the emancipation proclamation more than 150 years ago, but there is a great deal of work left to do in eradicating prejudice and bringing together the people of this nation.

Much of that work falls to the Department of Justice.

One of the reasons that this Department was created in the first place was to help protect the civil rights of African-Americans in the South and to fight the very same persecution that helped cause the Great Migration.

Note how Barr, no soft-hearted, weak-kneed liberal, acknowledged the racism that was the seed of blacks coming to America and the policy legacy that it created: first President Lincoln and the Civil War and then the Department of Justice. Compare that to Trump's second chief of staff, John Kelly, when discussing the history of the Civil War with white social conservative orthodoxy champion Laura Ingraham on the inauguration of her show, *The Ingraham Angle*, on Fox News.[2] During the interview, Kelly was asked about a local church removing a sign that memorialized that George Washington and General Robert E. Lee were members. Kelly said,

Well, history's history. And there are certain things in history that were not so good and other things that were very, very good.

I think we make a mistake, though, and as a society, and certainly as individuals, when we take what is today accepted as right and wrong and go back 100, 200, 300 years or more and say, "What Christopher Columbus did was wrong."

Ah, you know 500 years later, it's inconceivable to me that you would take what we think now and apply it back then. I think it's just very, very dangerous. It shows you just how much of a lack of appreciation of history and what history is.

I would tell you that Robert E. Lee was an honorable man. He was a man that gave up his country to fight for his state, which in 150 years ago was more important than country. It was always loyalty to state first back in those days. Now it's different today. But the lack of an ability to compromise led to the Civil War, and men and women of good faith on both sides made their stand where their conscience had them make their stand.

But even more blunt was white social conservative orthodoxy champion Dennis Prager who asserted with absolute moral certainty,

I love this country. I think having been to 130 countries has made me aware, from, but it did from a very early age, I knew it was special. You have to compare America to other places. You can't, you can't, do what the left does and compare America to some utopian dream. "You know America allowed slavery." Yes, America did allow slavery. But America abolished slavery too. And since every country on earth allowed slavery, the question is not who allowed slavery it's who abolished slavery. And had America abolished slavery at the outset there wouldn't

have been a United States of America to do all the good
that it has done. Because America would not have incorporated the southern colonies if it had abolished slavery
from the beginning.[3]

To Kelly, the Civil War was about the inability of men to compromise, and to Prager, slavery based on skin color has no relation at
all to the greatness of a nation said to be founded on individual
liberty and freedom. Just as a side note, in Chapter 4, I discuss
how white social conservative rhetoric and narratives regarding the
Civil War and the distinction in using the word America versus
Union provides an explanation for how white social conservatives
like Kelly and Ingraham can defend and honor the generals who
fought for the right to own black slaves.

To Prager, what's the big deal about slavery anyway? White social
conservative orthodoxy asserts that slavery, at worse, was "wrong"
but was necessary. But to General Barr it was evil, period. As Prager
makes clear, slavery was not an original sin to be ashamed of. Why?
Every nation on the planet throughout history had slaves, so what's
the big deal? White social conservatives like Prager assert that the
significant history of America during the colonial and postcolonial
era was the arrival of poor whites, indentured servants, who came
to America to find a better way of life and economic opportunity
and religious liberty. This is the true story of America. As to the
minor story of dragging blacks to America as slaves to serve whites,
Prager explained,

Half the people who settled the U.S., I don't know if
it's half it might have been more might have been less.
But it's an immense number of people who came over to
America came over as bonded indentured slaves if you
will, servants. That's how they got out of poverty. But if
you want to feel good about yourself you say no slaves,
same with America. Had America said no slavery there
wouldn't have been an America. The world would not

have been a better place had there not been an America! Okay![4]

Consider the white social conservative orthodoxy ease and lack of concern over the evil of slavery based on skin color when Prager admitted that whites in America at the time of the founding would rather have forgone the formation of America than give up their slaves. The point is not the fact that America would not have come into existence if slavery was opposed, but that blacks were so easily sacrificed as a price for the formation of America. The point is how easily white conservatives consider that price to be so little in consequence.

When it comes to race and crime, white social conservative orthodoxy asserts that race is explanatory to crime. Blacks are criminogenic. Consider the remarks of Trump acting director of Immigration and Customs Enforcement (ICE) Mark Morgan, who was subsequently appointed to be the acting director of Customs and Border Protection (CBP). On white social conservative orthodoxy champion Tucker Carlson's Fox News show, Morgan said that when he looked at Central and South American migrant juveniles who were captured and held at immigration detention facilities, "I've been to detention facilities where I've walked up to these individuals that are so-called minors, 17 or under. I've looked at them and I've looked at their eyes, Tucker—and I've said that is a soon-to-be MS-13 gang member. It's unequivocal."[5] It's that simple. Criminality of minority and brown people is self-evident on sight; it's unequivocal.

This type of dehumanization of people of color has a long history. As I discuss in Chapter 3, for centuries European Christianity was interpreted to support the enslavement of blacks as biblically justified and under European law slavery of blacks was lawful. For example, in the *Zong Massacre Case* (*Gregson v. Gilbert*) in 1783 the great chief justice Lord Mansfield held that the taking of black life was at best only equal to the killing of horses. In *Dred Scott v. Sandford,* the U.S. Supreme Court ruled in 1857 that there was no law regarding the protection of blacks that whites were obligated to respect. In defense of Mansfield his decision did not assert that as a moral issue blacks were less than whites, he stated that under the law they were inferior. Mansfield, unlike the Supreme Court, was no supporter of the institution of slavery. In 1772 Mansfield held in *The Somerset Case* that slavery was so odious of a practice that only a law specifically authorizing it could allow the practice to exist in England. Because there was no such law Somerset could not be held as a slave in England and was set free. The case effectively ended the practice of holding slaves in England and the *Zong Massacre Case* led to laws limiting insurance industry liability to pay slave ship losses in the international slave trade (The Slave Trade Acts of 1788 and 1799). England abolished the legality of English participation in the international slave trade in 1807 under the leadership of William Wilberforce, and later through the Slavery Abolition Act of 1833 abolished slavery in its colonies in 1834. The United States outlawed participation in the international slave trade in 1808. Of all the slave owning nations of Western European tradition, only the United States required a war to end the practice of slavery. All others ended the practice by court order, legislation, or by royal decree.

The significance of *The Somerset Case* is that it provided an additional reason for the colonies to seek independence from Great Britain.[6] Why? Because Mansfield's opinion that slavery was not supported by the common law and could only be supported by written positive law[7] was binding on the entire British Kingdom including the colonies. A case that questioned the morality, practice and legality of slavery was a threat to the slave system of the thirteen colonies. Parliament's refusal to pass legislation to affirm the legality of slavery coming off the attempts by England to tax the colonies between 1763–1770 and May 1773–June 1774 led to the Virginia General Assembly passage of the *Virginia Resolutions Establishing A Committee of Correspondence* (March 12, 1773) which led to the formation of the Continental Congress in September 1774.

The *Zong Massacre Case* was reflective of Eighteenth-century unquestioned presumption regarding the little inherent value in the lives of blacks. Mansfield wrote that killing blacks was, at best, no more wrong than killing horses without justification. His opinion was not an anomaly of history and this dehumanization of blacks in which they were inferior to whites under the law would last for centuries and this long history has contemporary policy implications. As I discuss throughout this book, rhetoric and narratives regarding race produces policy outputs and outcomes. Consider the modern policy implications of criminal justice, discussed in Chapter 7, in light of the recorded conversation[8] between Governor Ronald Reagan and President Nixon in 1971 when Reagan was commenting on African support for China in the United Nations (U.N.) which conflicted with U.S. policy.[9] Reagan asserted that the U.N. was "morally bankrupt" and was "nothing but a debating society." He suggested to Nixon that U.S. policy should be that it would not vote in the U.N. and would not be subject to U.N. votes since leaving the U.N. altogether was not politically practical, although more desirable.[10] After which he complained about African support for seating China rather than Taiwan at the U.N., he said, "To see those, those monkeys from those African countries, damn them, they're still uncomfortable wearing shoes." Nixon laughed and affirmed observing, "and then they—the tail wags the dog there, doesn't it? The tail wags the dog."[11]

So said the authors of the get-tough-on-crime, war-on-drugs, states'-rights, due-process-in-criminal-justice opposing, southern-strategy policies of the 1970s and 1980s. How much easier is it to initiate policies that incarcerate blacks and marginalize them when they are dehumanized to the level of monkeys who barely can handle shoes and have the nerve to participate in international policy—they are the tail wagging the dog. As discussed in Chapter 7, John Ehrlichman, Nixon's senior policy advisor, made it clear that the purpose of the war on drugs was to associate "blacks with heroin" on the national news in order to discredit them and disrupt their communities to marginalize them politically.

Note the significance of all these views. The racism and the history that Barr recognized is of little account to Kelly and of no account at all to Prager. At least CBP Director Morgan was honest when he said that migrants from South and Central America are criminals by definition. This approach to making black pain and injustice irrelevant in the scheme of things is highlighted in the debate over the Confederate flag and monuments of Confederate generals. In Chapter 4, I explore and explain why the defense of Confederate generals and discounting the history of slavery is orthodoxy for white social conservatives and how it's used to downplay the significance of what America fought against in the Civil War. My point is that this orthodoxy provides a home for the racism that supported explicit advocacy that blacks are inferior and were intended to be slaves and the modern implicit racism that provides emotional and policy justification for disproportionate black incarceration that ruled the politics of the 1970s through the first decade of the following century. In this book, I expose these types of subtleties in American political rhetoric and policy.

This book is written in a conversational—sometimes augmentative—approach to ask, why are blacks disproportionately arrested and incarcerated? The rhetoric of states' rights, individual responsibility, black inferiority, white supremacy—these two are not the same thing—along with the policies of involuntary servitude, slavery, the great society, and interpretation of the Fourth, the Fourteenth, and the Thirteenth Amendments all provide answers to that question.

It is my hope that you, the reader, will gain from this book an appreciation of how American political and social history provides a backdrop to the developmental history of American criminal justice and, within that context, why blacks are disproportionally incarcerated in it. My goal is to make clear that the answers to the primary question are not as simple as white social conservative orthodoxy asserts. Blacks are not criminogenic. My hope is to open the readers' eyes to how politics is born from rhetoric and narratives of what is believed to be true. In a fully functional constitutional republic like America, policy is born from the politics of elections, which reflect proposed and competing rhetorical political narratives. In America, it matters who wins presidential elections. From those elections and the political values that prevail come Supreme Court Justices and lower federal judges and legislation that becomes the foundation of federal policy that is followed and adopted by the states.

How this dynamic of politics, policy, and perceptions (treatment) of blacks has functioned, from 1619 and the slave laws that followed in the 1700s all the way to the get tough on crime laws of the 1980s and 1990s, all provide a context for why and how blacks view the criminal justice system as suspect. It's this story that I wanted to tell.

Introduction

I often tell my students that American history, in general, and criminal justice policy history, specifically, are a complicated mix of theories of why people commit crime, distinctions on what crimes deserve harsh treatment, who is designated a criminal, and issues of race.

The point being that American justice is best understood as a developing story parallel and concurrent to American political history. The goal of this book is to tell the story of American criminal justice with a focus on its impact on blacks in America.

It's without dispute that blacks are disproportionately arrested and incarcerated in America. It's also without dispute that blacks and whites perceive the criminal justice system differently. Blacks are more likely to hold suspicion of the system and are more likely to believe that it's discriminatory in its treatment of blacks. Whites are more likely to perceive the system as fair and just or at the very least not structurally discriminatory against blacks. The distinction between views is most often manifested when police use of force is discussed. The significance of the dispute is not in the different perceptions but why those differences exist.

It is proposed in this book that the answer regarding why those differences exist is in the history of blacks in America and specifically the treatment of blacks by the criminal justice system after the Civil War. The reality in how blacks were pursued for criminal behavior or accused of criminal behavior that was not true or how blacks could be lynched on the mere accusation of taking liberties with white women all provide a partial explanation. Modern treatment of blacks after the civil rights movement of the 1960s involved the use of federal government law enforcement to incarcerate blacks for what was up until then local criminal activity for local prosecutors to handle. The rise of the Drug Enforcement Agency and later the war on drugs in the 1970s followed by the 100:1 crack to powder cocaine and mandatory minimum laws of the 1980s further focused black attention on the disparities of criminal justice incarceration.

From 1619 when the first blacks were brought to Virginia as slaves, to 1865 and the end of slavery, the purpose of blacks in America was to serve the needs of whites. By the early 1700s, slave laws made slavery a status that could only be held by blacks. Poor whites were prevented from working with free blacks on common economic interests. By the early 1800s, any shame that was attached to Christian whites holding slaves was abandoned in the South. Resulting from the rhetoric of Senator John Calhoun, the father of states' rights resistance to national government protection of the rights of blacks; Senator Jefferson Davis, president of the Confederacy; and the Supreme Court in its famous *Dred Scott* decision, by the middle 1800s, poor whites were conditioned to perceive blacks as inferior but more importantly, they were conditioned to see themselves as superior to blacks. That superiority bonded them to rich white plantation owners who owned slaves. During this period, the issue of slavery had divided America with no reprieves, and in 1861, the devil demanded payment for his dance. By the end of the war, more than 300,000 American soldiers had died to rid America of slavery. But racism was another matter. America from the early 1700s had adopted into its social psychology that blacks were inferior, socially, politically, economically, and genetically. While the North and South disputed whether slavery was wrong, in both the North and South, it was mutually agreed that blacks were not equal. Slavery was wrong but racism was truth.

A century after the end of the Civil War, racism endorsed by the letter of the law was abandoned. As a matter of law, blacks were now equal under the law. But equal in society, equal in treatment, equal in empathy—that is something else.

In America, social empathy and sympathy are reflected in political rhetoric, narratives, elections, and policy. In America, we settle what is important, who is important, and how we discuss what is important through elections. Specifically, we decide that through elections of presidents. Presidential elections are reflections of the political mood of America every four years. Unlike elections for congresspeople or senators, elections for president are national elections in which people reflect onto the candidate of their choice what they like or what they don't like or what they oppose regarding the nation as a whole. Presidential elections represent what Americans think about America and what they believe the nature of American life is or should be. Tens of thousands—at least that's what politicians hope—of people go to political rallies and stand in the rain, the heat, the cold, the snow, for hours, if not days, to see their values reflected and affirmed in the candidate running for president. They support the policies and hear the rhetoric that affirms their beliefs but more significantly, they see reflected in the candidate the policies they oppose. Americans vote for president based on how they see that candidate mirror themselves. These elections, in turn, create policy. This book seeks to look at how these sympathies and policies supported the modern development of American criminal justice.

This book is designed to look at how criminal justice policy was birthed, in part, from the larger political history of race and racism in America. This book looks at why race and criminal justice are linked. The short answer is that criminal justice and those who enforce it—the police—have historically been used as a tool of social control. Before the Civil War, policing in America was born out of the slave patrols in the South and slave catchers in the North.

Blacks, free or slave, feared the police out of concern for being returned to slavery or simply arrested and sent into slavery. After the Civil War, a system of involuntary servitude occurred in the South, which lasted until the dawn of America entering World War II. In this system of involuntary servitude, actual guilt of crime was tertiary to the imprisonment or forced labor of blacks in the South. Post-World War II, America's fear of urban crime, drug gangs, and later crack houses and gangs running wild fostered criminal justice policies that resulted in 51 percent of the total prison population being made up of blacks in 1993 and 1994. More significantly, it resulted in the social-political assumption that the disproportionate incarceration was supposed to occur because blacks commit most of the crime in America. This belief is orthodoxy in white social conservative political rhetoric.

Throughout this book, I use the term white social conservative. I use this term as a description of a worldview. The term is not used to assert that those who are white and are social conservatives in their politics are racist per se. I use white social conservative as a term that explains a worldview of politics that can accommodate racism without disdain or acknowledgment. White social conservatives, and black social conservatives who see the world through white social conservatives' eyes, can easily lack sympathy or empathy for racist outcomes and can easily justify those outcomes using nonracist explanations. When I use the term white social conservative, I am addressing how this worldview works in relation to blacks in American history overall and specifically how criminal justice policy was developed in American political and policy-making history.

This book seeks to explain how America, within 30 years of ending a century of Jim Crow, could easily and without shame accept the reality of its prisons being 51 percent black when blacks accounted for only 13 percent of the U.S. population. This result has a historical context regarding how blacks are perceived and that the 51 percent incarceration result is not an accident of history; it is the result of specific policies created over two centuries. But more importantly, it's the result of social choices and societal fears. Fears of racial, social, economic, and political change. The purpose of this book is to examine how this fear and resentment of blacks occurred and how it interacted with the development of criminal justice policy, as well as how white social conservative rhetoric and narratives supported the policies that developed as a result of these social dynamics.

Each chapter in this book is designed to integrate American history with the historical development of the American criminal justice system, in which the former gives context to the formation of the latter. Each chapter of this book is designed to walk the reader through various topics within the overall purpose of the chapter. Each topic, although logically connected, is separated by text breaks. These text breaks will be used to alert the reader that a new but related concept is being introduced. In an effort to fairly reflect the values and ideas of white social conservatives, I will use full and/or expanded quotations so as to provide context for countering arguments and/or showcasing implicit racial biases or explicit racism. At various places, these quotations will allow me to provide alternative and contradictory responses. In other words, it is my goal to engage the arguments made by white social conservative orthodoxy.

Chapter 1 provides an overview and summary of the policy outcomes of the modern criminal justice system and the political rhetoric and narratives of white social conservatism that blacks are simply criminogenic, and that's why they are disproportionally arrested and incarcerated. Chapter 2 follows up with research from various strands of social science and political history to refute the assertion that blacks are criminogenic and explains how crime is the result of social structural dynamics as well as social and individual behavior.

Chapter 3 begins my review of American history and how race and racism were implanted in the development of America and its formation of criminal justice. In this chapter, I review how the process of involuntary servitude replaced slavery and how the criminal justice system after the Civil War enforced laws that were designed to criminalize blacks and place them in a status almost equal to slavery. I also introduce how the concept of black inferiority was developed by the intentional twisting of the Christian faith to justify the proposition that God designated blacks to be the servants of whites. Although it is readily admitted that Christianity and the Bible were used to justify slavery, white superiority and black inferiority; it is asserted that there is a broad distinction between the true tenants of Christianity and the scriptures compared to the "white man's religion" in which the Christian faith was perverted to justify slavery by white Christian protestant slave owners. Although this perception of black inferiority and white superiority within protestant teaching was finally abandoned in the late twentieth century, the residue of this proposition—black inferiority—has found support in the development of implicit racism. A concept discussed in later chapters of the book.

Chapter 4 introduces the modern political rhetoric of conservatives and liberals and how that rhetoric defined both the Republican and Democratic parties in the 1960s, as well as how the rhetoric of both parties merged race (blacks) and poverty and then merged both to crime. In this chapter, I discuss how that merging resulted in the federalization of criminal justice in the late 1960s through the early 1970s. This rhetoric that blacks and crime are synonymous allowed for the policies of the 1980s and 1990s, which resulted in blacks being the majority of those in prison by the middle 1990s. This chapter explores how this merging of race, crime, and poverty gives context to how white social conservatives perceive blacks in general and both how and why they defend and honor the Confederacy. There is a rhetorical and narrative logic to how contemporary white social conservatives can overlook the fact that the Confederacy used military force to destroy America in order to establish a republic of slave owners.

Chapter 5 follows this development with a discussion on how the definition and purpose of American criminal justice has changed from the penance era in 1790 to the post-second punitive era of today. This chapter traces the development of criminal justice policy regarding the use of prisons, the development of the professionalization of criminal justice as a system, and how America has defined what justice is when defining it by outcome versus process. Chapter 6 focuses on one specific aspect of criminal justice that exposes the divide in perceptions of its operation: the police and police use of force. In this chapter, I provide an enhanced analysis of the *Washington Post Police Shooting Dataset* and discuss the limitations of the protection of the Fourth Amendment regarding police use of force. The chapter concludes with a review of various incidences of police use of deadly force and how the criminal justice system processed accusations that police shot and killed blacks without legal justification.

Chapter 7 returns to American politics and criminal justice policy to examine the modern policies of the 1980s and 1990s that resulted in the modern incarceration of blacks in America. In this chapter, I explain how the presidencies of Ronald Reagan and Bill Clinton built the modern foundations of American criminal justice policy and operation. It was under both presidents, one a Republican and one a Democrat, that America abandoned the ideals of rehabilitation and adopted those of incapacitation, incarceration, and retribution. This chapter reviews how these operating theories of criminal justice governed criminal justice policy for decades. In this chapter, another key player in the development of modern criminal justice policy is introduced: the Supreme Court. In modern criminal justice, the Court was a lead institution in the rise of the rehabilitative era in which the protections of the Bill of Rights were incorporated into the Fourteenth Amendment and made applicable to the states. By the middle 1980s, the Court had abandoned the due process model and adopted the crime control model that gave police expanded powers in crime investigation, decoupled the warrant requirement from search and seizure, adopted a disdain for the exclusionary rule adopted by the Court in the 1960s, and generally supported the get-tough-on-crime policies of Reagan and Clinton.

Chapter 8 brings the reader to the present era in which America has abandoned approval of building prisons at all costs and disproportionately filling them with blacks. During this post-second punitive era, American politics found acceptance that the policies of Reagan and Clinton needed mitigation. This modern view is discussed within the context of the policy disputes between Attorneys General Eric Holder and Jeff Sessions regarding how prosecutors should make decisions regarding drug charges and using sentencing enhancements to increase the total number of years a drug possession charge should entail. With the fall of Sessions as attorney general and the views he held, I discuss the return of rehabilitation ideas that found support under President Trump, which were built upon the policies of Presidents George W. Bush and Barack Obama.

Chapter 9 concludes with a broader discussion on how theories of black inferiority are still present through implicit bias in popular culture. Examples of popular movies, research on providers of medical services, and political rhetoric and resulting policies are discussed within the context of how blacks are perceived. In this chapter, I conclude that the policies of the 1980s and 1990s will not return, and modern criminal justice policies have readopted rehabilitation to mitigate the policies of incarceration and retribution. Lastly, although implicit racism is still a problem in political rhetoric and criminal justice outcomes, America has developed a more open-minded view of the racial injustice (inequities) of those outcomes, has abandoned the idea that blacks are supposed to be incarcerated—white social conservative orthodoxy and rhetoric notwithstanding—and has accepted the proposition that police use of force resulting in black youths dead in the street deserves more than a cursory investigation and assumption that the police were justified.

chapter one

Race and Criminal Justice

An Introduction

"Blacks, whether originally a distinct race, or made
distinct by time and circumstances, are inferior to the
whites in the endowments both of body and mind."

(Thomas Jefferson, 1781)

"The dangerous error ... that all men are born free and
equal ... had strong hold on the mind of Mr. Jefferson
... which caused him to take an utterly false view of the
subordinate relation of the black to the white race in the
South; and to hold, in consequence, that the latter, though
utterly unqualified to possess liberty, were as fully entitled
to both liberty and equality as the former; and that to
deprive them of it was unjust and immoral."

(Senator John Calhoun, 1848)

"In the opinion of the court, the legislation and histories
of the times, and the language used in the Declaration of
Independence, show that neither ... persons ... imported
as slaves nor their descendants, whether they had become
free or not, were ... part of the people ... included ... in
that memorable instrument. ... They had for more than a

1

century before been regarded as beings of an inferior order, and altogether unfit to associate with the white race either in social or political relations, and so far inferior that they had no rights which the white man was bound to respect, and that the negro might justly and lawfully be reduced to slavery for his benefit. ... This opinion was at that time fixed and universal in the civilized portion of the white race."

(*Dred Scott*, 1857)

"One of the reconciling features [of the] domestic slavery of African bondsmen, is the fact that it raises white men to the same general level, that it dignifies and exalts every white man by the presence of a lower race."

(Senator Jefferson Davis, 1859)

Our new government is founded upon exactly the opposite idea; its corner-stone, rests upon the great truth, that the negro is not equal to the white man; that slavery—subordination to the superior race—is his natural and normal condition. This, our new government, is the first, in the history of the world, based upon this great physical, philosophical, and moral truth ... With us, all of the white race, however high or low, rich or poor, are equal in the eye of the law. Not so with the negro. Subordination is his place. He, by nature, or by the curse against Canaan, is fitted for that condition which he occupies in our system.

(Confederate Vice President Alexander Stephens, 1861)

"When a man has emerged from slavery ... has shaken off the inseparable concomitants of that state, there must be some stage in the progress of his elevation when he takes the rank of a mere citizen and ceases to be the special favorite of the laws ... Mere discriminations on account of race or color were not regarded as badges of slavery."

(*Civil Rights Cases*, 1883)

"We consider the underlying fallacy of the plaintiff's argument ... that the enforced separation of the two races stamps the colored race with a badge of inferiority. If this be so, it is ... solely because the colored race chooses to put that construction upon it."

(*Plessy v. Ferguson*, 1896)

Regarding the United Nations, "to see those, those monkeys from those African countries, damn them, they're still uncomfortable wearing shoes. The tail wags the dog there, doesn't it? The tail wags the dog."

(Governor Ronald Reagan and President Richard Nixon conversation, 1971)

"You want to know what [the war on drugs] was really all about? The Nixon campaign in 1968, and the Nixon White House after that, had ... enemies ... black people [and in] getting the public to associate ... blacks with heroin ... [w]e could arrest their leaders, raid their homes, break up their meetings, and vilify them night after night on the evening news. Did we know we were lying about the drugs? Of course, we did."

(John Ehrlichman, 1994)

"Disfranchisement has a disparate impact on blacks and Latinos because blacks and Latinos are disproportionately likely to be involved in crime." (2019) "Even if you grant the 'structural and historical issues' [explanation], the police can't solve this problem—really no one can, because these issues are now baked in the cake—but the police in particular can't because their job is to enforce the law, not to engage in housing policy." (2018)

(Black social conservative appointee to the U.S. Civil Rights Commission by President George W. Bush)

"In the face of grave oppression and grave injustice, African Americans have built, strengthened, inspired, uplifted, protected, defended, and sustained our nation from its very earliest days."

(President Donald Trump, 2019)

I heard a white social conservative say in an interview once that history does not start today, and there is a past to America. I could not agree more. The quotes listed above along with others discussed in detail subsequently in this book provide a social and political context for the development of American criminal justice policy. The racial dynamics of American justice did not just start with the rise of crack cocaine in the 1980s or the Great Society policies of the 1960s. Even President Trump admitted in 2019 (see Chapter 9) the enslavement of blacks because they are black predates the drafting "all men are created equal" and "we the people." Black incarceration by American justice developed as a desired policy outcome for decades after the Civil War. History matters because it brings truth. Injustice can only be put in its place when it's acknowledged, as Bryan Stevenson correctly observed, "Truth and reconciliation are sequential. You can't have reconciliation without first having the truth."

In the HBO documentary *True Justice*, Bryan Stevenson, executive director of the Equal Justice Initiative, relates a story of when he was a child, he and his little sister went to Disney World. Part of the church trip to Disney involved staying at a hotel. Being eight years old, he had no concept of racism in public accommodations. So, when he arrived, he ran with his sister to the hotel pool. He had never been in a hotel pool before, and he and his sister jumped in and played. They were so excited that they did not notice the hell that broke loose in the pool. He said that he soon realized that white parents were pulling their children out of the pool en mass. When there was only one white child left, he looked at him swim toward him, but his father grabbed the boy out of the pool by his arm. Stevenson looked at the father and asked what was wrong, to which the father said, "You're what's wrong, nigger." Stevenson relates that he ran to his mother in tears, and when he told her what happened, being a typical strong black woman, she told him to go right back into that pool. Don't you let them chase you out. He said he remembers being in the corner of the pool, holding his sister's hand, and doing all he could do not to cry. He asked after telling the story, "What do you do with a memory like that?" What does he do with it cognitively, what does he do with it emotionally, what does he do with it psychologically. The significance is in both asking the question and then working out an answer. White social conservatives and black conservatives that see the world through white eyes, respond why do anything with it at all. Slavery and Jim Crow and back to the bus and no blacks in the pool is a thing of the past.

There are multiple points to Stevenson's story but consider these two. First, it created a memory that has lasted for decades in a man who graduated from Harvard and has won five cases before the U.S. Supreme Court on expanding protections of people on death row. No small achievement in a court not known for its empathy toward those on death row arguing racial injustice in both trial and sentencing procedures—a point we will return to in later chapters. But the other significant point is the question Stevenson asked regarding the story: "The question becomes: Do the white kids remember the day they were forced out of the pool by their parents because two black kids got into the water?" In the shadow of this eloquent question, I would ask, does America remember slavery and the system of Jim Crow emotionally? Does it remember it psychologically? Stevenson does! Black people as a whole do!

But more importantly, does it remember it politically? An even more pressing question is not whether America remembers, but does America care about its racial past, and does America understand—or want to understand—how slavery and the system of Jim Crow affects contemporary policies and politics? For example, as Barr correctly said, millions of blacks migrated to the North because of the injustice and terror inflicted in the South, and as Stevenson observed,

In Chicago, Detroit, they went to those communities as refugees from generational terror in the South. ... Without an understanding of that, we don't understand how to deal with income inequality, education, a host of other issues.

This era of lynching would not have happened if we had a legal system committed to protecting African Americans from lawlessness and violence. Our courts failed, the law failed. If we don't acknowledge that, we're not going to be much better in the 21st century.[1]

We will return to the link between Jim Crow and the failure of the law to protect blacks later in the book.

Stevenson's story provides a historical context and explanation of contemporary criminal justice. Consider the explanation given by another famous person.

In 1868, 35 of 37 state constitutions expressly prohibited excessive fines. Nonetheless, as the Court notes, abuses of fines continued, especially through the Black Codes adopted in several States. The centerpiece of the Codes was their attempt to stabilize the black workforce and limit its economic options apart from plantation labor. Under the Codes, the state would enforce labor agreements and plantation discipline, punish those who refused to contract, and prevent whites from competing among themselves for black workers. The Codes also included antienticement measures punishing anyone offering higher wages to an employee already under contract.

The 39th Congress focused on these abuses during its debates over the Fourteenth Amendment, the Civil Rights Act of 1866, and the Freedmen's Bureau Act. During those well-publicized debates, Members of Congress consistently highlighted and lamented ... the Black Codes and similar measures. ...

For example, under Mississippi law, adult freedmen, free negroes and mulattoes without lawful employment faced $50 in fines and 10 days' imprisonment for vagrancy. Those convicted had five days to pay or they would be arrested and leased to any person who will, for the shortest period of service, pay said fine and forfeiture and all costs. Members of Congress criticized such laws for selling black men into slavery in punishment of crimes of the slightest magnitude. [Congress concluded] "It is idle to say these men will be protected by the States."

... Alabama's aristocratic and anti-republican laws, almost reenacting slavery, among other harsh inflictions impose ... a fine of fifty dollars and six months' imprisonment on any servant or laborer (white or black) who loiters away his time or is stubborn or refractory. ... Florida punished vagrants with a fine not exceeding $500 and imprisonment for a term not exceeding twelve months, or by being sold for a term not exceeding twelve months, at the discretion of the court. At the time, such fines would have been ruinous for laborers. [As one congressman observed,] "A thousand dollars! That sells a negro for his life."[2]

So, wrote not a liberal historian or an advocate of prisoners' rights or an advocate of national power to address the evils of states' rights, but so wrote the *chief states' rights original intent* justice on the U.S. Supreme Court, *Justice Clarence Thomas.*

Justice Thomas was not alone in acknowledging the significance of racial discrimination in the history of criminal justice. As two recent appellate briefs to the Supreme Court observed regarding the denial of citizenship rights to blacks based on skin color,

Free blacks were not entitled to bear arms ... based on their status as lacking citizenship. "Free persons of color have never been recognized here as citizens; they are not entitled to bear arms, vote for members of the legislature, or to hold any civil office." *Cooper v. Savannah*, 4 Ga. 72 (1848).

Scott v. Sanford, 60 U.S. (19 How.) 393 (1857), notoriously held that African Americans had no rights that must be respected. It argued against recognition of their citizenship because it "would give to persons of the negro race, who were recognized as citizens in any one State of the Union, the right to enter every other State whenever they pleased ... ; and it would give them the full liberty of speech ... , and to keep and carry arms wherever they went." Id. at 417.

....

In sum, having no arms right was an incident of slavery. Even free blacks were required to obtain a license to possess or carry a firearm, and the license could limit possession to one's premises. Such laws were based on the denial of the rights of citizenship to African Americans.[3]

African Americans have historically been excluded from the rights and privileges associated with full personhood in this country. The right to a jury trial—and to participate as a juror—is no exception. Of course, enslaved Black persons were deprived of the rights of citizenship. ... [A]s Reconstruction ground to a halt, ... the states of the former Confederacy seized the opportunity to devise new ways to suppress jury-service and jury-trial rights as they simultaneously suppressed the right to vote. [Confederate and southern states] accomplished both goals by vesting discretion in registrars regarding eligibility to vote, pegging eligibility for jury service to that determination, and then providing by statute that selected jurors be of good intelligence, sound judgment, and fair character. For both voting and jury-service rights, registrars exercised that discretion in a predictable, discriminatory way.

Nevertheless, this Court failed to invalidate this suppressive tactic.[4]

In an opinion written by Justice Brett Michael Kavanaugh, a Trump appointee, the Court acknowledged this history, explaining that although the Fourteenth Amendment and Supreme Court jurisprudence had held in 1880 that prohibiting blacks from jury service was illegal, as a historical fact,

> many jurisdictions employed various discriminatory tools to prevent black persons from being called for jury service. And when those tactics failed, or were invalidated, prosecutors could still exercise peremptory strikes in individual cases to remove most or all black prospective jurors.
>
> In the century after *Strauder* [*v. West Virginia*, 100 U. S. 303 (1880)], the freedom to exercise peremptory strikes for any reason meant that the problem of racial exclusion from jury service remained wide-spread and deeply entrenched. Simple math shows how that happened. Given that blacks were a minority of the population, in many jurisdictions the number of peremptory strikes available to the prosecutor exceeded the number of black prospective jurors. So prosecutors could routinely exercise peremptories to strike all the black prospective jurors and thereby ensure all-white juries.[5]

Justice Kavanaugh wrote that in the face of this century-long history, "In *Batson v. Kentucky*, 476 U. S. 79 (1986), this Court ruled that a State may not discriminate on the basis of race when exercising peremptory challenges against prospective jurors in a criminal trial." But, nonetheless, in the prosecution of Flowers

> in the six trials combined, the State employed its peremptory challenges to strike 41 of the 42 black prospective jurors that it could have struck—a statistic that the State

acknowledged at oral argument in this Court. ... Third, at the sixth trial, in an apparent effort to find pretextual reasons to strike black prospective jurors, the State engaged in dramatically disparate questioning of black and white prospective jurors.[6]

Justice Kavanaugh defended the prohibition of racial discrimination in jury pool creation, jury selection, and the role of the judge in the process. He wrote,

In the eyes of the Constitution, one racially discriminatory peremptory strike is one too many.

....

[T]he *Batson* Court rejected *Swain*'s [*v. Alabama,* (1965)] statement that a prosecutor could strike a black juror based on an assumption or belief that the black juror would favor a black defendant.

....

The Equal Protection Clause forbids the States to strike black veniremen on the assumption that they will be biased in a particular case simply because the defendant is black.

....

Third, the *Batson* Court did not accept the argument that race-based peremptories should be permissible because black, white, Asian, and Hispanic defendants and jurors were all "equally" subject to race-based discrimination.

....

The suggestion that racial classifications may survive when visited upon all persons is no more authoritative today than the case which advanced the theorem, *Plessy v. Ferguson* [(1896)]

....

Under the Equal Protection Clause, the Court stressed, even a single instance of race discrimination against a prospective juror is impermissible.

....

[I]n the real world of criminal trials against black defendants, both history and math tell us that a system of race-based peremptories does not treat black defendants and black prospective jurors equally with prosecutors and white prospective jurors.

....

Batson ended the widespread practice in which prosecutors could (and often would) routinely strike all black prospective jurors in cases involving black defendants.

....

In criminal trials, trial judges possess the primary responsibility to enforce *Batson* and prevent racial discrimination from seeping into the jury selection process.

....

The trial court must consider the prosecutor's race-neutral explanations in light of all of the relevant facts and circumstances, and in light of the arguments of the parties.

....

The trial judge must determine whether the prosecutor's proffered reasons are the actual reasons, or whether the proffered reasons are pretextual and the prosecutor instead exercised peremptory strikes on the basis of race.

....

The Constitution forbids striking even a single prospective juror for a discriminatory purpose.

After affirming that the purpose of *Batson* was to eliminate the general practice of using peremptory challenges to remove black jurors and that *Batson* rule applies to gender discrimination, Justice

Kavanaugh wrote that the, "Constitution forbids striking even a single prospective juror for a discriminatory purpose," and having found that the prosecution had done so at least once and that the prosecution had a history of striking black jurors in the various trials of Flowers, the Mississippi Supreme Court decision affirming the sixth conviction of Flowers was reversed.[7]

Both before and after reconstruction, it was a historical practice in the American criminal justice system for prosecutors to create all-white juries through law and then by the use of peremptory challenges. My point is this practice is not dead. In 2019, 33 years after *Batson* and 51 years after the end of formal Jim Crow, the Court—through the mouth a Trump appointee no less—had to tell the Mississippi courts in *Flowers v. Mississippi* that in America, under the Fourteenth Amendment, the use of prosecution peremptory challenges to create all-white juries is prohibited.

Justice Thomas wrote that the purpose and operation of the American criminal justice system, post-1865, was the systematic enforcement of laws and policies designed to incarcerate blacks and place them in a state of involuntary servitude in full compliance with the prohibition of slavery under the Thirteenth Amendment. So observed the same man who said to an all-white male Senate committee, to the cheers of white and black social conservatives, that they were engaged in a high-tech lynching of a black man.

After the Civil War, the states, through state law backed and enforced by local police officers and state courts, implemented an economic and political system designed to keep the former slaves in a state of near slavery. Blacks were prohibited from serving on juries,[8] from carrying weapons,[9] and states adopted non-unanimous jury conviction laws[10] to ensure convictions of blacks accused of crimes. Minor crimes, such as vagrancy and loitering, were punished by fines that the former slaves could not pay and were intentionally used to imprison them. But this system also had an economic benefit. After the slave-owning aristocracy lost their war of rebellion, they still had plantations to farm and cotton and tobacco to harvest. The need for large labor populations did not change. The available pool of labor, the former slaves, were still available. The problem was that the labor pool no longer could be counted on to work for free. This is where the criminal justice system came in. But understanding its entry requires understanding that slavery was, in fact, not totally eradicated from American law after Lincoln prevailed in the Civil War.

The Thirteenth Amendment passed by Congress on January 31, 1865, and ratified to the U.S. Constitution on December 6, 1865, had a qualifying phrase to its abolition of slavery. The great amendment says, "Neither slavery nor involuntary servitude, *except as a punishment for crime whereof the party shall have been duly convicted*, shall exist within the United States, or any place subject to their jurisdiction." Put simply, forced labor can be a punishment for crime after conviction. The amendment allows for the enslavement of the condemned.

In the post-Civil War era, plantation owners who needed labor would work with local law enforcement to have former slaves arrested and convicted for minor crimes, and then when they could not pay the fines, the plantation owners would pay them and the court would order the convicted to work off the value of the fine paid. A concurrent system of these Black Codes was criminal surety, in which a former slave would be arrested, and a surety bond would be paid to secure the release of the accused. The accused would pay off the bail by working for the plantation owner. One could ask, what did the court and local sheriff get out of this deal. Both took an administrative fee from the fine paid by the plantation owner. The criminal justice system, specifically the police, had a financial interest in making arrests of blacks—a concept that would be abandoned by the 1940s but reemerge in the 1980s as asset forfeiture.

This system of imprisonment and forced labor by criminal fines and bonds operated unopposed by the federal government—which under federal law was illegal and unconstitutional—from 1865 until the middle 1940s. Only when this system of near slavery enforced by the criminal justice system became untenable while fighting Nazism in World War II, followed by the era of the Cold War, did the criminalization of blacks for economic gain see the dustbin of history.

——————————————— ◆◆◆ ———————————————

Just because Bryan Stevenson and Justice Thomas remember how the American criminal justice system developed and just because as an academic fact this history exists without dispute, that does not mean that white social conservative orthodoxy accepts that this history means anything. To those who hold this orthodoxy, there is no link between slavery, lynching, police use of force, the Jim Crow system of involuntary servitude, the system of imprisonment and forced labor by criminal fines and bonds and modern criminal justice policy. And, as discussed in this book, white social conservative orthodoxy is not skin based—it's a worldview that can be held by blacks. According to white social conservative orthodoxy, history does start today when it comes to blacks, crime, and the nature of its functioning. Consider the enunciation of this orthodoxy in the mouth of a black social conservative.

> Unfortunately, "people of color" are overrepresented as crime suspects, and violent crime is more prevalent within the black community than within white or (especially) Asian communities. It may be that "White Americans overestimate the proportion of crime committed by people of color ... white respondents in a 2010 survey overestimated the actual share of burglaries, illegal drug sales, and juvenile crime committed by African-Americans by 20–30%," but that does not change the fact that African-Americans are overrepresented in criminal activity. The white respondents may have been wrong about the exact numbers, but they were correct in assuming that African-Americans are disproportionately involved in crime.

In 2016 ... 97 whites per 100,000 whites were arrested for violent crimes, and 351 blacks per 100,000 blacks were arrested for violent crimes ... 295 whites per 100,000 whites were arrested for property crimes, and 691 blacks per 100,000 blacks were arrested for property crimes. So in fact, black neighborhoods generally are more violent and have more crime than white neighborhoods.

The data make clear that whites are slightly underrepresented among criminals relative to their share of the population (there are, of course, specific crimes where whites are overrepresented), Asians are dramatically underrepresented relative to their share of the population, and blacks and Native Americans are dramatically overrepresented. In murder and non-negligent manslaughter, violent crimes, and property crimes, blacks range from 28 percent to 53 percent of those arrested, despite comprising only 13 percent of the population. Native Americans and Alaska Natives are only 1 percent of the population, but they account for 2 percent of those arrested for violent crimes and property crimes.

In short, the data make clear that blacks are overrepresented among victims of police shootings, but they are underrepresented relative to their overrepresentation in crime, particularly violent crime. 22.5 percent of those killed by police in 2017 were black. But 26.8 percent of all individuals arrested in 2017 were black. The report then shifts gears to acknowledge that yes, black neighborhoods have higher crime rates, but that fails to take into account "systemic issues" that are to blame. "The "black-on-black" crime narrative as an explanation for police excessive use of force disregards the structural and historical issues that formed these neighborhoods, as well as the social and economic factors that currently sustain them." Even if you grant the "structural and historical issues," the police can't solve this problem—really no one can, because these issues are now baked in the cake—but the police in particular can't because their job is to enforce the law, not to engage in housing policy.

The report then claims that the assertion that African-Americans are disproportionately likely to be involved in crime "is also problematic because there is not an empirically sound way to 'take a true measure of criminality within a population'" because the police are allegedly hopelessly biased. Then let's take a look at the National Crime Victimization Survey, which asks individuals to report when they have been victims of crimes and to identify the sex and race of the offender, if known. The NCVS captures crimes that victims did not report to the police. According to the most recent NCVS publication regarding offenders, which covers the period from 2012–2015, survey respondents reported an annual average of 5,883,800 nonfatal violent victimizations per year. The respondents reported that 43.8 percent of the offenders were non-Hispanic whites, 22.7 percent were black, and 14.4 percent were Hispanic. So even according to victims—many of whom are black themselves—African-Americans are over-represented among criminal offenders. The Commission report's approach however is, "Who do you believe—me or your lying eyes?"
....

This is important because since African-Americans are disproportionately likely to be involved in crime, they are also disproportionately likely to encounter police officers. Even the most law-abiding black men are, through no fault of their own, likely to encounter the police more frequently than white men. As Heather Mac Donald stated in her written testimony to the Commission, "This incidence of crime means that innocent black men have a much higher chance of being stopped by the police because they match the description of a suspect than white men. The police do not wish this; it is a reality forced on them by the facts of crime."

....

[T]he police are more likely to use force (whether lawful or excessive) against individuals who are involved in crime, and since African-Americans are more likely to engage in crime than whites, the police are more likely to use force against them. People who live in majority-black neighborhoods see the police use force against other neighborhood residents because those residents are engaged in crime, but they may not realize that the police do not as often use force against individuals in majority-white neighborhoods because fewer people in those neighborhoods are involved in crime. Reports such as this one that obscure the black-white crime disparity only encourage confusion on this point.[11]

This was the response of the lone dissenter in the 2018 report issued by the U.S. Civil Rights Commission that investigated disproportionate arrests and police use of force. According to this black social conservative George W. Bush appointee, blacks are criminal by nature, criminogenic, and that explains both the how and why they are disproportionally arrested and subjected to police use of force. History starts today. Innocent blacks who are stopped, frisked, and interrogated by police only have other blacks to blame. To black social conservatives like Bush's appointee, what does the history of slave patrols in the South, slave catchers in the North, Jim Crow, and the system of involuntary servitude have to do with black crime or police use of force today? The history of blacks and crime and treatment by the criminal justice system starts today. White social conservative orthodoxy asserts that blacks are stopped and arrested and incarcerated because they are criminogenic, not because racism exists. Again, I want to make the point white social conservative orthodoxy is not skin based. It was a black man, not a white man, on the Commission that wrote and asserted that blacks are criminogenic and disproportionate arrests and police use of force (contact) on blacks is the result of black disproportionate criminality. Racism does not require white skin to be racism.

The idea that blacks are disproportionately criminal is nothing new. From the post-Civil War era to today, blacks have been socially viewed as disproportionately criminal. The modern perception of linking blacks and crime in the American social and political consciousness began in the 1960s as a result of the summer riots of 1964–1968. The general public saw in the riots in urban neighborhoods—that's code for black neighborhoods—blacks, young black males in particular, running wild burning stores and buildings and only coming under control at the command of the National Guard. This perception became all the worse in the 1980s–1990s when the plague of crack cocaine engulfed urban neighborhoods with its corollary plague of unrestrained availability of guns sold in these same urban neighborhoods that supported unending mindless gun violence.

Reflecting on the opinion of George Bush's appointee, it should first be realized that in America, crime has always had a black face. Fear of blacks and their uprising dates back to the first slave laws of the middle 1600s to control the population of slaves that was soon more in number than their white slave owners. These laws prohibited slavery of whites. These laws specifically applied the status of slave to blacks and placed blacks outside of the protection of the law. These slave codes prohibited teaching blacks to read or write and prohibited the marriage of blacks to whites. These laws also prohibited the transference of inheritance to blacks born from the rape of black women by their slave masters (or their sons or slave overseers) and made slavery a status inherited through a black mother. All of these laws were enforced by the courts with criminal sanctions. With the end of slavery, whites feared this new uncontrolled black population. Black codes and Jim Crow economically, politically, and criminally caged blacks into a second-class citizenship that only ended as a matter of law in 1968. But this fear of blacks remained and found new outlets in modern criminal justice policy. A point we will return to later in the book.

As to the statistics cited by Bush's black appointee, the narrative that blacks commit most of the crime in America is derived from the fact that blacks are disproportionately arrested. The fallacy in this argument is that the former is not true, and the latter is not explained or defined by criminal activity. Arrest data is secured by the Federal Bureau of Investigation (FBI) and reported in the Uniform Crime Report (UCR). Consider the following.

First, according to the FBI UCR web page, "The UCR Program collects information on crimes reported by law enforcement agencies regarding ... violent crimes [and] all other crimes except traffic violations."[12] The UCR is not a measure of actual crime commission; it's a measure of police activity—making arrests—but it's used as a proxy for actual crime committed in the United States.

Second, UCR arrest data is a reflection of police investigations that result in arrests; it's not a reflection of actual guilt—it is not a reflection of conviction. At the stage of arrest, the standard of proof is only that the police believe a crime occurred, and the person arrested did it. This burden of proof—probable cause—is the second-lowest burden in American law. Two steps above hunch and no proof at all. Arrest data is really a measure of police investigative skills and police deployment. As discussed next, police deployment is about where the police are placed and what crimes they actually observe and then respond to. This deployment bias increases the likelihood of arrests of blacks and reduces the likelihood of the arrest of whites.

Third, the key thing to understand about UCR data is that it is not a measure of what it is claimed to be measuring. When we talk about crime in America, we are using arrest data as a proxy for crime commission. But as defined by the UCR itself, the UCR data is about crimes reported by the police to the FBI. The UCR is not about and does not reflect all crimes committed. Why? Because not all crime is reported to the police, much less all crime reported to the FBI by the police. Also, the UCR only reflects street crimes.

It does not report corporate, environmental, and financial crimes. The point is this, when we talk about crime in America white-collar crime is specifically omitted.

Lastly, the UCR data can be manipulated based on how reporting agencies (local police departments) enter the crime data.[13] Criminal offenses can be defined and coded to show increases or decreases in certain types of crimes based on the politics and needs of the agencies. Federal funding can increase or decrease based on the types of crimes reported. Local politics can dictate the need to prove increased or decreased crime patterns.

In addition to these four limiting factors, when discussing crime rates, police deployment can affect the data at the actual arrest stage and who gets arrested, which is then reported to the UCR system.

Consider the following hypothetical example. Police are ordered to reduce prostitution in the city and the crime is committed in neighborhoods A and B. Neighborhood A is majority black and neighborhood B is majority white. The police know that in neighborhood A, prostitutes engage in their trade in the open. Let's say that neighborhood A has 20 prostitutes working in it. Neighborhood B also has 20 prostitutes working in it, but they work in massage parlors and in the local university because they are college girls conducting high-level and discreet prostitution. So, the crime of prostitution is equally distributed in both neighborhoods, but prostitution in A is more public and annoying to its citizens than in B. The police need to make arrests to pacify the local politicians and the public. The police saturate neighborhood A because it's easier to catch street prostitutes than high-level call girls. The police also run a sting on a massage parlor in neighborhood B. Now, let's assume the total number of arrests for prostitution is 20. A total of 12 blacks (from neighborhood A) and 8 whites (from neighborhood B) are arrested. Thus, the crime rate for prostitution shows that 60 percent (n = 12) of prostitution is committed by blacks and 40 percent (n = 8) is committed by whites. The conclusion, blacks commit more prostitution.

The data does not reflect the 60 percent (n = 12) of prostitution committed by whites in neighborhood B. It's actually hidden from the data. If the police saturated neighborhood B with the same intensity and efficiency as applied to neighborhood A, then 12 whites and 12 blacks would be arrested and prostitution would, by race, be equal in both percentage and appearance. But instead, the data shows prostitution with a black face. The result being that whites are underrepresented in the prostitution crime rate and the political rhetorical result is whites are less criminal regarding prostitution. Blacks are shown to be more criminal than they actually are, and whites are seen as less criminal.

Add to our hypothetical that the black population citywide is only 13 percent. Whites, in our hypothetical, make up 75 percent of the population. Overall, population is one of many benchmarks used to put crime data in context to determine if the result is indicative of racial bias. So, the 13 percent is compared to the 60 percent, and the political rhetorical result is blacks disproportionately commit more prostitution. Thus, when the incarceration rate for blacks in prison is disproportionate to their general population, the rhetorical response is, the disproportionate representation is correct because blacks disproportionately commit prostitution. Put simply, prisons should be disproportionally populated by blacks, and the reason for that disproportionality is not racial bias. Rather, it's the natural result as Bush's appointee's asserted: "African-Americans are overrepresented in criminal activity."

The use of crime data without consideration of deployment and investigative focus of the police encourages multiple fallacies in understanding crime patterns and simplifies blame regarding who commits crime. My point is not that crime stats don't have utility but only that they are used as a proxy for crime patterns, and they are not actually measuring crime patterns. They are actually a measure at best of police clearance rates. And even with that, they are a measure of what the initial stage of the criminal justice system determines regarding crime. There is a large gulf between the police saying a person is guilty and a jury saying so beyond a reasonable doubt. Consider the significance of the difference between arrest and conviction with this simple conversation. When a cop arrests a man and his friend pleads with the officer saying, "You're making a mistake." The officer turns and responds, "That's why we have trials, mister."

But accepting the conventional use of FBI UCR arrest data as a proxy for the crime in America, the FBI arrest data clearly establishes that blacks don't commit most of the crime. Bush's appointee misquoted the data and is simply wrong that "black neighborhoods generally are more violent and have more crime than white neighborhoods." His error, in part, is wrong because of his focus on the race within the neighborhood rather than the social and economic dynamics of the neighborhood. Note the appointee's assertion, "black neighborhoods ... more violent ... than white neighborhoods," not poor or economically marginalized neighborhoods are more violent than economically and socially stable neighborhoods, regardless of race. Race is the determinative factor to him. If race was the determinative factor of crime, then integrated middle-class neighborhoods would have high rates of crime simply because blacks live there. If race was a determinative factor, all black middle and upper middle-class neighborhoods with $300,000 plus homes (yes, such things do exist) would still be saturated with crime and police deployment including the use of SWAT teams to execute warrants. The point of course is that they are not so saturated. Black middle and upper class neighborhoods are just as crime free as their white equals.

The proper determinative factor for understanding the level of crime in a neighborhood is economics and the sociology and psychology of concentrated poverty. Put another way, neighborhoods are violent because they suffer economic ills not because they suffer the presence of blacks. But because of historical Jim Crow policies in urban areas, economic isolation, deprivation, and concentration of blacks in such neighborhoods, there has been a conflation of race, crime, and poverty into one dynamic within American political and social consciousness. White social conservatives, and liberals for different political reasons, view majority black neighborhoods as poor neighborhoods and thus crime infested by definition. The fact that black middle-class and upper-middle-class neighborhoods exist with low crime rates escapes the logic of people like Bush's appointee. The existence of such neighborhoods, by definition, conflict with the neat and politically palatable syllogism that white social conservatives enjoy and gain comfort from. The comfort is that America's racial history has no practicality or applicability to today's crime problem. Blacks are more criminal than whites. Racism and its legacy are not something to be acknowledged and rectified in policy formation regarding crime. Crime is inherent to blacks, and that is what prisons are for.

Returning to UCR crime data, the significant error by Bush's appointee is that according to the most recent data report from the FBI (2017), most of the crime committed in America is committed by whites, not blacks. The differential criminality of various ethnic groups that Bush's appointee says proves that blacks are crimino-genic actually cuts the other way, and its whites that should be the group to be feared. According to the data, whites are more likely to commit rape, aggravated assault, or any other violent crime. Whites account for 70 percent of criminal arrests, while blacks account for 27 percent. Whites accounted for 59 percent of all violent crime arrests, while blacks accounted for 37 percent. Again, assuming the conventional interpretation of crime statistics, arrest data show whites are more criminal and violent than blacks.

In 2017, whites accounted for twice as many rapes as blacks (12,187 compared to 5,182), twice as many burglaries (104,671 compared to 46,227), twice as many thefts (501,231 compared to 215,630), twice as many car thefts (46,621 compared to 21,415), and more than four times as many arsons (5,051 compared to 1,788). Overall, whites committed twice as many violent crimes (236,590 compared to 151,744) and more than twice as many property crimes (657,574 compared to 285,080). Whites accounting for double the amount of crime than blacks is true for almost all FBI crimes, including assault, forgery, fraud, embezzlement, receiving stolen property, vandalism, sex crimes (not rape and prostitution), drug crimes, spousal abuse, driving under the influence (drunk driving), drunkenness, and vagrancy. The crime of aggravated assault shows whites only slightly more violent than blacks (191,205 compared to 101,432). The only two crimes in which blacks account for more arrests than whites are robbery (40,024 compared to 32,128) and homicide/non-negligent manslaughter (5,025 compared to 4,188).

Conservatives like Bush's appointee assert, "Because the white population and black population are not the same size ... What matters is the rate of violence."[14] Then he asserts that because blacks make up 13 percent of the population and whites make up 77 percent of the population, the rate of crime committed by blacks is disproportionate to their population. But he made this argument within the context of "prevalence of violence in communities." The error is that national population rates tells you nothing about what the prevalence of crime in specific communities should be. More importantly, America is still segregated in many cities. Thus crime in urban black neighborhoods is supposed to be dominated by blacks. That's who lives there. A neighborhood with 80 percent blacks should make up 70–80 percent of black criminals in that neighborhood. Just as white rural areas have mostly white criminals. People generally play, live, and shop in the same geographic area. Criminals are the same. That's why police look in the neighborhood for suspects when a robbery occurs. People function where they are comfortable. Bush's appointee asserted that the National Crime Victimization Survey shows "respondents reported that 43.8 percent of the offenders were non-Hispanic whites, 22.7 percent were black, and 14.4 percent were Hispanic." That's because the majority of all crime is intraracial, and victims are victimized by those who live close to them. Crime, like all social interactions, occurs within the routine activities area one resides in.

Consider a corollary point. The disproportionality argument is intentionally rigged to the detriment of blacks and creates the false narrative that whites do not commit crime. The disproportionate arrest rate of blacks is translated, in political terms, into disproportionate criminal activity, making the face of crime black. White crime is made politically, and rhetorically, invisible, and white-on-white crime is not rhetorically discussed as a public policy problem. Because whites are underrepresented, white crime is supplanted in political conscious-ness for the popular narrative of black-on-black crime. The notion of high rates of black-on-black crime is a rhetorical device to create fear of blacks as a whole and specifically in whites. It's meant to invoke in whites the question, if blacks do these crimes to each other, what will they do if they come into our neighborhoods? In the popular narra-tive, when white social conservatives and commentators talk about violent crime or gun violence, they offer as an example Chicago and Baltimore or some other city (code word for black). They don't offer as an example Wyoming, Kansas, or rural areas of gun violence or drug crimes because those areas are examples of white crime. When white (and black) social conservatives talk about black crime, it's couched in group descriptions and generalities regarding black behav-ior. But when white crime is discussed, it's couched in individualistic language. Black crime is the result of group cultural depravity and the lack of fathers in the home; white crime is the result of individual evil at worse but more likely mental illness or bullying. The racism is in the language of the two narratives. Crime committed by whites is seen as *sui generis* or individual, but crime committed by blacks is seen as general social deviance among blacks.

Consider the rhetorical dynamic when comparing school shoot-ings versus shootings in Chicago. The latter are urban and black and the explanations include deviant black culture, lack of discipline in the schools, and lack of fathers. The former are rural, suburban, and white, and the explanations include individual victimization because of school bullying, individual mental health needs that are not addressed, and white avoidance of disproportionate suspension of blacks and other minorities from schools. The narrative of white avoidance of disproportionality in in-school suspensions is that if schools would suspend all violent kids regardless of disproportion-ate impact, the few white violent students who commit the school shootings would be suspended as well. Consider the questions not asked during a school mass shooting. The questions are not "what is the state of the white family or white culture in the schools that are resulting in these shootings?" But when discussing urban crime, black culture is always the focus. Policy questions are birthed by political concepts. Political concepts are birthed by social narratives. Social narratives are reflections of political rhetoric. In cases of mass shootings, majority committed by whites, the rhetorical description of the shooter is always the person was sick—i.e., mentally ill. In cases of shootings in urban neighborhoods, the rhetorical description of the shooter is always the person is criminal—i.e., evil. The policy output for white mass murder events generally include calls for gun control and preventing those with mental health issues from having access to guns. But the policy output for black shooting events in urban neighborhoods is more police saturation and the reduction in the use of bail.

White mass murder is rhetorically a primarily mental health issue and subsequently a criminal justice issue. Black murder is rhetorically a primarily criminal justice issue and never a mental health issue. The racism is imbedded in the proposed explanations of the shootings and the proposed policy solution distinctions between both events.

◆ ◆ ◆

Leaving aside arguments over crime statics, Bush's appointee wrote dismissively in his lone dissent that the majority of the U.S. Civil Rights Commission report "shifts gears to acknowledge that yes, black neighborhoods have higher crime rates, but that fails to take into account 'systemic issues' that are to blame. ... [That] structural and historical issues that formed these neighborhoods, as well as the social and economic factors that currently sustain them"[15] should be considered when reviewing local crime patterns and behaviors. He concluded, "Even if you grant the 'structural and historical issues,' the police can't solve this problem—really no one can, because these issues are now baked in the cake—but the police in particular can't because their job is to enforce the law, not to engage in hous-ing policy."[16] Leaving aside such a dismissive attitude regarding the history of Jim Crow, the structural dynamics created by Jim Crow, and how these dynamics create social problems, Bush's appointee misses the point that neighborhood dynamics that foster crime are more complicated than housing policy and that police behavior can aggravate or mitigate those dynamics.

As any freshman-level introduction to criminology course, much less advanced study, makes clear, the explanations for why people commit crime are complicated and highly diverse. Poverty is a complex mix of societal ecological structural factors, as well as in-terpersonal and individual psychological and social factors. In other words, poverty in America is a combination of how one thinks and where one lives. Crime results from individual, social, structural, and life-course variables; crime is explained by the complicated interactions between people, among people, and between people and society. Neighborhood violence is explained by rational choice theory, social learning of aggression, crime pattern and crime tri-angle (routine activities) theory, chronic intergenerational poverty, intergenerational intra-neighborhood gang violence (and vendettas), the allure of violence and drug money, inability of the police to prevent street-level violence or open-air drug (heroin, cocaine, and crack) selling in the 1980s, and chronic organized drug and weapons trafficking in rural neighborhoods and urban inner cities.

These explanations supplement the fact that all behavior, including criminal behavior, is the result of the interaction of in-formal institutions of social control (family, church, employment, and schools), and the formal institutions of social control (police, courts, and corrections). These informal institutions transfer positive values and behavior from one generation to another, and when these institutions fail to maintain social order, the formal institutions attempt to supplement the deficit. Informal institutions transfer definitions and enforcement of positive social behavior, and when these institutions fail, criminal and other negative behaviors become pronounced.

All neighborhoods have a personality and sociology. Communities that are safe and secure produce behavior in accordance with that safety. In stable and safe communities, aggression and violence are not the primary answers to interpersonal disputes nor are they the means to establish respect between residents. Neighborhoods that are not safe and secure produce behavior in accordance with that lack of safety. Aggression and violence become the primary answers to interpersonal disputes and means to establish respect, which translates into personal safety. Structural and chronic poverty creates a heightened need for survival, and this need for survival creates the need for power and safety, which manifests in heightened violence. Put another way, the heightened need for vigilance for safety and security creates heightened levels of emotional and physical stress, which results in emotional trauma, which manifests itself in negative behavior (i.e., violence or hopelessness).

The constant need to maintain personal safety in an environment that does not provide a feeling of personal safety and one that provides risks to personal safety as a norm will also produce mental health trauma because of the culture of violence that the lack of personal safety produces. The trauma comes from either experiencing violence and sometimes mindless purposeless violence or doing the violence. This trauma can manifest itself in depression, post-traumatic stress disorder (PTSD), drug dependency, mindless aggression, hopelessness, or any combination of these. Research has shown that the lack of security and stability can cause brain chemistry changes because of stress, and chronic stress can cause permanent psychological and behavioral adaptations, such as hypervigilance, automatic aggression response to environmental stimuli, and self-destructive behaviors.

These mental health reactions to structurally aggressive communities are experienced by all members of the community and all age groups. Very young children can develop these mental health issues without the cognitive memory of why they feel a certain way or react under stress in a maladaptive way. More significantly, intense trauma results in the development of PTSD, which can be caused by intense exposure to violence (i.e., murder, aggravated assault) or the sudden violent death of a loved one. PTSD can cause maladaptive behavior—including criminal and self-destructive behavior. Another source of trauma in young children and older ones is the sudden removal of adult family members from violent "flash-bang" police raids and arrests by military armed and uniformed SWAT teams in the home or by the subtler trauma of the inconsistent presence of adult family members, parents, because of recurrent incarceration. This trauma is compounded by the inconsistency of release, reoffending, and return to prison by parents or other family members, which creates a chronic lack of stability in the family dynamic. The instability produces insecurity in children, which leads to maladaptive behaviors.

The trauma of an insecure family structure, as well as trauma because of witnessing a violent act, murder, for example, has a negative impact on the normal emotional processing of the loss of the loved one. It's this failure to grieve normally that creates emotional maladaptation to loss, which can lead to other negative behavior. The problem of maladaptation to the grief and trauma is amplified by each additional act of violence without emotional or cognitive relief, which results in the violence being normalized in the minds and culture of the community. Death and violence become the norm not the exception, and then people adapt their behavior to that reality in kind.

When looking at crime and violence, it's important to remember that urban cities don't suffer crime or have access to mental services uniformly. Crime and violence in urban cities are concentrated in certain neighborhoods (sometimes being different on the individual block level) that have been abandoned politically, socially, and economically, and they tend to have limited mental health services to deal with the traumas of life. While in other parts of the city, mental health services and the medications that follow are available for middle-class residents who suffer from all types of mental health issues and the maladaptive behaviors that go with them. While working-class, middle-class, and upper-class communities, black and white, have access to mental health and lawful prescriptions for medication to deal with depression, anxiety, and other issues; marginalized communities—again both black and white—resort to alcohol and various types of illegal drugs to self-medicate these mental health disorders.

Isolated communities that suffer from physical and emotional trauma because of violence as a norm also suffer from concurrent problems of chronic unemployment and the insecurity that unemployment brings, which manifests into a mentality of gaining financial security at all costs—i.e., drugs, gangs, and crime, as well as other types of violence. This mentality and behavior reaction results in focused and intense law enforcement and the social disruptions to families that occur when family members are chronically involved with the criminal justice system. These dynamics create an environment that is more prone to support behaviors that dehumanize and decivilize people rather than humanize and civilize them. I don't mean that inner city and rural communities are uncivilized but that the positive middle-class values that are fostered in economically stable middle-class communities are not supported or fostered in marginalized communities and the negativity that results decivilizes the environment regardless of the desires of the residents in that environment.

One additional point should be considered when understanding crime on the neighborhood level. As any teacher will tell you, students achieve what they can see. People who write books about success and make a living giving motivational speeches assert that the first step in success is seeing yourself better than you are. It's the ability to know things can be better and that hard work and temporary sacrifice of immediate pleasure will result in a better future. One of the aspects of social isolation is the inability to see better. Cognitively, if seeing "better" is not socially provided by the environment, a person cognitively and psychologically will not see that where they are is not all that there is in life. When I was a government policy planner, and before then a juvenile presentence investigation officer, I was amazed that children who lived two hours away from a beach had never seen the ocean and did not know they were a two-hour drive from one. The children did not have plans for a post-high school life because it was not brought to their attention that they were supposed to have one. All people, all successful people, are successful because somewhere in their lives someone positive told them and instilled in them positive views of life and expectations that they were to be successful. No one who is successful lacks the story of that one person—most of the time more than one—who said something and did something that put them on the road to success. These experiences cognitively and psychologically allow a person to see past difficulty and know that there is an entire world that they *can* have access to. In marginalized and abandoned environments, that ability to see past difficulty is not inculcated into people as it is in stable and socially integrated environments. Put simply, you can't achieve what don't know and don't see. The lack of the ability to do better starts with an inability to see better.

Consider the famous explanation of why elephants don't escape from captivity and remain held by a chain they have the physical power to break. When the elephants are babies, they are chained to the ground. The babies fight and pull on the chain, but they are not big enough to break it. They are stuck. Over time as they grow up, they become used to the chain and learn to function with the chain. As they grow, they see that all the other elephants their age have similar chains and the older ones also have chains. By the time they are adults, the physical chains are breakable, but they are now conditioned to the chain and its limitations, and they no longer fight against it. They live with it, and the chain is normal. They don't know how to break free of the chain, and, more importantly, they don't know it can be broken. The chain is now in their heads, which is more important than being on their legs.

Consider Plato's allegory of the cave.[17] Plato, who would teach Aristotle, reflects on the story from his teacher Socrates. The story goes that people are chained in a cave, and there is a light behind them that reflects a world. But the people are chained in such a way that they can't turn around and can only see the reflections on the wall of the cave in front of them. This is the entire life of the prisoners. They are born into chains staring at the wall. Plato further explains that the people have developed systems of rewards and honors and commendations for people who can predict the images as they change over time on the wall. He explains that the people function by the wall and what they see. The wall and what they see on it defines their total reality.

The story continues by asking what happens when one prisoner breaks free, turns around, and looks into the light that caused the images on the wall. He explains that the prisoner who is drawn by the light goes to the mouth of the cave to see the sun. The first problem is that the light in the prisoner's eyes hurts his eyes. The prisoner must endure the pain until his eyes adjust. The story explains that the prisoner endures the pain, and on the other end of the pain, the prisoner sees an entire world, and he realizes that the cave and images are not real. There is better than the cave. After enjoying this newfound reality, Plato asks would the prisoner return to the cave and engage the images on the wall as if they were real. The answer, of course, is no. But Plato then asks, should the prisoner go back and tell the others that the real world is behind them. Plato proposes that the answer is yes. So when the prisoner returns, Plato asks what would happen if the prisoner breaks the chains of the prisoners and forces them to see the sun and the real world. Plato concludes, first the people who are benefiting from the images will reject the world the prisoner says exists. Second, those who are forced into the sunlight will reject it because of the pain in their eyes and run back to the comfort of the dark. Lastly, the prisoners who are chained will kill the liberated prisoner for disrupting their world.

The nature of being in a marginalized and isolated environment is that it gets into the mind, and people become the elephant or those who kill the messenger when told there is sunlight behind them.

In all this, race has nothing to do with it.

chapter two

Race and Crime

Misidentifying the Cause of the Problem

U rban crime and disorder is not a social dynamic explained by a single factor. Social disorder is the result of trauma, lack of mental health services, chronic unemployment, omnipresence of deviant behavior, chronic unemployment, social aggression as a norm, heightened hypervigilance for safety, the presence of purposeless violent behavior, chronic intensive law enforcement, intergenerational family involvement with the criminal justice system, emotional and psychological disorders (i.e., depression, PTSD, antisocial personality disorder, childhood personality disorders), family dysfunction (absence of fathers), and hopelessness. All of these factors support and amplify each other in creating an environment that is conducive to the worst of human behavior. The point is this: crime in poor urban communities is much more complicated than the simplistic and racist assertions made by white social conservatives that crime is the exclusive result of the immorality of black culture, lack of fathers in the home, and failure to enforce discipline in the schools. The dynamics of poverty are at the heart of the problem, and poverty itself is more complicated than white social conservative orthodoxy stating that poverty is the result of laziness.

While at the American Enterprise Institute, Bob Woodson, a classical traditional black social conservative (see chapter 3 for definition) and president of the Center for Neighborhood Enterprise, provided a nuanced discussion of poverty and the moral issues attached to behavior found in poverty.[1] He explained that poverty is a different social dynamic for different people because of different causal situations. Some people are in poverty because of economic reversals in life. The loss of a job, loss of a spouse's second income, or suffering an economic downturn. The second group includes those who are caught in a cycle of poverty and government assistance, and because of the rules of governmental assistance, they can't take personal initiatives that increase their income. The third group consists of those who are mentally or physically disabled and need long-term help. The members of the fourth group are poor because of bad life choices and character flaws that keep them in a state of poverty. Woodson argued that conservatives think all poor people in urban areas are in group four. Conservatives point to people, black people, who are in group four and use them as the face of welfare, crime, and the futility of social programs. Even more, they argue, group four is the direct result of the social programs of Lyndon Johnson's Great Society. These policies, along with the societal abandonment of supporting marriage as both a moral and social system to maintain the family and social and economic success, are the sole reasons for group four. As Bush's appointee on the U.S. Civil Rights Commission concluded, "The police can't solve this problem—really no one can, because these issues are now baked in the cake."

The problem, of course, is that Woodson's group four is neither the sole explanation of poverty (urban or rural) nor the result of the Great Society. Nor is group four the explanation of black incarceration, as many social conservatives assert as a matter of orthodoxy. This orthodoxy asserts that crime is not the result of the urban policy during the Jim Crow era, but it's caused by the failed policies of the Great Society, and historical racism is not an explanation of black disproportionate incarceration. Let's discuss each assertion in turn.

Urban Policy During the Jim Crow Era

It is dishonest to assert that government policy and American sociopolitical and economic history have had no role in explaining the incarceration of blacks. Leaving the social and political impact of slavery aside, consider the effect of a century of Jim Crow, segregation, and the imposition of economic and legal impediments on the ability of black families to gain and maintain wealth intergenerationally in a capitalist system. The pre and post Reconstruction era lasted from 1865 to 1867 and 1877 through 1968, a total of 93 years. In other words, for almost an entire century, blacks were excluded from American economic history. More importantly, those 93 years encompassed the period of the rise of America from a third-rate nation to an undisputed world superpower. In a capitalistic system, especially in the United States, wealth and economic success are intergenerationally created and transferred. By wealth, I mean wealth in all its various forms: financial, social, educational, professional, academic, moral, political, and societal. The century that America developed all of its economic and social advancement, beginning with the rise of the textile industry in 1793 and ending with the rise of the robber barons and the gilded age in the 1920s, blacks as a matter of law were excluded. During this period American cities grew and formed the foundations of America's wealth and blacks were generationally excluded from fully adding and enjoying and benefiting from this growth. The exclusion of blacks from a century of development and advancement created social, societal, and structural dysfunction and isolation that remains after its cause, Jim Crow, was abated. Jim Crow, which replaced the system of slavery, was the social and political system—which excluded blacks—from one of the most important periods of American history. The time between America being a third-rate country on the international stage (1865) and when it was the undisputed world leader after World War II (1945).

Consider the historical impact of *racial neighborhood exclusions*[2] (early 1900s), followed by *legal restrictive covenants*[3] (1920–1948), followed by *racial restrictive covenants in fact* (1948–1968), and *redlining*[4] (1934–1968) of black neighborhoods through the Fair Housing Administration (FHA) policies of insuring private housing and neighborhood development loans in white-only locations in major urban cities. This system of redlining resulted in the physical, as well as social, political, and economic, isolation of black neighborhoods.[5] These policies were compounded by government support of the *rise of segregated white suburbs* and the concentration of black populations in the cities, the *exclusion of blacks from the benefits of the G.I. Bill*, and housing support granted to white servicemen after World War II, in addition to the housing practices of *blockbusting* (real estate companies and banks forcing whites out of city neighborhoods under the threat of housing devaluation because of blacks moving in), *real estate value manipulation* (getting whites to sell their homes at a loss, which were then, in turn, overvalued and resold to blacks), and *racial steering* (manipulating who moves into neighborhoods based on race and class). These policies resulted in the creation of concentrated poverty (political, physical, social, and economic) in selected sections (neighborhoods) of society. Add to this the use of *racial profiling*[6] as a crime suppression strategy.

Although the racism and the legal structures of these policies have been negated, the physical structural (ecological) results of these policies are still in effect. The physical design and operation of the major urban cities in the United States all originated in the late 1800s through the 1950s, which means they all originated during the apex of American apartheid and predate the 1960s and the policies of the Great Society. The concentration of poverty in sections of urban neighborhoods is no accident; it resulted from policy. Consider that legal segregation in America only ended in 1968, 192 years after the Declaration of Independence and 103 years after the Civil War. As a matter of statutory law, the full political, economic, and social opportunities of America being made available to blacks is only 50 years old.

Great Society

It is white social conservative orthodoxy that all urban and social ills are directly attributable to the Great Society. As discussed in greater detail in Chapter 4, the politics of the Great Society merged blacks with crime in American political rhetoric and policy. White social conservatives make the political connection of race and crime with the assertion that crime results from deviant family structures in the black community. This lack of traditional family structure with a father as the head of the home providing financial and disciplinary support and control of young black males has served as the defining explanation for crime for generations of social conservatives. This theory was adopted from a policy paper written in the Johnson Administration soon after the passage of the Civil Rights Act of 1964.

In March 1965, *The Negro Family: The Case for National Action*, otherwise known as the *Moynihan Report*, was leaked to the press, and it ignited a firestorm of controversy regarding the status of the black family and the effect of that status on American society as a whole. In 1965, Patrick Moynihan, assistant secretary of labor in the Johnson Administration wrote an internal government policy report to provide support for the unveiling of the declaration of the war on poverty. Ten years after the beginning of the modern civil rights movement, with the Supreme Court decision of *Brown v. Board of Education* in 1954 and culminating in the landmark passage of the Civil Rights Acts of 1964 and 1965, policy attention shifted from ending racial Jim Crow and segregation to a focus on economic disparities and the failure of black families to attain the American Dream.

In his famous "Freedom Is Not Enough" speech at Howard University in June 1965, President Johnson said, "The voting rights bill will [establish the freedom to vote]. ... But freedom is not enough. You do not wipe away the scars of centuries by saying: 'Now you are free.' ... You do not take a person who, for years, has been hobbled by chains and liberate him ... and then say, 'You are free to compete with all the others,' and still justly believe that you have been completely fair. ... To this end, equal opportunity is essential, but not enough, not enough." This speech, along with Johnson's war on poverty speech before Congress in January 1964, began four years of social programs, which resulted in Medicare, Medicaid, federal school loans, food stamps, and a host of other social welfare policy initiatives between 1964 and 1968. Patrick Moynihan authored Johnson's 1965 speech. Being at the cusp of leadership of major policy implementation, Moynihan was sidelined when his report was leaked to the press.

The report made two conclusions regarding the state of the black family. First, the black family was dysfunctional and was getting worse regarding its instability. Second, the damage to the black family could be addressed through direct social programs, the top being employment for the black male and allowing the black male to be the patriarch of his family with support from the black female, just as it was in white families. Two factors caused the damage to the black family, according to Moynihan.

The first factor was centuries of slavery and Jim Crow and their impact on the structure of the black family. As Moynihan explained, "Three centuries of injustice have brought about deep-seated structural distortions in the life of the Negro American" and that the "Negro situation ... commonly perceived by whites in terms of the visible manifestation of discrimination and poverty" needed to evolve to consider "the effect that three centuries of exploitation have had on the fabric of Negro society itself." Moynihan asserted that the negative functioning of the black family—low employment, high single-mother birthrates, and low income—should be understood as the result of Jim Crow, not the endemic inferiority or criminality of blacks.

The second factor was the matriarchal nature of the black family in which the black male was neither the breadwinner nor the male role model of manhood for young black males. This lack of black male presence in the home leads to failure in school and the delinquent behavior of young black male children. Moynihan asserted that because the "negro community has been forced into a maternal structure … out of line with the rest of the American society," it has a weak family structure, suffering from "a tangle of pathology." At the center of the tangle of pathology is black male unemployment and the failure to hold a responsible position in the home, which resulted in "25% of Black families not [being] intact[,] 24% of Black children born illegitimate [, and] 25% of Black families were single female headed households."

White social conservatives of the 1960s, as they do today, ignored the first factor and adopted the second factor as political orthodoxy on the level of Moses coming down the mountain with the two tablets written by God himself.

The report was only intended for internal government review as an empirical justification for the policies of the war on poverty. The report aimed to justify the need for national action. Moynihan received national condemnation for his effort. Liberal blacks cursed him and his report as blaming the victim and justifying racist ideas regarding the black family. Feminists, both black and white, cursed the report for blaming women for the problem of the family and supporting a patriarchal view of America that was under direct challenge by the women's movement of the middle and late 1960s.

Because of the backlash, the report was abandoned by the Johnson Administration and Moynihan left the administration. By the 1980s, the report had reemerged as being prescient and evidence that the policies of the 1960s were a failure. As President Ronald Reagan asserted in January 1988, "the Federal Government declared war on poverty, and poverty won." White social conservatives in the 1960s argued that social programs do not help the poor, and the problems of blacks are of their own making to be fixed by them alone. White social conservative orthodoxy advocates, both black and white, assert today that with the end of legal Jim Crow, the responsibility and fault of the black family structure belongs to blacks themselves. The pathology within the black family, was and is, reinforced by social programs that remove the value of work and personal responsibility from blacks specifically and the poor generally. White social conservatives today, as they did in the 1960s, ignore the slavery/ Jim Crow historical context Moynihan used to assert that poverty was attached to black family structure. In doing so, conservatives distort the report by asserting that Moynihan was right—the issue of poverty lay with the black family. As discussed in Chapter 1 and later in this book, explanations for black poverty and black incarceration are not that simple.

Historical Black Disproportionate Incarceration

If social conservatives are correct that historical racism and the resulting social policies supporting racism from 1619 through 1968 have no place in explaining crime and black disproportionate incarceration, then the incarceration of blacks should only correlate with the middle 1960s, the rise of the Great Society programs, and public policy of direct welfare payments to single mothers.[7] The Great Society programs, white social conservatives assert, are the *direct* cause of the fall of the black family and *the* explanation for disproportionate black crime—which results in disproportionate black incarceration. As shown in the following tables, black disproportionate incarceration predates the 1960s, the Great Society, the 1980s, and the rise of crack cocaine, and it even predates the Great Depression and World War II.

Official data from the Department of Justice shows that, as early as 1926, blacks experienced consistent escalating disproportionate incarceration. As shown in Chart 2.1, from 1926 through 1986, the percentage of blacks incarcerated increased from 21 percent in 1926 to 44 percent in 1986.

CHART 2.1 Race of Admissions to State and Federal Prisons 1926–1986

YEAR	1926	1930	1935	1940	1945	1950	1960	1964	1970	1975	1980	1986
BLACK	21	22	25	28	31	30	32	33	39	35	41	44
WHITE	78	77	74	71	68	69	66	65	61	64	58	55
EVENTS		The Great Depression 1929–1939		World War II		The Korean War 1950–1953 The Civil Rights Movement 1954–1968			The War on Drugs			
PRESIDENT	Coolidge and Hoover	Roosevelt				Truman, Eisenhower	Kennedy	Johnson	Nixon, Ford, and Carter		Reagan	

Source: Patrick Langan, Race of Prisoners Admitted to State and Federal Institutions, 1926–1986, U.S. Department of Justice (1991).

The disproportionate incarceration of blacks occurred before the Great Depression, despite the need for manpower during World War II and the Korean War, and well before the 1960s and the rise of the Great Society. It is white social conservative orthodoxy that states that the disproportionate incarceration of blacks is not because of racism but the disintegration of the black family, the abandonment of black children by black men, and the federal government providing welfare to unwed black mothers. But census data shows that in 1950, black marriage rates were almost equal to white marriage rates (64 percent compared to 67 percent).[8] But as the data shows, there was a disproportionate incarceration of blacks in 1950 (30 percent) when blacks accounted for 12 percent of the total population.

Census data showed that black women were more often married than white women prior to World War II. Census data shows that black men and women between 1890 and 1950 were getting married at younger ages than white men and women. Between 1890 and 1940, the percentage of white men and women who were never married by age 35 was higher than black men and women.[9] The lack of marriage is not the causal social dynamic of crime that white social conservatives assert because blacks were disproportionally incarcerated despite being married long before the advent of the Great Society and Johnson ascending to the presidency. Although the black marriage rate fell in the 1960s, the decline predates the Great Society. In 1960, the rate of black marriage was 61 percent (compared to whites at 70 percent), and by 1970, the rate was 56 percent (compared to whites at 68 percent). In 2018, the rate of black marriage was only 38 percent (compared to whites at 56 percent).[10]

When Johnson entered politics as a freshman member of the House of Representatives from the State of Texas in 1937 under President Franklin D. Roosevelt, blacks accounted for 25 percent of the total prison population, which was increasing from 22 percent in 1930, while blacks were only 9.7 percent of the total U.S. population. The disproportionality of blacks in the criminal justice system not only well predates the arrival and ascendency of President Johnson in 1964 and the policies of the Great Society but also has been an American historical constant both before and after the Civil War.

This historical constant of incarceration of blacks is the result of social and political policies over time. As discussed in Chapter 4, from 1619 to 1865, these social and political policies included slavery and laws to control the movements of free blacks. These policies included the *Fugitive Slave Acts* (1793 and 1850), the *Negro Seaman's Acts* (1820s), and the advent of *southern slave patrols* (the origin of policing in the South), for which the single purpose was to enforce slavery by controlling the behavior and movement of blacks.[11]

In the antebellum era, the South instituted slave patrols, and the North instituted slave catchers—both provided the foundation of policing in America—with the sole purpose of enforcing order on rural slave plantations, patrolling southern roads to prevent slave escapes, and capturing escaped slaves in the North, returning them under court orders and warrants. In the postbellum era, southern police would enforce *vagrancy laws* to force blacks into working relationships on plantations, and the courts would enforce *criminal anti-enticement laws, contract enticement enforcement laws, emigrant-agent laws,* and *false-pretense laws* that would make sure that as a functional matter, blacks did not leave the plantations.

Criminal anti-enticement laws made it a crime to hire blacks who were in the employ of others; it established proprietary claims over black bodies.

Emigrant-agent laws placed criminal fines on employment agents who were tasked with seeking workers from other states.

False-pretense statutes criminalized blacks leaving employment for other opportunities based on the theory that the blacks had committed fraud when they took the first position by not intending to comply with the terms of the employment to the detriment of the employer.

Contract-enforcement laws imposed a criminal fine for failure to satisfy the terms of a contract—a fine blacks could not pay.

Vagrancy statutes facilitated the arrest and fining of blacks for not being in employment (*apprentice laws*). The inability to pay these fines facilitated the system of *peonage* and *criminal surety*. Peonage and criminal surety provided financial incentives for local police and courts to incarcerate blacks. White plantation owners would pay the fine or bail (criminal surety) and receive the equivalent of slave labor to pay off the fine or bail paid by the plantation owner.

Both the contract-enforcement laws and vagrancy laws created a situation in which blacks could pay the fine by "voluntarily" signing their labor over to a plantation owner to work off the debt of the fine or the bond imposed by the court. If no plantation owner would pay the fine in exchange for the black labor, *convict leasing* would be used.[12] The convict-leasing system provided forced labor in coal mines, swamps, and other areas in which white labor could not be found.

This system of laws to control slaves and then freed slaves, first by the slave codes (late 1600s), followed by the Black Codes (1865–1866) and Jim Crow (1880s–1965) together formed a historical constant of the criminalization of blacks and a social and political constant of black disproportionate incarceration. These laws together created a system of bondage (slavery) and involuntarily servitude of blacks lasting for centuries, both before and after the Thirteenth Amendment. This system of laws and practices did not end until the 1940s! This system used the criminal justice system as a tool of social control that functioned to disproportionally incarcerate blacks regardless of their actual criminal behavior.

The social acceptance of disproportionate incarceration of blacks survived the fall of Jim Crow and with the rise of the war on drugs and later the rise of conservative politics in the 1980s and 1990s the historical constant of black incarceration continued. As shown in Charts 2.2 through 2.4 from 1987 through 2017, regardless of the politics or parties of the presidents, blacks have been

CHART 2.2 Race of Admissions to State and Federal Prisons
1987–1997

YEAR	1987	1988	1989	1990	1991	1992	1993	1994	1995	1996	1997
BLACK	47	48	50	49	50	50	51	51	50	49	49
WHITE	52	51	49	49	47	48	47	47	48	48	48
PRESIDENT	Reagan		George H.W. Bush				Clinton				

Source: Bureau of Justice Statistics, Correctional Populations in the United States
(1996, 2000).

disproportionally incarcerated. Federal data shows a consistent
yearly increase of the percentage of blacks in prison from 35 percent
(1975) during the presidency of Gerald Ford to 41 percent at the
beginning of the presidency of Ronald Reagan (1981) to 50 percent
at the end of the presidency of George H.W. Bush (1992) to
51 percent under the presidency of Bill Clinton (1993 and 1994).

Under the entire presidency of George H.W. Bush and during
the first term of President Clinton, blacks accounted for half of the
total prison population of America while accounting for 13 percent
of the total U.S. population.

By the end of the eight-year presidency of Bill Clinton, the
percentage decreased from 51 percent to 46 percent, and it continued to decrease from 46 percent to 41 percent by the end of the
eight-year presidency of George W. Bush. Under President Barack
Obama, the percentage continued to decrease from 41 percent to
33 percent. The reduction of the percentage of black incarceration

CHART 2.3 Race of Admissions to State and Federal
Prisons 1998–2008

YEAR	1998	1999	2000	2001	2002	2003	2004	2005	2006	2007	2008
BLACK	46	46	46	46	45	44	41	40	41	39	41
WHITE	33	33	36	36	34	35	34	35	40	36	34
HISPANIC	18	18	16	16	18	19	19	20	15	20	20
PRESIDENT	Clinton			George W. Bush							

Source: Bureau of Justice Statistics, BJS Prisoners in 1992–2016.

CHART 2.4   Race of Admissions to State and Federal Prisons 2009–2017

YEAR	2009	2010	2011	2012	2013	2014	2015	2016	2017
BLACK	41	40	38	36	36	36	35	33	33
WHITE	34	34	34	33	33	33	34	30	30
HISPANIC	20	24	23	22	22	22	21	23	23
PRESIDENT	Obama								Trump

Source: Bureau of Justice Statistics, BJS Prisoners in 1992–2017.

that occurred under President Clinton did so only when the politics of "get tough" on crime began to subside in 1998 and after the end the crack epidemic in 1994. For the first five years of the Clinton presidency, black incarceration was between 51 percent and 49 percent, only to remain flat at 46 percent for the remainder of his term in office.

The percentage of black incarceration did not begin to decrease significantly until the presidency of Barack Obama. Under President Obama, black disproportionate incarceration decreased to its lowest point since 1964 (33 percent) from 41 percent in 2009 to 33 percent in 2016. The decrease occurred as a result of the passage of the Fair Sentencing Act of 2010 and the policies of Attorney General Eric Holder. The Fair Sentencing Act of 2010 reduced the sentencing laws for possession of crack cocaine. Eric Holder issued prosecution policies that reduced the imposition of enhanced sentencing and charging offenses that activated mandatory minimum sentencing. These policies, along with the Supreme Court holding that the federal sentencing guidelines were not mandatory,[13] worked to alleviate criminal justice policies that were responsible for the disproportionate incarceration of blacks for more than two decades.

◆◆◆

The current disproportionate incarceration of blacks is not an accident of history but the result of a specific American social political history. As discussed later in this book, during the subsequent

25 years after World War II, American sociopolitical history brought turbulent change. This period involved the rise of the civil rights movement and the resulting social revolution of black equality under the law and in society, as well as the fall of the social Jim Crow system of white supremacy and black inferiority under the law. This revolution was followed by the political revolution of the Great Society in 1964 in which the federal government took a direct role in reducing poverty and all types of economic inequality in the United States.

These social and political changes were followed by the successful political blowback of social conservatives, urban white working-class northerners, and southern Democrats beginning with the elections of 1966. This political blowback was supported by the merging in the American mind of social disorder, crime, and civil rights—all of which merged crime and blacks (especially young black men) as synonymous in the American political consciousness. This merging began with the ascendency of states' rights, limited government, and crime control politics of Goldwater (1964) in Republican Party politics; the conservatization of American national politics by 1968; the rise of Nixon's silent majority; the utilization of the southern strategy, which resulted in the presidencies of Nixon (1968) and Reagan (1980); the disarray of the Democratic Party in 1968; and the expulsion of social conservative Democrats from the Democratic Party in the 1972 election.

These sociopolitical events formed the foundation for the modern political discourse of American politics in which the two parties divided the American electorate. The Republican Party caters to white males (both suburban and urban high school–educated working class), states' rights, limited government, social conservatives, constitutional originalists, Christian evangelicals, former segregationists, opponents of the rise of a strong national government, and law and order voters. The Democratic Party is dominated by various progressive, racial, gender, ethnic, urban, suburban, middle class, and working-class interests. The party became dominated by civil rights advocates, anti-war, strong national government, Great

Society, due process, and rehabilitation voters. Crime and race became one of the key demarcation lines between the two parties; the Democratic Party reflects the politics of civil rights and liberal attacks on the treatment of blacks within the criminal justice system, and the Republican Party reflects the social blowback against the policies and goals of the civil rights movement and conservative defense of the incarceration of blacks within the criminal justice system as being normal because of the criminogenic nature of black behavior.

The disproportionate incarceration of blacks, which predates World War I, has continued under subsequent presidents, and the political ascendency of American suburban white middle-class fear of crime in general, and specifically urban crime in 1964, was further reinforced by the advent of crack cocaine–motivated violent urban crime in the 1980s. The crack cocaine epidemic in the urban cities resulted in the "get tough on crime" policies adopted by the federal government and all 50 states in the middle to late 1980s through the end of the 1990s. These "get tough on crime" policies included three-strikes laws, increased building of maximum and super-maximum security federal and state prisons, mandatory sentencing laws, and truth in sentencing initiatives. The Comprehensive Crime Control Act of 1984 signed by President Reagan and the Violent Crime and Law Enforcement Act of 1994 signed by President Clinton together created the modern American criminal justice system and the modern explanation for black incarceration.

The **Comprehensive Crime Control Act of 1984** increased federal penalties for marijuana, ended parole in the federal system, and created the mandatory sentencing guideline system with the creation of the Federal Sentencing Commission, in addition to reinstituting the death penalty. The **Violent Crime and Law Enforcement Act of 1994** increased the number of local police; instituted the policy of truth in sentencing, which required states to pass laws that offenders sentenced to prison had to serve at least 85 percent of their sentences; and instituted the "three strikes and you're out" policy in which offenders would be sentenced to life imprisonment without the possibility of parole upon the conviction of a third felony. These Clinton policies, along with the *anti-violent crime initiative* in which the federal government would prosecute what was traditionally considered local crimes (drugs and gun crimes) and prosecute them under federal law, which had more severe prison sentencing guidelines, resulted in mass incarceration rates, as well as prison overcrowding that plagued criminal justice for more than a decade.

The politics of the 1960s and 1970s, along with the policies of Reagan and Clinton, socially and psychologically conditioned American society to define blacks as criminals and to expect to find them under criminal justice control. The political party loyalty realignments of the middle 1960s through the election of 1980, along with the economic changes that occurred in the 1970s and 1980s fostered various policies that negatively affected blacks and supported their disproportionate incarceration and isolation. In the 1970s, cities suffered deindustrialization because of manufacturing moving into the suburbs and then out of the country by the late 1980s through the 1990s. The resulting loss of working-class jobs and the victories of the civil rights movement allowed the black middle class to leave the cities ("black flight") in the middle to late 1970s. These changes resulted in the loss of middle-class social, political, economic, and tax base support in many urban areas—leaving many urban black neighborhoods in structural and social poverty.

These social and economic changes in the early 1950s and through the 1960s racialized American politics for various reasons. *First*, white flight, which was the response to the Second Great Migration (1940–1970), resulted in the development of white-only suburbs, like Levittown, which began the modern development of racially segregated neighborhoods. *Second*, political blowback occurred against the Democratic Party in the midterm elections of 1966 in which northern suburban and working middle-class whites, along with white southern Democrats, turned against the growth of the Great Society and the civil rights policies of President Johnson.

Third, starting in 1964, a political realignment occurred in which black voters shifted from the party of Lincoln, the Republican Party, to the Democratic Party. *Fourth*, the realignment of blacks to the Democratic Party was matched by the transference of southern white Democrats to the Republican Party, which began with the southern democratic opposition to President Truman in 1948.

White southern Democrats' reaction to President Truman began with his apostasy, that the federal government had a role and responsibility to protect individual rights, black rights, from local and state intransigence regarding discrimination and lynching. The significance of Truman's 1946 executive order forming the President's Committee on Civil Rights in the same year is that it resulted in the desegregation of both the federal workforce and the armed forces (executive orders 9980 and 9981, respectively) in 1948 and the later formation of the U.S. Commission on Civil Rights and the Civil Rights Division in the Justice Department through the passage of the Civil Rights Act of 1957.

The realignment of blacks to the Democratic Party and the transference of southern white Democrats to the Republican Party, which began with Truman, became irreversible with the Democrats passing the 1964 Civil Rights Act[14] with support from northern liberal Republicans. The liberal Republican wing of the party that supported the 1964 Civil Rights Act would be completely purged out of the party by 1980.

Fifth, the political-ideological realignments of both parties began with the 1948, 1964, and 1966 elections in response to the Republican Party adopting the rhetoric and policies of southern Democrats' assertions[15] of states' rights[16] as advocated by Sen. Strom Thurmond[17] (D. South Carolina), Gov. George Wallace[18] (D. Alabama), Gov. Orval Faubus[19] (D. Kansas), Gov. Ross Barnett[20] (D. Mississippi), Sen. Barry Goldwater[21] (R. Arizona), Sen. Richard Nixon[22] (R. California), and Gov. Ronald Reagan[23] (R. California). This realignment was further supported by the Republican Party's adoption of the states' rights theory of interposition, the modern version of the pre-Civil War southern concept of nullification in response to the civil rights movement of the 1950s and 1960s and white opposition to forced integration and bussing[24] in the 1970s.

Sixth, the Republican Party adoption of the southern strategy achieved the twin goals of winning national presidential elections by cultivating both the northern and southern white male vote and the political restricting and segregation of the black vote to urban areas. *Seventh*, in the 1972 election, after a heated and divisive political primary and convention, the Democrats selected George McGovern, and like the Republicans in the selection of Goldwater in 1964, the selection of McGovern changed the operating political orientation of the Democratic Party by expelling the foreign policy conservative wing of the party (what would come to be the neoconservatives ("neocons") within the Republican Party) leaving social liberals and progressives in a dominant position within the party.

In 1968, the Democratic Party continued to suffer the abandonment of the South that began during the 1948 election, crystalized during the 1964 and 1966 elections when George Wallace, after losing the nomination of the Democratic Party, formed the American Independent Party and won[25] 46 electoral votes and, in the popular vote, won almost ten million votes. More significantly, Wallace in 1968 won five southern states (Louisiana, Arkansas, Mississippi, Alabama, and Georgia), coming in second to Nixon in South Carolina, North Carolina, and Tennessee.[26]

In 1968, the entire Confederate South voted Republican. The Democrats' loss of the South to the Republicans (see Appendixes 2 and 3) was complete and permanent. In the 1968 and 1972 elections, Nixon pioneered the strategy of using white fear of crime, implying, while allowing others to outright assert, that the source of crime and disorder in America was the inner cities (i.e., blacks) and the policies of the Great Society. The 1972 election rhetoric of running a campaign to restore "law and order" and being the party of the "silent majority" to win white male votes became the standard operating strategy for decades within the Republican Party.

In no election since 1972 has a Republican run for president and in some way did not raise the issue of law and order. The Republican Party would have one more realignment election in 1980 with Ronald Reagan. Reagan would solidify, unify, and organize the control of the Republican Party under a new and broad coalition of constituencies. The coalition that elected Ronald Reagan would also finalize the marginalization of northern establishment liberal Republicans in the party. This winning coalition consisted of the southern Democrats of Strom Thurmond (1948), Barry Goldwater (1964), and George Wallace (1968). These voters were supplemented by the northern, urban, and rural working-class moral majority white male voters who supported Richard Nixon (1968, 1972). These two groups were supplemented by the Reagan voters. These voters were composed of social conservative, white evangelical protestant Christian, deregulation supply-side economics, small government, crime control pro-urban (city) law enforcement (as supposed to federal law enforcement), reduced federal government (states' rights), and foreign policy neocon voters. The Reagan coalition would rule Republican politics until the rise of the Donald Trump electorate in 2016.

This history of the political parties provides a background for the development of the criminal justice policy initiatives of the white social conservatives and the Republicans, as well as the explanation for the modern continuation of using the criminal justice system as a tool for the social control of blacks and the resulting disproportionate incarceration of blacks. From 1964 through the 1990s, the political rhetoric for supporting the suppression of urban street crime, if not direct responsibility for suppressing it, shifted to the national government. This policy change occurred in no small part because of the urban race riots in Harlem (1964), Philadelphia (1964), Watts (1965), and Atlanta (1966); the "long hot summer" riots of 1967, which included the riots in Newark (1967) and Detroit (1967); and the riots of 1968, including riots in Washington, D.C., Chicago, and Baltimore. These riots helped solidify the linkage between crime and blacks in the American mind and linked civil rights and Great Society initiatives with crime and race.

Add to the political blowback from the civil rights movement and the urban riots the linkage of crime and blacks that occurred as the result of the structural and criminological centralization of drug use and drug gang violence in urban cities in the 1960s, the rise of crack cocaine, and the violence that followed in urban cities in the 1990s. The urban riots of 1964–1968 helped establish the rise of conservative politics in 1964 and its ascendency by 1972. The fear caused by the race riots provided a platform for conservatives (Republicans) to take control of the national political landscape, which culminated in the nationalization of federal funding of state and local urban crime suppression with the passage of the **Omnibus Crime Control and Safe Streets Act of 1968**. From 1968 to the present, this policy shift resulted in various criminal justice policies, such as the war on drugs, the rise of the nationalization of drug control with the creation of the Drug Enforcement Administration, the passage of the **Comprehensive Drug Abuse Prevention and Control Act of 1970**, and the "get tough on crime" policies of the 1980s and 1990s.[27]

These sociopolitical events were compounded by black dissatisfaction with the Great Society's inability to produce an actual reduction of poverty in urban cities. The failure of the Great Society's programs to make actual and significant change in the levels of poverty in the inner cities coupled with incidents of continued police brutality resulted in the urban riots (1964–1968), which resulted, as discussed earlier, in white suburban middle- and working-class voters' abandonment of the Great Society and the Democratic Party in the 1966 and 1968 elections. White abandonment of the Great Society and its growing resentment of the riots after the passage of major civil rights legislation that ended a century of Jim Crow social policy coupled with white middle-class fear of black radicalism (Black Panthers), which replaced the peaceful civil disobedience strategy of Martin Luther King Jr., further intensified the social-psychological link of civil rights demonstrations with riots and riots with crime, disorder, and blacks in the American political consciousness.

Black Incarceration and the Historical Foundations for Racism in American Criminal Justice Policy

W hite social conservatives assert that America is a great country. Of that, I have no debate. Critical race theorists assert that America is a racist country. As a historical matter, I would not dispute that racism was an accepted proposition in American society from the 1630s and without a doubt from the 1720s through the 1950s. White social conservative orthodoxy asserts that America's racist past is behind her. To that, I would say the worst may be behind her but the results of it are not. *My point is all this can be true at the same time*, in the same context, in the same policy discussion, and in the same political rhetorical narrative. America is great because she is complicated and nuanced.

America established that the great theories of the Enlightenment can be implemented in organizing and maintaining a large and diverse nation. America established that rule of law can control the natural inclinations of humankind in which the strong oppress and take advantage of the weak. America established that government power comes from the people it governs and that they decide policy through regular and consistent elections. The purpose of government is to protect life, liberty, and happiness. America's most significant contribution to the science of governance is the utility and strength of a written constitution. America is the oldest written constitutional system on the planet. Note that all new nations that have come into existence after World War II have adopted the American model of having a written constitution that defines and legitimates the government. America established the principle that unconstitutional is illegal, immoral, and unjust by definition regardless of the legality in the making of the law. America proved that capitalism and democracy can exist and function without devolving into despotism. The Bill of Rights proves that government, to quote James Madison, can be made to control itself.

America also proved that capitalism, democracy, and the ideals of individual freedom can function alongside the enslavement of a people for centuries. Of all of the Western nations that engaged in slavery, only America had to endure a civil war to end the practice. France, Germany, Spain, Great Britain, even Russia ended slavery by peaceful means. While the rest of Europe internalized slavery as an economic tool, America internalized slavery on racial terms. Black skin, by definition, was inferior to whites and that justified slavery. This theory of inferiority, fully adopted in the South by the 1820s, was adopted by the North in the 1870s, and blacks were subjected to second-class citizenship for a century. The same nation that fought General Robert E. Lee and Stonewall Jackson—both fought to destroy the United States to create a slave republic, which in its constitution established slavery as a constitutional right—was building monuments to them in the 1920s. Native Americans through war, disease, relocation, and cultural decimation found themselves pushed off and pushed out of land that they had owned centuries before 1492 so that America could achieve its desire of being a nation from sea to shining sea.

American history is composed of great human advancement and great human debasement. It is this truth that makes America complicated and nuanced. Complicated and nuanced in her history. Complicated and nuanced in the implementation of her highest ideals. Complicated and nuanced in her politics. Complicated and nuanced on the issue of race. Consider that the America that engaged in racism for centuries—slavery and Jim Crow—in 40 years moved from blacks being second class to whites by divine design to electing a black man as president of the United States—twice! But during that same 40-year time period, the country adopted policies that resulted in the incarceration of blacks more than three times their proportion of their population in America. America accepted a black face for their government and asserted that the face of violent crime is also black. Only a complicated and nuanced nation like America could hold both ideals and politics at the same time.

If American history as a whole is complicated and nuanced, equally complicated and nuanced is American racial history within the context of social policy in general and criminal justice policy specifically. Blacks are disproportionally arrested and incarcerated in America. That fact is without dispute. The dispute is on how and why. Is it because of black criminality, which is disproportionate to their population, or is it the result of racism on the part of the police and courts? Can it be both? Is crime the result of social policy or individual behavior? Can it be both? In criminal justice, these questions—and the proposed answers—are argued and debated at every conference and in the academic and professional journals of the profession.

After attending a criminal justice conference in Baltimore, I took an Uber, and the driver was a first-generation immigrant from Nigeria. The gentleman looked at least 60 years old. I did not ask, that would have been disrespectful. As we talked, he told me that he had lived in Baltimore for decades, and I asked him about the city. He told me that in Baltimore, they have "silly laws" that allow people to buy houses, board them up, pay "the little tax," and do nothing with them. He said that occurs in the black neighborhoods and that it brings urban blight and crime. He said "these people come and hold the houses and do nothing, and it makes the neighborhood bad."

As we continued to talk, I asked him what he thought about the riots as the result of the Freddie Gray incident. He said, "Oh, if I get started it will be a long time." He proceeded to tell me that the problem in "our community, we do it to ourselves." He said they have, again, "silly laws" in which we can't discipline our children. He said, "I am the father in the house and my wife is the mother of the house. If my child comes into the house 8, 9, or 10 at night, I am going to be the father in the house." He said, "I beat them, and after he stops crying, I tell him what he did wrong and make him promise not to do it again. I tell him every day what is wrong." The problem, he explained to me, was that "if you don't, you lose control of them at five." He proceeded to say that our children don't have discipline, they get criminal records, and then they can't become police officers. Note his subtle point that being a police officer is an honorable profession and something black kids should aspire to. He pointed out to me that "our children don't understand that the law is not their friend." The law being the police. His point was that "our children" are not disciplined and thus don't react properly to the police.

He then transitioned in his conversation and observed that Baltimore is a black city and yet the police are all white: "From lieutenant to captain to above we are losing our city." With ease of thought, he shifted and said that the police have the "blue law," and even when blacks become police officers, they don't do anything when they see white police officers beat up blacks. He, of course, meant the blue wall of silence. But his point was that the blacks in the police department need to protect other blacks from abusive white police, and they don't, and that leads to resentment and riots. He then linked the lack of discipline of "our children" with blacks leaving the community to live in rich neighborhoods. He said he asks rich blacks who get in his car why they left the community. He pointed out that they are needed to help make the community. He also explained that there was not enough connection between the black people living in the city and the politicians. When I asked about his children, he said his three sons graduated college and were engineers.

I was struck by the simple elegance of this first-generation man in his grasp of the intersectionality of social structure theories, individual responsibility, and public policy and how they all interact to explain race and crime. He had no problem, and found no contradiction, in saying that in America, crime is the result of a combination of racial, social, societal, structural, and individual factors. He blamed individual parents, individual children, black middle-class flight, and their disengagement from working-class and poorer black communities. He observed that urban policy and "silly laws" create urban blight, which brings crime. The lack of the black community taking responsibility to establish positive engagement with local politicians, the lack of local politicians being responsive to local black community concerns and needs, and the abuse and discrimination by police in hiring officers all explain why the riots occurred and how America functions.

One of the reasons he so easily explained the complexity of social policy theory is because he exemplified classical traditional black social conservative theory which is different from black conservatives on Fox News and conservative talk radio. Classical traditional black social conservative theory, as supposed to white social conservative theory, finds congruence with the evil and good of America with no contradiction or conflict. Black classical conservative theory accepts that America was a slave nation and the only nation that had to have a civil war to end slavery and then implemented a century of laws that made the former slaves second-class citizens and the focus of criminal penology and all of this history matters in contemporary policy debates and yet fully accepts the greatness of American democracy and the freedoms that exist despite its racist past. America is both, and one does not negate the other. White social conservative theory lacks this ability to accept both. That's why when white social conservatives, and black conservatives who see America through white conservative eyes, hear America bashing when slavery or Jim Crow is raised. They hear America being attacked.

More subtly, when blacks talk about white racism during slavery and Jim Crow, white conservatives hear they are racist.

Here is the reason for this: white social conservatives see themselves and America as one; they see America and white as one. Attacking white social conservative policy is attacking America, per se. More significantly, pointing out injustice in America or America's racial history is attacking America, per se, and thus attacking whites, per se. For example, consider the response from the dean of white social conservative champions, Rush Limbaugh, when he commented on star athletes who complained about racism or discrimination in America.

> It's getting tiresome to listen to a never ending parade of people on the left, rip this country, criticize this country, blame this country and when none of what they are saying is applicable. This is not the land of grievance. This is the land of opportunity. This is the land of wealth and prosperity, like nowhere has ever been in American or world history. And we are tired of it.[1]

White social conservatives also detest the accusation of racism, which they assert is nothing more than a political tool to silence them. Consider what Steven Miller, senior advisor to President Trump, said on *Fox News Sunday*[2] regarding claims of racism in Trump's policies, racism in his campaign rallies and the responses of his supporters at those rallies, and his tweets attacking four black and Hispanic congresswomen.[3]

> I think the term "racist," Chris, has become a label that is too often deployed by left, Democrats in this country simply to try to silence and punish and suppress people they disagree with, speech that they don't want to hear. The reality is that this president has been a president for all Americans. ...
>
> ....

I fundamentally disagree with the view that if you criticize somebody and they happen to be a different color skin, that that makes it racial criticism. ...

....

If you want to have a color blind society, it means you can criticize immigration policy, you can criticize people's views, you can ask questions about where they're born and not have it be seen as racial.

....

The core issue is that all the people in that audience and millions of patriotic Americans all across this country are tired of being beat up, condescended to, looked down upon, talked down to by members of Congress on the left in Washington, D.C., and their allies in many corners of the media.

White social conservatism has a worldview regarding the history of race and racism in America. As Limbaugh said, "We are tired of it." As Miller said, attacking people of color for being anti-American is not racism, and racism only exists in the rhetorical narratives of the left. But what they also resent is who is doing the complaining. On July 14, 2019, President Trump tweeted in response to comments made by four freshmen women of color collectively known as "the squad"— Rep. Ilhan Omar (a citizen born in Somalia), Rep. Alexandria Ocasio-Cortez, Rep. Rashida Tlaib, and Rep. Ayanna Pressley:

So interesting to see "Progressive" Democrat Congresswomen, who originally came from countries whose governments are a complete and total catastrophe, the worst, most corrupt and inept anywhere in the world (if they even have a functioning government at all), now loudly and viciously telling the people of the United States, the greatest and most powerful Nation on earth, how our government is to be run. *Why don't they go back and help fix the totally broken and crime infested places from which they came.* Then come back and show us how it is done. These places need your help badly, *you can't leave fast enough.* I'm sure that Nancy Pelosi would be very happy to quickly work out free travel arrangements!

The president openly asserted who do these black and Latina women think they are to comment publicly on the leadership and policies of the sitting Speaker of the House—that's where the Nancy Pelosi reference came from—much less contesting his immigration initiatives. According to the Trump worldview, they should be grateful America made a place for them, especially Omar who was a refugee from Africa, in the first place. As Nixon and Reagan complained, the tail wagging the dog.

The following day in a tweet, Trump said, "When will the Radical Left Congresswomen apologize to our Country, the people of Israel and even to the Office of the President, for the foul language they have used, and the terrible things they have said. So many people are angry at them & their horrible & disgusting actions!" Trump did not back down, when asked at a press event: "If he was concerned that 'people saw the tweet as racist, and that white nationalist groups are finding common cause with you on that point,' Trump replied, 'It doesn't concern me because many people agree with me.'"[4] He said of the four congresswomen, "If you are not happy in the U.S., if you're complaining all the time, very simply you can leave right now. Come back if you want, don't come back. Its O.K. too. But if you're not happy you can leave. ... These are people who in my opinion who hate our country ... if they are not happy, they can leave."

Tweeting the same day, Trump continued, "We all know that AOC and this crowd are a bunch of Communists, hate Israel, they hate our own Country, they're calling the guards along our Border (the Border Patrol Agents) Concentration Camp Guards, they accuse people who support Israel as doing it for the Benjamin's, ... they are Anti-Semitic, they are Anti-America, we don't need to know anything about them personally, talk about their policies. I think they are American citizens who are duly elected that are running on an agenda that is disgusting, that the American people will reject."

As will be discussed in Chapter 9, Trump's political support comes from the fact that he can break all social protocols and norms of political discourse with impunity, and he reflects what white social conservatives wish they could say but don't because they would not escape the consequences. As David Duke said in Charlottesville, "That's why we voted for him."

Leaving Trump aside, white social conservatives, as shown by Limbaugh's response, take criticisms of America personally. In white social conservatives' ears, if slavery and racism are evil, then America was evil, then they are evil. This is why white social conservative theory rejects arguments that disproportionate incarceration of blacks is the result of systemic racism. First, they reject the word racism, because that was abandoned in the 1960s. Second, they reject the word systemic because racism can only be systematic—enforced by law—and that was abandoned in the 1960s.

White social conservatives don't want to hear that Washington owned slaves, that Jefferson owned slaves, that Jefferson wrote that blacks are genetically and socially inferior, or that Jackson owned slaves. They don't want to hear about slavery, Jim Crow, the trail of tears, the internment camps of the Japanese, the Tuskegee experiments, the history of lynching, the destruction of Native Americans, the massacre at My Lai, that Martin Luther King advocated for social and economic equality including the imposition of a required minimum living wage, or why Reconstruction was abandoned. No, white social conservatives only want to hear about Washington being a man of prayer before battles; that Jefferson wrote the Declaration of Independence; that Jackson established democracy; that as a matter of history, the moral center of the founding generation was protestant Christianity; that abolitionists were Christian; that blacks in the Massachusetts 54th regiment and the Tuskegee Airmen fought bravely for America under her flag; that Martin Luther King had a dream about only being judged by the content of character and not by skin; that America ended centuries of racism decades ago; that America fought and wiped Nazism off the face of Europe and world history; that America liberated Nazi death camps; and that America is a land of opportunity and freedom from oppression. *Here is the point. All this, both bad and good, are equally true.* But white social conservatives can't hold both truths together at the same time. Only the latter (the good) matters, not the former.

The implicit racism that hides in white social conservative theory is in intentional failure to acknowledge the significance, both historically and contemporaneously, of the evil *with* the good. The *with* is the point. Because when they downplay and ignore the history of blacks who suffered under the evil of slavery and racism, there can be no reconciliation with the champions of white social conservative orthodoxy who ignore the impact of historical racism. The embracement of what Trump represents only makes the possibility of honest and useful political discourse all the more less likely.

The distinction between white social conservatives and traditional classical black social conservatism is that the later has no problem with saying America is the greatest nation on earth, but we don't pretend that unflattering history does not matter, that blacks did not suffer for most of American history under racial injustice, and that history has contemporary consequences. All three truths can be held in the traditional black conservative mind at the same time. They can't be in the white social conservative mind. My Uber driver exampled the ability of black classical traditional social conservative theory to see America's racial flaws as a given, but as my father told me, those contradictions had nothing to do with my individual behavior. My father and mother told me, as my Uber driver clearly told his own children, "If the white man must know one and one is two to get the job, you need to know two plus two is four." Yes, America is a racist country, but that does not mean you can act the fool. My translation of my father's point. It is true that racism is a dynamic of America, and there is systemic injustice in how blacks are treated, but this truth is not the exclusive explanation of the various disparities blacks suffer from. Racism is not always causal, but it's correlated and associated within race-neutral factors. In some situations, racism is the dominant explanation for disparities and social inequalities that blacks suffer from. But in other situations, race is a nuance within otherwise race-neutral factors because of how these race-neutral factors developed in American political and policy history.

Consider the relationship between the founding of America and blacks in American history: between 1619 and 1865 is 246 years; between 1789 and 2020 is 231 years; between 1865 and 1968 is 103 years; between 1968 and 2020 is 52 years.

The enslavement of blacks in the colonies and then in the United States (1619–1865) lasted 246 years, which means slavery and the racism that undergirded it is 15 years older than the entire constitutional history of the United States!

The history of the Black Codes, Jim Crow, and blacks being second-class citizens by statute (103 years—1865 and 1968) is slightly less than half as old as the entire constitutional history of the United States (1789–2020).

Blacks being free from Jim Crow (statutory second-class citizenship) (1968–2020) is only 52 years old in a country that is 231 years old.

Now consider this historical, political, economic, sociological, and psychological development, as well as the operation of the government institutions built on them and their relation to blacks when blacks have only been equal under the law for 52 years of a nation that is 231 years old. This is what President Obama meant when he said racism is in America's DNA.[5]

———————————— ◆ ◆ ◆ ————————————

In May 1607, the Virginia Company of London established the first colony on the North American continent in Jamestown, Virginia. The Virginia colony was established 13 years before the arrival of the Puritans in Cape Cod, Plymouth, Massachusetts, in November 1620. The Jamestown settlement was a financial venture to establish an English foothold on the continent, to establish a system of trade for North American raw materials.

The Jamestown colony during its first few years was not successful; in fact, the inhabitants nearly starved to death. But in 1613, John Rolfe introduced tobacco as a cash crop in Jamestown.[6] Tobacco proved to be the colony's salvation when it became the most profitable export industry in the colony, and by 1617–1618, more than 40,000 pounds of tobacco was shipped to England. Tobacco was the first of many colonial products farmed to meet European demands for luxury and commercial goods. Farming tobacco proved to be profitable, but it was very labor intensive and "white Virginians, who increasingly shunned field work" needed laborers, and they used African slaves to work "long hard hours in the fields" to solve the problem of a lack of availability of white labor.[7] Even before the first colonies were settled in the North American continent, the European colonization of South and Central America and the use of large agricultural lands for the harvesting of tobacco and sugar fostered the need for the importation of more than ten million Africans by the European nations to farm these agricultural estates in the Americas.

The international slave trade involved various European nations that forced the immigration of millions of Africans to the Americas and the Caribbean.

- The Portuguese between 1441 and 1836 imported 5.8 million

- The French between 1549 and 1818 imported 1.4 million

- Great Britain between 1562 and 1807 imported 3.3 million

- The Netherlands (Dutch) between 1619 and 1814 imported 555,300

- Denmark between 1649 and 1802 imported 85,000[8]

The international slave trade route was a triangle. The first angle was from Europe to Africa in which the European slave traders would trade guns, ammunition, and other finished goods for

African slaves. The second angle was from Africa to the Americas and the Caribbean—the middle passage. This angle involved the selling of African slaves for goods for Europe—tea, spices, cotton, tobacco, and other goods. The third angle was the return of these goods to Europe, which were processed as finished goods for sale and trade. The international slave trade was centuries old by the time the first Africans were brought to Jamestown. As with the colonies in the Americas, slavery would be needed in North America soon after tobacco was introduced in 1613.

On August 20, 1619, only 13 years after the colony was established, 20 African slaves arrived in Jamestown, Virginia, from Angola.[9] They were originally enslaved by Portuguese slavers and placed on the *San Juan Bautista* destined for Veracruz in the colony of New Spain but were intercepted by two English ships which took about 60 of the slaves as bounty, and one of the two ships, the *White Lion*, landed in Point Comfort (Jamestown) looking for supplies. They were subsequently used as laborers in raising tobacco. The arrival of the slaves proved to be very beneficial to the developing tobacco-growing agricultural aristocracy of Virginia. Tobacco, and the large tracks of land required for harvesting it, birthed the southern system of plantations, the plantation aristocracy in the South, and the rise of generational wealth fueled and defined by slavery. Within 12 years of the importation of these 20 slaves, more than half a million pounds of tobacco were exported. "The first great American enterprise had been established."[10]

In the early history of southern use of labor to harvest tobacco and later cotton, labor included white indentured servants, as well as African slaves. During this early period, indentured servants could be black or white. But "by the mid-seventeenth century it was becoming clear that Africans and white servants received different treatment."[11] By the 1640s, whites in Virginia who escaped from service were punished by having time added to their service, but blacks were sentenced to a life of service. By the 1660s, slave laws were being passed in the colonies, including changing the common law of rights of inheritance for blacks by linking their legal and social status to the mother rather than to the father with the result being that black children, produced when white slave owners raped their slaves, did not have the legal status of white children. These laws were followed by laws against interracial marriage and laws that made children of white women who married their black slaves the property of the owner of the black slaves.[12] These laws also created the *slave patrols*, which were tasked with preventing slave revolts, slave escapes, returning runaway slaves, and keeping free blacks under social control.

By the 1670s, Virginia was fearful of the growing black population and feared poor white and black slave alliances that could result in rebellion against the growing southern aristocracy. Laws were made to discourage poor white and black associations, and these laws formed the foundation of the social dynamic of poor whites being placed on a higher social status than blacks. These slave laws mirrored antebellum laws, which prohibited slaves from running away, prohibited people from hiding slaves, and required people to return runaway slaves under the **Fugitive Slave Laws** of 1793 and 1850 and the **Fugitive Slave Clause** of the U.S. Constitution.[13] These federal laws supported the system of slavery dating back to the early nineteenth century,[14] and the postbellum Black Codes were the southern answer to the Thirteenth Amendment. Both the Black Codes and the slave laws were predated by the southern slave codes, which were passed after *Bacon's Rebellion* (1676) to separate the shared social and economic interests of the indentured classes (African slaves and white indentured servants). Bacon's rebellion involved a revolt by settlers of Virginia, led by Nathaniel Bacon, against Governor William Berkeley. The significance of the rebellion in American racial history is that the rebellion included blacks as equals with whites. The slave laws were designed to prevent this idea of equality in action from occurring again. The first laws were passed in 1705 in Virginia and then followed by Maryland, North Carolina, South Carolina, and Georgia. These slave codes used the criminal justice system to support the system of slavery.[15] In Missouri, the Slave Code of 1804 required free blacks to carry their papers of manumission and, in 1835, Missouri passed legislation that required all free blacks to be employed and under the supervision of a white employer, specifically "requiring any free black aged seven to twenty-one to be legally bound as an apprentice or servant"[16] under pain of criminal penalty.

By the mid- to late seventeenth century, black slaves replaced white indentured servants as the main source of imported labor in the colonies. By the middle 1770s, the colonies had passed laws that only allowed Africans to be enslaved and classified them as aliens, having no legal rights, and mandated that black slavery was perpetual through maternal generations. Race (black skin) was used as the physical, visual, and legal designation for slavery; black skin was the demarcation line between the applicability and the inapplicability of the law and its protections of whites and blacks in America, respectively. The American context of race, from the date of early slavery, was that blacks were no more than a means to an end and were not equal to those who came to the colonies, whether rich or poor. While it is true that all early immigration occurred through ships, blacks came in the bottom of them and were treated as such when they arrived. Identification of their status was based and defined by skin color.

By the middle 1770s, enforcement of these laws provided a purpose for local law enforcement, which were composed of poor whites and white slave overseers hired by the slave aristocracy. Policing of blacks in America reflects a larger American historical context. That American context is more than a century older than the writing of America's founding documents and its writers.

◆ ◆ ◆

The Black Codes and the Origins of Black Incarceration within American Criminal Justice

Blacks in chains have been a social constant both before and after the Civil War. Originally, blacks were "incarcerated" through the system of slavery. When slavery ended in 1865, it was replaced by the southern development of the *Black Codes*. These laws were passed in 1865–1866 and allowed the former Confederate States to pass laws that prevented blacks from voting, owning property, or enjoying the rights of citizenship. These laws were abolished during radical Reconstruction, 1867–1877, but were later replaced by the system of *Jim Crow*, which put blacks in a system of second-class citizenship that lasted until the late 1960s.

The system of both the Black Codes and Jim Crow was built on the assumption that blacks needed to be controlled and forced to work. Even during the time of radical Reconstruction, 1867–1877 when the North asserted military control of the former Confederate States, there was an "assumption that blacks would not work without compulsion."[17] The significance of the Black Codes is that they replaced the control of blacks through slavery with control through criminal justice statutes. These statutes made blacks susceptible to slavery through conviction, which the Thirteenth Amendment authorized. The Thirteenth Amendment prohibits slavery, except as punishment for conviction of crime. These Black Codes, which were followed by Jim Crow laws, supplemented the broader American policy determination to nullify as many of the post-slavery rights black citizens enjoyed as possible.

The Jim Crow system, which was a broad set of social laws that prevented blacks from enjoying full citizenship, involved various criminal justice statutes. These laws included *mandatory contract laws*, backed by *vagrancy laws*, that required blacks to enter year-long agricultural labor contracts under threat of being convicted of vagrancy.[18] These laws provided a permanent labor force for the agricultural needs of the South. Slavery or no slavery, the cotton, tobacco, and other farm-based products had to be planted, cultivated, and harvested from the ground. Before 1865, slavery was the source of labor. After 1865, when the sharecropping system did not provide enough labor, criminal conviction would make up the slack. Jim Crow used *criminal surety* to require blacks convicted of vagrancy to work for plantation owners to pay off the bond paid by those plantation owners. These criminal statutes supplemented other laws that put blacks in a system of slavery by another name. These laws included *criminal anti-enticement laws,* which forbade employers from hiring contracted workers, which were backed up by *contract enforcement laws* that criminalized blacks taking a better job opportunity.[19] Another system of controlling the right of blacks to contract their labor were *false-pretense laws,* which defined taking another job when wages had been promised for labor as fraud.[20] These contract laws served two purposes: to protect landlords from sharecroppers abandoning the land before harvest (i.e., to protect the landlord's investment) and to maintain a stable labor force that could no longer be controlled by simple slavery.

The significance of the system of these laws is that criminal law was used to enforce contract law. While the use of criminal sanctions as a remedy for civil disputes was an abandonment of Western legal history, the criminalization of contract law solved a practical problem and maintained the social structure of white supremacy in the South. After the Civil War, although landlords maintained the right to sue a sharecropper for leaving or otherwise not fulfilling the terms of the contract, as a practical matter, this right had limited utility. Assuming the absconded sharecropper could be found and returned, because he had no money or valuables, what purpose would a financial judgment from the court be to the landlord? These criminal laws made it a crime to leave a plantation. What a civil lawsuit could not accomplish, criminal law could. The criminal anti-enticement laws, contract enforcement laws, and false-pretense laws forced blacks to stay on the land and work, even when better opportunities presented themselves because failure to do so would result in criminal conviction. Blacks became permanently attached to the plantations with little difference from the antebellum period.

To supplement the criminal surety, mandatory contract laws, criminal anti-enticement laws, contract enforcement laws, and false-pretense laws, southern criminal justice passed specific criminal statutes that were designed to inject blacks into the criminal justice system. These laws included "pig laws" and employment and apprentice laws (*anti-vagrancy statutes*).[21] *Pig laws* were statutes that redefined formally misdemeanor or trivial offenses as felonies and imposed harsh sentences and fines. These laws were selectively enforced against blacks to inject them into the criminal justice system and into forced labor through *peonage, criminal surety*, and *convict leasing*. These laws passed in the 1880s were maintained four decades into the twentieth century.[22]

Peonage

Peonage is forced labor to pay off a financial debt owed to another. Peonage was a tradition brought to the United States through the Louisiana territory when it was ceded to the United States from Spain and France in the Louisiana Purchase in 1803,[23] through the annexation of Texas in 1845, and the subsequent conquest of Mexico during the Mexican-American War (1846–1848).

To prevent the spread of the practice, Congress passed the Peonage Act of 1867, which prohibited the practice of peonage in the New Mexico Territory specifically and in the United States generally.[24] The federal law against peonage was passed (March 1867) 16 months after the assassination of Lincoln (April 1865) and 15 months after the ratification of the Thirteenth Amendment (December 1865) outlawing slavery. The Peonage Act was the first federal legislation to criminally outlaw involuntary servitude. Under the Peonage Act, involuntary service could not be compelled to liquidate financial debt. The law specifically prohibited local law enforcement from enforcing peonage by making it illegal to "hold, arrest, or return, or cause to be held, arrested, or returned, or in any manner aid in the arrest or return of any person or persons to a condition of peonage."

After the North withdrew from the Confederate South, still an agricultural economy, the South needed labor to work the remaining plantation fields. The defeat of the South did not change the economic dynamics of the South. Blacks were free but still had to work, and the status of economic dependence and intellectual ignorance that they were forced to endure before the war did not immediately change after the war. Blacks were still poor, undereducated, and only skilled in agricultural work or jobs that supported the southern plantation system. After the Civil War and during Reconstruction, they worked and struggled to educate themselves and when they became economically independent of white landowners, they posed a threat to the system of white supremacy. When the North abandoned blacks to the former leaders of the Confederacy, southern criminal justice and the system of Jim Crow after Reconstruction would retard black achievement of self-sufficiency and social equality for a century. Without federal enforcement of civil rights after the Civil War and Reconstruction, blacks were left to the mercy of state and local government officials, politics, and policy interests. A lesson not lost on blacks—then or today.

The history of the **American postbellum criminal justice** *system and disproportionate incarceration of blacks in America* **begins** *with state policies to circumvent the federal law against criminal peonage.*

The origin of **American policing begins** *with the slave patrols in the South, slave catching in the North, and enforcement of criminal surety, mandatory contract laws, criminal anti-enticement laws, contract enforcement laws, false-pretense laws, employment and apprentice laws (anti-vagrancy statutes), pig laws, and convict leasing in the South and failure of federal enforcement of the Peonage Act postbellum.*

Both federal civil and military authority were required to enforce the Peonage Act. Thus, from the earliest days of the postbellum period, it was the duty of the federal government to enforce laws preventing state-sponsored activities that put individuals in a state of involuntary servitude. Although peonage was illegal under federal law, it was not enforced after the fall of Reconstruction. When the North withdrew from the South, peonage was integrated with the Thirteenth Amendment, and the South passed laws that focused on criminalizing black economic and social behavior so that blacks could be forced to comply with employment contracts under the threat of criminal prosecution, or blacks were required to liquidate criminal fines paid by others at bail and sentencing hearings. The legal basis for this was that involuntary servitude was authorized by criminal convictions. Blacks went from slaves to criminals. The slave plantations changed to penal plantations. In Louisiana the famous Angola prison is a living and functioning monument and testimony to this history of black incarceration.

Peonage occurred through the dual dynamics of the creation of criminal violations that required fines or high bail before trial. Blacks who did not have such funds were released under criminal surety bonds paid for by white property owners in need of labor. Blacks were then forced to work for those whites to liquidate the debt. The southern criminal justice system used the conviction of minor crimes as a tool to force blacks to work for white planta- tion owners to plant and maintain crops to pay off debt incurred through imposition of criminal fines.

This system of laws, along with the segregation laws, lasted decades into the twentieth century. The systematic use of peonage was part of a larger system of social, economic, political, and legal oppression in the South after the Civil War. This oppression included the use of whitecapping, lynching, intimidation in voting, and simple murder of blacks on sight. *Whitecapping* was a method of intimida- tion by poor whites who had lost their land because of debt. These poor whites would depose blacks of their land by force or threat of force. This system of fear and oppression, both legal and illegal, was allowed to flourish under federal government indifference well into the twentieth century. As Pete Daniel explains in his book *The Shadow of Slavery*, the southern economic system was "a debt-labor system characterized by violence and the corruption or acquiescence of local police officers was openly tolerated. In a section of the country characterized by illiteracy and poverty, vulnerable victims were in profusion, and most of the peons were black."[25]

The system of peonage was supportive of the broader system of indebting blacks and the use of the local police force to maintain their compliance within the agricultural system of the postbellum period. After the Civil War, the agricultural system of the South suffered, in part, from a lack of cash to pay for labor. To address the lack of cash for both tenant and landowner, two systems developed: the sharecropper and tenant farmer. These systems were different in fact, practice, and law.

Blacks were sharecroppers not tenant farmers. *Tenant farmers* paid rent for the land and owned the produce of their planting and harvest. The distinction also applied to how the farmer was expected to be treated. The tenant farmer owned his time and strategy for securing the harvest; the landowner received his payment through agreed-upon rent. The tenant farmer "owned" his personhood regarding the labor required to secure the harvest.

Sharecroppers lived on the land, borrowed supplies from local store merchants for planting, and then split the produce of the land with the landowner. The loans black sharecroppers secured were collateralized against their half of the harvest. The problem the sharecropper regularly found himself in was that the yield was never enough to cover the half taken by the landowner and the loan owed to the merchant who provided the sharecropper with the seed, food, supplies, and other necessities for the planting season. The loan would be carried over to the next season compounded by the new loan needed for the new year. The sharecropper was placed in perpetual debt. Any attempt to escape the debt would be met with criminal contract violation charges and the system of peonage/criminal surety or convict leasing.

The sharecropper, as far as the landowner was concerned, was a wage worker and as such was under the supervision of the landowner. The landowner expected the sharecropper to work as he did under slavery. The sharecropper was under the control of the landowner overseer as he was under slavery. He could not remove his wife and children from enforced work nor from the intentions of rape of his wife and daughters by the overseer. This system was what southern legislation contemplated when the Black Codes were legislated.[26] The criminal justice system provided its support to the sharecropping system through enforcement of local Black Codes and the Jim Crow system through the local sheriff, which replaced the slave patrols. Sheriffs enforced peonage, vagrancy laws, and criminal surety to force blacks to work the plantation system.

The significance of the injustice of peonage was that it was illegal under federal law since 1867, but it was allowed to function almost unabated until the dawn of World War Two. The lesson drawn from peonage is that it lasted because of the national government's abandonment of blacks on the altar of national unification with the South.[27] The federal government did not engage in a serious effort to intervene and stop the states from operating under criminal peonage until the progressive era, resulting from U.S. Justice Department prosecutions[28] and by the Supreme Court ruling in *United States v. Clyatt* that criminal justice peonage was unconstitutional in 1905.[29] Although peonage was held unlawful in 1905, the Confederate States were recalcitrant in supporting their right to enforce peonage and criminal contract laws. The criminal penalties imposed on blacks accused of committing criminal fraud by intentional abrogation of contract led to the Supreme Court rulings in *Bailey v. Alabama* (1911) and *United States v. Reynolds* (1914), which stated that state laws that allowed private contracts to be enforced by criminal sanctions were unconstitutional.[30] But what the Court says is unlawful and what the national government enforces is not always the same thing. The system of peonage and criminal contract laws, along with sharecropping, did not disappear from southern criminal justice until the practice came under direct attack by federal enforcement of the Peonage Act in the 1940s.

Criminal Surety, Enticement Laws, and Other Systems of Involuntary Servitude

Criminal surety, along with convict leasing,[31] occurred shortly after the end of the Civil War. The system involved using convict labor to meet state, local, and private labor needs. *Criminal surety*, established by state statute or by customs dating back to the ante-bellum period of the Confederate South, authorized county governments and local police officers to allow private agricultural, construction, coal mining companies, and/or private plantation owners to pay the bail of accused people in exchange for promises of labor from these misdemeanants, and sometimes felons.[32] Charges would be stayed in exchange for labor for a set period of time, which could be weeks to months. The South passed statutes that redefined formally misdemeanor or trivial offenses as felonies and imposed harsh sentences and fines. These *pig laws* were selectively enforced against blacks to inject them into the criminal justice system.

One of the ways to keep the former slaves in a status close to slavery was to control employment because that minimized economic independence. Between 1865 and 1867, ten southern states established *anti-enticement laws*.[33] These laws made it a crime to try and hire away a laborer already under contract to another person. The result of these laws was the control of the black labor force, specifically its mobility. These statutes were passed in Alabama, Georgia, Florida, North Carolina, Arkansas, South Carolina, Louisiana, and Mississippi before and after the fall of Reconstruction.[34] These laws not only outlawed the hiring of blacks under contract but also many authorized the employer to send the police or private "man catchers" to secure runaway contracted blacks and return them to the employer.[35] Tennessee (1917), Virginia (1924), and Texas (1929) also passed anti-emigrant-agent laws during the first great migration (1916–1920s) to prevent blacks from leaving the South to go to the North.[36]

While anti-emigrant-agent laws were designed to control whites and to prevent them from "stealing" blacks from their white landlords who needed black labor, *contract-labor statutes* were specifically designed to keep blacks in their place by requiring them to have employment under penalty of criminal sanction. Young blacks who could not prove employment or were not employed were "apprenticed out" to white plantation owners. These *apprentice laws* provided revenue for the local county sheriffs because they shared with the local court the fee paid by the white plantation owner to have the youth assigned to them. States enforced these apprentice and contract labor laws with *proof of employment statutes* that required blacks to carry papers proving that they left their employers legitimately and that they were gainfully employed.[37] These laws were little different than the *manumission statutes* that required freed blacks to carry their freedom papers to show on demand of any white man or police officer to prove they were free during the days of slavery.

Although these statutes fell out of favor during Reconstruction, they reemerged in the 1880s and 1890s after the North abandoned blacks to the mercy of southern Democrats in 1877. To keep black employment stable, the southern states passed laws that made it unlawful for a black to look for better employment while under contract.[38] These *false-pretense laws* (criminal contract fraud) criminalized breach of contract under the guise of asserting that the failure to comply with a contractual obligation was an act of fraud with the intent to injure the employer. The use of civil contract breach as a strategy to criminalize black labor disputes to bring blacks to heel was too much even for the separate but equal Supreme Court, and in 1911, the Court held[39] the false-pretense laws unconstitutional.[40] But many former Confederate States (North and South Carolina, Florida, and Georgia) remained incalcitrant and maintained false-pretense statutes until the 1940s.

It was one thing to have methods to enforce a contract already made; it was something else to force blacks to enter into those labor contracts. That is where the criminal justice system came in with laws outlawing vagrancy, loitering, and lack of proof of employment. These Black Codes, passed in 1865–1866 in North Carolina, Florida, Louisiana, Georgia, South Carolina, Alabama, Virginia, Texas, and Mississippi defined the crime of vagrancy in sweeping terms, which included anyone without a labor contract.[41] The *vagrancy laws* made being out of work or unable to prove employment a crime punishable by fines, and it provided a source of forced labor of blacks when the need for labor increased because of economic conditions.[42] The *apprentice laws* focused on black children and forced them to work for white employers under the theory that black youths needed to be prevented from idleness and crime. The courts would receive a fee from whites taking the responsibility to "train" black youth in a trade. The fact that blacks, through various *commercial and trade restrictive laws,* were banned from the various white trade associations and being unable to own property almost guaranteed unemployment, which led to vagrancy violations, which subjected them to criminal surety, peonage, and convict leasing. The criminal surety laws gave a convict a choice: sign the labor contract and work for a person for six months or a year or serve months in a jail or prison work camp at hard labor.[43]

This system of involuntary servitude: peonage, vagrancy statutes, forced labor contracts, the sharecropper system, convict leasing, and criminal surety had their high-water mark between the late nineteenth and early twentieth centuries. But as the nation moved from the Great Depression to the war of the Greatest Generation and its fight against Nazism and, after the war, its fight against communism, the legality and political and social support for the system of involuntary servitude of blacks began to come to an end.

Jim Crow would be dead two decades after the guns were silenced in 1945. But the lasting and enduring damage of the system was the systemic disproportionate confinement of blacks in the criminal justice system. The history of the involuntary servitude makes clear that, from 1865 through World War II, blacks were sought by the criminal justice system to benefit former slaveholders, business interests, and government labor needs. Actual criminal behavior of blacks was secondary, if not tertiary, in explaining black incarceration. But with the systematic policy of the social control of blacks (slavery, followed by the Black Codes, and Jim Crow) dispensed with by the late 1960s, the systemic political and social assumption that blacks are criminals and need to be controlled remained. This assumption has resulted in social policy outputs and outcomes that support a belief that blacks are supposed to be disproportionately represented within the criminal justice system.

Convict Leasing

With the death of Reconstruction because of the disputed election of 1876 and the compromise of 1877,[44] known as the second great corrupt bargain,[45] in American history, any pretense of black equality to whites disappeared. The need for labor to rebuild the South, both in agriculture and the newly developing industrial capacity because of the building of railroads and coal mining, a systematic need for continuous labor at low cost in the life-threatening work of private industry produced a secondary system of black servitude almost equal to slavery—the convict-leasing system.

During slavery, blacks had economic value to both the slave owner and the southern society as a whole; as convicts, blacks again had economic value to both the plantation owner and/or the coal mine owner in need of cheap labor and to southern society as a whole—their labor was a source of governmental revenue. Although convict leasing was a major factor in meeting employment needs in the postbellum south, its roots date to the antebellum period of the 1840s–1850s in which slaves were imprisoned and sentenced to periods of hard labor as an alternative to hanging them for crimes.[46] Prisoners who were slaves were worked and sold as the non-convicted slaves were.

The overarching concept of convict leasing, regardless of operation, is that the convict has financial value to the criminal justice system. Convict leasing removed from the purpose of criminal justice the principles of rehabilitation of the offender or retribution on the offender and replaced it with the purpose of securing financial profit. Southern policing had enough of an original sin in that it was birthed from the sole purpose of oppressing free blacks, and law and order was solely defined by controlling the slave population and preventing slave escapes and rebellions. But after the Civil War, slave patrols became southern police forces, and the purpose of the southern police was to arrest blacks for financial gain, regardless of actual guilt.

After the Civil War, sheriffs and constables maintained the classical southern way of life, which included keeping the former slaves subservient and maintaining white supremacy. In this post-Civil War system of social control, southern police and local judges were paid through fines and bonds,[47] which through peonage and criminal surety were paid by white plantation owners. The system of police having a financial incentive to make arrests did not end with convict leasing and peonage in the 1940s. Since the 1980s, police financial incentive to make arrests exists through the federal and state system of asset forfeiture and arrest requirements of Justice Department state-local police drug units. Currently, in many localities, government operational budgets are supplemented by police issuing parking tickets and other fines for minor violations, which also carry fines for failure to pay. These fines are used to supplement the annual budgets of the localities. This system of "taxation through fination" is enforced by the issuing of bench warrants when the fines and fees are not paid. The violence resulting from the shooting of Michael Brown by Darren Wilson in Ferguson, Missouri, in August 2014, was partially explained by chronic community outrage at the systematic use of the Ferguson police to issue citations and the court to collect the fees, mostly from the majority poor black residents, to cover the operational budget of the city.[48]

Under the convict-leasing system of the postbellum period, the charges made against blacks included serious felonies, but mostly they were petty crimes, such as vagrancy, gambling, and loitering or violations of civil contracts resulting in an unpaid debt or a charge of breach of contract (intentional financial fraud).[49] These petty crimes or civil contract claims, when convicted, would require fines, which the accused could not pay. "If the black man was unable to pay the fine, a local white man would 'graciously' pay the fine allowing the black man, and occasionally a black woman, to work off the debt over time. Once in this system, time could be added to the original contract simply by accusing the peon of another crime. The key to the entire process was the swift arrest, trial, and sentencing of the black person and the absence of witnesses and lawyers for defense."[50] This system of criminal peonage was supplemented by the state or county renting convicts to industry for a fee—convict leasing. The convict was trapped: first he worked to pay off the fines of the conviction which were paid by the landowner—peonage—then when he escaped or refused to work past his originally sentenced period, he was arrested, convicted for violating the contract (only the person holding the debt could determine if his time was served), and subsequently rented out to the same landowner under convict lease.[51] Of course, the sharecropper knowing how this system worked would chose to stay on the land and work in perpetual debt rather than risk being arrested for vagrancy or contract fraud and then put to work through convict leasing or be under a judicial order to work for a plantation owner under peonage, criminal surety, and/or forced apprenticeship.

By the late nineteenth century, the states of the Deep South were renting out state prisoners for labor when not using them for state labor projects. State use of convicts for labor on state projects birthed the practice of chain gangs, work gangs, and imposition of the sentence of 20 years of hard labor. And in the southern prisons, a man could be beaten and worked to death in a convict-lease work camp, if not killed by disease first,[52] and race was at the heart of the harshness of the southern system.[53] The convict-leasing system began in 1844 in Louisiana and started to formally end in 1928 when abandoned by Alabama. The convict-leasing system, like the criminal-peonage system, did not functionally begin to end until the 1940s when Attorney General Francis Biddle issued orders for federal prosecutions under circular 3591 on December 12, 1941. The point being is that these systems did not end, like slavery before them, until the federal government's power was imposed. A lesson not lost on either states' rights white social conservatives or those who advocate for civil rights.

————————————— ◆ ◆ ◆ —————————————

I often tell my students that the criminal justice system as we know it today did not just appear out of the sky. The American criminal justice system is part of the larger social and political dynamic of American politics and social decisions. The criminal justice system reflects America's determination of what is crime, what is criminal, who is to be punished, and how criminals are to be treated. But more importantly, the answers to these and other questions are not static. They are fluid based on the social politics of the moment.

In understanding the politics of the moment, which results in specific criminal justice policy, it is important to realize that the politics and policy are not the end of the process. Before policy and before politics, there are political narratives and political rhetoric. How right and wrong are perceived (political narratives) by society is translated into what society advocates for (political rhetoric). That advocacy is translated into politics (the power to make government decisions—who wins elections), which is operationalized into government action (policy). In a functioning constitutional republic like the United States, politics is operationalized through elections. Those who win them make policy, and those who lose elections go home and write memoirs.

One of the policies that flow out of political discourse is the law and how the courts support the letter as well as the purpose of the law. In the American context, there is a linear history of the enforcement of the law regarding blacks. The history includes the judicial enforcement of the slave laws, then the Black Codes, then Jim Crow, and later the "law and order" statutes of the 1980s and 1990s. This historical process began with the judicial pronouncement that slaves under the law are equal to horses in regard to their treatment.

In the movie *Belle*, regarding the transatlantic slave trade and the law allowing insurance companies to provide financial insurance against losses of the cargo of slave ships, it was observed that "it is the utter injustice ... the industrial slaughter of so many. No. It is more than that. It's the shame of a law that would uphold a financial transaction upon that atrocity."[54] The movie *Belle* centered on the life of Dido Elizabeth Lindsey, the grandniece of Lord Chief Justice William Mansfield. The time period for the movie was

1783 when Lord Mansfield decided the *Zong Massacre Case*.[55] The case involved an incident in which slave traders threw live slaves overboard and then claimed they had to save the lives of the crew because of a lack of water for both the slaves and the crew. During the trial, Mansfield accepted this argument of necessity and informed the jury that slaves, like other property aboard a ship, could be thrown overboard and be under insurance protection. Mansfield equated the lives of slaves with the lives of horses when he wrote, "The matter left to the jury, was whether it was from necessity: for they had no doubt (though it shocks one very much) that the Case of Slaves was the same as if Horses had been thrown overboard." He made clear that regarding the death of horses or slaves, if "the Slaves are kill'd they will be paid for ... as if horses were kill'd ... but you don't pay for Horses that die a Natural Death."[56]

Mansfield held that evidence discovered after the trial showed that the ship was not in distress, as claimed, and that it had rained before the slaves were thrown overboard. Mansfield ordered the jury verdict for the shipowners to be overturned for a new trial. The reporter of the case wrote that this case probably led to the law that prevented insurance companies from being required to pay for the loss of slaves based on their deaths because of natural causes, ill-treatment by the crew, or being thrown overboard for any reason.[57] The significance of this case in the history of blacks and the law as enforced by the court is that what Mansfield said regarding the value of black lives, that they were equal, at best, to the lives of horses, was true under the law! Black lives, to paraphrase a current assertion, did not matter as a matter of law. The U.S. Supreme Court would affirm this status in the famous *Dred Scott* case in 1857 in which it held not only that there was no law regarding the rights of blacks that a white man must respect but also that as a matter of original intent, blacks were not covered by the Declaration of Independence, which states "that all men are created equal ... endowed. ... with ... Rights ... [including] Life, Liberty and the pursuit of Happiness" and were not citizens under the U.S. Constitution. The Civil War reversed the later, and Jim Crow affirmed the former.

The idea that blacks were property and treated as such allowed for their dehumanization. The principle of black inferiority under the law survived slavery and formed the foundation for the system of discrimination in America based on race that formed the passage of Jim Crow laws in America. With the subsequent fall of Jim Crow after the civil rights movement, the idea of black inferiority and need for social control survived and found implementation through the criminal justice system. There is a continuity of social control based on the inferiority of blacks that runs from slavery through the crime control policies of today. One of the factors underlying this continuity is one of the original justifications for slavery—biblical assent, if not biblical command, that God intended blacks to be servants of whites.

White Christian Europe had a religious philosophical problem when it adopted slavery. Historically, slavery was the result of war in which one of the prizes of victory was the enslavement of the vanquished. But slavery based on this classical theory of war did not assert that the slave was less human than his new master. Slavery was the punishment for lost wars. But the enslavement of Africans for the purpose of transport to the new world was a different matter. Africans were not a conquered people because of traditional war; they were kidnapped for the purpose of economic exploitation. This was a problem because the Bible makes clear that man stealing, kidnapping, is a sin. Thus, the Europeans needed to interpret the Bible in such a way that slavery was lawful under the Bible. The answer, in part, is found in the story of Noah and later the law that God gave the Israelites in the new land. The reason why this matters is that America was settled by Christians, and Christian principles are at the foundation of American history. European slave masters and American colonists had to merge slavery with Christianity to enjoy both.

In the book of Genesis, Noah, his wife, his three sons (Ham, Shem, and Japheth), and their wives were rescued from the flood. After the family found solid land, Noah got drunk and passed out naked. The scriptures report that Ham saw Noah naked and looked upon him, but when Shem and Japheth knew of their father's position, they covered him without looking at his nakedness. When Noah woke up and knew what Ham had done, he cursed Ham's son Canaan declaring that he shall serve the sons of Shem and Japheth. The sons of Shem led to Abraham, the patriarch of the Jewish nation. The sons of Japheth include Europeans and Asians. The sons of Canaan are the colored peoples of the world, including those of Africa and the Middle East.[58] This story, along with the fact that God gave the land of Canaan to the Jews both before and after they were delivered from Egypt, buttressed the belief that God had made his choice between the children of Noah; Shem first, Japheth second, and Ham to serve both. White European theology concluded that blacks were, by God's will, cursed to the status of slaves to the descendants of Japheth. White Europeans, the sons of Japheth, were within their rights by God to take African slaves and sell them to white Christians in the colonies in North America at will and at their mercy with no concern of the judgment of God.[59]

The belief of American Christian slave owners that Africans were slaves by divine decree was also supported by the self-perception by the puritan settlers of North America that they were the new chosen people of God, and they were entitled to treat the indigenous peoples of North America and Africans brought to North America as the Hebrews of the Old Testament treated the indigenous peoples found on the other side of the Jordan. They read in the Bible that God said to Moses, "Completely destroy them—the Hittites, Amorites, Canaanites, Perizzites, Hivites and Jebusites" and "the Israelites captured the Midianite women and children and took all the Midianite herds, flocks and goods as plunder. They burned all the towns where the Midianites had settled, as well as all their camps. They took all the plunder and spoils, including the people and animals."[60] American Christian slave owners reasoned, as Moses acted in the land of the Jordan, so can we in Africa. They reasoned the Old Testament allowed the children of Israel to hold and take slaves from the conquered nations, and God specifically blessed the patriarch of the Old Testament, Abraham, who owned slaves.

American slave Christian theology also asserted that in the New Testament God commanded that slaves were to obey their masters not as eye pleasers but as unto God. Although Paul asked Philemon for the freedom of the slave Onesimus and admonished Philemon when he said that because Onesimus was a brother in Christ, and he should be treated as such, the point is Paul sent the slave back to his master. They pointed to the fact that Paul offered to pay for his freedom and specifically did not command that his freedom be given.[61] This was not the only misreading and misapplication of Paul that white Christianity reasoned from him. They ignored the fact that Paul rejected racism as well as slavery. In the second chapter of the book of Galatians, we are told that when Peter, a Jew, was found not sitting and eating with Gentiles (non-Jews, whites) because they were non-Jews (white), Paul publicly rebuked him and his hypocrisy of claiming to be a follower and teacher of the word of Christ yet not sharing it with non-Jews (whites) with honesty and integrity. For Paul said, in Christianity, "there is neither Jew nor Gentile, neither slave nor free, nor is there male and female, for you are all one in Christ Jesus."[62] Because we are all equal before God through Jesus his Son, all Christians should be treated as such. White European and American Christians were not the first to ignore this principle for their own economic and social gain, but they surely ignored it when dominance of the world shifted to them when Christianity took center stage as a social and political dynamic in European world history.

This misrepresentation and manipulation of the scriptures was transferred from Europe to American thinking. American white Christians reasoned that the Bible itself, both in the Old and New Testaments, not only did not prohibit slavery, but it acknowledged and approved of the practice of owning slaves and required slaves to comply with their status. They reasoned that, because the Bible condoned slavery and because it did not condemn the practice, it was not immoral or prohibited for white Christians to kidnap, buy, and hold African slaves.[63] The dehumanization and racism developed by American Christians based on the notion that blacks were the sons of Ham and as such were supposed to be slaves by the decree of God only made the institution of slavery worse in America, because it was based on racism as opposed to European slavery, which was based on conquest and economics. Economic justification was the primary distinction in European slavery, racism was a secondary justification as Europe moved away from religious foundations for social dynamics. In American slavery, by the early 1800s, blacks were an economic means to an end, but the justification was based on racial inferiority as designated by God. In 1865, slavery (an economic means to an end) was ended, but the inferiority perception long after prevailed.

This justification of slavery in American history is important because one aspect of racism in America is that it was conflated into American religious history and that is one reason why racism has prevailed in American social history even when its operational tools—slavery, Black Codes, and Jim Crow—have been relegated to the dust bin of history. The implicit belief that blacks are criminal and should be disproportionately incarcerated replaced the idea that blacks are supposed to be enslaved and are naturally inferior to whites because that is the judgment of God. And, as discussed in the next chapter, this idea of black inferiority was fully advocated by one of the most famous men of the founding generation: Thomas Jefferson.

The Bible as a whole, and Christianity specifically, does not support the racial imposition of slavery put forth by the white Christian enslavers of Europe and later America. To briefly answer their misrepresentations, I submit the following for consideration.

First, the history of slavery is the story of how "man took dominion over man. ... *God made men; men made slaves!*"[64] As it is written, "The Lord saw that the wickedness (depravity) of man was great on the earth, and that every imagination *or* intent of the thoughts of his heart were only evil continually."[65] In answering why Moses had to make allowances[66] for the Jews regarding their behavior, Jesus said, "Because your hearts were hard *and* stubborn."[67] Put simply, slavery was not God's idea.

Second, the Old Testament makes kidnapping a death penalty offense.[68] Slavery by kidnapping is not supported in the Bible, Old or New Testament.

Third, Noah, not God, cursed the son of Ham! Nor is it recorded in scripture that God affirmed Noah's curse.

Fourth, as a matter of biblical structure,[69] the curse did not establish a scriptural tradition. The curse is not mentioned post-Noah, and Noah, unlike Abraham and Moses, is not a prophet or a patriarch of the scriptures; the advocacy of white Christian confederates notwithstanding.[70]

Fifth, the curse was issued by a drunk who cursed his grandson for the sin of his son. The word of drunk does not carry biblical significance.

Sixth, even if one assumes that the curse of Noah has biblical significance, all curses under the Old Testament were atoned[71] for through the resurrection of Jesus as written in the New Testament.[72]

Seventh, the New Testament, when slavery was mentioned, required masters to be just to their slaves, for it reminded them that all Christians are slaves to Christ. Although the scriptures make clear, as white Christians proclaimed, that slaves were to obey their masters, the context of the scripture is that they were to obey and serve their masters as Jesus served God and that slaves—as did their masters—should do all things for God as He watches all. The obedience was not obedience based on slavery itself.[73]

Lastly, the New Testament makes clear that the heart of God on the matter of Christians owning slaves was that He desired them to be freed and accepted as brothers of the faith.[74] Christianity is about redemption from sin through Jesus. Christianity redeems, not condemns; it makes one free; it does not enslave the body of one to another.[75]

Christianity brought this truth to the American slave: the knowledge that he was a child of God and, as such, had to be treated that way. This truth emboldened the abolitionist movement and in the face of this truth, Jefferson wrote, "I tremble for my country when I reflect that God is just: that his justice cannot sleep forever." And in the face of this truth, Lincoln concluded in his Second Inaugural Address regarding the carnage of the American Civil War, "the judgments of the Lord are true and righteous altogether."

chapter four

Rhetorical Orthodoxy of Conservatives and Liberals

I t has been said by many a life coach and motivational speaker that thinking produces words, and they, in turn, produce decisions and actions, and those, in turn, produce habits and behaviors, which, in turn, produce character and destiny. Many a conservative has asserted that America was birthed from an idea, and America is defined by what it believes. America is not a nation created by the history of thousands of years; America was created by a set of specific ideas adopted at a specific period of time. What defines America, conservatives tell us, is its ideals and principles and its actions. All of which define its character as great and good. I am in complete agreement.

But not all of those ideas were good or just or admirable. Those unjust and evil ideas, just as the great ones of the Declaration of Independence, defines America's actions, its cultural habits, and its behavior, which resulted in the American character. American exceptionalism is defined by its ability to hold both great and evil ideas in the same narrative and to have committed great acts of self-sacrifice, altruism, and generosity, as well as great atrocities. This duality is exampled in the writings of a man who is at the very founding of the great ideals of America. Consider one of his most famous (at least it should be) writings.

> The circumstance of superior beauty, is thought worthy attention in the propagation of our horses, dogs, and other domestic animals; why not in that of man? Besides those of colour, figure, and hair, there are other physical distinctions proving a difference of race. They have less hair on the face and body. They secrete less by the kidnies, and more by the glands of the skin, which gives them a very strong and disagreeable odour. This greater degree of transpiration renders them more tolerant of heat, and less so of cold, than the whites.
>
> A black, after hard labour through the day, will be induced by the slightest amusements to sit up till midnight, or later, though knowing he must be out with the first dawn of the morning. They are at least as brave ... But this may perhaps proceed from a want of forethought, which prevents their seeing a danger till it be present. When present, they do not go through it with more coolness or steadiness than the whites.
>
> They are more ardent after their female: but love seems with them to be more an eager desire, than a tender delicate mixture of sentiment and sensation. ... In general, their existence appears to participate more of sensation than reflection. ...
>
> Comparing them by their faculties of memory, reason, and imagination, it appears to me, that in memory they are equal to the whites; in reason much inferior ... and that in imagination they are dull, tasteless, and anomalous. ... But never yet could I find that a black had uttered a thought above the level of plain narration; never see even an elementary trait of painting or sculpture. In

music they are more generally gifted than the whites ... Misery is often the parent of the most affecting touches in poetry ... Among the blacks is misery enough, God knows, but no poetry. ...

Their mixture with ... whites ... proves ... their inferiority. ... We know that among the Romans ... the condition of their slaves was much more deplorable than that of the blacks. ...

Yet notwithstanding these and other discouraging circumstances among the Romans, their slaves were often their rarest artists. They excelled too in science, insomuch as to be usually employed as tutors to their master's children. ... But they were of the race of whites. It is not their condition then, but nature, which has produced the distinction. ...

The opinion, that they are inferior in the faculties of reason and imagination ... it must be said, that though for a century and a half we have had under our eyes the races of black and of red men ... I advance it therefore ... that the blacks, whether originally a distinct race, or made distinct by time and circumstances, are inferior to the whites in the endowments both of body and mind.

This unfortunate difference of colour, and perhaps of faculty, is a powerful obstacle to the emancipation of these people. ... When freed, he is to be removed beyond the reach of mixture.[1]

So, wrote, not the grand wizard of the Ku Klux Klan or the founders of the Confederate States as they asserted the reasons for the secession from the Union in 1861, but so wrote *Thomas Jefferson.*

These words were written in 1781 by the same author who wrote only five years earlier, "We hold these truths to be self-evident, that all men are created equal, that they are endowed by their Creator with certain unalienable rights, that among these are life, liberty and the pursuit of happiness." Yet, while believing that blacks by

birth were inferior to whites in all things—except musical ability—
he wrote that slavery both before and after independence was an
evil. In his original draft of the great Declaration of Independence,
he listed among the abuses by the king worthy of separation that

> he has waged cruel war against human nature itself,
> violating its most sacred rights of life and liberty in
> the persons of distant people, who never offended him,
> captivating and carrying them into slavery in another
> hemisphere, or to incur miserable death in their trans-
> portation thither. ... Determined to keep open a market
> where Men should be bought and sold, he has prostituted
> ... every legislative attempt to prohibit or to restrain this
> execrable commerce: and ... he is now exciting those very
> people to rise in arms among us, and to purchase that
> liberty of which he has deprived them by murdering the
> people upon whom he also obtruded them; thus paying
> off former crime committed against the liberties of one
> people, with crimes which he urges them to commit
> against the lives of another.

Jefferson's famous slave clause of the Declaration of Independence
was opposed by the southern colonies, and under their threat not
to sign the declaration if the clause was included, it was deleted.
This was the first of many compromises to make and maintain
America at the expense and sacrifice of the human and "endowed
... unalienable rights" of blacks.

Five years after writing the slave clause, he wrote that the "whole
commerce between master and slave is ... the most unremitting despotism on the one part, and degrading submissions on the other."
He lamented that under such a system, the children of slave owners
learn from this evil, the "worst of passions, and thus nursed, educated, and daily exercised in tyranny, cannot but be stamped by it
with odious peculiarities." Reflecting on this system, which allows
"one half the citizens thus to trample on the rights of the other,"

he concluded, "Indeed I tremble for my country when I reflect that God is just: that his justice cannot sleep forever."[2]

Fifty years after Jefferson, a son of the south responded to those who lamented on the evil of slavery and its trampling on the rights of blacks, reflecting the new south and its position on slavery. The south was abandoning the proposition that slavery was evil and emphatically defended their God-given right to enslave blacks with no shame or fear.

On January 10, 1838, Senator John Calhoun of South Carolina—the father of states' rights and nullification politics—proposed (on the floor of the U.S. Senate) in his *On the Importance of Domestic Slavery* speech[3] six resolutions asserting states' rights and the theory of limited powers of the national government. It was with this speech and subsequent speeches defending slavery and later secession that states' rights, defiance of the federal government, and subjugation of blacks merged. States' rights and assertions of limited powers of the national government was birthed into American politics within the specific context of opposing federal power to end the chief aspect of racism in America at the time: the existence and spread of slavery into the western territories. This context is important to understand because states' rights and limited government became the argument of southern democrats in the 1930s through the 1950s who opposed the goals of the civil rights movement in the 1960s and 1970s. In the 1860s, states' rights and limited government was asserted to support succession. A century later, the rhetoric of George Wallace and Strom Thurmond adopted the rhetoric of Calhoun and by the late 1950s through the 1960s and this rhetoric evolved into the new political sophistication and branding rhetoric under David Duke, Richard Nixon, and the southern strategy. This progression is how states' rights, became the rhetorical code for the protection of segregation and limiting the federal government power to govern how states treat the civil rights of minorities.

Movies have the ability to clarify historical events. In 2018, the movie *BlacKkKlansman*, portrayed the real-life story of Ron Stallworth, a black police officer who infiltrated a KKK branch in

1978–1979 under the national leadership of David Duke. In a very poignant scene, Stallworth was having a conversation with a white police officer who explained the significance of David Duke in the political climate of the late 1970s at the dawn of the Reagan era.

> Racism is moving away from the old violent racist styles, that's what David Duke is peddling. Racism is becoming mainstream ... always in a three piece suit, never seen in hood or robe in public ... [and it has] sights on a higher office. Politics, how so? Politics, it's another way to sell hate. Think about, affirmative action, immigration, crime, tax reform. No one wants to be called a bigot anymore, I guess Archie Bunker made that too uncool. So, the idea is under all these issues, everyday Americans can accept it. Support it. Until eventually, one day he gets somebody in the White House that embodies it.

The art of politics is to get people to share your policy outcomes, even when they don't support your justifications and reasons for those outcomes. The point of politics is to get their support, not their reasons for supporting you. The art of political rhetoric is to give people a reason to support your policy outcomes for various and sometimes contradictory reasons. The reason political platitudes work is because people can hear whatever they want in them. The reason political code language works is because it allows people to support racist outcomes and claim not to be racist because their reasons, on their face, are totally race neutral and may even be morally defensible. For example, the rationalization to support war on drugs or support of the crime control model and limited government. The policy outcome produced the same results that occurred in the glory days of peonage, criminal surety, and the pig laws discussed in Chapter 3.

Racism is not concept exclusive (i.e., racism is not exclusively defined as Klansmen in robes with ropes walking down Pennsylvania avenue). The distinction between America in the 1920s and today is that racism can exist in outcomes without conscious or intentional Klan-level bigotry. Racism can exist in policy outcomes without racist inputs. This is what is meant by concept of racism without racists.[4] Racism can hide in morally defensible ideas. Racists can hide racism in race-neutral ideas because they know what the political outcome will be. As discussed next, it was this subtly that Goldwater, Wallace, Thurmond, and Nixon took advantage of in the late 1960s and early 1970s. The same mouths that said nigger in the 1940s said crime control in the 1970s. The same mouths that opposed the death of Jim Crow in the 1950s and 1960s at the word of the Supreme Court, cursed the Court for being soft on crime in the 1970s. The same mouths that opposed the federal government's passage of the Civil Rights Acts of 1964, 1965, and 1968 opposed federal government imposition of integration of urban schools in the 1970s and later affirmative action in the 1980s.

The point is that racism in America has been separated from the George Wallace/Strom Thurmond 1940s–1950s brand. George Wallace himself proved this in his 1968 election campaign. He abandoned his segregation today, segregation tomorrow, segregation forever rhetoric with the rhetoric of crime control, limited government (limited federal government), opposition to forced bussing, and unrestrained support for local police. Nixon, as Wallace did, campaigned on attacking the Supreme Court for being soft on crime. The rhetoric changed, the policies changed, but those who heard it and supported it were the same as those who heard and supported the Wallace politics of opposition to the civil rights movement of 1954–1964. But the new rhetoric also created a space for those who rejected Klan-level racism. Not racism, but Klan-level racism. Although Klan-level racism was abandoned by the mainstream of America in the 1970s, that does not mean that Klan-level racism abandoned America.

On August 12, 2017, a mob of Ku Klux Klan (KKK), neo-Nazis, and white nationalists descended on Charlottesville, Virginia to protest the taking down of a confederate statute of Robert E. Lee. They were armed with bats and sticks. A counter group gathered to oppose the march of the white nationalists after they held a night march the day before. A fight ensued between the two groups. David Duke was one of the group leaders, and he explained to the press,

> I believe that today in Charlottesville, this is a first step toward making a realization of something that Trump alluded to early in his campaign, which is this is the first step towards taking America back.
>
> We are going to fulfill the promises of Donald Trump. That's what we believed in. That's why we voted for Donald Trump, because he said he's going to take our country back.

The riot that occurred as a result of the white nationalist being confronted with equal force became a topic of contention between President Trump and the press on August 15, 2017. The riot culminated with the death of Heather Heyer, who was intentionally run down in the street by a car driven by one of the neo-Nazi marchers. Trump was asked about the march, and he made the following statement at a press conference:

> All of those people—Excuse me—I've condemned neo-Nazis. I've condemned many different groups. But not all of those people were neo-Nazis, believe me. Not all of those people were white supremacists by any stretch. Those people were also there because they wanted to protest the taking down of a statue, Robert E. Lee.
> ....
> But, many of those people were there to protest the taking down of the statue of Robert E. Lee. So this week, it is Robert E. Lee. I noticed that Stonewall Jackson is coming down. I wonder, is it George Washington next week? And is it Thomas Jefferson the week after?
> ....

Well I do think there's blame. Yes, I think there is blame on both sides. You look at both sides. I think there is blame on both sides. And I have no doubt about it! And you don't have doubt about it either!

....

And you had some very bad people in that group. But you also had people that were very fine people on both sides. You had people in that group—excuse me, excuse me—I saw the same pictures as you did. You had people in that group that were there to protest the taking down, of to them, a very, very important statue and the renaming of a park from Robert E. Lee to another name.

....

George Washington was a slave owner. Was George Washington a slave owner? So will George Washington now lose his status? Are we going to take down—excuse me—are we going to take down statues to George Washington? How about Thomas Jefferson? What do you think of Thomas Jefferson?

In political rhetoric, context is everything, and to this day, supporters and opposers of Trump debate on what Trump meant when he said, "You also had people that were very fine people on both sides." Trump and his supports say that the context was that there were people in Charlottesville who were protesting the taking down of the statue and were not part of the Klan march, and they—the people who protested that the statue should be taken down—were the very fine people.

The problem with this context is that it's not true. The peaceful people who were protesting the taking down of the statue were not the ones marching in neo-Nazi and KKK uniforms and carrying KKK and white nationalists' signs on August 11 and 12, 2017. A racist mob of marchers replaced them. The Klan and neo-Nazi marchers came looking for a fight with those opposed to them, and they got the fight they wanted. The context of the press conference was about the violence caused by Nazi marchers not the people protesting the statue a day before the Klan's night march. It was that context, the Klan march, that the press was asking Trump about. It was within that context that Trump said there were very fine people on both sides when everyone knew better. What Trump supporters refuse to do is admit that the context of the riot was the values of the Klansmen versus those who oppose them. The context was not about the legitimacy of statues of Confederate generals who defended the destruction of America over slavery. But the problem is deeper because what the Klansmen were protesting—the removal of the statue and advocacy for white supremacy—has vocal and political resonance with Trump voters and social conservatives. Trump voters and white social conservatives perceive no problem in honoring those who fought America over the abolition of slavery and what slavery represents in American history: black inferiority to whites *per se*. My question is this: how can people who support the honoring of men who sought to destroy America in order to create a republic based on the slavery of blacks because they are black be "fine people" in the first place.

Consider this: supporters of Generals Robert E. Lee and Stonewall Jackson say that these generals, among others, were defending their states and their homes. Fine. So did General Eugen Rommel, the desert fox, of the Third Reich. So did the architect of the Pearl Harbor attack by the Japanese, Admiral Isoroku Yamamoto. They were defending their homes and nations. They were courageous and skilled warriors too. Yet there are no monuments in America to their honor and glory in their war against America. There are no such statues in Germany or Japan either!

The fact that they fought to protect nations that asserted Nazism and imperialism and killed American soldiers in the war is enough to prevent statues from being erected in their honor. But Lee and Jackson are different! Why? Because to American white social conservatives (and black conservatives who see the world through white conservative eyes), what Lee and Jackson fought against (union without slavery as Lincoln came to understand the war to be about) is not noble beyond dispute. More significantly, what Lee and Jackson fought to protect (states rights' and union with slavery) is not evil beyond dispute to white social conservatives. To them, as I heard a white social conservative radio host explain, slavery is a historical event and no more and you can't apply today's standards (slavery is wrong) to the past (his point being slavery was not wrong then).

Consider what statues are designed to memorialize. Memorial statues are designed to honor some person or concept that is worthy of national esteem. That's why Lincoln, Washington, and Jefferson have national monuments. That's why the Statue of Liberty dominates the Hudson. That's why Hamilton has a statue in front of the Department of Treasury building. That's why the U.S. Capital is littered with statues of past Congressmen, Senators, and other great American figures and heroes. That's why Chief Justice John Marshall has a statue in the Supreme Court, and the Supreme Court has statues outside of the building honoring the many sources of law and justice. And in this company, white social conservatives put Lee and Jackson! Really?! Men whose claim to fame was to burn down America to build a slave republic on its ashes.

But here are two subtleties of the implicit racism undergirding the Civil War statue controversy. First, note that when white social conservatives talk about the Civil War, they talk about the southern generals (not the Confederacy) who fought the Union—note, the "Union" not "America." Implicit racism on the political rhetoric level is found in word choice; the words that are used and not used matters. "America" in white social conservative rhetoric means noble and great. The "Union" in white social conservative eyes represents northern opposition to states' rights. In the South, the war is still referred to as the war of northern aggression. The fact that it was the South that attacked Fort Sumter and initiated the Civil War is beside the point in regard to southern myths about the war. The point is in white conservative theory, nobility is attached to the word "America," not the word "Union." This supplements the second subtly. White social conservatives see Lee and Jackson and other Confederate generals as men who fought against the Union—not America—and that fight was over the black question: slavery. Because the generals only fought the Union (nothing noble) and did not fight against America (all noble), white social conservatives assert that these generals can be honored. The fact that they fought to preserve slavery (and all its assumptions) is of no consequence to white social conservative orthodoxy.

The Civil War settled that slavery was no longer compatible with America's future. Once the temper of the North cooled, the breach and wounds of the war were healed on the backs of blacks sealed by the abandonment of Reconstruction and the application of the healing salve of Jim Crow on those wounds. Fine. As the scriptures tell us, the evil of man is without measure, and the history of man proves that he can be wicked to those he oppresses. But white social conservatives' denials of the cause of the war—the evils of slavery and the proposition of black inferiority—notwithstanding, the implicit racism regarding the Confederate monuments lay in the failure to admit the purpose of erecting them in the first place. They were not erected days and weeks after the war or even days or weeks after the fall of Reconstruction. They were erected across the South in the first two decades of the twentieth century at the height of Jim Crow, the lynching of blacks on sight, and the marching of the Klan down Pennsylvania Avenue, and they were used to defend the myth of the Lost Cause of the Confederacy. They were erected to honor the men who engaged in war to defend the creation of a slave republic, which was to be built on the destruction of America—a constitutional republic based on individual freedom. They were also erected as a political message to remind blacks in the South to stay in their place. The implicit racism in defending these monuments and disregarding why they were erected in the first place (not to mention defending the Confederate flag) is in the failure to acknowledge the evil of Jim Crow or to act as if it didn't happen or to act like it doesn't matter. Just as a side note, if one thinks white social conservative theology can't be absolute in defining evil, consider their views and politics on abortion.

Until Charlottesville, rhetorically and politically, there was no moral equivalency between Klansman with bats marching in a southern town and those who oppose them with bats of their own. Trump changed that. His comments legitimized the moral equivalency between the two groups. The underlying message, Trump opponents heard was, nice people on both sides included the marchers and values of David Duke. Duke heard the same, for he tweeted on the same day of the press conference, "Thank you President Trump for your honesty & courage to tell the truth about #Charlottesville & condemn the leftist terrorists in BLM/Antifa."

◆ ◆ ◆

Returning to the conflating of racism, states' rights, and limited powers in American political rhetoric; Calhoun argued that the federal government was limited, that it was formed by the states, not "we the people," and that it was the abolition of slavery, not slavery itself, that was evil, and the federal government should seek to protect, not interfere with the southern and western states' implementation of slavery. The Calhoun Resolution (January 1938) was a follow-up to his February 6, 1837, *Slavery a Positive Good* speech on the floor of the U.S. Senate in which Calhoun defended the economic, social, political, and natural order of life in regard to slavery in the South. On February 19, 1847, Calhoun again asserted that the federal government was the creation of the states not the people and would prophesy the assertions made by the Confederate South less than two decades later. In this speech, *The Importance of His Resolutions on the Slave Question*, he warned the nation that the continued opposition to slavery, as a moral and political issue, by the North would break the union. Calhoun made clear that the South joined the union under the clear understanding that the institution of slavery would be protected. He quoted the Constitution, which only allowed the federal government to end participation in the international slave trade. The federal government had no power—constitutionally or morally—to, interfere, with the proper system of domestic slavery.

A year later, in *the Oregon Bill* speech, Calhoun made clear that "ours is a Federal Constitution. The States are its constituents, and not the people." In his June 7, 1848 speech Calhoun responded to the proposed Oregon Bill which prevented the expansion of slavery into the Oregon territory. In this speech, he shifted to the justification of slavery and defended the superiority of whites over blacks in southern society as a unifying factor of whites, regardless of their level of wealth or education. He argued that no white man in the South would lower himself to the level of menial labor. That status belongs to blacks. This refusal, he explained, was shared by all whites, and on this refusal, all whites are equal: "With us the two great divisions of society are not the rich and poor, but white and black; and all the former, the poor as well as the rich, belong to the upper class, and are respected and treated as equals."

Calhoun stated that if the nation breaks up over the issue of slavery and a future historian asks why, "he will trace it to a proposition ... which, as now expressed and now understood, is the most false and dangerous of all political errors. The proposition to which I allude ... that "all men are born free and equal." This error, Calhoun explained, was supported by the South as well as the North when the Declaration of Independence was written, but now, "to this error [the] proposition to exclude slavery from the territory northwest of the Ohio may be traced ... and through it the deep and dangerous agitation which now threatens to engulf, and will certainly engulf, if not speedily settled, our political institutions, and involve the country in countless woes." In this famous speech Calhoun rejected Jefferson's lamentations regarding the practice of slavery in America and Jefferson's conclusions that it was evil, and asserted that any thought that "all men are created equal" includes blacks was a falsehood that the current debate over the expansion of slavery was making clear.

Calhoun would not be alone in this belief. On the eve of the Civil War on March 2, 1859, on the floor of the U.S. Senate, Senator Jefferson Davis, the future president of the Confederacy, said,

> I reply to the statement, and I reply in no offensive sense. The Senator makes a statement that the white laborers of the South are degraded. I say there was never anything less true, either in the Senate or out of it. I say that the lower race of human beings that constitute the substratum of what is termed the slave population of the South, elevates every white man in our community.
>
> ....
>
> It is the presence of a lower caste, those lower by their mental and physical organization, controlled by the higher intellect of the white man, that gives this superiority to the white laborer. Menial services are not there performed by the white man. We have none of our brethren sunk to the degradation of being menials. That belongs to the lower race—the descendants of Ham, who, under the judgement of God speaking to the prophet Noah, were condemned to be servants.
>
> To propose that we should change our industrial system, that we should bring negroes up to a level with the white man, would be such an offense that the lecturer who would come to teach such philosophy would be fortunate indeed if he should escape without some public indignity.[5]

These views would be echoed in 1860–1861 by the Secession Ordinances (see Appendix 1) of the various southern states that left the union after the election of Lincoln and the Civil War that would follow. With the defeat of the South, the idea that the states not the people formed the union would be eradicated from American political discourse until the inauguration of Ronald Reagan in 1980. But the idea of black inferiority and white supremacy as a unifying social concept for America would not only help bind America back together after the war but also find new avenues and remain in America's political discourse for another century under the system of the Black Codes and Jim Crow.

I start my review of the rhetorical orthodoxy of white social conservatism theory with Jefferson and Calhoun because they formed the foundation for the rhetoric and politics of states' rights within the context of opposing the humanity and equality of blacks. This rhetoric remained after the Civil War and helped originate and foster the growth of the politics of the 1950s through the 1980s. The political rhetoric and merging of fears of the national government, the advocacy of states' rights over the power of the national government, the fear of crime, and the assertion that law enforcement was exclusively the province of the states and local government into one coherent conservative theory for presidential election victory was developed by Thurmond, Wallace, Goldwater, Nixon, and Reagan.

It is true that conservative theory in America can trace its seeds to Jefferson and the Anti-federalists. The Anti-federalists opposed the creation of the Constitution in the first place because it created a strong national government. Jefferson opposed Hamilton's plans to focus the economic strength of America on international trade, maintaining an international credit rating, the tying of the states together through the national government assuming their revolutionary war debts, and demanding that America stay neutral in the war between France and Great Britain. All of these actions, as viewed by Jefferson, strengthened the politics and policies of a strong national government and favored international trade and textile over local agricultural slave industry as the source of American financial commerce. Jefferson agreed to the debt consolidation plan only when Hamilton agreed to put the capital of the nation in southern territory. That way, according to Jefferson, the South could keep a better eye on it.

History would show that a weak national government served the interests of the southern aristocracy, which was built entirely on slavery. Only when the interests of America and the slave owner aristocracy were no longer commensurate did the South secede. Only when the North acceded to the racism that undergirded slavery did the nation bind its wounds. It would be another century before black inequality, black abuse by the South, and southern intransigence to federal law under the constitution was ended. Only when southern intransigence was no longer viable and subjected to the power of the national army did the South relent. Only after the application of federal government power over the states were blacks elevated from second-class status under the law.

When Dr. Martian Luther King marched in Selma, and spoke in Montgomery, Alabama,[6] he reflected on race in America and found agreement with Calhoun and Davis regarding the utility of racism and how its use defined American politics and how southern democrats held poor white voters despite the fact that they gained nothing except superiority to blacks. Dr. King explained,

> The segregation of the races was really a political stratagem ... to keep the southern masses divided and southern labor the cheapest in the land. You see, it was a simple thing to keep the poor white masses working for near-starvation wages in the years that followed the Civil War. Why, if the poor white plantation or mill worker became dissatisfied with his low wages, the plantation or mill owner would merely threaten to fire him and hire former Negro slaves and pay him even less. Thus, the southern wage level was kept almost unbearably low.
>
> Toward the end of the Reconstruction era ... the Populist Movement ... began awakening the poor white masses and the former Negro slaves to the fact that they were being fleeced by the emerging Bourbon interests. [T]hey began uniting the Negro and white masses into a

voting bloc that threatened to drive the Bourbon interests from ... political power in the South.

To meet this threat, the southern aristocracy began immediately to engineer this development of a segregated society. ... [T]his is very important. ... Through their control of mass media, they revised the doctrine of white supremacy. They saturated the thinking of the poor white masses with it. ... They then directed ... laws that made it a crime for Negroes and whites to come together as equals at any level. ...

If it may be said of the slavery era that the white man took the world and gave the Negro Jesus, then it may be said of the Reconstruction era that the southern aristocracy took the world and gave the poor white man Jim Crow. ... [A] psychological bird that told him that no matter how bad off he was, at least he was a white man, better than the black man. ... And his children, too, learned to feed upon Jim Crow. ...

Thus ... the establishment of a segregated society. They segregated southern money from the poor whites; ... they segregated southern churches from Christianity ... and they segregated the Negro from everything.

Dr. King explained that racism has a purpose, it's not simply an ideological development or personal worldview. Racism meets a social and political need. King explained that racism undergirded an economic and political need both before and after the Civil War, as well as before and after Reconstruction. White supremacy said to poor whites, you are equal in only one thing, but it's an important thing; you're white, so you are better than blacks no matter how poor and uneducated you are. Today, white supremacy says no matter what whites do, the face of crime is always black. During Reconstruction, whites were told black financial equality with whites is to be feared by whites; today, whites are told black violence needs to be feared. This is the subtly behind gun rights, for conservatives assert the people need guns to protect their homes from the criminal hordes. While guns, under the Second Amendment, for self-defense and protection of one's home has its place; the politics of gun rights and crime in white social conservative rhetoric (remember what Bush's appointee asserted) masks white fear of crime in America which to them is black. For centuries after the Civil War, the Southern Democratic Party maintained this political rhetorical dynamic. By the late 1960s, this rhetorical dynamic transitioned to the Republican Party. In either party, the focus was the white, rural, non-college-educated, poor voter.

————————————— ◆◆◆ —————————————

In my History of Criminal Justice class, I explain to my students that it is conventional liberal orthodoxy that the blame of the modern disproportionate arrest and incarceration of blacks is laid at the feet of Republicans; dating from the politics of Barry Goldwater, Richard Nixon, and before them George Wallace and Strom Thurmond. But the truth is that the beginning of the modern criminal justice system policies that have led to the disproportionate incarceration of blacks and the policy linking of crime to race was first asserted by the liberal northern wing of the Democratic Party under Lyndon Johnson. Johnson asserted that as a policy matter, crime and race were linked through poverty, and the economic and social policies of the Great Society were crime prevention policies. It was Johnson in 1966 who said to deal with urban crime—black people—the issue of poverty must be addressed. This has been the orthodoxy of the Democratic Party and Progressives to this day.

From 1954 through 1964, the focus and political energy regarding race was centered on ending Jim Crow. Beginning with the 1954 Supreme Court victory over *Plessy v. Ferguson* and the doctrine of separate but equal and ending with the Civil Rights Act of 1964, the legal system of Jim Crow was on its way to the dustbin of history. The victory was made, in part, due to mass civil disobedience in the form of marches and sit-ins and challenging local police to enforce Jim Crow. The strategy was to break the law and to be seen doing it. Blacks en mass breaking the law. Blacks had the moral high ground in doing so, but they were breaking the law none the less. This would matter when crime in the 1960s began a decade-long increase, and by 1968, a militant version of black resistance was replacing Kings' nonviolence approach. The Black Panthers and Black Power were in their heyday. National leaders like Nixon and FBI Director Hoover feared what would follow if blacks were angry, unified, and armed. Such was the impetus for the FBI COINTELPRO strategy to monitor, infiltrate, and break various radical black organizations in the early to middle 1970s. Such was the impetus of Nixon and his law-and-order politics and his war on drugs policies.

While blacks were challenging Jim Crow, the nation as a whole was suffering a mass increase in crime. Between 1960 and 1964, violent crime increased by 26.2 percent, and property crime increased by 35.6 percent. By 1964, conservatives, having taken over the Republican Party with the nomination of Barry Goldwater, were now asserting what would become election orthodoxy for the remainder of the century: fear of violent crime and that Democrats were soft on crime. The rising crime rate was linked to social disunion and that included black crime in general and black social disobedience and marches specifically. As a political matter, civil disobedience became merged with social disunity, and both were linked with crime. The face of both, in the American political mind, was black. In 1964, the Democrat's chief domestic policy was the Great Society: a series of programs that were designed to end poverty. They included expansion of social security, creation of Medicare and Medicaid, college loans, food stamps, federal funding for elementary and high schools, support for rural education, head start, and various other urban and rural renewal and social programs. After two years of these programs (1964–1966), crime had increased 18 percent and property crime had increased 15.9 percent.

The Johnson Administration was besieged with the politics of crime and assertions that crime is the result of soft social programs, the weakening of individual responsibility and the American family, the weakening of the police, and soft on crime Democrat judges. Republican orthodoxy was set. Democrat orthodoxy on crime policy was established when President Johnson, on March 9, 1966, addressed Congress on crime and law enforcement.[7] Johnson asserted that crime was a national problem that required national solutions. He stated that the following policies must be continued.

1. Law enforcement must receive additional federal funds for education and professional development through the Law Enforcement Assistance Act of 1965.
2. Prisoners must be given ways to improve themselves while in prison so that they don't commit more crimes upon release, which was the purpose of the Prisoner Rehabilitation Act of 1965.
3. Crime must be studied, and theories must be developed to change criminal behavior and the social conditions that foster it, which was the purpose of the creation of the National Crime Commission and the District of Columbia Crime Commission (1965).
4. The FBI Academy must continue to increase the number of local police trained in advanced police techniques through the National Academy.
5. Organized crime must be pursued and dismantled.

Johnson said with the aforementioned policies in place, new initiatives were required.

1. Implement programs that recognize that crime is not local but national because criminals move across local and state lines.
2. Improve crime prevention and detection strategies used by police.
3. Stop the flow of firearms into the hands of criminals: "I recommend a pistol registration act prohibiting the sale of deadly weapons to those who have been convicted of violent

crimes, to those with a history of mental instability, and to habitual alcoholics."

4. Modernize federal criminal law to better address interstate crime and organized crime.

5. Reform the bail system—end preventive detention.

6. Continue to support rehabilitation in jails and prisons.

7. Provide drug addiction counseling and treatment.

8. Use of computers to unify information and make criminal justice more efficient.

Johnson then concluded with his observation that crime is the result of social injustice. Here is where he stated that crime will not be stopped unless its root causes are addressed. By 1966, crime was seen as urban in the American mind. When Johnson stated that the root causes had to be addressed, he stated racial discrimination, social injustice, and poverty were the root causes. Johnson concluded his address by observing,

> Our commitment to ensuring social justice and personal dignity for all Americans does not flow from a desire to fight crime. We are committed to those goals because they are right.
>
> But social conditions which foster a sense of **injustice** or exploitation also **breed crime.**
>
> ....
>
> The **programs** now underway **to eliminate** the degradation of **poverty,** the decay of our cities, the disgrace **of racial discrimination,** the despair of illiteracy—are all **vitally important to crime prevention.**
>
> ....
>
> The vast majority of our citizens who suffer poverty and discrimination do not turn to crime.
>
> But **where legitimate opportunities are closed, illegitimate opportunities are seized.** Whatever opens opportunity and hope will help to prevent crime and foster responsibility.

Effective **law enforcement** and **social justice** must be pursued **together**, as the foundation of our efforts **against crime.**

The proposals I am making today will not solve the problem of crime in this country. The war on crime will be waged by our children and our children's children. But the difficulty and complexity of the problem cannot be permitted to lead us to despair. They must lead us rather to bring greater efforts, greater ingenuity, and greater determination to do battle.

In his 1966 speech before Congress, he said when poverty is alleviated, crime will be reduced. It has been Democratic orthodoxy ever since that the explanation of crime generally—black urban crime specifically—is social and economic inequality. It has also been liberal orthodoxy ever since that crime control requires gun control. The Republicans were not totally dismissive of Johnson's speech. They accepted the assertion that crime is a national problem worthy of national resources. Nixon and Reagan would implement this theory with national force being applied to drug use and utilization of federal law and prisons to deal with local gun and drug crimes. The Republicans also accepted Johnson's premise that blacks and crime were linked. They just rejected the economic link. It has been Republican orthodoxy since the Great Society that blacks are criminals because of their own cultural deviance, not because of racism and economics. Republicans asserted poverty does not result in crime; deviant behavior results in crime. As for black deviant behavior—that's what prisons are for. Johnson linked crime and race as a social problem to be fixed to gain support for the Great Society. Educated urban liberals told white America that these programs would make them safer from crime. By 1968, this assertion was rejected, and the law-and-order politics of Goldwater and Nixon bore fruit, and Nixon was elected president.

◆◆◆

The divergence of the two parties in America, although crystalized in the 1960s with Lyndon Johnson and the Great Society in 1964, the Republican nomination of Barry Goldwater in 1964, and the election of Nixon in 1968, did not originate in the 1960s but began with the Great Depression (1929) and the rejection of the pure laissez-faire economic policies of the preceding 50 years. Liberals abandoned the proposition that the national government has no role in the economic regulation of the country and asserted that unless the government did something to deal with the Wall Street excesses of the 1920s, which led to the crash of the 1929 and the resulting economic depression, America could slip into the despotism (Communism, Fascism, and Nazism) that was engulfing parts Europe.

Through the policies of President Roosevelt, the national government took a role in the economic systems of America that it had never had before. Roosevelt, first elected in 1932, asserted that the purpose of the federal government was to provide a minimal level of financial security for all Americans while supporting the operation and individual ideals of free market capitalism. Traditional values and economic conservatives opposed Roosevelt and the philosophy behind the New Deal programs from its inception. President Roosevelt prevailed in three subsequent elections (1936, 1940, and 1944), and the New Deal programs became a staple of modern American life.

After World War II, the nation had not only defeated Nazism and Fascism but also the Great Depression and emerged as a world superpower with an economic and industrial base that was second to none. But more importantly, Americans developed the worldview that American dominance in the world, Pax Americana, and economic security were the norm, not the exception. More importantly, the Roosevelt years had built into the American political system the idea that the national government was the primary governmental institution. In 1946, the federal government assumed responsibility for maintaining full employment and maintaining economic stability. By the end of World War II, all political and economic roads led to Washington, D.C. The federal government was no longer first among equal states; it was first with no equals, and the state governments were secondary in the new federalism. By 1946, the federal government under the rhetoric of the New Deal had put its weight behind economic fairness, if not equality. Within a decade, it would also put its weight behind ending Jim Crow. The rejection of this new reality is the foundational definition of modern social and economic conservativism.

Social conservatives in the 1950s were convinced that America was moving in the wrong direction for a multitude of reasons. The post-depression policies of Roosevelt, which had supplanted classical Republican perspectives on the role of government, were compounded by the apostasy of the national government ensuring that blacks were to be treated as equals under the law. Between 1948 and 1962, the Democratic Party was splitting between southern Democrats (Strom Thurmond and George Wallace) and northern Democrats (Harry Truman and Hubert Humphrey) over the issue of segregation. In 1947, Truman said to the NAACP that he would create a presidential commission on civil rights to make recommendations for national legislation to support civil rights. In 1948, Humphrey would say at the national party convention that the party platform would oppose poll taxes and other Jim Crow laws in the South. Thurmond would form the States' Rights Democratic Party (Dixiecrats) in 1948 and run on a platform to oppose the policies of desegregation and win South Carolina, Alabama, Mississippi, and Louisiana. This is where the southern migration from the Democratic Party would begin. By 1963, Democrat George Wallace, at his inauguration as governor of Alabama, would make clear he that he wanted segregation today, segregation tomorrow, segregation forever.

The northern liberal Democrats were challenging the system and the compromise that the party itself had imposed on the nation after the Civil War. The South would surrender slavery and live under a government that had the power to end it—but Jim Crow would prevail, and blacks would be second-class citizens in both the North and South; and the Democratic Party would own southern politics. By the early 1950s, this compromise, that occurred in 1877 was now being challenged by the national Democratic Party. The southern Democrats rebelled, and over the next 15 years, they would abandon the liberal wing of the party and find adoption in the Republican Party. Over this same period, social conservatives would take control of the Republican party (1964) and the liberal wing of the party would be completely expelled by 1980.

This history of social and political change and the rise of the supremacy of the federal government at the expense of state government became pronounced during the civil rights movement in the 1950s with its the goal of causing the fall of the 100-year-old social/political system of segregation. The federal government supported the end of Jim Crow with the use of military troops and the U.S. Marshals to bring the southern states to heel in 1957 (suppressing the near riot of whites opposing integration and use of the National Guard to prevent the Little Rock Nine from attending the Little Rock High school in Arkansas), in 1962 (suppressing the white riot at University of Mississippi over the admission of James Meredith), in 1963 (moving Wallace out of the doorway of University of Alabama), and in 1965 (the protection of the second Selma Edmund Pettus Bridge march after the police riot in which the marchers were beaten with nightsticks). The Supreme Court's support of the rising civil rights movement was made all the worse in conservative eyes by the Court that was not only requiring the states to allow black children to be seated with white children, because we (the Supreme Court) say so, but while doing so, the states could not force those children to say the Lord's Prayer in school.

During the 1950s and early 1960s, conservatives as a group united in their opposition of the growing federal government and the social changes occurring in society. These conservatives included William F. Buckley and his magazine the *National Review*, Ronald Reagan, Richard Nixon, Milton Friedman, the editors of the *Wall Street Journal*, Strom Thurmond, and George Wallace, just to name a few. The rhetoric of Thurmond and Wallace is significant.

These conservatives came onto the political and social stage with conservative principles that attacked not only the liberalism of the 1960s (and the civil rights acts of the 1960s) but also both political parties, which supported and/or tolerated these movements rather than opposing them at all costs. During this period, conservatives led by Thurmond and Wallace and followed by Goldwater and Reagan established a unifying theory of what American conservatism should and would be. They united under the banner of states' rights, opposition to the Civil Rights Acts of 1964, 1965, and 1968, and forced integration. They defended at all costs the principles of limited government, as well as individual economic and social responsibility.

By the time of the ascent of Johnson and his election in 1964, America was adopting liberal policies on every sphere of society, but there had also developed a growing backlash to those very policies. President Johnson's landslide victory in 1964 masked the growing resentment of the rise of social liberalism as manifested by the victories of the civil rights movement. By 1964, white flight from the cities had begun, and the rise of the suburbs like Levittown, New York, began the social and political separation that would later create the silent majority (and the southern strategy) that elected Nixon in 1968. The elections of 1964, 1966, and 1968 would cement social conservatism into the Republican Party.

In 1964, Barry Goldwater won the Republican Party nomination for president. His nomination established the control of the party by free market, anti-Great Society, personal responsibility, crime control model, limited federal government, strong military, low taxes, anti-integration and socially conservative, traditional family values–oriented voters, and politicians. In 1966, conservative white middle-class blowback gave the Republicans a significant victory in the midterm elections and foreshadowed the fall of President Johnson and the Great Society. In the midterm elections of 1966,

> Republicans were revived and on the brink of an era of
> increasing political success, including near-domination of

presidential elections that Democrats have occasionally overcome but have not yet ended four decades later.

A number of events took a toll on Johnson's popularity by late 1966, including lack of demonstrable success in Vietnam, race riots and other civil disturbances at home, and an increasing sense that the Great Society was running amok, spending too much and centralizing too much.

When all was said and done, the GOP gained 47 House seats, three Senate seats, eight governorships, and 557 state legislative seats. Republican governors controlled 25 states, the most since the early 1950s. Republicans actually won a majority of the aggregated national vote for U.S. Senate. Of the 38 House districts where Democrats had replaced Republicans in 1964, only 14 remained in Democratic hands in 1966.[8]

By 1968 (especially after the urban riots of 1967), politics in America had abandoned the hopeful and optimistic ideals of the early 1960s and became more hostile to the policies of President Johnson and the social policies of the left. By 1968, both the left and the right of the political spectrum opposed the Vietnam War, and support for civil rights was being abandoned by both white middle-class suburban voters and black urban youth. The civil rights movement, in the minds of white social conservatives, had merged civil disobedience with the politics of left-wing radicalism, both of which were merged with white middle-class fear of crime. All three were merged with fear of blacks in general and black males specifically within the American political and social mind. By the end of 1968, the nation had turned away from the Democrats.

By 1968, John F. Kennedy, Martin Luther King Jr., and Robert F. Kennedy had been assassinated, and the civil rights movement took a militant approach to American society. The promises of the Johnson Administration had not come to fruition, and blacks were beginning to abandon the integration and the nonviolent perspective of King as a method to achieve economic success. The social fabric of the nation changed not only because of the civil rights movement but also because by the middle and late 1960s, the second wave of the women's movement was fully engaged, and the dawns of the militant black rights movement and the gay rights movement were approaching. Put simply, things were getting out of hand, and the nation turned to Nixon. President Richard Nixon took office in 1969 on a law-and-order platform in which the silent majority sought to turn back America and American society from the influence of the 1960s, the counterculture, and the decade of Woodstock.

The reelection of Nixon in 1972 continued to centralize conservatism in the Republican Party and solidified liberal control in the Democratic Party. As the 1964 election gave traditional conservatives control of the Republican Party during their convention, the 1972 divided and cantankerous Democratic convention established control of the party to the social liberals. The nomination of McGovern split the party and forced out the conservative democrats (foreign policy conservatives/Wilsonians (neocons), the Nixon "hard hats" (urban and suburban non-college-educated, working-class white males), and middle-class educated white males, all of whom would find a home in the Republican Party.

By the election of Reagan in 1980, a coalition of the various strands of conservative thought found a unifying figure in Reagan and found a figure who could win. To this day, all conservatives, regardless of stripe, revere Reagan because of his accomplishment in 1980 and his reelection landslide in 1984 (winning 49 out of 50 states).

The strategy that carried the Republican Party from a devastating loss in 1964 to dominance in the 1980s has been called the southern strategy. The southern strategy is built on the proposition that in American politics, the goal is to achieve political power, to win elections, and to implement conservative policy. Elections are won or lost on group conflicts. Put another way, elections are not won by voting for what you like but rather by voting against what you hate. If a voter is convinced the nation is moving in the wrong direction, that voter will vote against the party that is in power that is linked with that wrong direction. One progressive theory on how people vote for presidents and elected officials and how they, in turn, hold their voting base, and the policies that follow is the relationship and interaction of selfishness, greed, and racism.[9] In American politics, elections encompass the relationship between self-interest and national ambition (selfishness), individual and national economic ambition and wealth creation (greed), and dynamics of race (racism). American history, unlike European history, is defined by date certain events and political decisions that resulted in the American character. Consider the impact of the following historical policy choices and the America that resulted from them. Rejection of Jefferson's slave clause due to the South's refusal to support the Declaration of Independence with its inclusion, the fugitive slave laws, slavery, debates between Jefferson and Hamilton over the national debt, the rise of the Jeffersonian Republicans as a foil against the Federalists, the fall of the Federalists in the elections of 1800 over the debate of the Jay Treaty and avoidance of war with Britain, the Louisiana Purchase in 1803, the slavery compromises of 1820, 1850 and the Kansas-Nebraska Act of 1854, the annexation of Texas in 1845, the Mexican-American War (1846–1848), the election of 1860, the Civil War, the election of 1864, the rise and fall of reconstruction, the rise of Jim Crow, black inferiority, white supremacy, the politics of the progressive era, the rise of wall street and government regulation of wall street and the politics of trust busting, the election of 1932, the rise of the new deal, the elections of 1960 and 1964, the rise of conservative politics (states' rights and opposition to federal protection and enforcement of civil rights) in the republican party in 1964, the rise of conservative economics (supply-side theory) in 1980, the election of Obama in 2008, and the resulting backlash elections of the tea party in 2010 (republicans win the House) and 2014 (republicans win the Senate), Trump in 2016 and the progressive backlash elections in 2018 (democrats regaining the House). All of these events (and others) involve the interaction and relationship of individual and societal political taste voting. These tastes define what individual voters will tolerate to secure their desires and priorities in policy outcomes. As Trump's national campaign manager, Kellyanne Conway, astutely observed, "There is a difference for voters between what affects them and what offends them. And they are going to vote on what affects them 99.9% of the time."[10]

Voting is also explained by the fact that people vote based on the group they are in and the values that are attached to the group they are in. The group can be defined by religion, ideology, gender, class (economic) or race. By 1964, the New Deal coalition of southern poor whites, urban whites, and blacks to a limited extent, which had dominated the politics of the Democratic Party was breaking up over the adoption of civil rights by the national leadership of the party. With the Democrats adopting policies that increased the number of blacks in the party, southern Democrats and then Republicans—led by Wallace, Thurmond, Goldwater, and Nixon—sought to dislodge southern white Democrats from the party to convert them to vote for Republicans. By the election of Nixon in 1968 and 1972, the strategy included the use of dog-whistle politics of tough on crime, and by the 1980s, it added opposition to affirmative action and abortion to hold white voters. The southern strategy sought to create a new Republican majority by combining white and middle-class voters in the South, west, and suburbia.[11]

The southern strategy between 1968 and 1972 took advantage of white resentment and unease of (1) black advancement—which many believed occurred at their expense—and (2) the general cultural changes in America: the rise of women's rights, gay rights, integration, liberal moral sexual behavior and attitudes, and the general abandonment of the 1930s' and 1940s' visions of the role of women and men in society. The shift in southern voting began in 1948 (see Appendixes 2 and 3), and the southern strategy bonded these voters into a voting majority that took hold with Nixon in 1968 and bore full fruit with the election of Reagan in 1980.

The election for president, unlike local elections for governor, senator, or congressman, is a measure and vote on national policy and what voters think America is and should be. Presidential elections are referendums on the state of society as a whole and are reflective of whether change is desired or whether change is opposed. Presidential elections and the parties they symbolize also settle political debates. Some elections have been historically determinative in the development of America. The election of Washington in 1789 established the model of what America wanted the president to be. The election of 1800 decimated the Federalist Party. The election of 1828 ushered in the Age of Jacksonian democracy. The election of 1860 ushered in the Civil War and the election in 1864 settled that the America wanted the Civil War to conclude with the Confederacy defeated and America remaining whole. The election of 1876 and the corrupt bargain of 1877 settled that Reconstruction was over. Subsequent elections also provide the background for understanding policies that made blacks second-class citizens and why blacks were and are disproportionately incarcerated throughout American history.

As discussed in Chapter 3, southern Democrats agreed to support the Republican candidate, Hayes, in the disputed election of 1876 in return for the Hayes and the Republicans agreeing to remove the last of the federal troops from the South and returning home rule to the southern Democrats. This deal decimated the economic and political gains blacks had made during Reconstruction, ushered in the rise of Jim Crow, and cemented southern Democratic Party control of the South. From the 1876 election through the elections of 1944, with the exception of the 1928 elections, the Democratic candidate for president won in the South without dispute. But the dominance of the party in the South began to change with the 1948 elections (see the tables in Appendixes 2 and 3) in which Thurmond and the Dixiecrats won four of the Confederate States, Alabama, Louisiana, Mississippi, and South Carolina against the national Democratic candidate Truman and his support of civil rights. As the national Democratic Party shifted to support civil rights, southern Democrats in the South began to leave the party. In 1952 and 1956, the Republican won half and then the majority of the South, respectively. In 1960 and 1964, the Republicans won half of the

South. In 1968, the Democrats lost the entire South, with the spoils split between Wallace and Nixon. By 1972, the loss was complete, with the Republicans wining the entire South.

Not counting elections with favorite-son candidates, the South began to abandon the Democratic Party en masse in 1964, and by 1972, the abandonment was complete and has never returned. With the exception of 1960 (Kennedy), 1964 (Johnson), 1968 (Humphrey), and 1976 (Carter) **Texas** was lost to the Democrats from the 1952 elections. **Virginia** and **Oklahoma** were similarly lost with the exception of Johnson in 1964. **Alabama** was lost after the passage of the Civil Rights Act of 1964 and starting with the 1968 election the republican candidate for president always won with the exception of Cater in 1976. **Arkansas** and **Tennessee** were similarly lost with the exception of Carter in 1976 and Clinton in 1992. **Mississippi, North Carolina,** and **South Carolina** were also lost after the passage of the Civil Rights Act of 1964 with the exception of 1976 with Carter. With the exception of Clinton in 1996, the entire South voted for the Republican candidate, and subsequent to the 1996 election, the entire South, with the exception of Florida, has been solid Republican. *Johnson was correct when he stated that after passing the Civil Rights Act of 1964, the party had turned over the South to the Republicans.*

The southern strategy in the late 1960s through the early 1970s, aside from fighting integration and the agenda of the post-1968 civil rights movement, translated the language of segregationist racism into conservative rhetoric of states' rights and law and order. The racial rhetoric of Wallace and Thurmond in the 1940s through the early 1960s was replaced by the race-neutral crime and law-and-order rhetoric of Wallace, Goldwater, Nixon, and Reagan in the late 1960s through the 1980s. Segregation today, tomorrow, and forever was replaced by calls for law and order, limited government, the war on drugs and crime, opposition to affirmative action, and reverse discrimination. Republican politics took advantage of resentment among southern Democrats that the Democratic Party was no longer a "white man's party." The campaign of Wallace in 1968 injected into conservative rhetoric and orthodoxy a resentment of social and political elites in both parties and the narrative of the forgotten man in the political discourse in both parties. A theme that Trump would achieve victory with almost five decades later.

Nixon in a 1968 radio address would mirror this narrative with his assertion of the "salient center," which the following year became the "silent majority,"[12] which in 1980 under Jerry Farwell became the "moral majority." All of these brand names represented the same type of voter. They are the people of middle America, living in middle America, who do not demonstrate, who do not picket or protest, who did not riot, who respected authority, and who were open to being convinced to vote for either party. These were also the voters who resented the speed of change in society (end of segregation and imposed integration) and the hippie protesters of 1968. They were the people who supported law enforcement, feared urban crime and riots, resented the conclusions of the *Kerner Commission* that blamed black violence and riots on white America, and were voters who both resented the protesters of the Vietnam War and the failures in conducting the war in Vietnam. They were the voters who believed America was moving down the wrong track, both morally and socially. Nixon and Wallace both realized that if the rhetoric of raw racism could be substituted for law and order, as well as removed from arguments defending states' rights and conservatism in general, these white voters (in the North, South, and Midwest) could be enticed into the Republican Party. They were successfully enticed in 1968 and 1972 and have not left since.

By the second decade of the new century, the southern strategy had changed into Republican white voters resenting social elites—in both parties and in the media—who they perceived as looking down on them. These voters of the South and Midwest turned on the "Republican establishment," which they perceived as selling out working-class white voters, who had supported them for decades with their votes and got nothing in return. These voters resented the Republican establishment for their alliance with social and corporate elites who supported international trade that produced wealth in New York and political power in Washington but had failed to make life better for the white middle class. In this rebellion, these voters formed the Tea Party faction within the Republican Party, which was birthed by the failures of the George W. Bush Administration, the Iraq War and the financial crash of 2007–2008, and the resentment of a black man being elected as president. The Tea Party rebellion against the party establishment continued because of the continued failure of establishment Republicans to defeat the policies of Obama after winning the House in 2010, the failure of the establishment Republican candidate to defeat Obama in the subsequent presidential election in 2012, and failure to repeal the policies of Obama after winning the Senate and holding the House in 2014. These Tea Party voters continued their rebellion against the Republican Party establishment and produced the election of Donald Trump in 2016.

◆ ◆ ◆

One of the anchors of Republican theory is that the national government, from the days of Franklin D. Roosevelt, had grown too large and powerful and usurped the legitimate powers of the states and local governments. By the 1980s, the one exception to this theory was crime. On the issue of crime, the federal government and all of its coercive power were to be unleashed. In the 1980s, that unleashing of power was on urban areas, and the targets of this national federal law enforcement attention were blacks, and the result of this attention was the modern development of black disproportionate incarceration.

chapter five

The American Criminal Justice System

A Birds Eye View on Design and Purpose

.

I often explain to my students that the criminal justice system is the result of social policy, politics, and history. To understand why the criminal justice system is trusted by some and not by others, both historical and contemporary events must be consulted. Understanding the criminal justice system also requires understanding that it is not a unitary system. All the parts don't work to the benefit of the others. The system is made of multiple and sometimes conflicting parts. The system is also the result of local politics, traditions, availability of financial resources, and history of government administration.

Consider two of the three main parts of the criminal justice system: the police and the courts. The police are the gatekeepers of the system. Entrance into the criminal justice system, for the most part, occurs when the police make an arrest and seize a person and through arrest processes him or her into the pre-trial process or issues a summons commanding a person to appear in court to answer a charge under threat of arrest for failure to appear in court. In the popular imagination, the police are efficient and arrest only the guilty. Consider the first question that we instinctively ask when we see someone arrested: "What did he do?" The police have the power of life and death, for they are the only members of society who have the right to use force against the unarmed with a presumption of legality. We give them this power to maintain order and safety in society as a whole. History and contemporary events dictate how we view police as a result of how they use this power and on whom.

Prosecutors, defense attorneys, juries, and judges make up the second major part of the system—the courts. Together, these subparts determine if under the law the accused is guilty. Note I said under the law not in fact. The criminal justice system can't determine if, in fact, the accused is guilty because the system was not there when the crime occurred, if it did. The system comes in when a charge is made. With imperfect information and the human dynamics of good and evil hearts, the courts must determine if it's proved that a crime occurred and the accused did it. Thus, the goal of the system is not to determine if, in fact, a crime occurred but under the rules of law did the prosecution prove a crime occurred and the accused did it. The prosecutor must prove guilt beyond a reasonable doubt. The defense attorney, as many have explained to me, is not concerned with whether his or her client is in fact guilty or innocent. His or her job is to make the prosecutor prove guilt or to secure a sanction that is acceptable to the accused. Defense attorneys use the law and procedural rules to protect the accused, guilty or innocent.

Judges, in theory, don't care if the accused is innocent or guilty. They don't care because their role is to make sure that the law is properly applied in their courtrooms. Their job is to make sure procedural justice is applied without prejudice to any party. The law is the point, not the accused. The proper application of the law defines justice. Juries are the finders of fact. They determine whether the prosecution proved that a crime occurred, and the defendant did it. The jury represents the judgment of the community.

So much for Schoolhouse Rock level civics!

Understanding the complexity of the criminal justice system begins with understanding that it is a multidimensional institution and a political machine that has multiple, and sometimes contradictory, purposes. Think of the criminal justice system as a machine with three dominant wheels: the police, courts, and corrections. Within these wheels, there are various interlocking smaller wheels, gears, and belts that move people from arrest to incarceration. Politics governs which wheels are perceived as more significant and worthy of support. Thus the wheels and subparts have their own political constituency that is both coveted and used for the benefit of the machine as a whole and/or for the benefit of a particular part of the machine. This is why police and prosecutors are more honored than defense attorneys. Prosecutors are portrayed in American media and political thought as honest, overworked defenders of justice who are usually constrained in their jobs to protect society by liberal judges who tie their hands with technicalities. Defense attorneys are portrayed as defenders of people they know are guilty and manipulators of the law to get them off so they can commit other crimes. This is why politicians are elected to higher office after serving as prosecutors, and they provide funding for prosecutors to prove they're hard on crime. As discussed, later in this chapter, the 1980s and 1990s were defined by the politics of get tough on crime. Politics also governs how laws are used to define the purpose of the machine—a point we will return to in a moment.

Understanding criminal justice also requires the acknowledgment of its power within American society. That acknowledgment aids in understanding the differential in white and black fear of the various parts of the criminal justice system. The criminal justice system is the singular most powerful institution within American governmental structures. The criminal justice system is the only governmental system in the United States that has a range of power that can, at its beginning stage (the police), seize an American citizen and deny him/her the right to walk away (deny the right to liberty) and can take the life of the person. This power over life, both the denying of liberty and the taking the life of an individual, held by the criminal justice system can be exercised both at its beginning by the police on the street or at its end in prison in which a warden can order the imposition of drugs to cause death during an execution after decades of legal proceedings.

The criminal justice system stands as more than an institution with power over life and death; it reflects the greater politics and philosophy of America. The criminal justice system has no powers that the political and historical forces of America over the past two centuries have not given it. The criminal justice system reflects what Americans feel is required to feel safe. This fear and desire for safety and safety from what and from whom is the background for race and criminal justice.

The criminal justice system is a creation of the government for a specific purpose. In 1968, Herbert L. Packer published his famous book, *The Limits of the Criminal Sanction*, which provided a theoretical framework for understanding how the American criminal justice system operated and what the purpose and goal of the system were. He proposed that two opposing models can define the system: due process and crime control. These models were originally used to explain how the criminal justice system functions and how the various parts interact. By the 1980s and 1990s, these two models expanded to provide a foundation for moral explanations of crime and why crime occurs, as supposed to sociological explanations, which had dominated academic and public discourse from the 1950s through the 1970s. As discussed earlier, these differing models can explain how criminal justice policy is justified politically and morally.

The two models are described in absolutes so as to provide the social and political distinctions regarding the purpose of the criminal justice system. Of course, the criminal justice system functions, in fact, under an interaction between both models, with the results taking from both.

Advocates of the crime control model assert that the explanation of crime is, in fact, that crime is an individual moral issue. Crime results from a lack of behavioral moral clarity. The focus of analysis is the individual. Crime is explained as the result of subgroup cultural failures. Crime is about the values an individual chooses to adopt. The crime control model places primacy on maintaining society/social order and protecting civilization from anarchy and lawlessness. There are five basic social assumptions of the crime control model regarding the purpose of the criminal justice system. First, the purpose of the system is to protect society from crime and disorder. Second, secure and punish the guilty. Third, the police don't arrest the innocent. Fourth, the police should get the benefit of the doubt regarding the legality of actions they take. Fifth, justice is defined by the outcome. The focus of the crime control model is not the accused but protection of society as a whole. The role of the courts is to certify and confirm what the police know: the accused is guilty. The accused must be punished. Justice occurs when courts and police are in accord regarding the accused.

Advocates of the due process model assert that the explanation of crime is, in fact, that crime is the result of social dynamics and relates to how society treats the individual. Crime results from unfair and unequal societal structures imposed on the individual. The focus of analysis is society. Crime is explained as the result of poverty and social and economic injustice. Due process places primacy on controlling societal power and protecting the individual from tyranny and oppression by the government. As with the crime control model, there are five basic concepts of the due process model. First, protect individual freedom and liberty from the power of government to take away that freedom and liberty under the guise of punishing the guilty. Second, the guilt of the accused is not established at arrest but only at trial after the government has actually proved the guilt of the accused. Third, the police can arrest the innocent. They do so for various reasons, some benevolent and some malevolent. Fourth, the accused should receive the benefit of the doubt allowed by law. Fifth, justice is defined by the process of the system, from arrest to trial. Justice is how the accused is treated, not the final outcome of finding guilt.

Another way of understanding the difference between the two models would be to consider the following dynamics of power within the criminal justice system. There are only two governmental institutions in America that can physically take hold of people, control their lives, and take away their ability to act as they please (freedom and liberty); to force them to act and behave in a certain manner; to change their names; to redefine their status in society; to control their associations; to move them to locations at will; to force them to fight or surrender their rights to protect themselves from physical threat, and to take their lives from them. These two institutions are the military, in times of the draft and war, and the criminal justice system. The military in time of war can get you killed. It can put you in situations of serious life-threatening danger with no social consequences. Because the draft is no longer implemented, the criminal justice system remains the only agency in America that, under the law, can define and control an individual on its own determination with no appeal outside of the system. With a voluntary military, to be subject to danger, you must voluntarily place yourself in the military. The criminal justice system can come and get you and inject you into its world on its own determinations and by its own rules.

The criminal justice system can put you in prison and subject you to violence, physical and sexual, by the hands of other prisoners. In prison, you eat when told and what you are given, you are housed in whatever it deems acceptable, and the system can keep you in such an environment for days, weeks, months, years, or for the remainder of your natural life. In times of war, the military can put you in physical danger of being injured by the enemy. You eat when you are told and what you are given, and you can be in an environment of combat for days or weeks. You can be captured or killed. My point is not that military service is prison, but there are only two institutions, the draft into the military and the criminal justice system, that can subjugate your individual freedom to serve a societal institution with its own interests and goals. The former is no longer imposed and the former can engulf a person by its own rules and on its own terms.

Because of the significant power of the criminal justice system, the due process model asserts that the purpose of criminal justice is to control this power in the interest of the individual who is injected into it by police actions. The crime control model discounts and minimizes the power of the system and prioritizes the need to protect society from criminals. It assumes that the criminal justice system, its individual parts, and the system as a whole, has no interest in the innocent, because its purpose is to protect society from criminals. The assumption is that it functions with the desire to seize the guilty with limited resources. To focus on the innocent would be a waste of resources.

Regarding the power of the criminal justice system to change lives and impose formal and informal (collateral) sanctions, crime control model advocates assert that it is of no consequence to society as a whole, because only the guilty suffer the sanctions, and they deserve to suffer. Crime control focuses not on the suffering of the criminal but the suffering of the victim of the criminal. The life of the criminal being immeasurably altered is of no or little account compared to the life of the victim being altered by the offender. The focus of sympathy belongs to the victim, not the offender. To the crime control model advocate, justice is done when the factually guilty (assumed by the arrest, because it would be inefficient to arrest the innocent) are found legally guilty by the court (which is its only purpose). Thus, innocent until proven guilty really means the court has not sanctioned and affirmed what is the truth—the accused is guilty.

The due process model rejects the initial assumption that the criminal justice system only secures the guilty. Due process assumes that the system can and does make errors and is not efficient in separating the innocent from the guilty. Thus, the purpose of a trial is not to affirm a police arrest but to require the government to prove guilt as a matter of fact and law, and until that is done, the individual is legally and factually innocent.

These models help explain why certain criminal justice policies are supported when others are rejected. Due process model holders pay more attention to rehabilitation and control of police than crime control model holders. Crime control model holders reject criminal procedures that seem to control police actions and how evidence can be secured and used in court. Due process holders focus on how the wheels and belts of the criminal justice system function and if the wheels and belts are fair to the accused. Crime control model holders focus on whether the result—the outcome—protects society as a whole. They focus on societal and victim protection more than whether the system was fair to the accused.

The due process model rejects retribution over rehabilitation, while crime control rejects rehabilitation as a purpose of the criminal justice system in the first place. To crime control model holders, the purpose of the criminal justice system is retribution (revenge—social payback), incapacitation (making sure the offender can't commit additional crimes), and incarceration (banishment from society). Crime control rejects the proposition that the system can rehabilitate or fix the offender. Only the offender can fix or change his behavior. Crime control has little concern for the nature of prisons, while due process places more attention on how prisoners are treated. Due process places significant value on appeals after conviction and seeks to expand that ability as a policy matter to control the power of the government through the criminal justice system. Crime control model advocates seek finality in convictions and to limit appeals of convictions as much as possible to secure the goals of retribution, incapacitation, and incarceration. Due process model holders tend to support judicial oversight of prisons and the expanded ability of prisoners to enjoy constitutional protections from the decisions and policies of prison officials' determinations of prison conditions. Crime control model holders seek to limit judicial application of constitutional rights to prisoners and those convicted of crimes on the premise that such people have lost the constitutional rights that law-abiding citizens enjoy as a matter of principle. Felons and convicts, both in prison and on probation/parole, are the property of the state, not free citizens, and they should be treated as such for the safety of those who obey the law and have a right to protection from criminals.

———————————— ◆◆◆ ————————————

When the first American settlements were established in May 1607 (Jamestown, Virginia) and November 1620 (Cape Cod, Massachusetts), they brought with them the ideals and principles of justice practiced in Great Britain. The Puritans in Massachusetts brought the concept that crime and sin were synonymous and that public power was required to punish sin. Crimes were defined by sin, as defined in the scriptures of the Bible, specifically crimes defined in the books of Exodus and Deuteronomy.[1] As defined by Moses, punishments were corporal in nature, and in the colonies, they included whipping, the use of the stocks, branding, banishment, and public humiliation. The punishments did have a rehabilitative premise. The purpose of corporal punishment was to break the pride and will of the sinner to convince him or her to soften his or her heart and repent. Repentance was significant in the colonists' thinking of crime and sin, because "all have sinned and come short of the glory of God." The colonists applied a Christian proposition to rehabilitation, repentance. The Christian proposition was that, through repentance, a person can be reconciled with God and society. Once a sinner became repentant, justice and equity[2] required that he or she be accepted back into the community as a full member because the goal of corporal punishment, as Paul told the Corinthians, was restoration through repentance. After the colonies freed themselves from Great Britain, the question arose as to how criminals should be treated.

After the colonies freed themselves from Great Britain, America began to develop its own unique perspectives on the science of prisons and what the purpose of prison was. As shown in the figure below, the timeline of criminal justice theory can be discussed in six distinct periods which encompass the professionalization of the various parts of the criminal justice system, the rise of professional policing, prosecutors, rules of evidence and formalized criminal procedures for trial, the development of theories of criminality, prison design based on theories of punishment, as well as development of criminal statutes designed to increase sanctions and incarceration. This history developed concurrently with the rise of slavery and Jim Crow and this concurrent development provides explanations for why American criminal justice was used as a replacement for the social control of blacks for a century after the fall of slavery.

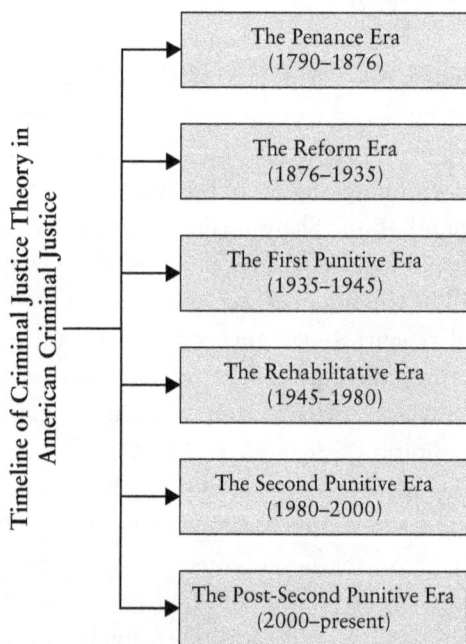

FIGURE 5.1

The Penance Era (1790–1876) involved the beginning of the use of prisons as a place to incur repentance and the rehabilitation of a criminal in the United States. Corporal punishment as a response to criminal behavior was abandoned for the proposition that forced solitary confinement would soften the heart of the offender through isolation and prayer. The offender would be isolated from the criminal associations that he or she may have been exposed to and, with pure isolation and the presence of a Bible and time, the evil of his or her ways would come to the offender and, upon repentance, the person would no longer commit crime. The theory of the penance model is rehabilitative. Incarceration was not to protect society or to inflict pain and suffering on the offender as punishment, but penance was built on the premise that the individual was responsible for his or her actions, and through imposed discipline and enforced silence, rehabilitation would occur. During this time, America used prisons for mass incarceration.

The penance era can be divided into two periods. The first is *the penitentiary period* (1790–1825) in which the Quakers developed the theory of penance through isolation, which was operationalized in *the Pennsylvania system* at the Walnut Street Jail opened in 1773 and Eastern State Penitentiary opened in 1829. This is where the word penitentiaries came from. The second period during *the mass prison period* (1825–1876) advanced an alternative theory, known as *the Auburn system*. The Auburn system of penance was implemented at the Auburn State prison opened in 1818 and Sing Sing prison opened in 1826, in which isolation was abandoned for rehabilitation through forced silence, corporal punishment, hard labor, and prisoner regimentation. Over time, the Auburn system replaced the Pennsylvania system as the primary theory of prison construction and operation in the North. Of course, as the North developed the penance theory, the South used slavery and forced labor as the operational strategy for criminals in its criminal justice system.

The reform era (1876–1935) marked the abandonment of the religious Christian explanation of crime (crime is sin) and the adoption of the medical model for explaining crime. It was during this period the prisoner industry, in which prisoners were required to work at trades to develop skills that they could use when released, was first attempted as a mode of rehabilitation. This theory of rehabilitation was deemed a failure due to cost, lack of positive rehabilitative results, and complaints of unfair competition from private industry. The *Ashurst–Sumners Act* (1935) made interstate commerce in prison-made goods illegal. During the reform era, the professions of criminal justice (probation and parole officers, judges, youth workers, social workers, police officers, criminal defense attorneys, juvenile court officers and judges, full-time prosecutors, prison wardens, and court administrators) formalized the operation of formal societal criminal justice. During this period, plea bargaining began to become a method of resolving criminal charges, and criminal trials became longer, more complex, professionalized, and systemized with the rise of written rules of evidence and formal court procedures and operations. During this period, the concepts of indeterminate sentencing, probation and parole boards, prison reform, prisoner good time toward early release, separate prisons for women, gender-specific theories of crime and rehabilitation, separate courts for juveniles, the development of the distinction between juvenile delinquency and court adjudication versus adult criminal conviction, and separate detention of juveniles from adults were implemented under the concept that dealing with criminal offenders, like dealing with the sick, was for professionals.

The Auburn system was replaced with rehabilitation through education, diversion from prison, release from prison because of good behavior, and the theory that crime is like being sick with pneumonia. If isolation because of the pneumonia is required, it should last no longer than is required to make the person better, after which the patient should be released with additional medicine and sent home to loved ones who will continue his or her care. Likewise, criminal behavior is a sickness of behavior, and if prison (a hospital by analogy) is required, the person should be held only as long as the professionals (prison wardens) determine it is required to fix the behavior (illness). When the offender is no longer a danger to society, the person should be released under the care of a criminal justice professional (parole officer) who will supervise the release and make sure relapse of criminal behavior does not occur.

During the reform era, American criminal justice adopted the parole system pioneered by British reformer Alexander Maconochie in the 1840s and the Irish system of classifying prisoners by threat level pioneered by Sir Walter Crofton in 1854. In 1841 America made its contribution to the reform era worldwide with the invention of probation pioneered by John Augustus in Boston through his work with offenders he asserted should not be placed in prison but could be rehabilitated under court supervision. Overall, these concepts supported the medical model. If a person has a bad cold, you don't expose him or her to people with pneumonia so that the person gets infected with a more serious disease. You control the cold with medicine but let him or her go home. In line with the medical analogy, in the criminal justice context, the offender who is not a direct threat to society has a professional (probation officer) who will work to control the behavior of the offender so that the person will become a productive member of society. The overall assumption during the reform era is that the criminal can be fixed. The purpose of the criminal justice system was to fix the offender, not to punish him or her for its own sake, because you don't punish a person with pneumonia; you heal the person. The moral condemnation theory of the penance era was replaced by the illness theory of reform. While, in the North, the principles of the reform era took hold with the retention of mass incarceration and industrial prisons, the South used convict leasing, chain gangs, and prison labor camps. Reform did not take place in the South; rather, it retained and maintained a system that put blacks in a state of neo-slavery.

The first punitive era (1935–1945) marked America's first abandonment of rehabilitation and reform for retribution as the governing theory for the criminal justice system and use of prisons. During this period, America suffered crime waves across state lines and birthed the need for the federal government to become a key agent of criminal justice and crime control. The dark side of the Roaring Twenties brought increases in bank robberies, prostitution, kidnappings, auto theft, racketeering, gambling, and drug trafficking, all committed by criminals who crossed state lines with faster cars and the use of guns more powerful than those carried by local police. The 1920s had birthed organized crime, which had a nationalized criminal reach during prohibition (1920–1933), with famous criminal names like Al "Scarface" Capone, George "Bugs" Moran, Bonnie and Clyde, "Machine Gun" Kelly, Lucky Luciano, John Dillinger, and other organized crime families in Chicago and New York, along with corruption in government (Teapot Dome Scandal of 1923).

In addition to the rise in violent interstate crime, the lack of middle-class and working-class American compliance with prohibition and the resulting rise of bootleggers, rum runners, and speakeasies produced in America the normalization of open defiance of the law (scofflaws) and a reduced belief that certain laws had legitimacy. This belief reduced societal law and order. The growth in violent and organized crime, along with the uncertainty and disorder of the Great Depression moved American sensibilities on crime from rehabilitation to incapacitation, incarceration, and retribution. During this period, the FBI was created (1935) out of the Department of Justice Bureau of Investigation (1908). The Bureau of Investigation, in 1924, was placed under the command of J. Edgar Hoover, who governed it through its renaming as the FBI in 1935 and continued to govern it until he died in 1972.

With the rise in fear of crime, the purpose of prison was not to rehabilitate; instead, it focused on the incapacitation and incarceration of criminals with the political rhetoric of just deserts and the policy of warehousing offenders. The purpose of the criminal justice system was protection of society, and that birthed the rise of maximum security prisons on the state and federal levels, with the most famous being the opening of **Alcatraz** (August 1934). Alcatraz was the model for the theory that the purpose of prison was to make the offender "pay his debt to society" with the return of regimentation and prisoner control. Alcatraz also operationalized the **concentration model** of prisoner control. Alcatraz was designed to hold the most dangerous and incorrigible prisoners within the federal prison system in one place—the theory of the concentration model was to confine the most dangerous in one place and that would increase the safety of all other prisoners in the system. Although this model would be abandoned during the rehabilitation era, it would return in the second punitive era and form the basis for supermax prisons in the 1990s.

The first punitive era involved the rise of striped uniforms and long prison terms at hard labor and replaced the idea of fixing the offender as one would heal a patient with pneumonia. The significance of this period was the rise of the role of the national government in criminal justice and crime control, which up until this period was always a local matter. The rise of the FBI helped foster the rise of professionalism of law enforcement in general under Hoover. During this era, policing in America transitioned from an institution known for political corruption to a profession that used police car patrols, exams for entry and promotion, departments separated from political control, and utilization of scientific methods of investigation and criminal identification. The use of science and the development of police science began with the adoption of the Bertillon system (identifying and classifying criminals by physical measurements) in 1887 and the advent of fingerprints as the primary system of identifying criminals in 1903. These advances led to the professionalization period (1920–1970) of policing which would continue through the rehabilitative era. The professionalization of policing would occur alongside the general return of rehabilitation and would abandon the police deployment of community support-based crime prevention model of Robert Peel (the guardian model) adopted during the reform era. During the professionalization period, the warrior model of community control and crime investigation and suppression would replace the guardian model of policing. The warrior model adopted a militaristic organizational approach to achieve professionalism in policing, and this model was first pioneered and operationalized in the Los Angeles Police Department (LAPD) under Chief William Parker (1950–1967). This warrior model would be continued under Chief Daryl Gates (1978–1992). The LA Police Department would serve as a model for policing across the United States from the 1950s through the 1990s.

The rehabilitation era (1945–1980) was birthed, in part, because of the lessons of World War II. In Germany, Italy, Spain, and France, dictators rose to power in functioning democracies. The military and police forces were unleashed on civilian populations to maintain order, and individual liberty was to be sacrificed for the good of society as a whole. The Axis Powers took this principle to its most logical conclusion and gas chambers and political prisons spread across Europe. The lessons learned in the United States and Western Europe were that government power must be controlled at all levels and that the rights of the individual under the law and through the courts must be valued above governmental claims of needing to prevent crime and disorder. The crimes of Nazi Germany proved that totalitarian tyranny can function in a republic under procedural rule of law. This lesson reintroduced the ideals of the due process model in criminal justice policy and the return of rehabilitation as the governing theory of American prisons. The lessons of the war provided a reminder that positive law (written law) is not the sole definition of legality nor is it the exclusive venue to justice. The purpose of the law is to uphold the higher concepts of justice as well as equality. Justice is accomplished through the application of the higher principles of the law and the supremacy of the law over governmental power to act. Unjust laws that are efficient and legally passed can still be unjust, and such laws should not be obeyed. These lessons were not lost on the generation of Thurgood Marshall, Martin Luther King, and the black leaders of civil rights after World War II.

The rehabilitative era regarding criminal justice occurred in concurrence with the rise of the civil rights movement, the second wave of the women's movement, and then the homosexual rights movement in the early 1970s. The rise of the 1960s and the values of Martin Luther King Jr., John F. Kennedy, Robert Kennedy, Lyndon Johnson, and the due process revolution at the hands of the U.S. Supreme Court (discussed in Chapter 7) all provided the background for the idea that American prisons and criminal justice policy should focus on the offender.

During the 1960s, the rise of the treatment model, akin to the reform medical model, reached its golden age. Crime was not only perceived as a social sickness that should be treated like an illness; crime resulted from social, structural, racial, and economic injustice imposed upon people who had no choice but to commit crime. During this period, every possible concept of rehabilitation and theory that crime is the result of social and societal structure found advocacy and policy justification. This period saw the rise of prisoner rights advocacy groups and prison reform, including religious rights for inmates, prisoner advisory boards, and the right to have access to law libraries in prisons for appeals. This period also involved the rise of diversion programs and community correction initiatives, alternative sentencing, community-based programs, drug treatment programs, various types of alternatives to incarceration, the deinstitutionalization of the mentally ill from state mental hospitals, the rise of re-entry programming, the constitutionalization of the juvenile justice system, and work-release and furlough programs. In the golden age of rehabilitation, it was believed that crime was socially imposed, and criminals had rights in prisons that mirrored the rights they had before conviction.

Beginning with the politics of Goldwater in 1964, the urban riots of 1964–1968, and the election of Richard Nixon and the rise of "law-and-order" politics in the early 1970s, the optimism of the early 1960s was being abandoned. The golden age of the rehabilitation era was slowly replaced with public skepticism over whether rehabilitation programs worked, a general resentment of the social changes that the 1960s had inflicted upon white middle-class social and Christian values, and the rise of the militarization of policing. During the middle to late 1970s, the narrative that crime occurs because of the lack of law enforcement and the coddling of criminals was replacing the theory that crime was the result of social and structural injustices. The rise of law-and-order politics culminated in the election of Ronald Reagan in 1980, which marked the beginning of a new era in American social politics in general and, specifically, in criminal justice policy.

As discussed in Chapter 4 and later in Chapter 7, the modern development of the criminal justice system and federalization of criminal justice policy began during the Johnson Administration. In an effort to gain support for the Great Society, Johnson asserted in 1966 that his policies would reduce urban crime—black crime. The Johnson Administration began the federalization of the politics and policy of law and order when, on August 20, 1964, President Johnson signed the **Federal Criminal Justice Act of 1964**. That act provided funding for indigent defense counsel. This act was followed by the president signing the **Law Enforcement Assistance Act of 1965** on September 22, 1965, which provided block-grant funding for the education and support of local police officers. But a year later, the politics of crime had shifted, and the need for law and order—control of the streets from criminals, i.e., blacks—had to be addressed. Johnson met the challenge when he gave his special message to Congress on crime on March 9, 1966.

Congress complied with the president. On June 22, 1966, President Johnson signed the **Bail Reform Act of 1966**, which was to "assure that all persons, regardless of their financial status, shall not needlessly be detained pending their appearance to answer charges, to testify, or pending appeal, when detention serves neither the ends of justice nor the public interest." Two years later, at President Johnson's urging, Congress passed the **Omnibus Crime Control and Safe Streets Act of 1968**. The new law provided more than $400 million in block grants for police training, authorized the president to order wiretapping for national security and homeland defense purposes, prohibited private employers from wiretapping employees, overruled the *Miranda* decision by allowing the admission of confessions at trials when those confessions were voluntarily secured from a defendant regardless of whether the actual warnings required by the Supreme Court were given, and outlawed interstate sales of handguns, along with raising the minimum age to buy a handgun in interstate commerce to 21 years old. The *Miranda* provision was not used by federal law enforcement, and when it was, the Supreme Court held it unconstitutional in *Dickerson v. United States* in 2000.

Under the national radar of the politics of the war on poverty and the Great Society, crime policies slowly shifted law enforcement toward a more militant and militarized approach to crime. In the 1950s, the LAPD, under Chief William Parker, established the professionalization model for his officers. Chief Parker believed that crime was the sole result of disrespect for the police. He believed that crime resulted from the disregard and disrespect of the law. The problem of crime was easily resolved. The police officer was a warrior who enforced the law with brute force upon the criminal. Communities were safe because they were under control. Communities that were not under control were to be made so by force. Chief Parker believed that blacks were not under control. Civil disobedience resulted in criminal behavior. The law is the law—whether those are laws enforcing segregation and Jim Crow or laws prohibiting burglary and theft. The law was to be obeyed. Parker's view found a similar perspective in the director of the FBI, John Edgar Hoover. Between these two men, a new generation of police officer ethos was being created in the public eye. The warrior model was the template of the modern police officer and purpose of the policing. Crime was about social disorder, and the warrior police officer was the sole agent to solve and prevent disorder. Where Parker and Hoover parted company with President Johnson was on whether the police were the sole agents responsible for solving social disorder. Johnson believed the entire criminal justice system was the wall that prevented crime and disorder. The warrior model under Parker and Hoover believed the thin blue line, the warrior cop, is the sole separation between society and an ever-encroaching jungle. A concept that would find support in the mouth of a president in 1980.

Another public official would introduce and support a key tool of law enforcement and maintenance of law and order by brute force: Governor Nelson Rockefeller and his policies of no-knock warrants and use of stop and frisk of pedestrians on the street. The *no-knock warrants statute* allows the police to secure a special warrant that enables them to enter a house without knocking and allowing the owner or occupant time to answer the door. The *stop-and-frisk statute* allows the police to stop a person on the street and detain upon suspicion of crime. Both pieces of legislation became effective on July 1, 1964. Over the next decade, both policies underlying the statutes were adopted by the states, the federal government, and the U.S. Supreme Court as legitimate law enforcement tools to address crime. The problem with both laws is not their existence but how they were implemented. Over the proceeding decades, reports and cases would arise showing how the police entered and destroyed the homes of people under the authority of no-knock warrants and blacks being stopped with little more reason than that they were black, and blacks tend to be criminal.

The middle- and late-1960s also birthed another aspect of the militarization of the police—the need for the police to deal with armed, organized, radicalized political criminal gangs, mass shooters, and radical racial groups, like the Black Panthers. There was a need for special police units. This need resulted in the formation of the *LAPD Special Weapons and Tactics (SWAT) Team,* the brainchild of then LAPD Inspector Daryl Gates. The idea of SWAT was birthed after the *Charles Whitman massacre at the University of Texas at Austin clock tower* on August 11, 1966. The lack of preparedness of law enforcement to deal with Whitman and the urban riots of '64 and '65 instilled in Gates the need for police departments to have officers trained in military tactics to deal with disturbances that regular officers were not trained or equipped to handle. Aside from the epiphany of SWAT in the mind of Gates, the "riots in Watts and other urban areas" left an impression on middle-class suburban voters who feared the "rising black criminal class," but who had felt immune from criminal violence, were dissuaded of that immunity by "Whitman's rampage on a college campus. ... And all of this came as the country was still reeling from Richard Speck's trial for torturing, raping, and murdering eight nurses from South Chicago Community Hospital a month earlier.

The criminal threat no longer seemed to be limited to the inner cities."[3] Middle-class America wanted to feel safe, and the rise and support of militarized police would provide a source of comfort. Although Gates found it hard to convince his superiors that SWAT should be supported, the urban riots of 1967 and 1968 and the police riot at the 1968 Democratic Convention in Chicago provided fertile ground for law enforcement acceptance of the SWAT idea. In December 1969, Gates and the LAPD SWAT team entered the national limelight with its raid on the Los Angeles headquarters of the Black Panthers.[4]

Gates and his SWAT team raided the headquarters of the Black Panthers to execute a warrant for possession of illegal firearms. The Panthers were ready for a fight because of the killing of Fred Hampton, the deputy chairman of the Illinois chapter, by the Chicago police.[5] The raid resulted in three hours of exchanged gunfire, and after Gates secured permission from the Department of Defense to use a Marine grenade launcher on the house the Panthers surrendered, all in front of the national media.[6] This raid, along with the LAPD SWAT raid on the Symbionese Liberation Army, famously known for the kidnapping of Patty Hearst, in November 1973 made both Gates and SWAT sensations in the national consciousness and within law enforcement.[7] By the early 1980s, every police department in America had some type of SWAT-trained officer corp.

Under Nixon and the rise of the crime control model, the police were to be honored, supported, and funded as the warriors against crime. The ethos that the police were warriors against what Reagan called "the jungle" ever encroaching upon civilization was exemplified by the image of the LAPD officer. During the 1970s, the LAPD formed in the national popular consciousness the example of what the warrior cop should be. Popular police dramas of the 1950s through the and 1970s, such as *Adam 12*, *Dragnet*, *The Rookies*, and *SWAT*, all used the LAPD as the model for fictional police departments or dramatized the LAPD directly. These television series, as well as the series *The FBI*, which dramatized actual FBI investigations, and shows like *Hawaii Five-O*, *CHIPS*, *Starsky and Hutch*, and *Barretta*, all supported the crime control model of the police. Police officers were brave, overworked, and, despite working within a system that favored criminal defendant rights—letting them go on "technicalities"—they were, above all, honest, incorruptible, and did not use force unless it was required. Suburban, middle-class white and black voters who were exposed to the police and the criminal justice system only through television were prone to support Nixon and, later, Reagan's view that law and order was exclusively maintained by the men in blue, as shown on TV. The police warrior model was defined in terms of the strong and tough but fair arbiter of justice on the street who guarded the gates from the barbaric hoards. Police abuses of blacks were neither seen nor believed by these voters. This dynamic allowed for the second punitive era policies of the 1980s in which the police in general, and militarized SWAT units in particular, were unleashed to deal with the scourge of the 1980s—crack cocaine and the crime and violence that came with it.

With the 1968 assassinations of Dr. King and Robert Kennedy, American politics was changing. Both parties in Congress defined law and order as the need to control and suppress crime. The Supreme Court was abandoning the due process revolution as exemplified by its decision in *Terry v. Ohio* in which the Court held reasonable articulable suspicion was all that was required for police to stop a person the police believed could be involved in criminal activity. The Court in *Terry* affirmed the New York stop-and-frisk statute. The American public was becoming convinced that crime should be defined as a social disorder and disobedience, not the result of social injustice or economic inequalities.

In the wake of a decade of civil rights marches and civil disobedience, 1968 witnessed the abandonment of nonviolent civil protest for civil rights and the advocacy for a militant civil rights movement. The Great Society had not ended social disorder and the 1968 riots became a major political issue in the 1968 elections. In the politics of crime, race became the euphemism for disorder and a threat to law and order with the war on poverty being blamed by both the left and the right for having failed to reduce poverty, which was supposed to reduce crime and increase public safety. With the failure of the war on poverty and Great Society programs becoming clear, but race being irrevocably linked to crime, the crime control model as an answer to crime was ready to make its appearance with the election of Richard Nixon. If social programs won't reduce black crime, law enforcement will.

By the 1968 presidential election, crime was a defining election topic. During the campaign, Nixon was famously quoted as saying the "solution to the crime problem is not the quadrupling of funds for any governmental war on poverty but more convictions." After receiving the Republican Party nomination for president, Nixon asserted that crime was the main question for America to answer. Nixon announced that the "silent majority" of America was ready for a change in which its politicians would seek more law and order and less America blaming for the chosen deviant behavior of a few. As Johnson established the orthodoxy of liberal theory of crime reduction in his 1966 address to Congress, Nixon established the orthodoxy of social conservatives in his acceptance speech at the 1968 Republican convention.

After winning the election, Nixon opened the first salvo in the war on crime by backing proposals to allow no-knock warrants and stop and frisk in the District of Columbia. On July 29, 1970, he signed the **D.C. Crime Bill**, which authorized the D.C. police to conduct no-knock warrants, field urine testing during drug raids, and preventive detentions. The law also expanded police wiretapping authority and allowed the police to seize evidence that was not listed in warrants. Nixon then turned to illegal drug use. He famously declared a war on drugs and signed the **Comprehensive Drug Abuse Prevention and Control Act of 1970** on October 27, 1970. The legislation revolutionized federal power to deal with illegal drug use. The legislation abandoned all previous national illegal possession legislation and placed enforcement of illegal drug use within the Justice Department on a constitutional theory that Congress could outlaw illicit drug use under the commerce clause rather than the tax power of Congress. Title II of the Act, the

Controlled Substances Act, created a system of making drugs illegal to use and established a schedule system for all drugs in which schedule one drugs were illegal to use or possess.

Nixon then reorganized federal law enforcement to wage this newly declared war on drugs. The lead federal agency in illegal drug interdiction prior to the creation of the Drug Enforcement Administration (DEA) in 1973 was the Bureau of Narcotics and Dangerous Drugs (BNDD), a creation of the merging of the Bureau of Internal Revenue, the Bureau of Drug Abuse Control, and the Federal Bureau of Narcotics in the 1960s. Three years after the passage of the Comprehensive Drug Abuse Prevention and Control Act, Nixon, under the Reorganization Plan No. 2 of 1973, created the DEA and made it the primary agency to enforce federal illegal drug use laws. The DEA was composed of the merging of the BNDD and the Office of Drug Abuse Law Enforcement, an agency Nixon created within the White House in January 1972, in addition to securing agents from the U.S. Customs Service and the Office of National Narcotics Intelligence. The Controlled Substances Act was amended to allow the DEA, jointly in consultation with the Department of Health and Human Services and the Food and Drug Administration to define which drugs would be classified as schedule one drugs and, thus, be illegal to use or possess.

Nixon was not alone in his attack on crime through a war on drugs. The crime control model found support from Governor Nelson Rockefeller with the passage of his no-knock and stop-and-frisk policy legislation in 1964 and, in 1973, New York passed the first modern *mandatory sentencing statutes* for drug possession, the **Rockefeller Drug Laws of 1973**. The Rockefeller Drug Laws of 1973, for the first time, elevated drug possession and distribution crimes as equivalent to violent crimes, such as murder, rape, and arson. The drug law created a system of equating the drug dealer with the violent criminal. This strategy greatly increased the number of criminals sentenced to long prison terms for nonviolent drug offenses. This approach to drug crimes would drive the increases in the U.S. prison population for decades.

The second punitive era (1980–2000) ushered in the end of the rehabilitative period as the first punitive era ended the reform era. With the rise of crime, urban crime ("black on black" crime) and the general change in political sentiment and the abandonment of the idea that prisoners could be fixed, America returned to the policy that the purpose of the criminal justice system and prisons was the incapacitation and incarceration of prisoners and justice required retribution, not rehabilitation. The rise in violent crime, violent juvenile crime, gun violence, sensational cases of child abductions, and the crack epidemic of the 1980s ushered in a return of incapacitation, incarceration, the protection of society, and make the offender "pay his debt to society." These political sentiments gave rise to the policies of determinant sentencing for violent crime and drug offenses; the policy of juvenile transfer, the transferring serious juvenile offenders and juvenile "super predators" to adult court, so they could be tried and punished like adults; the total abandonment of parole and good time policies; and the rise of supermax prisons. During this period, the federal government provided states with billions of dollars to build prisons and supermax prisons (23-hour lockdowns). Federal funds were provided to states that implemented various crime-control policies, including the establishment of sex offender databases, passage of legislation giving victims of crime the right to be heard at sentencing hearings, and passage of truth-in-sentencing statutes. The result of these policies was significant increases in prison populations for longer periods of time.

This period also introduced the policy of sentencing guidelines that imposed mandatory sentencing of offenders for crimes. The guidelines were designed to remove discretion from judges in sentencing offenders, which was hailed by both liberals and conservatives. Liberals or due process model holders supported sentencing guidelines because the guidelines ended vast variances between sentencing for individuals of different races who had committed the same offense (racial bias by judges). Conservatives or crime control model holders supported sentencing guidelines to prevent the imposition of "soft" sentences by liberal anti-police judges. The impact of increased incarceration rates because of the mandatory sentence guidelines were supplemented by the policy of three strikes. Under this policy, offenders who were convicted of a third, and sometimes a second, serious offense would be sentenced to life without the possibility of parole.

The post-second punitive era (2000–present) did not return to the rehabilitation era as a theory of criminal justice and prison operation, but the post-second punitive era allowed for the softening of retribution politics while maintaining the idea of incapacitation and incarceration. As the lowering of the national and local crime rates occurred, policies that allowed for the reduction in mandatory minimum sentences for drugs appeared under the *Fair Sentencing Act* (2010), and during this period, the Supreme Court ruled in *U.S. v. Booker* (2005) and *Kimbrough v. U.S.* (2007) that the federal sentencing guidelines were advisory but not mandatory. The treatment of the guidelines as advisory allowed for judges to have discretion in sentencing and allowed them to develop programs designed to divert offenders from incarceration through specialty courts. Specialty courts were initiatives in which court personnel received training to deal with certain types of offenders and these offenders were exclusively handled by these courts. The idea was for the courts to craft rehabilitative plans and when necessary retributive outcomes to deal with the specific issues the offenders had. These courts included DUI courts, mental health courts, truancy courts, first offender courts, and domestic violence courts.

The withdrawal from the policies of the second punitive era occurred, in part, from the reality of the high cost of mass incarceration, and with state and federal budgets no longer supplemented by deficit spending to build and maintain prisons, the utilization of rehabilitation as a less expensive way to deal with offenders forced political change. Early in this period the idea that offenders can be fixed or rehabilitated was still abandoned but the idea of retribution at all costs had also been abandoned. Within the second decade of the new century, public policy was changing and rehabilitation became politically palatable under presidents Bush (*The Second Chance Act of 2007*), Obama (*The Fair Sentencing Act of 2010*) and Trump (*The First Step Act of 2018*).

During the heyday of the second punitive era, the disproportionate incarceration of blacks was defended by the assertion that it was the sole and natural consequence of deviant black behavior and culture. In other words, it was not a problem to be fixed by reforming the criminal justice system but a reality to be accepted, so long as the black community did not change the behavior of young black men. The problem was cultural and not because of the operation of the criminal justice system. During the post-secondary punitive era, the disproportionate incarceration was recognized as a problem to be fixed, not accepted as normal.

This period is discussed in greater detail in Chapters 7 and 8. In 1995, America reached the one million mark of people incarcerated in federal and state prisons. By 2005, America broke the two-million mark for the total number of people incarcerated in federal, state, and local jails. America per capita has more people incarcerated than in any other Western industrialized nation on the planet. The point is that this did not occur by happenstance. This is the result of policy. This policy outcome of mass incarceration also created a social psychological dynamic that affects all members of society. How? High incarceration and justifications for it define how people who are the focus of incarceration are seen and perceived by society as a whole. They are seen as violent, suspect, and worthy of police contact to protect society as a whole. Even Bush's black appointee discussed in Chapter 1 acknowledged that "law-abiding" blacks have more contact with police than "law-abiding" whites. It's how this contact functions in a crime control model political climate that is discussed in the next chapter.

chapter six

Police Use of Force in Theory and Practice

The fear of crime in America was a potent political tool that had held the Republican Party voting base together from Nixon through George W. Bush. It was also a political reality that changed the politics of the Democratic Party to require them to catch up on the "get tough on crime" rhetoric and politics of the post-1960s America. This dynamic forced the party to abandon the defense of the politics and policies of the Great Society of President Johnson. In the 1980s, the new focal point of law-and-order politics was the politics of crime and race in the era of crack cocaine in black urban neighborhoods. Because of the nature of crack drug trafficking and the gang and gun violence that came with it, the constant of disproportionate arrests and incarceration of blacks was taken to a new level. To the detriment of blacks, the plague of crack initially concentrated in urban neighborhoods, and the criminalization of crack was the funnel in which thousands of young men of color were poured into the criminal justice system. With the groundwork laid by Nixon and Rockefeller, those young men of color would be incarcerated for decades, if not life, under the new drug policies and laws under Reagan, Bush, and Clinton.

The fears of black men and crime not only supported the rise of the policies of the second punitive era but provided political cover for the excesses of the warrior model and police use of force, especially the use of force by police shooting unarmed blacks. Police use of force is governed by the Fourth Amendment which establishes that the "right of the people to be secure in their persons, houses, papers, and effects, against unreasonable searches and seizures, shall not be violated" and the Supreme Court has determined that when the police use force—anything from a verbal command to obey an order to the police shooting a person—the Fourth Amendment alone governs whether that use of force—a seizure—was justified under the constitution.[1] A seizure occurs, according to the Supreme Court, when a reasonable person believes they can't leave. A seizure involves the entire continuum of force, from being subjected to a stop and frisk[2] to being shot by the police. Before defining the limits of Fourth Amendment law—let's look at a Fourth Amendment story.

> On November 22, 2018, Emantic Fitzgerald Bradford was sitting alone in the restaurant area of Riverchase Galleria shopping mall in Hoover, Alabama. While sitting he heard gun shots and being a former soldier and having a concealed carry permit attempted to respond to an active shooter. Bradford unholstered his gun, cocked a bullet into the chamber, and ran toward the person who was shot and the person who was giving aid. Bradford was running toward the shooter. At the same moment, four police officers who were assigned to the mall also heard the gun shots and also ran toward the situation. Both the police and Bradford were running toward an "active shooter" situation, but Bradford was in front of the police and the police were running behind him. When the police came upon the scene, they saw Bradford with a gun running toward the person shot and the person giving aid. Bradford's back was toward the police. The

police did not know who the shooter was but at the moment they entered the situation they saw an armed black man running toward two unarmed people. The police shot twice hitting Bradford in the back, killing him.

On February 5, 2019, the Alabama Attorney General issued a report that the police officer who shot Bradford would not face criminal charges because the officer acted reasonably under the circumstances. The Attorney General concluded that the law does not hold police culpable for being wrong in killing an innocent person, the law only requires that the officer act reasonably in taking the action that results in the killing. The Attorney General concluded that a reasonable police officer, with the information the officers had at the time, would have concluded that Bradford was the active shooter, who at the moment of being shot was about to shoot two unarmed people. The fact that the officer was wrong is of no consequence. The Fourth Amendment only requires reasonable action, not correct action viewed in hindsight.

The harsh reality is that the attorney general was correct. The Fourth Amendment only protects people from "unreasonable" seizure by the police. In *Tennessee v. Gardner* (1985) the Supreme Court held that police use of force, in this case shooting an unarmed escaping burglar, was governed by the Fourth Amendment and police use of force is a seizure. The Court held that police can use deadly force when dealing with an armed and dangerous suspect who poses a threat to the officers or others, but they can't use such force against a suspect simply because he is escaping. In *Graham v. Connor* (1989), the Court held that all police use of force was governed by the Fourth Amendment, but only the Fourth Amendment governs such force. The court rejected the assertion that the due process clause of Fifth and Fourteenth Amendments can address excessive use of force by the police. In *Graham,* the Court held that police use of force must be assessed by reviewing all of the specific facts of the specific situation (totality of the circumstances) that the officer was confronted with at the time the force was used, and with that, the court must determinate what a reasonable officer in that specific situation with those specific facts would have done. If the court finds that the acts taken were the same as what a reasonable officer would have taken, the police use of force will be reasonable under the Fourth Amendment.

Although police enjoy the benefit of the doubt, that does not mean that culpable responsibility is always escaped.

In the 2014 Laquan McDonald killing, Officer Jason Van Dyke was convicted on 16 counts of aggravated battery for 16 shots that were not needed in the confrontation with McDonald. Under Fourth Amendment analysis, each use of force, the 16 discharges of his weapon, for example, is independently assessed as to whether it (each discharge of his weapon) was excessive—i.e., unreasonable. In the McDonald shooting, the police shooting (16 times), was excessive and resulted in 16 counts of criminal culpability. Because the force was excessive, the force was unreasonable, thus illegal.

In the 2017 Justine Ruszczyk killing, Officer Mohamed Noor was convicted of second-degree murder for killing Ruszczyk when she approached his police car after calling for help for a suspected rape. Noor and his partner had parked their car in an ally near Ruszcyk's location and while in the car Noor withdrew his gun and when Ruszcyk knocked on the roof of the car, Noor shot her from the passenger side of the police car. Because Noor had no justification in taking out his gun and discharging it, the use of force was unreasonable, and he was found guilty of murder.

In the 2018 Botham Jean killing, Officer Amber Guyger came home after her shift ended, and while texting and not paying attention, entered the home of Jean thinking it was hers, and upon seeing Jean, Guyger shot and killed him. She was convicted for murder in October 2019 and sentenced to ten years.

On October 14, 2019, a neighbor made a non-emergency call to the Fort Worth, Texas police and said he saw his neighbor's door open. He said something might be wrong because it was open for a long time and asked the police to make a safety visit. When Officer Aaron Dean arrived at the house, he withdrew his gun, and upon seeing a shadow in the window shot through the window and killed Atatiana Jefferson. Jefferson, alone with her 8-year-old nephew, had secured her licensed conceal carry permitted gun when she heard noise coming from her backyard and pointed it towards the window. Dean failed to announce himself as a police officer and fired at Jefferson upon seeing her shadow. Officer Dean resigned the following Monday and was arrested and charged with murder the same day. In all of these cases, police use of force without legal justification placed the police in the same situation as an ordinary criminal.

Both *Gardner* and *Graham* established that under the Fourth Amendment, the court will look at the justification for the use of force and the method in applying the force. The former is about whether the police had a legal reason to justify the force. The latter is an independent analysis, which focuses on the level of force used, how the force was used, and the level of intensity of the force used. If the police officer is justified in using force on a suspect but the situation is such that a wrist lock would enforce compliance with the police, the use of a baton to the head would be excessive and a violation of the Fourth Amendment. In such a case, the officer would be culpable for assault.

Subsequent case law on police use of force has made it clear that analysis of police use of force is not to be done in hindsight. In other words, it does not matter if police officers, in fact, were wrong in their determination of the facts or the decision to use deadly force. All that matters is that they were reasonable in their actions at the time they took them. The Fourth Amendment is governed and defined by the word unreasonable, which is a context word. It looks at the specific situation and determines if the action taken was reasonable, not whether it was, in fact, correct. In the Bradford case, the police thought they were shooting an active shooter. The fact they were wrong is of no consequence. This is one of the key weaknesses in Fourth Amendment jurisprudence and the protection it provides. Because the police belief regarding Bradford was objectively reasonable under the circumstances at the time, the law provided no remedy, even though the officers were, in fact, wrong, and Bradford was, in fact, innocent.

Despite this weakness, the Fourth Amendment has a wide and exclusive area of jurisdiction over police and criminal justice actions. The Court has held that the Fourth Amendment governs all government "seizure" from arrest through the pretrial process[3] and pretrial detention[4] and that the standard of the Fourth Amendment (objective reasonableness) applies to claims of excessive force used by jail officers during pretrial detention.[5] The Fourteenth Amendment due process clause only protects pretrial detainees from excessive force when the intensity and purpose of that force rises to the level of punishment.[6] The Court has held that government action that rises to the level of punishment is action that inflicts unreasonable or unnecessary pain.[7]

The other weakness of the Fourth Amendment is that it does not take into account racial bias or prejudice or unconscious belief that blacks are more likely to be criminals. The point being, the law is not concerned with the history of race in America. Police shootings of blacks has historical baggage. That baggage includes the belief that blacks, especially young black males, are criminogenic. As discussed in previous chapters, this baggage was developed from the earliest days of slavery and the post-reconstruction era. This baggage has manifested in the social and political reactions to police shootings of blacks. Crime control model advocates give the police the benefit of the doubt. When police officers are not held accountable for the death of young black males, the perception by blacks is that little has changed regarding the social value placed on black lives. The recent history of police shootings in 2014–2017 and lack of holding police accountable—which in the American system is criminal conviction—gave rise to the politics of the Black Lives Matter movement and the conservative answer—Blue Lives Matter.

According to the *Washington Post Dataset* on police shootings, in 2015, police killed 995 people, in 2016, police killed 963 people, in 2017, police had shot and killed 987 people, and in 2018, the

CHART 6.1 Top-Ten States of Police
Shootings Resulting in Death 2015–2018

STATES	NUMBER	PERCENT
California	602	15.3
Texas	332	8.5
Florida	241	6.1
Arizona	199	5.1
Colorado	134	3.4
Georgia	128	3.3
Ohio	121	3.1
Oklahoma	118	3.0
North Carolina	103	2.6
Washington	102	2.6

police had killed 995 people. As shown in chart 6.1 enhanced analysis of the dataset shows that California, Texas, and Florida are the top-three states for police shootings that result in death.[8]

The incidents of police shootings by race showed that clusters of shootings by race are different by race. As shown in chart 6.2 the top-three states in which blacks were killed by percentage within race were Ohio, North Carolina, and Georgia. For whites, the top three were Oklahoma, North Carolina and Ohio, and Washington. For Hispanics, the top-three states were California, Arizona, and Texas.

As shown in chart 6.3 the top four cities in which police have used deadly force are Phoenix, Los Angeles, Houston, and Las Vegas.[9]

As shown in chart 6.4 the top three cities involving blacks being shot were Chicago, Houston, Columbus, Ohio and Los Angeles.

As shown in chart 6.5 blacks made up almost 25 percent of all police shooting resulting in death while accounting for 13 percent of the total U.S. population.

CHART 6.2 Top-Ten States of Police Shootings Resulting in Death by Race 2015–2017

STATES	WHITE	BLACK	HISPANIC	ASIAN	OTHER	UNKNOWN	NUMBER
California	151 (31%)	77 (15.8%)	213 (43%)	18 (3.7%)	13	15	487
Texas	104 (42%)	55 (22%)	78 (31%)	2 (.8%)	4	5	248
Florida	89 (50%)	59 (33%)	23 (13%)	1 (.56%)	2	4	178
Arizona	67 (49%)	8 (5.8%)	47 (34%)	0	9	5	136
Colorado	44 (48%)	9 (10%)	26 (28%)	3 (3.3%)	4	4	90
Ohio	49 (55%)	35 (39%)	0	2 (2.2%)	2	1	89
Georgia	45 (53%)	30 (35%)	7 (8.3%)	1 (1.2%)	0	1	84
Oklahoma	52 (62%)	16 (19%)	7 (8.3%)	2 (2.3%)	5	2	84
Washington	43 (53%)	12 (15%)	9 (11%)	4 (5%)	8	4	80
North Carolina	43 (55%)	30 (38%)	3 (3%)	1 (1.2%)	1	0	78

CHART 6.3 Top-Ten Cities of Police Shootings Resulting in Death 2015–2018

CITIES	NUMBER
Phoenix	60
Los Angeles	58
Houston	37
Las Vegas	36
Columbus	33
Chicago	31
San Antonio	29
Albuquerque	28
Miami & Tucson	24
Kansas City & Oklahoma City	22

CHART 6.4 Top Cities of Police Shootings Resulting in Death By Race* 2015–2017

CITIES	BLACK	CITIES	HISPANICS
Chicago	22	Los Angles	21
Houston	16	Albuquerque	13
Columbus	14	Phoenix	13
Los Angeles	11	San Antonio	12
St. Louis	13	Bakersfield	9
Miami Gardens, Washington, D.C. & Philadelphia	10	Tucson	9
Baltimore, Baton Rouge, Jacksonville, & Indianapolis	9	Denver, Fresno, Houston, Las Vegas	7
NYC	8	Miami, San Jose, Santa Ana	7
Atlanta, Kansas City, Milwaukee, & Charlotte	7	Reno	6
New Orleans, Oakland, & Oklahoma City	6	El Paso	5
Las Vegas	5		

* Asians showed one incident in each of 43 cities. Whites showed one incident in more than 1,000 different cities.

CHART 6.5 Police Shootings Resulting in Death by Race Distribution 2015–2017

RACE OF SUSPECT	NUMBER OF SHOOTINGS	PERCENT	PERCENT OF GENERAL POPULATION*	PERCENT OF VIOLENT CRIME ARRESTS (2017)**[10]
White	1,465	49.9	76.5	58.5
Black	722	24.6	13.6	37.5
Hispanic	538	18.3	16.4	–
Asian	47	1.6	5.6	1.5

* U.S. Census 2008–2012 estimates data (American Fact Finder tool generated).
** Table 43A Total Arrests FBI Crime in the United States 2017.

When looking at the situations and context, for police use of force resulting in death, the distribution was not equal by race. As shown in chart 6.6 the asserted reason for police use of deadly force is distributed differently by context. One of the more significant results of the analysis of the data is that traffic stops accounted for a third of all police shootings of blacks, and it was the third-most prevalent reason for blacks and Hispanics being shot by the police. For whites, traffic stops ranked ninth in situations resulting in a police shooting.

While situations that resulted in police use of deadly force were distributed differently by race and blacks are more likely to be shot during a traffic stop than by citizen complaints—calls for service; the data was uniform that the police perceived threat that resulted in police use of deadly force is the perception of gun or some other type of weapon. Analysis of the *Washington Post Dataset* showed that half (55.6 percent) of the explanations for police shootings was the presence of a gun and 81.5 percent of the threat perception involved some type of weapon. Because the police claim the threat of a weapon in almost all of the cases, that raises the question of discriminability.[11] The question being, under stress[12] and ambiguous situations, are police correct that a gun was present? Discriminability is the ability to discern a "gun" from a "wallet"

CHART 6.6 Top Shooting Context Situation Percentage Distribution by Race Percentage 2015–2017

WHITE	BLACK	HISPANIC	ASIAN
Domestic violence – 60%	Responding to robbery – 33%	Car chase – 24%	Car chase – 3%
Warrant execution – 58%	Resisting arrest – 31%	Home invasion – 23%	Domestic violence – 2.7%
Threating police – 52%	Traffic stop – 31%	Traffic stop Home invasion – 20%	Failure to comply with police instructions Hostage situation – 2%
Home invasion – 51%	Hostage situation – 27%	Threating police Civilian call/ assault – 19%	Shot at/attacked the police – 1.6%
Car chase Failure to comply with police instructions – 49%	Shot at/attacked the police Civilian call/ assault – 26%	Responding to robbery Resisting arrest Domestic violence – 18%	Civilian call/assault Threatened police – 1.4%
Shot at/attacked the police – 48%	Failure to comply with police instructions – 25%	Shot at/attacked the police – 17%	Traffic stop – 1.1.%

and respond accordingly. Discriminability also raises the question of whether a police officer in an ambiguous situation with a black youth under time pressure can tell a gun from a wallet.

As shown in chart 6.7 the police were wrong regarding the suspect having a weapon only 12 percent of the incidents. When measuring

CHART 6.7 Police Error in Weapon Discrimination 2015–2017*

	NUMBER	PERCENT
Yes—police mistook object for weapon	322	12% Police were wrong
No—person was armed	2,361	88% Police were correct

* Cases of unknown race and unknown police error omitted.

CHART 6.8 Police Error in Weapon Discrimination 2015–2017*

	WHITE	BLACK	HISPANIC	ASIAN
Yes—police mistook object for weapon	155 (48% wrong) 11% of total whites	102 (32% wrong) 14% of total Blacks	63 (19% wrong) 12% of total Hispanics	2 (0.6% wrong) 4% of total Asians
No—person was armed	1,268 (54% correct) 89% of total whites	598 (25% correct) 85% of total blacks	452 (19% correct) 88% of total Hispanics	43 (1.8 correct) 95% of all Asians

* *Cases of unknown race and unknown police error omitted.*

police discriminability error by the suspect not being armed with a gun or weapon the police were correct 88 percent of the time. Just to be clear, police correct discriminability does not establish the legality of a shooting, nor does incorrect discriminability establish the illegality of a shooting under the Fourth Amendment or the law defining homicide and justification in using deadly force. But the failure to distinguish a weapon from a wallet goes to the propensity of the police to use deadly force in ambiguous situations and how that propensity changes when race is applied to the ambiguous situation. As shown in chart 6.8 when police error was distributed by race, police error rate was constant, but police were more likely to be wrong when the suspect was black than white.

Overall, police were wrong—i.e., the police mistook an object for a weapon in 12 percent of the incidents. When viewed within race, the police discrimination showed variation. When viewed within race, police were wrong 14 percent with black suspects but only wrong 11 percent when dealing with whites. As expected, when looking at total incidents of police shootings by race more whites than blacks were shot. Blacks were shot more than Hispanics and Asian suspects were the least in police shootings. Overall, population distribution accounts for the differences in incidents by race.

When police officers were wrong, the situational context was different across racial groups. As shown in chart 6.9 traffic stop was

CHART 6.9 Distribution of Context Situation When Police Were in Error by Mistaking an Object for a Weapon by Race Percentage 2015–2017

WHITE	BLACK	HISPANIC	ASIAN
Civilian call/assault and Threatened police (16%)	Resisting arrest (17%)	Resisting arrest and responding to robbery (14%)	–
Resisting arrest (14%)	Civilian call/ assault (12%)	Civilian call/ assault (12%)	–
Domestic Violence (10%)	Traffic stop and Threatening police (11%)	Traffic stop and Threatening police (11%)	–

in the top three situations only for blacks and Hispanics. Resisting arrest was the top situation for blacks and Hispanics. Threating police was the top situation for whites. Traffic stops were fifth in ranking for situational contexts in which the police were wrong regarding a weapon that resulted in whites being shot and killed, it was third among blacks and Hispanics.

Overall, traffic stops were seventh in the list of contexts that resulted in police shootings. For whites, traffic stops were ninth, but for blacks, they were third. When looking at traffic stops and police error in discriminability, traffic remained third for blacks and was fifth for whites. My point is there are rational reasons why blacks are more frightened by police during traffic stops than whites. They are, in fact, more likely to be shot in such situations than whites.

As shown in charts 6.10 and 6.11 when reviewing the context of shootings, discriminability and the mental health of the person shot by the police, again racial incongruence was found.

The data showed that of blacks who showed mental illness (16 percent) in 23 percent of incidents police were wrong regarding a weapon. Of whites who showed mental illness (66 percent) in 65 percent of incidents police were wrong regarding a weapon.

CHART 6.10 Mental Illness 2015–2017*

	WHITE	BLACK	HISPANIC	ASIAN
Yes	455 (66%)	110 (16%)	105 (15%)	13 (1.9%)
No	1010	612	433	34
Total	1465	722	538	47

* *Cases of unknown race and unknown police error omitted.*

CHART 6.11 Mental Illness 2015–2017*

	POLICE ERROR IN WEAPON DISCRIMINATION	WHITE	BLACK	HISPANIC	ASIAN
Yes	Yes—police mistook object for weapon	58 (65%)	21 (23%)	8 (8.9%)	2 (2.2%)

* *Cases of unknown race and unknown police error omitted.*

Of Hispanics who showed mental illness (15 percent) in 8.9 percent of incidents police were wrong regarding a weapon. Of Asians who showed mental illness (1.9 percent) 2.2 percent of incidents police were wrong regarding a weapon. When the police were wrong in perceiving a weapon, they were much more likely to be wrong when dealing with blacks and Asians with mental illness than with whites and Hispanics with mental illness.

◆◆◆

Police use of deadly force, as a historical matter, was not the only method in which blacks were killed within the context of their perceived behavior or threat. One of the systems used in America to discipline blacks and maintain white supremacy was the use of lynching. Between 1877 and 1950, 4,084 blacks were lynched in the South[13] alone and more than 4,400 blacks were lynched nationwide.[14] Blacks were lynched for various reasons including being an economic threat to whites, not showing proper deference to whites on the street, or by having inappropriate contact with whites (casual social transgressions) or retaliation for resistance to Jim Crow (the dominant reason between 1910 and 1940). Lynching also occurred as a source of public enjoyment of white mobs and as a method of systematic removal of blacks from a neighborhood. Lynching was not only an act of violence against blacks to keep them in line and in terror after the Civil War, but it was used as an extrajudicial remedy to enforce criminal laws. Lynchings occurred as a result of an accusation of theft or a violent crime, or the classical reason for lynching the suspicion or accusation of the rape of a white woman (25 percent of all lynchings were committed for this reason alone).[15]

Southern police during this period either abandoned black prisoners to be taken from jails and lynched or they actively participated in lynching events. In many instances, white mobs did not wait for a trial or arrest and lynched black men on nothing more than a white woman's accusation. Southern police were also known to abandon black neighborhoods to white mobs that burned those communities to the ground. These events occurred through the early 1920s. On the national level, southern Democrats filibustered proposed laws making lynching a federal crime for more than three decades between the 1920s and 1950s. The use of lynching as an extra judicial criminal justice tool did not escape the political rhetoric of Washington, D.C.

At the dawn of the twentieth century, the American century, the federal government was embroiled in the question of whether lynching should be outlawed. President Theodore Roosevelt in his December 3, 1906, Annual Address to Congress said regarding lynching,

> The members of the white race on the other hand should understand that every lynching represents by just so much a loosening of the bands of civilization; that the spirit of lynching inevitably throws into prominence in the community all the foul and evil creatures who dwell therein. No man can take part in the torture of a human

being without having his own moral nature permanently
lowered. Every lynching means just so much moral dete-
rioration in all the children who have any knowledge of
it, and therefore just so much additional trouble for the
next generation of Americans.

　　Let justice be both sure and swift; but let it be justice
under the law, and not the wild and crooked savagery of
a mob.

Leaving aside his paraphrasing of Jefferson's observations regarding what slavery does to society, consider the point the president
made. White men should not engage in lynching, because it represents the breakdown of civilization and the moral nature of white
men. The fact that in a lynching, a black man has been murdered
is a superfluous point. But significantly, note how the president
bypasses the truth behind lynching; it occurs against black men,
because they are black and because they are accused of touching
white women. He whitewashed the truth of lynching by focusing on
the more general moral argument that it is extrajudicial and raises
the evil specter of the mob.

　　This is how implicit racism works, you abandon the actual evil
(whites lynching blacks because they are black) and focus on a
more abstract truth (lynching is wrong because it's an illegal extrajudicial act). The latter is true but it's irrelevant compared to the
true evil which is the former.

　　A contemporary example of subtle (or not so subtle) racism on the
policy level is America's reaction to the opioid addiction epidemic
of the second decade of the new century. The National Institutes of
Health reports that in "the late 1990s, pharmaceutical companies
reassured the medical community that patients would not become
addicted to prescription opioid pain relievers, and healthcare providers began to prescribe them at greater rates. This subsequently
led to widespread diversion and misuse of these medications before
it became clear that these medications could indeed be highly addictive." These assurances proved to be false. Thousands of deaths and

more than twice as many cases of addiction to opioids, first through prescriptions of oxycodone and oxymorphone for pain relief, which was followed by addiction to illegal drugs like heroin, and synthetic opioids such as fentanyl, has run havoc in middle-class white America. According to the National Institutes of Health, "Every day, more than 130 people in the United States die after overdosing on opioids. In 2017, more than 47,000 Americans died as a result of an opioid overdose, including prescription opioids, heroin, and illicitly manufactured fentanyl, a powerful synthetic opioid. That same year, an estimated 1.7 million people in the United States suffered from substance use disorders related to prescription opioid pain relievers."[16] The response has been to call addiction to opioids a medical problem—a disease—which requires a national policy to control the production and overprescription of legal opioids, as well as a national effort to educate people on the dangers of addiction to opioids even when needed for pain suppression.

All this is true, but when an equally addictive drug, crack cocaine, ran havoc in poor black and Hispanic communities from 1981 through the middle 1990s, the public policy response was to build more prisons to house drug offenders sentenced to draconian lengths of incarceration. White addicts have received sympathy and treatment for their drug addiction, blacks received the full weight of the criminal justice system.

When President Roosevelt did acknowledge the issue of race and lynching in his speech, he asserted that blacks need to see black rapists as people not worthy of protection. He said,

> Every colored man should realize that the worst enemy of his race is the negro criminal, and above all the negro criminal who commits the dreadful crime of rape; and it should be felt as in the highest degree an offense against the whole country, and against the colored race in particular, for a colored man to fail to help the officers of the law in hunting down with all possible earnestness and zeal every such infamous offender.

The president, in 1906, told blacks in America that the "worst enemy of his race is the negro criminal," not criminals in general but the negro criminal. Not Ku Klux Klan members but the negro criminal. In a time of white lynch mobs, the national political acceptance of the Ku Klux Klan, and the illegal southern system of peonage supplementing the system of convict leasing in the South; the president told blacks, regarding blacks accused of raping white women, that it is the "highest degree of offense for the colored man to fail to help the officers of the law in hunting down ... such [an] infamous offender." This was the advice President Roosevelt gave blacks when it was common knowledge and experience that a black man accused of raping a white woman would not receive a fair trial, if he received a trial at all! In most cases of a black man accused of touching a white woman, much less raping one, he is more likely to have received adjudication in the night, under a tree, by the judicious tying of knot of a rope around his neck. He would hear "crucify him" from a mob, not "guilty" by an impartial jury.

Leaving that aside, consider the president's focus: black people lose more when blacks act criminally—a theme that has never left political discourse on black criminality. As Bush's appointee and white social conservatives assert with no complaint or apology, innocent blacks are more likely to be stopped by the police than innocent whites because of the disproportionate criminality of blacks in general.

The president concluded his remarks on lynching by admonishing that those who raise up lynch mobs increase black distrust of the American criminal justice system.

> Be it remembered, furthermore, that the individuals who ... arouse mobs and to bring about lynching ... greatly to increase the likelihood of a repetition of the very crime against which they are inveighing. When the mob is composed of the people of one race and the man lynched is of another race, the men who in their speeches and writings either excite or justify the action ... cause the people of the opposite race to lose sight of the abominable act of

the criminal himself; and ... excite in other brutal and depraved natures thoughts of committing it. Swift, relent-less, and orderly punishment under the law is the only way by which criminality of this type can permanently be suppressed.

Now consider what the President of the United States said at the dawn of the twentieth century. The more lynching of blacks for raping white women you have, the more blacks will get excited and go out and find white women to rape. Only in the total dehuman-ization of blacks to the level of the ape could this logic make sense. But this was the logic of early twentieth-century progressivism and its adoption of social Darwinism during the gilded age.

By the late 1940s through the 1950s, Strom Thurmond and south-ern Democrats in line with the policy outcome of the 1920s fought tooth and nail to prevent legislation from making lynching a federal crime. Their reason was not that lynching was wrong—but that it was not for the federal government to proscribe the practice. States' rights and limited government arguments were proposed to assert lynching, like the Jim Crow system, was a local matter to be addressed by the government closest to the people. Lynching, like slavery a century before, was a local matter not to be regulated or abolished by the federal government. White public enjoyment aside, southern lynch-ing met a criminal justice need—crime control—as well as a social need—control of the former slaves. The police and the criminal justice system were tools to achieve both needs. They both utilized the death penalty to maintain social order: the police by not stopping the use of lynching and the criminal justice system by using a more judicial method—the electric chair and later lethal injection after conviction.

States' rights notwithstanding, the U.S. Senate finally relented from its historical decades-long recalcitrance in resisting a federal law prohibiting lynching in 2018. Led by the only three black mem-bers of the U.S. Senate, Senators Cory Booker (D), Kamala Harris (D), Tim Scott (R), the Senate atoned for its sins of filibustering anti-lynching legislation on December 19, 2018, and on February

14, 2019, when the Senate by unanimous voice vote passed the **Justice for Victims of Lynching Act**, which classified lynching as a hate crime under federal law. As of writing, the House of Representatives has not passed the Act for presidential signature.

◆◆◆

The impact of a century of lynching and criminal justice system injustices has left its mark. Lynching is a model of injustice for how the criminal justice system works and how false accusations can be life ending, if not simply life altering. Even black conservatives like Clarence Thomas in 1991 invoked lynching when voicing cries of unfairness when being unjustly accused and treated.[17] This is why when blacks are shot by the police with seemingly no fair justification, the rhetoric of lynching is used. Lynching involved not only injustice at the hands or indifference of the police, it involves the fear of blacks and the devaluing of their lives when taken.

It is true that the racism of early twentieth century has been put in the dustbin of history. Let there be no debate on that. America has moved on from that level of racism. But that does not mean that the residue of that racism has moved on. The America of the second decade of the twenty-first century still views blacks as criminals. Enhanced analysis of the *Washington Post Police Shooting Dataset* shows that traffic stops only accounted for 6 percent of all police shooting incidents but accounted for 31 percent of incidents of shooting blacks and 20 percent of incidents of shooting Hispanics. This confirms research that for blacks and Hispanics, police traffic stops are more dangerous than for whites.

The statistical reality of differential risk of police use of force supplements the distrust of blacks of the criminal justice system when considering the system reaction and treatment of police when blacks are killed by the police. Consider some of the more infamous cases of police shootings and the results of the police shootings between 2014 and 2018.

On July 17, 2014, *Eric Garner* was surrounded by a squad of New York City Police Department (NYPD) officers enforcing a quality of life violation for selling untaxed individual cigarettes ("lucies") in front of a lawful storefront.[18] When the officers attempted to secure Garner, he backed away from the officers and asked to be left alone. Officer Daniel Pantaleo from behind grabbed Garner by the neck and with the weight of his body and the assistance of four other officers brought Garner to the pavement. With at least five officers on top of him, he cried out "I can't breathe!" Subsequently, Garner died of a heart attack. The Garner incident ignited protest but the District Attorney determined not to charge Officer Pantaleo with manslaughter because of the use of a chokehold which is banned by NYPD policy. Almost five years to the day of the incident, Attorney General William Barr determined the Justice Department would not charge Officer Pantaleo with federal criminal civil rights violations.[19] General Barr ruled in favor of the U.S. attorney for the Eastern District of New York over the recommendation of the Justice Department Civil Rights Division which recommended charging Pantaleo. The dispute was over the *mens rea* (mental state of mind) required by the federal statute that the officer must have acted willfully in the unreasonable force used, which resulted in the violation of Garner's civil rights. Acting willfully requires proof that Officer Pantaleo knew what he was doing was unreasonable and violated Garner's rights when he grabbed him. Barr and the U.S. attorney did not think they could meet the burden. The government must be able to prove that the officer performed an unlawful act (unreasonable use of force) but must also be able to prove that the act was done knowing that it was unlawful and committed anyway. The U.S. attorney was correct when he explained at the press conference, "willfulness may be inferred from blatantly wrongful conduct, such as a gratuitous kick to the head, an officer's mistake, fear, misperception, or even poor judgment does not constitute willful conduct under federal criminal civil rights law." With the Justice Department closure of federal involvement in the case, the NYPD placed Officer Pantaleo on administrative trial and the chief administrative judge Rosemarie Maldonado found him guilty of violating police procedures—use of a chokehold—and making false statements[20] and he was subsequent fired by NYPD police commissioner James O'Neill on August 19, 2019.[21]

On August 5, 2014, *John Crawford*, was a black man who was lawfully in a Walmart looking at a BB gun for sale in the store. Customers saw him holding the gun, and a white customer falsely called 911 and reported that a black man with a gun was menacing customers. Beavercreek, Ohio, police officer Sean Williams approached Crawford and killed him. The grand jury declined to indict Officer Williams. Although the court found probable cause to believe the customer falsely reported an armed threat, the special prosecutor determined not to charge the customer in the case.[22] In a sadder case, on November 22, 2014, *Tamir Rice*, a 12-year-old who was playing with a toy gun was reported by the 911 operator to the police that there was an armed person in the park menacing people with a gun. Tamir was shot to death by two police officers immediately after they stopped their car in front of him. The 911 operator resigned. The two officers were not charged with his death. In April 2015, *Eric Courtney Harris* was shot by volunteer officer Robert Bates of the Tulsa, Oklahoma, Sheriff's Office. Bates shot Harris in the back after he was tackled and held on the ground by other officers. Bates asserted that he meant to shoot Harris with his Taser but used his gun by mistake. Bates was convicted of second-degree manslaughter in May 2016 and sentenced to four years imprisonment in June 2016 and was released in October 2017.[23]

Consider *Akai Gurley* and *Timothy Stansbury*, who were both shot by NYPD officers on November 20, 2014, when they were entering a darkened stairwell in their own building. The NYPD publicly stated that neither of the men were doing anything illegal or threatening to the officers. The officers were in the building with their guns drawn because they were afraid of the building they were in and accidentally shot the two men upon seeing them. One of those officers, Peter Liang, was found guilty of manslaughter for the killing of Akai Gurley in February 2016, and after the Brooklyn district attorney recommended no jail time for the officer in March, Officer Liang was sentenced to five years of probation after the judge reduced the conviction to criminally negligent homicide in April 2016. The conviction was the first conviction of an on-duty NYPD police officer for the shooting of a civilian in a decade.[24]

Some of the more infamous cases in 2018 included the cases of *Stephon Clark, Thurman Blevins, Richard "Gary" Black Jr., Joseph Santos, and Antwon Rose.*

Stephon Clark was an unarmed black man who was believed to be armed by the police and was shot at 20 times and hit eight times mostly in the back by two Sacramento, California police officers on March 18, 2018, after pursuing him on a belief that he was involved in breaking into cars.[25] *Thurman Blevins* was shot and killed as he ran away from the Minneapolis police officers on June 23, 2018.[26] On July 30, 2018, the Hennepin County Attorney Mike Freeman announced that Officers Ryan Kelly and Justin Schmidt (who both fired and killed Blevins)[27] would not be charged with the death of Blevins because, in part, the video of the body camera showed Blevins running from the police with a gun in his hand after refusing to stop when ordered to do so.[28] Freeman, citing the criteria under *Graham v. Connor*, announced that it was reasonable for the officers to fear for their safety when perusing an armed fleeing suspect (the gun was in his hand) who failed to stop upon command.[29]

On July 30, 2018, *Richard "Gary" Black Jr.*, a white male who was a bronze star recipient, was shot in his own home after killing an intruder who attacked his grandson. The Aurora, Colorado, police were called by Black's wife who told the police when they arrived that there was a naked intruder in the house with her husband and what her husband was wearing.[30] According to the police chief, at the August 2, 2018, press conference,[31] the officers shot and killed Black after they saw him walking from behind a wall and passing in and out of a room holding a gun and a flashlight. According to the chief, Black was told five times to drop the gun which he did not do. The chief admitted that Black had a hearing disability and may not have heard the police command to drop his gun.[32] When an officer saw Black approach the police officers and point his flash light in the direction of the officers, who were at Black's front door, an officer shot Black.[33] The chief asserted that Black's wife only said to the police "he has a gun" and did not give the officers a description of the intruder.[34] Under *Graham v. Connor* the Fourth Amendment was not violated even though an innocent who was defending his home was shot and killed by the police. As noted earlier, the officers are not required to be right; they are only required to have acted reasonably based on the information that they had at the time they used force. The officers were confronted with a home invasion and an attack on a child, upon reaching the door they heard shots, they were confronted with a man who was armed and did not drop his weapon upon command, and they shot the man when he turned toward them with a weapon in his hand.

On July 28, 2018, *Joseph Santos* was shot and killed by a five-month rookie of the South Whitehall Township Police Department. Officer Jonathan R. Roselle was confronted with Santos who had jumped on his police car and punched out the windshield. Santos jumped off the car and walked away from the car. Upon being ordered by Roselle to get on the ground, Santos started to walk toward that car. Roselle was behind the police car and was pointing his gun at Santos. Santos, a 44-year-old Hispanic man, was un-armed and walking slowly toward the car. Roselle fired five times and killed Santos. On August 7, 2018, the Lehigh Valley District Attorney Jim Martin at a press conference[35] announced that Roselle was being charged with voluntary manslaughter explaining, "In my opinion, this was the act of a relatively inexperienced officer who held a subjective fear for his own safety but made a decision which objectively was unreasonable in light of the facts as they existed and appeared at the time he discharged his weapon and killed Mr. Santos" and asserted that Roselle himself said at the scene that he "fucked up. And he did not know what to do because Santos kept coming at him."[36] The shooting was captured on video.[37] Martin explained at the press conference that although he believed that Roselle honesty believed that his life was in danger (subjective test) that belief was not objectively reasonable for him to have at the time the deadly force was used (objective test).[38] Under Pennsylvania law, the killing of a person under an honestly held but mistaken and unjustified belief that the person posed a deadly threat fails the objective test and warrants a charge of voluntary manslaughter. Martin stated that Santos was not armed, was not attempting to flee from a violent felony, or was making threatening movements against Roselle. Roselle was shielded by his police car while facing an unarmed man and as Martin explained, Roselle was equipped with non-deadly force weapons, and he "had the option to engage Mr. Santos physically" with those weapons and chose not to do so. These factors, Martin concluded, established that it was not objectively reasonable for Roselle to believe that he had to use deadly force. As discussed throughout this book and in this chapter, the logic, reasoning, and conclusion of District Attorney Martin in the Santos shooting is an exception, and unfortunately, not the rule in determining police responsibility and accountability in police use of deadly force. In most cases of police use of force, prosecutors don't challenge an officer's assertion of fear and the assertion by the officer alone usually results in prosecutor failure to charge police after deadly force is used. As of writing, officer Roselle is scheduled go to trial in Lehigh County before judge Kelly Banach for voluntary manslaughter on September 24, 2019.[39]

Antwon Rose was shot in the back while running away from the East Pittsburgh, Pennsylvania, police on June 19, 2018. Rose was in a car that was stopped by police because the car was suspected in being involved in a drive by shooting. When the occupants of the car ran after being stopped, Officer Michael Rosfeld shot Rose in the back. Rosfeld stated that he thought Rose, or the other occupant of the car, was pointing a gun at him as he ran away after being ordered to stop. Neither Rose nor the other occupant were armed. Rosfeld was charged with criminal homicide on June 26, 2018, and was acquitted after a four-day trial on March 22, 2019.[40] Under Pennsylvania law and Supreme Court jurisprudence, the police can use deadly force on a fleeing suspect if that suspect poses an imme-diate danger to the police, the community, or is an escaping violent felon. Rosfeld argued that he shot Rose because, "I thought one of them was pointing a gun at me. They were dangerous felon suspects. They had just fired a gun at someone." He explained on the stand, "My intent was to end the threat that was made against me. I just wanted to end the threat to me. I followed the threat and fired. I just saw that person moving, so I assumed the threat was still there." In justifying the level of forced used and his intent, Rosfeld testified, "I meant to fire until the threat against me had been ended, whether it be if I missed and he surrenders, stops, gets on the ground. I just wanted to end the threat to me."[41] Put simply, "One of the suspects turned, pointed toward me what I thought was a handgun [and] we're trained to fire until the threat is eliminated ... I did it to protect myself and the community."[42] After three-and-a-half hours of deliberation, the jury found agreement with Rosfeld.

Some of the more famous killings in 2017 include the shooting of 15-year-old *Jordan Edwards* who was killed in Balch Springs, Texas, on April 29, 2017, and *Justine Ruszczyk*, an Australian who was killed in Minneapolis, Minnesota, on July 15, 2017. Edwards was shot by Officer Roy Oliver of the Balch Springs, Texas Police Department when he fired his rifle into a car of four black teenagers that were driving away from the police. Officer Oliver was indicted for first-degree murder on July 17, 2017. Oliver claimed that the car was aggressively approaching him, but body camera recordings established that the car was not. Oliver was indicted in July 2017 for murder and four counts of aggravated assault with a deadly weapon by a public servant in addition to two charges of aggravated assault relating to a use of force in an unrelated prior incident.[43] On August 28, 2018, Oliver was convicted for murder[44] and on August 29, 2018, he was sentenced to 15 years imprisonment.[45] A very rare outcome for police shootings of unarmed black males.

Ruszczyk, a white woman, had called the police to report a pos-sible assault near her home and was shot by police while speaking with them next to their car. Officer Mohamed Noor shot Ruszczyk from inside his police vehicle while sitting in the passenger seat as Ruszczyk was standing outside of the car and speaking to his partner who was seated in the drivers' seat. Noor was indicted on March 20, 2018, for intentional second-degree murder, third-degree murder (depraved heart indifference), and second-degree manslaughter (culpable negligence reckless behavior). Officer Noor was fired the same day. On April 29, 2019, Noor was convicted of third-degree murder and second-degree manslaughter.[46] He was sentenced to 12-and-a-half years in prison on June 7, 2019.[47] The sentencing judge, in her sentencing statement, reported that when she spoke to the jury they asked, "Why are officers more concerned about their personal safety than the safety of the public? ... Why should a civilian have to be afraid of approaching a squad car? ... The jurors were particularly concerned with Officer Harrity's statement [Noor's partner] that his priority was making sure he did whatever he had to do to get home safe each night."[48]

In a statement of repentance, rarely seen when a police officer shoots someone, Noor said, "The moment I pulled the trigger, I felt fear. When I walked around, I saw Miss Ruszczyk dying on the ground, I felt horror. Seeing her, there, I knew in an instant that I was wrong."[49] The judge was not moved. She noted that Noor showed regret for the consequences of his actions not the actions themselves. She stated that Noor in the presence investigation stated that he was justified because he acted to protect his partner.[50] Noor continued to justify his actions in his statement at his sentencing hearing in which he regretted the shooting of an innocent person, but asserted, "I shot because I was protecting my partner Mathew Harrity's life. I realized after that I was wrong. That mistake is my hardship to bear."[51] The error was not in shooting an innocent person, the error was taking out his gun without legal justification in the first place (thus unlawfully knowingly and recklessly creating a dangerous situation that could result in death), pointing his gun with the intent to kill, and then killing someone without justification. This distinction, both in law and fact, was not lost on the judge, but it was lost on Noor.

Noor chose to take out his gun, while sitting enclosed in his police car, during a radio call for help, and fired his gun across the body of his partner when Miss Ruszczyk startled him. He did so out of a standing fear of ambush. As the judge relayed regarding her conversation with the jury, the Minnesota police made clear at trial that officers had a constant fear of ambush and the jury wanted to know where did this fear come from, and why did Noor and his partner have such a fear in a low-crime neighborhood. Regarding this fear and Noor's actions in light of them, the judge explained that the act of shooting Miss Ruszczyk was intentional even if made under error in assessing the situation. Accordingly, the judge affirmed the conviction of murder third-degree (the killing perpetrated during the performance of a dangerous act—pointing the gun and firing it, resulting in death) and manslaughter second-degree (culpable negligence creation of an unreasonable risk—his unholstering of his gun and firing it, resulting in death). Because the manslaughter conviction was a lesser included offense, the judge only sentenced Noor for the murder conviction. The conviction was novel because it was the first conviction of an on-duty police officer in Minnesota, and it involved a black police officer who shot a white civilian. The novelty was not lost on some who observed that "He's Somali. He's black. And he's Muslim—that's a trifecta. The system has an easier time convicting a black man in a blue uniform."[52] But the significance of the conviction, in the eyes of many, was what occurred in this case should have occurred in the 2016 Castile case in which the Minnesota police were exonerated.

The moral significance of all these shootings was summarized by the father of Ruszczyk at her funeral. "Justine, my daughter, was killed by a bullet fired by an agent of the state."[53] When the officer who killed his daughter was convicted he observed that the conviction, "reflects the community's commitment to three important pillars of civil society: The rule of law, the respect of the sanctity of life and the obligation of the police force to serve and protect. We believe this guilty verdict strengthens those pillars."[54]

There is a difference between being shot and killed by a criminal and being shot by an agent of the state. The difference tends to be lost on white social conservatives. It is true, as they say with great enthusiasm, that more black males are killed by other black males than by police officers. But the distinction is in the fact that when a criminal kills a black male, there is moral and social and political value placed on the victim. The point being it matters who killed the black male because the killing by the criminal does not represent society, the killing by a police officer directly represents society. Society and the law make clear that the killing by the criminal was wrong and the life taken has legal value. But when the agent of the state kills a black male the killing automatically carries moral and legal justification. Politically, police shootings assume the black life was worth being taken. The moral support is given to the agent of the state. As previously discussed, in police shootings, it is the officer that has the support of the Fourth Amendment and enjoys the benefit of the doubt. The political outcome is that the black males' life is not found to enjoy the same legal value or social and political support. In other words, that black life does not matter, or at the very least, values less.

These shootings in 2017 followed two previous years, 2015 and 2016, which resulted in almost 2,000 people killed by the police. Many of the cases involved police killings of blacks during traffic stops or blacks dying in police custody. Some of the more famous incidents include the cases of *Keith Lamont Scott* (September 20, 2016, Charlotte, North Carolina), *Terence Crutcher* (September 16, 2016, Tulsa, Oklahoma), *Sylville Smith* (August 13, 2016, Milwaukee, Wisconsin), *Philando Castile* (July 6, 2016, Falcon Heights, Minnesota), *Alton Sterling* (July 5, 2016, Baton Rouge, Louisiana), *Daniel Shaver* (January 18, 2016, Mesa, Arizona), *Jeremy McDole* (September 23, 2015, Wilmington, Delaware), *Samuel DuBose* (July 19, 2015, Cincinnati, Ohio), *Sandra Bland* (July 13, 2015, Hempstead, Texas), *Freddie Gray* (April 12, 2015, Baltimore, Maryland), and *Walter Scott* (April 4, 2015, North Charleston, South Carolina). These shootings followed the infamous police killings of *Laquan McDonald* (October 20, 2014, Chicago, Illinois), *Ezell Ford* (August 11, 2014, Los Angeles, California), *Michael Brown* (August 1, 2014, Ferguson, Maryland), *Eric Garner* (July 17, 2014, Staten Island, New York), and the killing of *Trayvon Martin* (February 26, 2012, Sanford, Florida) by a white Hispanic community watch leader in a gated community.

The 2015, killing of Walter Scott in North Charleston, South Carolina, was especially compelling regarding black experience with police in that it involved a shooting resulting from a traffic stop. The officer shot at Scott eight times, hitting him five times in the back, while Scott ran away and then the officer attempted to plant his Taser on the dead body to claim self-defense. His assertion of self-defense failed when a video was posted showing him shooting Scott and planting the Taser. After a mistrial in which one white woman refused to convict the officer for murder, Officer Michael T. Slager plead guilty to federal civil rights charges. On May 2, 2017, he pled guilty to violating 18 U.S.C. § 242 Deprivation of Rights under the Color of Law in that he, as a police officer, acted under the color of law and

> deprived Walter Lamar Scott, Jr., of the right to be free from the unreasonable and excessive use of force ... a right secured by the Fourth Amendment to the United States Constitution [in] That the defendant acted willfully; and that bodily injury or death resulted ... [which] involved the use of a dangerous weapon ... The defendant used deadly force even though it was objectively unreasonable under the circumstances. The defendant acknowledges that his actions were done willfully, that he acted voluntarily and intentionally and with specific intent to do something that the law forbids.[55]

Officer Michael T. Slager was sentenced to 20 years in prison.

In the 2014 Laquan McDonald killing in Chicago, Illinois, police video showed him walking away from the police when he was killed. Officer Jason Van Dyke was indicted on December 15, 2015, with first-degree murder for shooting McDonald 16 times after McDonald was shot and on the ground.[56] On October 5, 2018, Van Dyke was convicted of second-degree murder of McDonald as well as 16 charges of aggravated battery (one for each gun discharge at McDonald).[57] In addition, three officers were charged on June 27, 2017, with conspiracy, official misconduct, and obstruction of justice, because they entered into a

> conspiracy to conceal the true facts of the events sur-
> rounding the killing [of McDonald by Van Dyke] in order
> to shield their fellow officer from criminal investigation
> and prosecution. In order to accomplish this goal, the co-
> conspirators lied about what occurred and mischaracter-
> ized the video recordings [in order to prevent the public
> from seeing the video]. The co-conspirators understood
> that public airing of the events ... including the video
> recordings, would inexorably lead to a thorough criminal
> investigation ... and criminal charges.[58]

On January 18, 2019, Van Dyke was sentenced to 81 months (6 years and 9 months) in prison for the second-degree murder.[59] On January 17, 2019, the three officers, David March, Joseph Walsh, and Thomas Gaffney were acquitted on the conspiracy, official misconduct, and obstruction of justice charges.[60]

The 2019 conviction of officer Mohamed Noor in the *Justine Ruszczyk* case, the 2018 criminal convictions of Officer Jason Van Dyke in the *Laquan McDonald* case and Officer Roy Oliver in the *Jordan Edwards* case, the 2017 federal plea bargain of Officer Michael T. Slager in the *Walter Scott* case, and the 2016 convictions of Officer Peter Liang in the *Akai Gurley* case and Officer Robert Bates in the *Eric Courtney Harris* cases are exceptions to the general outcome of police killings of blacks, which usually results in no charges being filed.

In 2015 and 2014, no officers were charged with murder because of on-duty killings, and "since 2005 there have only been 13 officers convicted of murder or manslaughter" but 2015 "was a year of reckoning [when] 18 officers faced such charges."[61] Criminologist Philip Stinson, who created a database on police deviance and secured a National Institute of Justice grant to study police criminal activity has reported "that on-duty police officers across the country shoot and kill someone about 1,000 times each year. Almost all of the cases end with a determination by a prosecutor that a police shooting was legally justified."[62]

> Since 2005, there have been 82 police officers across the country charged with murder or manslaughter resulting from an on-duty shooting. That includes 18 officers charged in 2015, 13 in 2016, and three charged with murder or manslaughter resulting from an on-duty shooting so far in 2017. It is a rare event for a police officer to be charged with a crime resulting from a fatal on-duty shooting, and even rarer for an officer to be convicted in one of these cases. In the past 13 years, only 29 officers have been convicted and most of those convictions were for lesser manslaughter offenses. Only one officer has been convicted of intentional murder during that time period ... There have been 15 officers convicted at a jury trial (the other 14 convictions were by guilty pleas). The criminal cases for 31 officers ended in a non-conviction.[63]

According to the *Washington Post*, since 2005, "54 officers nationwide have been criminally charged after they shot and killed someone in the line of duty. When prosecutors filed charges, there were often additional factors. In 80% of the cases, at least one of the following occurred: the victim was shot in the back, there was a video recording of the incident, other officers testified against the shooter or a cover up was alleged."[64]

When police shootings are not cleared as "justified," account-ability for the death has not resulted in incarceration, but rather in the police officers being acquitted, as they were in the Freddie Gray, Terence Crutcher, Philando Castile, Sylville Smith, Anthony Smith,[65] Daniel Shaver,[66] and Anthony Lamar Smith[67] cases. When criminal trials occur the results tend to be criminal trials resulting in a mistrial because of a hung jury, as in the first trial in the Freddie Gray case and the twice hung jury trials in the Samuel DuBose case. Other outcomes include the officers suffering administrative sanctions (being fired or suspended), as Officer Timothy Loehmann (fired) and Frank Garmback (suspended for ten days) were in the Tamir Rice case and Officers Blane Salamoni (fired) and Howie Lake (suspend for three days) were in the Alton Sterling cases. In some cases officers accept non-criminal sanction plea agreements, as in the Sandra Bland case.

In the *Sandra Bland* case, the Texas State Trooper accepted a plea of surrendering his state law enforcement license and agreeing never to seek a law enforcement position in exchange for the drop-ping of a misdemeanor charge of perjury regarding his justification for removing Bland from her car, which resulted in her arrest and later suicide in the Waller County Jail. According to the indictment, the trooper asserted that he "had Sandra Bland exit the vehicle to further conduct a safe traffic investigation [and] such sworn statement [was] false in that Defendant Brian T. Encinia removed Sandra Bland from her vehicle because he was angry she would not put out her cigarette."[68] Bland ended up hanging from a jail cell, because the officer was angered by her behavior. She was not contrite and submissive enough for him.

These cases and their final resolutions together provide support for the negative perception blacks have for the criminal justice system because of the lack of criminal culpability being imposed on police officers for the killing of blacks. In addition, there is a consequence for police use of force without accountability or sanction—it creates a fear of police in general and encourages police officers to believe that they can act without accountability.

On July 26, 2017, in Salt Lake City, Utah, police Detective Jeff Payne forcibly grabbed, pushed against a wall, handcuffed, and arrested head trauma room nurse *Alex Wubbels*, who failed to obey his request for a blood withdrawal from an unconscious patient when the withdrawal was against a written policy agreed to between the hospital and the Salt Lake City Police Department. She explained to the detective that, unless the patient was under arrest, the detective had a warrant, or the patient consented (the patient was unconscious at the time), she could not draw blood. Payne knew she was correct, because the Supreme Court in *Birchfield v. North Dakota* (2016) clearly wrote that "we conclude that a breath test, but not a blood test, may be administered as a search incident to a lawful arrest for drunk driving. As in all cases involving reasonable searches incident to arrest, a warrant is not needed in this situation [but] the search incident to arrest doctrine does not justify the warrantless taking of a blood sample."[69] Such a search requires a warrant, barring some other exception (see chart in chapter 7). Even more significant was the fact that the patient was not a suspect in the car accident. Payne wanted the blood sample simply because he wanted it.

When the nurse, Wubbels, showed Payne the written policy between the hospital and the police department in compliance (in part anyway) with the Supreme Court ruling defending her refusal and after her supervisor informed Payne that Nurse Wubbels was correct and that the officer was making a mistake and chided him for threatening her, Payne lost his temper with her presumption to tell him what she would not do under his direction and arrested her and pushed her into his police car. It was her attitude and lack of contriteness and submissiveness that resulted in her arrest.[70] Twenty minutes after the arrest, while sitting in his car, she was released, and she later received apologies from the police department chief and the mayor. Both the mayor and the chief admitted that the arrest was not lawful and the amount of force used to make the arrest was not appropriate. Payne was removed from the blood draw unit, placed on administrative leave pending a department investigation, which occurred simultaneously with a criminal investigation.[71]

When it was revealed that Payne said after the encounter that, "I'll bring them all the transients and take good patients elsewhere" to retaliate against the nurse and the hospital, he was fired from his part-time job as a paramedic. After an administrative investigation, Payne was fired and his supervisor, who authorized Payne's arresting of Nurse Wubbels, was demoted from lieutenant to officer.[72] The demotion of Lt. James Tracy was affirmed in April 2019.[73]

Nurse Wubbels, a white female, and Sandra Bland, were arrested and manhandled not for violation of the law but for not having an attitude sufficiently subservient to the liking of the police officer. It's the abuse of power and the sense of entitlement to abuse their power that is the point. That sense of entitlement has consequences, in the case of Bland—her death—and in the case of Nurse Wubbels—a physical assault and the loss of her liberty.

This sense of entitlement by the police to use force because of the attitude of a citizen and its historical lack of public accountability creates a logical fear of the police, because criminal culpability is not the result of police abuse of power. This lack of accountability can lead police to take liberties with how they treat people, both black and white, as well as explain why they take liberties. Consider the following case of a white woman who refused to move her hands because she did not want to be shot by the officer during a driving under the influence (DUI) traffic stop. On July 10, 2016, four days after the Philando Castile shooting, the following conversation occurred when Cobb County, Georgia, police lieutenant Greg Abbott conducted a traffic DUI stop.

> Abbott: Now Listen to me. Call the person who is coming to get you. Tell them they don't need to come. All right? Yes. OK. Go ahead and call them. I am going to take you to jail and then I am going to impound the car.
>
> Passenger: Before that [inaudible]
>
> Abbott: No

Passenger: I can't call them if you don't open the car door.

Abbott: Why can't you?

Passenger: I just want to put myself in that

Abbott: Use your phone. It's in your lap right there

Passenger: Okay, I will, I just don't want to put my hands down. I'm really sorry

Abbott: Is something wrong

Passenger: No, I've just seen way too many videos of cops shooting people

Abbott: But you're not black. Remember, we only kill black people. Yeah, we only kill black people, right? All the videos you've seen, have you seen any white people get killed?

Passenger: Yes

Abbott: You have.

Passenger: An eighteen-year-old white boy killed in twenty-three seconds [inaudible]

Abbott: Yeah

Passenger: [inaudible] I'm not saying you're a bad cop [inaudible]

Abbott: Right[74]

During a DUI traffic stop, a white police lieutenant with 28 years of experience, with the purpose of comforting a white woman who was drunk, told her that she did not need to worry and could lower her hands, because police only shoot black people.

Consider the dynamics of this encounter and what it means both socially and politically. Because she was not black, she had nothing to fear from the police. There is a reason why blacks fear police in general and specifically when alone during a police stop. Blacks define both police action and the criminal justice system through the lens of history. That history is defined by abuse and discrimination at the hands of government power based on skin color. And that abuse has been specifically unleased by the police dating back to 1619.

While police shootings are perceived by many whites in America as the result of blacks unwilling to respond appropriately to a lawful police officer command that must be enforced, blacks view use of force by the police that result in the shootings of young black men as nothing out of the ordinary. Blacks being abused by law enforcement dates back to the beginning of American policing—the beginning of that abuse being the slave patrols of the antebellum period, followed by police enforcement of the black codes and Jim Crow in the postbellum period (1865 to 1918), the "get tough" on crime policies of the late 1960s, the federalization of illicit drug policy in the 1970s, the rise of police drug task forces in the 1980s, and the imposition of police drug suppression "jump out squads" in black communities in the 1990s.

Consider policing from a philosophical inquiry, *Quis Custodiet Ipso Custodies*, "Who will guard the guards themselves?" The police have a power that the President of the United States does not have. They have power, on the street, to take the life and liberty of any person they choose. They can take life with less justification than is required to secure an arrest warrant, and they can take liberty with only slightly more required justification. When police take action, the question is how this power is controlled and is it controlled when it's applied to black males? The Fourth Amendment provides a very limited check on police power. The true control on police power is political. The enforcement of control of police power is dictated by the level of societal fear of crime and who commits that crime. Blacks tend to ask, "Who will watch our watchers—who will protect us from our protectors when it comes to police?" Whites tend to support the police because they are perceived as protectors of them.

Policing is a system of control and the use of force. Police work, as exampled by the Minnesota police testimony in the Ruszczyk case, is about the officers going home alive after an altercation. Police encounters are about police control and domination, which to the police officer equals officer safety. The loss of physical control leads to a fear of personal safety in the police officer. The lack of dominance equals lack of safety. This fear for safety leads to police aggression. The subconscious fear of young black males leads the police to perceive a threat and then act aggressively to maintain control. The result can lead to a black man face down on the hood of a car or dead in the street.

An example of this dynamic is the Crutcher killing. Officer Betty Shelby shot and killed Terence Crutcher on September 16, 2016, in Tulsa, Oklahoma, while being backed up by three other officers and a police helicopter. In a *60 Minutes* interview regarding the killing, Selby said, regarding why she chose to use deadly force when in an ambiguous confrontation with a black male bigger than she was and whom she feared had a gun, "If I wait to find out if he had a gun or not I could very well be dead. There is something that we always say: I would rather be tried by twelve than carried by six."[75] Consider the dehumanization of Crutcher and the privilege enjoyed by Shelby that she felt free to be so honest regarding the taking of Crutcher's life with nothing more than a police platitude.

Race, she said, had nothing to do with the shooting. The social psychology research on *bidirectional stereotyping* says otherwise. Bidirectional stereotyping involves the involuntary psychological uploading of negative racial stereotypes of blacks and physiological fear of blacks into subconscious thinking which colors cognitive perceptions and behavior. Research shows that when people are in ambiguous situations, in which all the information necessary to understand the situation and assess safety is not available, people will upload information into their subconscious or from their conscious memories of past events similar to the ambiguous one, to fill in the blanks. Bidirectional stereotyping occurs when a person associates an individual with a group dynamic or behavior on a psychological or emotional level. An individual black man in an ambiguous situation is associated with blacks in general and blacks in general are associated with crime or physical threat. Consider the Atatiana Jefferson case discussed earlier in this chapter. Officer Dean is told to go into a black neighborhood to answer an open structure call, and upon arriving at the location he immediately takes out his gun with no other justification than where he is. An "open structure" call could include anything from a person sick to a possible burglary. An "open structure" call does not, by itself, justify, either procedurally or legally, the ratcheting up of force to an upholstered gun. Further, his bidirectional stereotyping (black neighborhood = crime = danger) prevented him from following proper procedure in entering Jefferson's back yard; first, announcing his presence as a police officer and second, assessing the situation before shooting at the first object that came into his line of sight. The bidirectional stereotyping filled in an ambiguous situation and prevented Officer Dean from assessing it with actual reality; that the lights were on, toys were in the front yard, and the door was open not kicked in or otherwise damaged.[76] The lack of processing the ambiguous situation with known facts resulted in Ms. Jefferson shot dead through her own window in her own home.

In her interview, Shelby, in tears, said the confrontation began when she saw Crutcher standing next to his car, and she thought his standing still was "zombielike behavior" and that standing still next to his car led her to fear that Crutcher was on PCP. The helicopter pilot hovering over the scene when Crutcher was facing four armed police officers with their guns drawn, said Crutcher, "looks like a bad dude too." Consider what occurred in this case. A large black man standing motionless next to his car and she thinks PCP! A police officer looking down from a helicopter and sees four police officers with guns drawn on one black man and he sees "a bad dude." Both are in an ambiguous situation with a black man and criminal and danger uploads to fill in the ambiguity. They act accordingly and Crutcher ends up dead.

When Crutcher walked toward Shelby with his hands in his pocket and then removed them at her command, his behavior left her with the fear that he had a gun. She drew her weapon, not because he was being belligerent, but because he did not follow her command not to approach his car. She explained in the interview that as he walked toward his car, she thought he was looking for a gun that he did not have in his pocket. When he walked to his car and, to her, looked like he was putting his hands into the window, she shot him dead. The police watched him bleed to death in the street for two minutes before attempting to give aid. The police found no gun. They did find a small amount of PCP in his car and in his system.

When asked about how she felt about killing Crutcher and why it happened, she stated that his disobedience and walking away from her and looking at his car meant he was looking to do her harm. Shelby said that his movements alone justified his killing. Officer Shelby said Crutcher is dead because of his own actions. He caused his own death, and "if he would have complied. If he would have communicated with me. If he would have just done what I asked him to do." The jury agreed and acquitted her of manslaughter charges in May 2017. It's this dynamic of police fear that causes black parents in black communities to have "the talk" with their children, especially, their young black males. Racism does not have to be on the level of David Duke and a white mob of Klansmen and white nationalists marching in Charlottesville with torches and bats to be racism. As demonstrated in the Crutcher, Jefferson, and other cases discussed in this chapter and in this book, the process of bidirectional stereotyping and the political rhetoric that blacks are as a group criminogenic can lead to the death of blacks without the overt racism of David Duke.

chapter seven

The Get Tough on Crime Era

Contemporary Explanation of Black Incarceration

W hen President Carter left office in 1980, there were a total of 329,207 prisoners in state and federal prisons, and after the first year of the Reagan Administration, there were 369,009, an increase of 12.1 percent.[1] One year after Reagan took office the Justice Department, Bureau of Statistics (BJS) reported that prison incarceration in 1981, "surpassed the record 10.5 percent annual growth rate set in 1975. Between 1980 and 1981 the incarceration rate of sentenced prisoners rose from 139 to 154 per 100,000 U.S. resident population." The BJS explained that the increase in federal prisoners, "grew by nearly 3,800, or 16 percent, reversing a three-year decline begun in 1978 that had reduced the federal prison population by one-fourth. Federal authorities linked the 1981 growth to increased attention to bank robbery and drug offenses."[2] The BJS explained that the increase on the state level was the result of "a sterner public attitude toward crime and criminals. During the past 5 years 37 States have passed mandatory sentencing laws and 11 States have passed determinate sentencing laws, both of which frequently result in a longer average time served than indeterminate sentences. Many States have adopted more stringent regulations on the use of parole, and four States have abolished it altogether."[3]

Mandatory sentences require certain offenders to receive a specific or minimum sentence. Determinant sentencing requires a specific range of time to be served by the offender. For example, a mandatory sentence is five years in prison and a determinant sentence is a minimum sentence of five to ten years. These types of sentences are more stringent than indeterminant sentencing. An indeterminant sentence gives a broad range of sanction, for example, 0–20 years. Mandatory and determinant sentencing are fixed, while indeterminant sentencing is not fixed and allows for the use of parole, good time, probation, and other methods of reducing the amount of incarceration in prison. Mandatory and determinant sentencing as a practical matter requires the offender to serve actual time in prison.

Prison incarceration is the result of public policy. With the increase in crime in the 1960s and the abandonment of the rehabilitative era, 1980 ushered in the second punitive era. By 1988, the end of the Reagan Administration, the number of prisoners in federal and state prisons was 631,669.[4] An increase of 91.5 percent in the prison population in only eight years. The prison boom would continue under Presidents Bush and Clinton. By 1990 the prison population had increased to 771,243, a 133.8 percent increase from 1980.[5] In 1992, the last year of the presidency of George H.W. Bush the prison population was 883,593, a 167.9 percent increase from 1980 and a 28.4 percent increase in only four years.[6] In 1995 under President Clinton, the United States broke the million prison incarceration barrier with a total of 1,078,357 people in federal and state prisons.[7] By the year 2000, the number of incarcerations was 1,391,261 and by 2007, the number had increased to 1,598,316.[8] When adding jail populations, America broke the two million incarcerated barrier in 2005 with 2,195,500 people in federal prison and state/local jails and prisons.[9] At year-end 2001, the beginning of the presidency of George W. Bush, the U.S. prison population totaled 1,406,031.[10]

When President George W. Bush left office in 2008 the prison population was 1,610,446[11] but when President Obama left office in 2016, the prison population decreased to 1,506,800,[12] 6.87 percent decrease. The trend of U.S. prison population increases more than two-decades long finally ended. According to the BJS, "The number of prisoners under state and federal jurisdiction at year-end 2016 (1,506,800) was a 7% decrease (down 108,700 prisoners) from 2009 when the U.S. prison population peaked."[13] *"Federal prisoners made up 13% of the total U.S. prison population at year-end 2016 but accounted for 37% of the decline in the total prison population.* The number of federal prisoners decreased from 196,500 in 2015 to 189,200 in 2016. This was the fourth consecutive year of population decline among federal prisoners."[14] BJS reported that in 2016 there was "a decline of 19,800 prisoners (down 1%) from year-end 2015. State prisons held 12,600 fewer prisoners in 2016 than in 2015, while the federal prison population decreased by 7,300 (down almost 4%)."[15] Under the Obama presidency, the imprisonment rate of sentenced black adults declined by 31 percent from 2007 to 2017.[16] The imprisonment rate for sentenced prisoners under state and federal jurisdiction decreased 13 percent from 2007 to 2017 (from 506 to 440 per 100,000).[17] The Obama legacy of prison reduction has continued. The most recent data is from 2017 which shows the total of people in federal and state prison is 1,489,363.[18] The BJS reports that the "imprisonment rate for sentenced prisoners was the lowest since 1997, at 440 prisoners per 100,000 U.S. residents of all ages and 568 per 100,000 U.S. residents age 18 or older."[19] The United States still maintains an overall incarceration rate of two million people. In 2000 the total U.S. incarceration (including jails) was 1,945,400 and in 2016 it was 2,172,800.[20]

Between 1980 and 2008 America increased the number of people in federal and state prisons from 329,207 prisoners to 1,610,446, an overall increase of 389.2 percent! The first thing to realize when looking at such an increase is that such an increase can only occur by deliberate policymaking. As discussed in Chapter 4, the goal of the second punitive era was the implementation of the crime control model in which the purpose of the criminal justice system is to convict the guilty and to maintain public safety through the formal institutions of social control—police, courts, and prisons. The prison and incarceration boom of the 1980s and 1990s was built, in no small part, on the fear of urban crime and the paramount policy/political issue of the late 1980s through the mid-1990s— violent crime and the plague of crack cocaine that engulfed black and Hispanic neighborhoods. Presidents Reagan in the 1980s and Clinton in the 1990s built the two pillars of the get tough on crime politics of the second punitive era.

The 1980s–1990s and the Rise of Crime Control Model

President Reagan: Crime Control Takes Center Stage—the Great Society Is Dead

When Reagan came to office, he made clear what his policy would be regarding crime. Crime to the Reagan Administration was simply explained by the simple fact that the criminal justice system since the 1960s was more interested in coddling criminals than deterring them or punishing them. Criminals that were convicted were not punished severely enough to deter crime. The answer is simple. Change the law to require the courts to sentence criminals and not release them. Reagan announced his support for the policy of establishing sentencing guidelines on the federal level and ending probation/parole through the creation of minimum and mandatory sentences. The federal government did not originate establishing sentencing guidelines or the implementation of determinate and mandatory sentencing. By the time Reagan came to office in 1980, 37 states had passed mandatory sentencing statutes and 15 states had passed determinate sentencing laws.[21] It was the policy of the Reagan Administration to follow the example of these states.

In 1982 Congress passed HR 3963, an anti-crime bill, but it was vetoed by Reagan on January 3, 1983.[22] In his veto message, Reagan stated that he supported the Violent Crime and Drug Enforcement Improvements Act of 1982 (S 2572), which was not passed by the House. Reagan rejected HR 3963 because the bill fell short of his demands. He wrote that the bill did not deal with "bail reform, nor does it address sentencing reform. Both are subjects long overdue for congressional action." He rejected the bill because it would "hamper existing enforcement activity. I am particularly concerned about its adverse impact on our efforts to combat drug abuse." His main complaint was with the creation of "a drug director and a new bureaucracy within the Executive Branch with the power to coordinate and direct all domestic and international Federal drug efforts, including law enforcement operations." Even within law enforcement, Reagan despised the growth of the national government and rejected the idea of a "drug czar" and the "creation of another layer of bureaucracy within the Executive Branch would produce friction, disrupt effective law enforcement, and could threaten the integrity of criminal investigations and prosecutions—the very opposite of what its proponents apparently intend."

Overall, he stated the bill did not enact his proposed "legislation to strengthen law enforcement and restore the balance between the forces of law and the forces of crime. Changes in sentencing, bail laws, the exclusionary rule, the insanity defense, and other substantive reforms in criminal law were not passed by the 97th Congress. Such reforms, if enacted, could make a real difference in the quality of justice in this country." Congress complied with Reagan's demands and a year later passed the **Comprehensive Crime Control Act of 1984**.

The Comprehensive Crime Control Act was signed by President Reagan on October 12, 1984, and the bill revolutionized federal criminal justice. The act touched on almost every major law enforcement aspect of criminal justice.[23] Some of the key provisions of the act included the following changes.

Title One, the **Bail Reform Act of 1984,** repealed the Bail Reform Act of 1966 and authorized preventive detention if the court found that a defendant posed a danger to the community outside and independent of the defendant likelihood of appearing in court for future hearings. Title One allowed the government to appeal an order granting bail and established addition penalties for the commission of a crime while on bail.

Title Two, the **Sentencing Reform Act of 1984** established the Sentencing Guidelines Commission with a mandate to create a set of federal sentencing guidelines that would be mandatory for the judiciary. Title Two also established maximum terms of imprisonment for certain types of felonies and misdemeanors. One of the key policy initiatives that Reagan supported from 1973 was achieved in Title Two, which eliminated parole in the federal correctional system and provided for special sentencing for violent juvenile offenders. By statute, criminal sanctions were

> to reflect the seriousness of the offense, to promote respect for the law, and to provide just punishment for the offense; to afford adequate deterrence to criminal conduct; to protect the public from further crimes of the defendant; and to provide the defendant with needed educational or vocational training, medical care, or other correctional treatment in the most effective manner [and sentences] need to avoid unwarranted sentence disparities among defendants with similar records who have been found guilty of similar conduct [as well as meet] the need to provide restitution to any victims of the offense.[24]

America had officially changed the purpose of American correctional theory by reorganizing the purpose of criminal justice. The purpose was the incapacitation, incarceration, and retribution in addition to victim restoration. Only when these are achieved is rehabilitation and equal treatment in sentencing to be a goal. The values and priorities of the rehabilitative era were formally and officially, by statute, rejected. It would be well into the first decade of the following century before research into implementing rehabilitation was politically palatable under President George W. Bush. It would be another decade before rehabilitation returned as a viable policy initiative under Presidents Obama and Trump.

Title Three, the **Comprehensive Forfeiture Act of 1984**, authorized federal law enforcement to secure property gained through criminal activity—both personal and real property as well as authorized the government to seize property believed to be the fruit of criminal activity *before* conviction. It also changed the burden of proof for seizure of property. The law allowed for seizure based on probable cause and authorized judges to issue asset forfeiture warrants for property involved or gained through criminal activity.[25] This changed the law under the **Comprehensive Drug Abuse Prevention and Control Act of 1970** which required conviction before seizure of property gained through illegal drug activity. Under Title Two of the Comprehensive Drug Abuse Prevention and Control Act it was made a rebuttable presumption that any property of a person convicted under the Act was subject to forfeiture if the government established by a preponderance of the evidence that any property gained by the convicted defendant was the result of the illegal drug activity resulting in arrest.[26] Under the **Psychotropic Substances Act of 1978** all types of money, negotiable instruments, securities, or other things of value were added to the list of things subject to asset forfeiture.[27]

The **Comprehensive Forfeiture Act of 1984** also established the Department of Justice Assets Forfeiture Fund and the federal "equitable sharing" program in which state and local police agencies could secure up to 80% of a seized property when the seizure involved federal law enforcement in the investigation.[28] Many local agencies used this partnership to secure real property or other financial assets unavailable through local government funding or to bypass local political decisions regarding police agency funding.

Partnerships with federal agencies that resulted in "return" of forfeited property and money through joint state/local and federal operations were not subject to local policy decisions made by local governments.

Title Three also authorized the attorney general to transfer drug-related forfeited property to other federal, state, or local agencies. It authorized law enforcement to use forfeited property for official law enforcement purposes. Put simply, law enforcement was given a financial incentive to make arrests of those accused of drug and other types of crimes—resulting in a policy outcome not unsimilar to convict leasing, criminal surety and peonage, discussed in Chapter 3.

Title Seven authorized the attorney general to authorize the administrator of the General Services Administration to transfer to any state or local government federal government surplus property for correctional use. Title Ten established minimum mandatory sentences for the use of firearms during a federal crime of violence, made it a federal crime to attack or threaten a federal employee during the commission of his/her duties, or to kidnap such federal employee or his/her family. Title Eleven made it a crime to warn a person of an impending federal warrant issuance. Title Twelve allowed the government to appeal any district court order for a new trial.

Although the Comprehensive Crime Control Act of 1984 would prove significant in changing the nature of criminal sentencing in America—establishing a uniform mandatory sentencing system which was designed to reduce the discretion of judges after conviction—it did not increase the length of time to be served in prison. Reagan would solve that oversight by pushing for and receiving the **Anti-Drug Abuse Act of 1986**, which he signed on October 27, 1986. The key aspect of the Act was to change the criminal penalty for crack cocaine compared to powder cocaine. The bill famously created the *100 to 1 crack-powder disparity* in which 5 grams of crack and 500 grams of powder cocaine were punished with at least a five-year sentence, regardless of any mitigating factors. A conviction of possession of 50 grams of crack and 5,000 grams of powder cocaine were punished by a sentence of at least ten years. The new law also expanded asset forfeiture to include any and all property of equal value to the value of property subject to seizure that is no longer available.[29] The 1986 act was followed by the **Anti-Drug Abuse Act of 1988,** which President Reagan signed on November 18, 1988, which created a *five-year mandatory minimum* and a twenty-year maximum sentence for simple possession of *5 grams* and 50 grams of *crack* cocaine respectively for first-time offenders.

As discussed in Chapter 1, these laws, together, resulted in the increase in the disproportionate incarceration rate of blacks from 41 percent in state and federal prisons in 1980 to 49 percent in 1989, peaking at 51 percent in 1993–1994, and remaining at 50 percent in 1995. Blacks accounted for half of the total number of people in federal and state prisons when they only accounted for 13 percent of the total U.S. population. The explanation for this increase was the social and political landscape that crack created, along with the general "get tough on crime" policies and Justice Department policies on charge and sentencing enhancements under Presidents Bush 41, Clinton, and Bush 43.

Modern Black Incarceration in the Landscape of the Second Punitive Era

The modern foundation for the incarceration of blacks is the plague of crack and its arrival in the black community. In 1981, a new version of cocaine was introduced in Los Angeles, California. Powder cocaine had maxed out its demand by the late 1970s, and a new market was required. To increase the demand and reduce the cost of powder cocaine, the drug was mixed with baking soda or any other powder product and then cooked. This resulted in a crystalized version of cocaine that could be smoked and inhaled directly into the lungs and brain, resulting for some users, in a faster and more intense high from the drug. Further, this form could be sold at a very low cost. A pound of powder cocaine could be increased to three pounds of pre-crack product that, when cooked down to crystal crack "rocks," could be sold as low as a dollar and as high as five dollars for a single use. The crack user found a cheap quick high that required additional hits and drug sellers created a customer base that would return for additional product sometimes three to five times per day. The economic laws of capitalism worked, and a permanent and loyal customer base was created. With demand high and cost for manufacturing low, millions of dollars were generated on the sale of crack. By 1983, crack had spread to every major city in the United States.

Because crack was the way to get the non-affluent to use cocaine in large numbers, crack was a product tailor-made for the black and Hispanic inner-city drug user, while the affluent drug user still used powder cocaine. Crack cocaine also had a different physiological reaction for some users. It proved to be more addictive and established addiction faster than powder cocaine in some users. A single hit could produce dependency. Drug users shifted from heroin to crack and new drug users were created by experimentation with crack by first-time drug users.

Crack was a plague that aggravated the criminal problems that had already weakened the black community. The negative results of desegregation, the loss of working class non-college education jobs, white and black flight from the cities and the resulting concentration of poverty—in all its forms—moved the middle-class moral underpinning out of the black community. The federal government also altered the dynamics of urban communities through application of federal laws like Hobbs Act (1951),[30] Racketeer Influenced and Corrupt Organization (RICO) (1970)[31] and other statutes in the late 1960s through the 1970s which decimated large organized urban crime organizations and gangs that controlled the nature of criminal activity in the community. The Hobbs Act prohibits actual or attempted robbery or extortion affecting interstate commerce. The Hobbs Act was applied to street-level crimes like robbery, armed robbery, and drug dealing. The courts held that as long as the criminal activity has some connection to interstate commerce, federal jurisdiction can be established over what is otherwise a local street crime. RICO was designed to attack organized crime and establish culpability through agreed criminal goals implemented through a criminal enterprise. That enterprise can be a criminal organization (a street gang for example) or a legal organization used for criminal activity. As long as the activity of the enterprise has some contact with interstate commerce and the individuals in the enterprise commit a crime in the furtherance of the criminal purpose of the enterprise and are involved in the operation of the enterprise, the individual is culpable for all actions taken by the enterprise and its members. Because the courts have held that the interstate commerce requirement can be established by relatively minor connection (de minimis) to commerce, the Hobbs Act and RICO federalized prosecution of local street crime and organized drug trafficking.[32] The use of the Gun Control Act of 1968 (the impact of this law on sentencing is discussed in greater detail in chapter 8) further decimated the operations of large street-level crime and gangs by enhancing sanctions for underlying crimes of violence when committed with guns.[33]

The unintended consequence of this federal law enforcement activity to break large street gangs in the 1960s–1970s was that there was no longer a unified control of lower-level and younger gang members. Within larger gangs, the older members disciplined and controlled the violent tendencies of the younger gang members. When law enforcement broke the leadership of the larger gangs, control of the younger gang members was lost. Smaller gangs resulted from the breakup of the larger gangs and violence among the smaller gangs by younger members increased. At this time, crack appeared. The sale of crack did not require the significant criminal organization to profitably sell it, as heroin did. To sell crack, all that was required was some powder, some other material to mix it with, and a corner to sell it from. The smaller gangs had a product that sold for thousands of dollars at the street level. The laws of economics were applied, and positive law-abiding employment in black neighborhoods lost in the competition for employees. But because crack was a cash business, sellers were prone to robbery. Thus, entered the plague that accompanied crack, the significant increase in guns, and the resulting gun violence. Smaller gangs and individual drug dealers used semi-automatic weapons to protect themselves from robbery and maintain control of drug sale territory. The illegal gun industry that supported the drug industry was a business all to itself. Illegal guns flooded the inner cities. It developed strategies for gunrunning across state lines, straw purchases from gun shops, and gun manufactures sold automatic and semi-automatic weapons to gun dealers who they knew, or should have known, sold guns to gang members or their proxies. The National Rifle Association (NRA) fought tooth and nail to oppose gun laws in the 1990s under the assertion that gun ownership and sales are an absolute right under the Second Amendment. With the exception of the semi-automatic weapons ban in the 1994 *Violent Crime and Law Enforcement Act* signed by Clinton, the NRA has won every battle to pass gun control legislation for decades.

The result was a drastic increase in murder and shooting injuries in the black community, which—and this is the important part—was public for all of America to see. Young black males getting shot and shooting each other, which seemed purposeless, was sensational-ized on the local news. The local and national news in the middle 1980s was full of stories showing black men either dead on the street or in handcuffs on the hood of police cars. To make matters worse, stories on the local news showed reports of drug-addicted babies and mothers selling themselves to get the drug and innocent people getting shot when two young black males started shooting at each other with no ability to shoot straight—thus hitting everyone but the person they were shooting at. Crime news stories in the 1980s showed blacks in cars driven by rival black and Hispanic gang members and shooting indiscriminately, resulting in retaliation shootings of the same type. The political reaction was that this level of violence by unconstrained young black males was getting out of hand, and laws had to be passed to deal with it. Local police departments said that they were overwhelmed by the violence and needed both equipment and training, as well as support from the national government.

President Reagan, who decried federal intervention in local state and local matters (the very definition of tyranny), found no hesitation in providing federal help to the states to unleash the hammer of federal law enforcement on the black community. That help came from unleashing federal law enforcement in the form of federal prosecution for drug use—in this case, simple possession. The federal government passed the Anti-Drug Abuse Acts of 1986 and 1988. Under these laws, federal prosecutions resulted in sanctions that were much more draconian than state laws. More significantly, federal prosecutions could result in making an offender disappear. Conviction in federal court resulted in being sent to a federal facility anywhere in the country. State prosecutions only resulted in incarceration within the state which could allow the offender to maintain contact with his neighborhood and criminal associates. Reagan, Bush, and Clinton provided local police with federal assistance from the DEA and the FBI. In the middle 1980s through the middle 1990s, federal-state drug task forces were formed in which federal prosecutors would prosecute otherwise local drug and gun crimes in an effort to break up smaller drug gangs. Under Reagan, federal support also gave local police agencies access to military bases in which they received military training (SWAT training), equipment, and criminal intelligence training and technical support under the *Military Cooperation with Civilian Law Enforcement Agencies Act of 1981.*

The totality of these policies resulted in the entire local and federal criminal justice system being dropped on the black community and specifically on the heads of young black males. The black community suffered increases in prosecution for low-level possession of crack cocaine with minimum mandatory sentences in federal prisons. Urban communities were besieged with militarized police units, special drug units, joint federal, state, and local drug task forces, and militarized drug warrant units comprised of federal and local officers, as well as special probation/parole police units, which had the authority to enter the homes of people on probation and parole without the need for warrants *en masse* from the late 1980s through the 1990s under President Reagan, followed by Presidents Bush and Clinton. The black community was under siege either by crack violence on one side or federal and local law enforcement on the other. The target of attention, from either side, was the young black male. Drug gangs sought black males as either participants or customers, and law enforcement sought them as targets for arrest, imprisonment, and their property as sources of revenue through asset forfeiture.

To make this dynamic all the worse, the Democrats had surrendered to the Republicans the argument on the causes of crime, and they were in active competition with the Republicans on who could be tougher on crime. The political ground of "tough on crime" that was owned by the Republicans in the late 1960s through the early 1980s was now open to dispute by the Democratic Party by the late 1980s and 1990s. Neither party talked about the root causes of crime, and neither party advocated Great Society solutions to the crack epidemic in the black community. Under both parties, the answer was to let the prison building begin, both full well knowing who was ending up in them.

The plague of crack cocaine also provided evidence for the general perception that black males were criminogenic, that they were out of control, and that they had to be put under control. By the late 1960s/early 1970s the face of violent crime was black. The politics of that face formed part of the base of the southern strategy, and the earliest proponents of the strategy knew that all too well. Dan Baum in his article published in *Harper's Magazine*, wrote race was a determinative factor in Nixon's War on Drugs. Baum wrote in the April 2016 issue[34] about an interview he had with John Ehrlichman, Nixon's senior policy advisor, in 1994.

> I was writing a book about the politics of drug prohibition. I started to ask Ehrlichman a series of earnest, wonky questions that he impatiently waved away. "You want to know what this was really all about?" he asked

with the bluntness of a man who, after public disgrace and a stretch in federal prison, had little left to protect. "The Nixon campaign in 1968, and the Nixon White House after that, had two enemies: the antiwar left and black people. You understand what I'm saying? We knew we couldn't make it illegal to be either against the war or black, but by getting the public to associate the hippies with marijuana and blacks with heroin, and then criminalizing both heavily, we could disrupt those communities. We could arrest their leaders, raid their homes, break up their meetings, and vilify them night after night on the evening news. Did we know we were lying about the drugs? Of course we did."

The belief by many within the black community that the government allowed heroin and later crack cocaine to settle in black communities to give the government the justification to unleash law enforcement and the criminal justice system with the goal to incarcerate blacks disproportionately is a deep-seated belief, and it colors how blacks view crime control model advocates. Putting Ehrlichman's statement in historical context with peonage, criminal surety, convict leasing, and the CIA Inspector General concluding in its 1998 report that the CIA turned a blind eye to cocaine drug running conducted by the Contras, the belief is not unreasonable. As Baum correctly concluded, "Nixon's invention of the war on drugs as a political tool was cynical, but every president since— Democrat and Republican alike—has found it equally useful for one reason or another."

But regardless of its origin, crack was a plague in the black community, and my point is not that crack was not a problem that needed attention, but the only attention it got was cops, courts, and corrections. Only the hammer of government and the unleased warrior cop philosophy was applied to the problem. Politically, that could be done, because crack was viewed as a black drug and a black crime. The fact that whites used crack by the late 1980s and 1990s equally to blacks was of no consequence in the politics of crime control. News stories of crack babies[35] born addicted to crack and mothers abandoning them *en masse* for the need to get their next crack high were a nightly event. The entertainment industry in movies and rap music that romanticized the use of crack in the 1990s just made the problem all the worse with rap artists and movies glorifying those who sold crack as being authentically black.

Between 1991 and 1995 under the George H.W. Bush and Clinton Administration blacks accounted 51 percent of the total U.S. prison population. In 1995, America broke the one million mark of people incarcerated in federal and state prisons. The 1990s was the high-water mark in the get tough on crime rhetoric and policies of the *second punitive era*. No politician could get elected if they were perceived as soft on crime. Justice Department grants required state criminal justice policies and programs to be focused on reducing serious violent crime. During this period, catchphrases like "super predators" and "adult time for adult crime" supported policies for treating juveniles as adults for certain types of crimes and the general political attack on the operating principle of juvenile court (rehabilitation). This period also saw the overall nationwide abandonment of parole through "truth-in-sentencing" statutes that required offenders to serve most if not all of their imposed sentence. These types of statutes supported the impact of both mandatory and minimum sentences for certain crimes, all of which removed judicial discretion in setting prison terms and fostered overcrowding.

The Bush Administration: The Reagan Years Continue—"We Will Build More Prisons"

President George H.W. Bush continued the trend established by President Reagan. Soon after assuming the presidency, on September 5, 1989, President Bush announced from the White House the release of the nation's first *National Drug Policy*[36] which made clear that "our most serious problem today is cocaine, and in particular, crack." During his televised address he held up a plastic evidence bag and said, "this is crack cocaine seized a few days ago by drug enforcement agents in a park just across the street from the White House." Now consider the optics of this. The criminal trafficking of crack had gotten so out of hand that drug dealers were now brazen enough to sell crack in the open across the street from the White House. The crack epidemic was now a national problem.

This national problem, according to Bush, required a national solution. Bush announced that the nation had a new and comprehensive drug policy document. "Earlier today, I sent this document, our first such national strategy, to the Congress."[37]

The speech became embroiled in scandal when it was reported that the DEA, under White House orders, arranged for a drug dealer to go to the park by the White House to sell the crack. The DEA had to give the drug dealer directions because he had never been to the park before. The scandal notwithstanding, Bush had made his point—crack was a national law enforcement problem and it would receive national law enforcement response.

Theatrics aside, President Bush continued the policy of President Reagan that drugs, and crack specifically, was to be controlled by crime control policies. The Bush doctrine was clear in who would be on the receiving end of this enhanced law enforcement, crime control, and use of prisons approach to deal with crack cocaine. In his national address he stated quite simply, "while illegal drug use is found in every community, nowhere is it worse than in our public housing projects." Public housing, for various reasons, concentrated poor blacks in geographically poor neighborhoods. More prosecutors, more jails, more courts were unleashed on them. The president made clear that "Congress needs not only to act on this national drug strategy but also to act on our crime package announced last May, a package to toughen sentences, beef up law enforcement, and build new prison space for 24,000 inmates." Since "you and I both know the Federal Government can't do it alone" the president implored that, "the States need to match tougher Federal laws with tougher laws of their own: stiffer bail, probation, parole, and sentencing." By the presidency of Clinton, the states had complied.

Bush put his money on his doctrine. After requesting a $1.5 billion increase in law enforcement and $65 million in emergency funding to support international drug interdiction and crop eradication in Columbia, Bush asked for $321 million in federal spending on drug treatment. Although Bush advocated for treatment, he asserted a zero tolerance regarding those who used drugs with a specific focus on schools.

> I am proposing a quarter-of-a-billion-dollar increase in Federal funds for school and community prevention programs that help young people and adults reject enticements to try drugs. And I'm proposing something else. Every school, college, and university, and every workplace must adopt tough but fair policies about drug use by students and employees. And those that will not adopt such policies will not get Federal funds—period!

The president, in total, asked Congress for $8 billion in additional spending to deal with drugs and crack cocaine. He asked Congress for stronger law enforcement support and tougher laws. He was not rebuffed.

On November 29, 1990, President Bush signed the *Crime Control Act of 1990*, which focused on victims' rights (*Criminal Victims Protection Act of 1990*) and provided federal grants and funding for anti-drug task forces. But most significantly, Title Nine of the act (*Mandatory Detention for Offenders Convicted of Serious Crimes Act of 1990*) required mandatory detention for convicted drug offenders facing ten years or more who had filed for appeal of convictions, and Title Thirty provided support for placement of offenders facing 12 to 30 months' incarceration to accept in the alternative incarceration in a military-type boot camp (shock incarceration) for six months followed by release. Bush also signed the *National Defense Authorization Act of 1990*, which authorized the Pentagon to provide local police departments with surplus military equipment. The equipment included weapons, cars, armored vehicles, communication equipment, computers, bullet-resistant vests, uniforms, body protective gear, and riot suppression equipment. The *section 1208 program* provided such equipment for anti-drug operations. The 1208 program, which expanded military partnerships with local police authorized by President Reagan in the Military Cooperation with Civilian Law Enforcement Agencies Act of 1981, was expanded from anti-drug operations to any and all bona fide police uses by President Clinton in 1997.

President Bush continued the Reagan Administration strategy of focusing on demand and on Nancy Reagan's focus on adolescent and teen demand for drugs. In a national televised Nancy Reagan–type speech geared toward teens, President Bush focused on the moral issues of drugs and asserted that drugs were evil, they bring death and destruction, they bring crime, and they are the cause of babies being born with physical defects that will affect them for the rest of their lives. President Bush in his September 1989 address made the case that drugs were evil and that alone should deter youth from using it or tolerating those who do. But the president stated that if the carrot of morality was not enough to discourage kids from using drugs, the stick of criminal justice punishment was going to be applied.

The president told his adolescent audience things had changed regarding how the criminal justice system would deal with drug dealers and users. He made very clear that "the rules have changed. If you do drugs you will be caught, and when you're caught you will be punished. You might lose your driver's license—some States have started revoking users' driving privileges. Or you might lose the college loan you wanted—because we're not helping those who break the law. These are privileges, not rights. And if you risk doing drugs, you risk everything, even your freedom. Because you will be punished. ... Some think there won't be room for them in jail. We'll make room. We're almost doubling prison space. Some think there aren't enough prosecutors. We'll hire them, with the largest increase in Federal prosecutors in history. The day of the dealer is drawing to a close."[38] As Bush had made clear in his inaugural address in January 1989, on the moral level, "there are few clear areas in which we as a society must rise up united and express our intolerance. The most obvious now is drugs. And when that first cocaine was smuggled in on a ship, it may as well have been a deadly bacteria ..." Bush made clear what the policy of his administration would be regarding drugs, when he said, "take my word for it: This scourge will stop!"

President Bush's impact on the "get tough" policies of the late 1980s was limited because he only had one term. But the president gave significant support to laying the foundation of the get-tough policies that would govern the 1990s. President Bush's support for a crime control approach to drugs and violence and the support for police strike forces and increased prosecutions of drug users, along with the significant building of prisons, all made palatable the result of disproportionate incarceration of blacks. The drug war was a war on crack dealers and gangs—which, in the public consciousness, meant young black males. Thus, dropping the full power of the criminal justice and law enforcement machine on the heads of blacks garnered little sympathy. Bush's successor, a Democrat, took hold of the well-plowed land made clear by his predecessor. President Clinton signed legislation and advocated for policies in congruence with those of President Reagan that resulted in the incarceration of blacks that lasted for more than a decade after he left office.

The Clinton Administration: Democrats Take Command of the Get Tough on Crime Landscape

Since the late 1960s, the Democratic Party was stigmatized by the label that it was soft on crime. It was the party of President Johnson, the Great Society, welfare, and protection of the due process rights of murderers and rapists. It was the party of opposition to the rights of victims and the strengthening the power of police to be the thin blue line of civilization against the advancement of the jungle. President Clinton successfully changed that narrative. After winning the presidency, Clinton's contribution to the "get tough" policies of the 1990s was the passage of a comprehensive crime bill that rivaled the one signed by President Reagan in 1984.

In his first formal State of the Union Address on January 25, 1994, Clinton took control of the "get tough on crime" politics from the exclusive ownership by Republicans and demanded a crime bill with the following policy prescriptions; (1) a three strikes and you're out provision for repeat offenders, (2) increased police officers, (3) gun control, and (4) militarized drug treatment. President Clinton got his crime bill eight months later.

The **Violent Crime and Law Enforcement Act of 1994**, which President Clinton signed on September 13, 1994, was a comprehensive crime control theory–inspired piece of legislation. The act *eliminated Pell Grants for prisoners*, thus ending the ability for prisoners to gain a college education while in prison. Title Four of the Act, the **Violence Against Women Act of 1994**, established federal funding to prevent domestic violence, and it granted women who suffered violence with the ability to sue for civil damages in federal court. The act also increased the number of crimes that could receive the federal death penalty, required states to track sex offenders (*Jacob Wetterling Crimes Against Children and Sexually Violent Offender Registration Act of 1994*), and it put a *ban on the sale of semi-automatic and assault weapons* (*The Public Safety and Recreational Firearms Act* *of 1994).* The Act, through Community Oriented Policing Services Grants, sought to *put 100,000 police officers* on the street. The program provided funding for police agencies to increase the number of officers dedicated to community policing.

In his 1994 State of the Union speech Clinton, as did Presidents Bush, Reagan, and Nixon, before him, complained that convicted offenders were not being punished. Clinton sought to change this by linking federal funds to state laws that increased the percentage of time offenders were incarcerated. President Reagan's abandonment of federal parole in 1984 was now supplemented by state government abandonment of parole under Clinton's crime control law in 1994. The Act established the *Violent Offender Incarceration and Truth in Sentencing (VOI-TIS) program,*[39] which provided special federal grants to states that complied by passing laws that required prisoners to serve at least 85 percent of their sentence before being eligible for parole.[40] In Fiscal Year (FY) 1996 the VOI-TIS grant awarded $65,252,476 to states that passed truth-in-sentencing laws, in FY2001 $435,273,543 was awarded, and between FY1996 and 2001, a total of $2,707,534,780 was awarded to the states.[41] The *VOI-TIS grant* effectively ended parole from American criminal justice.

But the crowning jewel of the **Violent Crime and Law Enforcement Act of 1994** *was* the *three-strikes* provision. Codified under 18 U.S.C. § 3559(c) the statute imposed a life sentence for a violent felony if the convict had two prior serious felony convictions or two drug convictions. The Clinton Administration viewed the three-strikes statute as a key tool in dealing with violent crime. Two years before the passage of three strikes, it was Justice Department policy as made clear in the October 12, 1993 memo *Principles of Federal Prosecution* under Janet Reno that in regard to charging,

> It should be emphasized that charging decisions and plea agreements should reflect adherence to the Sentencing Guidelines. However, a faithful and honest application of the Sentencing Guidelines is not incompatible with selecting charges or entering into plea agreements on

the basis of an individualized assessment of the extent
to which particular charges fit the specific circumstances
of the case ... Thus, for example, in determining the most
serious offense that is consistent with the nature of the
defendant's conduct ... it is appropriate that the attorney for the government consider ... whether the penalty
yielded by such sentencing range (or potential mandatory minimum charge, if applicable) is proportional to
the seriousness of the defendant's conduct, and whether
the charge achieves such purposes of the criminal law as
punishment, protection of the public, specific and general
deterrence, and rehabilitation.

Reno's memo affirmed the standing policy issued under Attorney
General Dick Thornburgh on March 13, 1989, *Plea Bargaining
Under the Sentencing Reform Act*, in which he wrote, "A federal
prosecutor should initially charge the most serious, readily provable offense or offenses consistent with the defendant's conduct."[42]
Thornburgh's memo affirmed the original Justice Department policy
(Part C paragraph 1) promulgated by Attorney General Benjamin
R. Civiletti on July 28, 1980, *Principles of Federal Prosecution*,
which asserted that federal prosecutors "should charge, or should
recommend that the grand jury charge, the most serious offense that
is consistent with the nature of the defendant's conduct, and that is
likely to result in a sustainable conviction." In giving commentary
to this rule, Justice Department policy explained as follows.

Paragraph 1 of Part C expresses the principle that the
defendant should be charged with the most serious offense
that is encompassed by his conduct and that is likely to
result in a sustainable conviction. Ordinarily, this will be
the offense for which the most severe penalty is provided
by law. This principle provides the framework for ensuring
equal justice in the prosecution of federal criminal offenders. It guarantees that every defendant will start from the

same position, charged with the most serious criminal act he commits. ... In assessing ... the most serious offense ... the attorney for the government should bear in mind some of the less predictable attributes of those rare federal sentences that carry a mandatory, minimum term of imprisonment. In many instances, the term the legislature has specified certainly would not be viewed as inappropriate. In other instances, however, unusually mitigating circumstances may make the specified penalty appear so out of proportion to the seriousness of defendant's conduct that the jury or judge in assessing guilt, or the judge in ruling on the admissibility of evidence, may be influenced by the inevitable consequence of conviction. In such cases, the attorney for the government should consider whether charging a different offense that reaches the same conduct, but that does not carry a mandatory penalty, might not be more appropriate under the circumstances.[43]

In the pre-sentencing guidelines era, Justice Department policy took into account that certain types of minimum mandatory sentences could influence either the judge or the jury determination of guilt because the resulting sentence could be disproportional to actual criminal behavior of the defendant. This practical concern required persecutors to consider filing charges that did not have minimum mandatory sentences but were still reflective of the behavior of the defendant. This concern for the application of draconian sanctions that were disproportionate to the behavior of the defendant would survive the advent of the sentencing guideline regime established in 1984.

Reno's October 1993 memo clarified the standing policy from Civiletti and Thornburgh by making clear that federal prosecutors were to charge the "most serious offense" which she said was defined by "the nature of the defendants conduct" and federal prosecutors were to make an "individualized assessment" of possible charges available and determine if "particular charges fit the specific circumstances of the case" tempered by consideration of whether the resulting sentence under the guidelines "is proportional to the se-riousness of the defendant's conduct." Her policy memo would not survive the politics of the age. Reno herself would mitigate her own policy two years later in March 1995, and it would be abandoned *in toto* by Attorney General Ashcroft a decade later.

On March 13, 1995, the Clinton Justice Department, under Attorney General Janet Reno, issued a memo on March 13, 1995, *Memorandum for All United States Attorneys Subject: Three Strikes,*[44] instructing U.S. attorneys that the three-strikes law "should play a key role in every district's anti-violent crime strategy" in order to "to take violent criminals off the streets" through coordination with state and local prosecutors. The memo summarized that the administration's *Anti-Violent Crime Initiative*, which had "long used the Armed Career Criminal Act, 18 U.S.C. § 924(e), to achieve the prolonged incarceration of armed, violent offenders" was now supplemented by "a powerful new federal tool, the so-called Three Strikes, You're Out provision, to help us deal with violent repeat offenders." The Armed Career Criminal Act was Title Eighteen of the Comprehensive Crime Control Act of 1984, and it provided for en-hanced penalties, 15 years imprisonment, for felons who committed felonies with firearms who had prior convictions for violent crimes. See *Johnson v. United States* (2015) in the Supreme Court jurisprudence chart later in this chapter on the constitutional infirmities in defining the "violent felony" requirement in the Armed Career Criminal Act and *United States v. Davis* (2019) for similar infirmities in the "crime of violence" requirement in the Gun Control Act of 1968.

The three-strikes statute, the memo asserted, "provides a vehicle to take the most dangerous offenders out of the community and keep them out. This is particularly important in states where prison overcrowding results in early release even for violent criminals." The March 1995 memo is still current Justice Department policy.

Clinton Administration policy authorized U.S. attorneys to use three strikes on non-federal crime offenders by transferring offend-ers to the federal system and reducing state overcrowding legal problems. The memo instructed U.S. attorneys that any serious violent crime, defined as "murder, manslaughter, sex offenses, kidnapping, robbery, and any offense punishable by 10 years or more which includes as an element the use of force or that, by its nature, involves a significant risk of force," as well as unarmed robbery and the "distribution, manufacture, or possession with intent to distribute significant quantities of controlled substances, or equivalent state offenses" were covered under the three-strikes statute. Under this new policy, the federal government federalized street-level crime. Clinton did this with the full support of social conservative states' rights advocates. The same people who opposed the federal government interference with segregation and asserted the use of federal law enforcement in the local issues of the states was tyranny; now supported the use of those same forces when unleashed on local street criminals. The rhetorical field of crime control had been conquered and Clinton now owned the field.

The VOI-TIS truth-in-sentencing grants, along with the three-strikes law and the Clinton Administration policy of applying it, ushered in the nationwide passage of state three-strikes statutes and prosecutorial policies that increased prison populations. These new statutes and prosecution policies contributed to longer sentences for inmates through plea bargain-based convictions in which defendants pled guilty to avoid more stringent sanctions after trial because they were declared three-strike eligible. As to its impact, in states like California with stringent three-strike laws, "African-Americans comprise[d] 31% of inmates in the state's prisons, but 37% of offenders convicted under two strikes and 44% of three strikes offenders."[45]

The support and passage of the Violent Crime and Law Enforcement Act of 1994 and its impact on black incarceration paled in comparison to Clinton directly overruling the U.S. Sentencing Commission recommendation that the 100 to 1 ratio of crack-to-powder cocaine passed in 1986 should be changed.

In 1995, the U.S. Sentencing Commission issued a report, *Special Report to the Congress: Cocaine and Federal Sentencing Policy*, on cocaine and crack use and reviewed the various reasons justifying the 100 to 1 ratio created in the *Anti-Drug Abuse Act of 1986* and concluded that the statute was having a disproportionate impact on blacks.[46] The commission proposed to establish guidelines that would use the impact of the distinction between powder and crack cocaine on the community rather than focus exclusively on the 100 to 1 ratio for sentencing decisions by the court.[47] The commission recommended that the guidelines be adjusted to reduce the impact of the 100 to 1 ratio.[48] President Clinton and Congress were having none of this. For the first time in the history of the commission, Congress passed legislation rejecting a finding of the commission.

On October 30, 1995, Clinton signed **Public Law 104–38** entitled *To disapprove of amendments to the federal sentencing guidelines relating to lowering of crack sentences and sentences for money laundering and transactions in property derived from unlawful activity*. Upon signing[49] the legislative rejection of the commission and its findings, Clinton did not hide what he was doing. He made clear that,

> Today I reject United States Sentencing Commission proposals that would equalize penalties for crack and powder cocaine distribution by dramatically reducing the penalties for crack. ...
>
> Since I took office, my Administration has fought to stop drug abuse and to stamp out the crime and violence that are its constant companions. We are battling drug traffickers at every level of their networks—from the very top to the very bottom.
>
> ... We told criminals convicted time and again for serious violent crimes or drug trafficking that from now on, its three strikes and you're out. ...
>
> ....
>
> We have to send a constant message to our children that drugs are illegal, drugs are dangerous, drugs may cost you your life—and the penalties for dealing drugs are

severe. I am not going to let anyone who peddles drugs get the idea that the cost of doing business is going down.

President Reagan could not have said it better himself. President Reagan said the same thing when he signed the *Anti-Drug Act of 1986*:

> Well, today it gives me great pleasure to sign legislation that reflects the total commitment of the American people and their government to fight the evil of drugs. ...
>
> The magnitude of today's drug problem can be traced to past unwillingness to recognize and confront this problem. And the vaccine that's going to end the epidemic is a combination of tough laws—like the one we sign today—and a dramatic change in public attitude. We must be intolerant of drug use and drug sellers.[50]

In the face of proved disproportionate incarceration of blacks under the 100 to 1 ratio, Clinton said the harshness of the crack law is needed to remove crack from black neighborhoods and the impact, though devastating, is required to end the violence that occurs with crack cocaine. The two parties had found congruence. It would be a decade into the following century, 15 years, before the 100 to 1 ratio was reduced under President Obama in 2010 and made retroactive under Trump in 2018.

Over his eight years in office Clinton supported all types of "get tough on crime" legislation, including signing *Megan's Law* in 1995, the *Pam Lychner Sexual Offender Tracking and Identification Act of 1996*, the *Prison Litigation Reform Act of 1996*, *Antiterrorism and Effective Death Penalty Act of 1996* (which placed statutory limits on death penalty habeas petitions), and *the Jacob Wetterling Amendment Act of 1998*. But Clinton's signature social legislation was the *Personal Responsibility and Work Opportunity Reconciliation Act of 1996* (the welfare to work law, which allowed drug testing for people on Temporary Assistance for Needy Families-TANF). Three months after seeking and signing legislation reversing the Sentencing Commission, Clinton, in his 1996 annual address to Congress, asked for a "one strike and you're out" legislation regarding public housing.

Congress complied and passed the *Housing Opportunity Program Extension Act of 1996* and the *Quality Housing and Work Responsibility Act of 1998*. Under the **Quality Housing and Work Responsibility Act of 1998**, reaffirming a provision under the Anti-Drug Abuse Act of 1988, owners of federally subsidized housing and public housing agencies were authorized to place in leases a notice of authority to evict residents for illegal drug use or alcohol abuse and that prior illegal drug use or alcohol abuse can be terms for permanent ineligibility for public or subsidized housing.[51]

The **Housing Opportunity Program Extension Act of 1996** gave local Public Housing Authorities (PHAs) "new authority and obligations to deny occupancy on the basis of illegal drug-related activity and alcohol abuse."[52] In the Anti-Drug Abuse Act of 1988, Congress authorized Housing and Urban Development (HUD) and PHAs to put in all leases the following language,

> that any criminal activity that threatens the health, safety, or right to peaceful enjoyment of the premises by other tenants or any drug-related criminal activity on or off such premises, engaged in by a public housing tenant, any member of the tenant's household, or any guest or other person under the tenant's control, shall be cause for termination of tenancy[53]

The Clinton Administration asserted that the anti-drug use leasing requirement under the Anti-Drug Abuse Act of 1988 had not been properly enforced and that would end with his *"One Strike and You're Out"* policy. The Clinton Administration issued guidelines that required local PHAs to require criminal background checks for all people applying for public housing and to have procedures to evict any and all current residents for drug or alcohol use.[54]

In justifying this policy and the new HUD guidelines implementing the policy, Clinton said that "Public housing has never been a right; it has always been a privilege. ... The only people who deserve to live in public housing are those who live responsibly there and those who honor the rule of law ... Under the new rules ... for the first time there will actually be penalties for housing projects that do not fight crime and enforce 'one strike and you're out.' ... I know that for some, 'one strike and you're out' sounds like hardball. Well, it is. It is because it's morally wrong for criminals to use up homes that could make a big difference in the lives of decent families. ... After all, it's not as if nobody wants to live there. ... The people who are living there deserve to be protected ... For too many years, the chaos in some of our public housing units has been a national blind spot and a national disgrace. Most Americans probably think it has to be that way. Many of them who have had no personal experience with tenants may even believe most people who live in public housing are lawless, are not working, are not concerned parents. All of that is wrong. Now we are going to give the good, decent, law-abiding citizens in public housing the life they deserve, and we're going to give the kids the future they deserve by doing what we should have been doing all along ..."[55]

Under a Democratic president, the policy of removing people from public housing on conviction or suspected drug use found national support and presidential advocacy. The policy, according to President Clinton, was supported by the fact that public housing residency is a privilege, not a right. So much for the progressive theory that housing is a human right.

The One Strike and You're Out policy applied vicarious liability to all residents in public housing. The policy applied to all members of the household regardless of their knowledge of any criminal activity of any individual member residing in the house. This "no-fault" clause that applied eviction to an entire household for the sins of one member was affirmed by the Supreme Court in *Department of Housing and Urban Development v. Rucker* (2002).[56]

Leaving aside the ability to make an entire family homeless for the sins of one member, the real impact of the policy was that it was issued during the crime control period of the 1990s in which police had a financial incentive to make and secure more convictions of minor drug dealers and users. During this period, local police agencies secured federal anti-drug funding by establishing high arrest and conviction rates. During this period, poor black communities were suffering from intense anti-crime police activities, including the use of SWAT teams to execute drug warrants, the formation of local–federal drug task forces, which specifically targeted open-air drug trafficking in black communities, and the use of "jump-out squads" that would conduct random sweeps of residents to find and arrest residents with drugs. Prosecutors were engaged in using plea bargaining to secure convictions through overcharging and by pre-trial incarceration through opposition to bail for drug arrests. Prosecutors could secure pleas from suspects who feared incarceration or needed to be released to take care of family members. When prosecutors opposed bail or requested bail that would result in incarceration because of the inability to pay the court-ordered bond, offenders where more amenable to taking a plea—regardless of guilt—to be released. The "one strike and you're out" policy would make people who pled guilty to minor or reduced charges to get out of jail because of the lack of ability to secure bail ineligible to maintain residency in public housing and could result in entire families being evicted. Thus, from this policy, countless stories of family dislocation occurred over decades.

In the **National Defense Authorization Act of 1997** under *section 1033*, Clinton authorized the Pentagon to provide surplus military equipment to local law enforcement agencies. Under the 1033 program, the Pentagon provided local agencies with military weapons, including armored vehicles, helicopters, ordinance, gas and grenade launchers, and high caliber rifles to local police without charge. The 1033 program expanded the 1208 program under President Bush. The program was curtailed under President Obama by executive order in 2014, which was withdrawn by President Trump in 2017.

Clinton stole the "tough on crime" mantle from the Republican Party, and under his presidency, more people were incarcerated than under Reagan and Bush. In "President Clinton's first-term

(1992–1996), 148,000 more state and federal prisoners were added than under President Reagan's first term (1980–1984), and 34,000 more than were added under President Bush's four-year term (1988–1992)."[57] Under President Reagan, during his first term, the number of people incarcerated increased by 129,000, while under Bush, the number increased by 243,000, and under Clinton, during his first term, it increased by 277,000.[58] Comparing Clinton's and Reagan's eight years in office each, under Reagan, there was an increase of 448,000, but under Clinton, there was an increase of 673,000 people. Under Clinton, 225,000 more people were incarcerated than under Reagan.[59] Under Reagan, the incarceration rate per 100,000 was 247; under Bush, it was 332; and under Clinton, it was 476.[60]

The net result during the 1980s and 1990s under Reagan, Bush, and Clinton was that black incarceration rose from 41 percent under Reagan to a high of 51 percent under Clinton in 1994. The black incarceration dropped during Clinton's final years in office from 49 percent in 1997 to 46 percent in 2001. The reduction occurred simultaneously with the beginning of the end of the crack epidemic in 1993, culminating in 1996.[61]

Needless to say, that one of the results of the second punitive era between 1980 and 2000 was a significant increase in prison and corrections spending, as well as an increase in the prison population. In 1982, states spent $15 billion on corrections, and by 2002, states had spent $53.4 billion on corrections.[62] Each and every year for two decades, the amount spent increased.

In summary, various policy initiatives led directly to the modern disproportionate incarceration of blacks. These included the *Comprehensive Crime Control Act of 1984*, which established mandatory sentencing guidelines system and ended federal parole; the *Anti-Drug Abuse Act of 1986*, which established the 100 to 1 ratio of crack-powder disparity in which 5 grams of crack and 500 grams of powder cocaine were punished with at least five years; *the Anti-Drug Abuse Act of 1988*, which created the five-year mandatory minimum sentence for simple possession of 5 grams of crack cocaine for first-time offenders; the *Violent Crime and Law Enforcement*

Act of 1994, which established three strikes and truth in sentencing; the *Clinton Justice Department March 13, 1995, Memo*, which
established the prosecution policy that the three-strikes legislation
was to be used to achieve the specific purpose of increased incarceration; and *Public Law 104–38* the 1995 legislation that overruled the
U.S. Sentencing Commission. It would only be at the end of the first
decade of the following century (under President Obama) and the
second decade of the same century (under President Trump) before
tempering the impact of these policies was politically palatable.

In 1926 blacks accounted for 21 percent of those in state and
federal prison and at the dusk of the century (2001) blacks
accounted for 46 percent of the incarcerated population. From
1926 through 2001 each year showed an increase in disproportionate incarceration of blacks. That trend would not significantly
change until the second decade of the new century. This more than
seventy year trend would began to decrease in 2002 and by 2016
the percentage would be reduced to 33 percent. In the first decade
of the new century, the crime control policies of the past would
slowly lose political support, but they did not completely end. In
that decade there were still prisons to build and blacks continued
to disproportionately fill them.

President Bush and a New Century

President George W. Bush was the first president of the new century and the policy of the new administration was that funding
for the Department of Justice would "shift in spending from state
and local law enforcement to support our core federal law enforcement mission, and better target assistance to areas of greatest need,
such as crime in our schools, crimes committed with firearms, and
violence against women." To meet these responsibilities the Justice
Department would focus on building and maintaining prisons and
it requested $949.5 million increase in funding to support the fed-
eral detention of pretrial detainees and convicted offenders as well

as 77.2 million for the DEA and $240.14 million was requested for border and immigration enforcement (INS).[63]

The first president of the twenty-first century followed the policies of his predecessors with a general "get tough" approach to criminals in which the focus would be on increased federal funding for prisons and law enforcement. This would have been President Bush's response to what was perceived as the greatest threat of domestic violence—crime. September 11th would moderate the Bush Administration domestic law enforcement policy. After September 11, domestic security policy shifted from crime to counterterrorism. Federal law enforcement and domestic safety agencies were reorganized to focus on protecting America from terrorism and from this new priority came the founding of the Department of Homeland Security on November 25, 2002. Political focus changed from inner-city crime suppression to the war on terror. Federal funds shifted accordingly. Now, local police focused grant writing on securing federal funding to support domestic terrorism monitoring and suppression. This would drive American domestic policy for more than a decade into the new century.

But even under the shift in policy to deal with the war on terror, the crime control model of the 1990s found support. After the officers in the Rodney King beating were acquitted in 1992, two of the officers, Stacy Koon and Lawrence Powell, were convicted in federal court for violating King's civil rights. The District Court reduced the sentence of both officers from the presumptive sentence of 70 to 87 months to a sentence of 30 to 37 months, a downgrade of eight levels in the sentencing guidelines.[64] The District Court reasoned that the beating resulted in part because of Rodney King's wrongful conduct which the court held resulted in a five-level reduction and an additional three-level reduction was justified because (1) the officers would be subject to abuse in prison, (2) neither men would ever be law enforcement officers again and had suffered public humiliation because of the publicity of the case, (3) the officers had been "significantly burdened by being subjected to successive state and federal prosecutions," and (4) because the officers were not "violent, dangerous, or likely to engage in future criminal conduct" they were not a threat to society. "The court concluded these factors justified a departure when taken together, although none would have been sufficient standing alone."[65]

The government appealed the reduction and the Court of Appeals "reviewed '*de novo* whether the district court had authority to depart' [from the guidelines and it] reversed the five-level departure for victim misconduct, reasoning that misbehavior by suspects is typical in cases involving excessive use of force by police and is thus comprehended by the applicable guideline. As for the three-level departure, the court rejected each factor cited."[66] The Supreme Court on appeal held that the Court of Appeals used the wrong standard for review. Rather than using *de novo* which allows the court to review the issue on its own determinations, the Supreme Court held in *Koon v. United States* (1996) that a reviewing court should only determine if the district court abused its discretion. Under this burden, the legal question is whether the original court applied the law incorrectly. Abuse of discretion does not allow the reviewing court to substitute its opinion on how the case should have been resolved with the decision by the original court. Abuse of discretion is a much more deferential approach.

The Supreme Court held in *Koon* that the sentencing guidelines allowed district court judges to deviate from the presumptive guidelines when the court finds certain aggravating or mitigating circumstances should be considered that were not considered in applying the sentencing guidelines. The Court held that under the Comprehensive Crime Control Act of 1984 trial courts had not lost all discretion when issuing a sentence under the sentencing guidelines. The Court wrote that the District Court did not get the law wrong in the five-level downward departure because of King's conduct, but it did get the law wrong regarding the three-level reduction. The Court held that the career loss and threat to society factors cited by the District Court did not authorize departure but the remaining two factors, their susceptibility to abuse in prison and the successive prosecutions in state and federal courts did authorize departure. The case was remanded for a new sentencing hearing.

In 2003 President Bush approved congressional reversal of the proposition that judges could depart from presumptive guidelines. The **USA PROTECT Act**, signed by President Bush on April 30, 2003, reaffirmed the crime control model policies of the 1980s and 1990s which rejected judicial discretion in sentencing convicted criminals. The act reaffirmed the policy of "truth in sentencing" and rejected the idea that a check was needed to be placed on prosecutors and legislators regarding the harsh sentences of criminals. Specifically, the policies of the 1980s and 1990s made clear that the courts were not to be a check on either prosecutors or legislatures that increased sentences of offenders.

The USA PROTECT Act made five changes to the sentencing guidelines under the *Sentencing Reform Act of 1984*. The last three overruled *Koon v. United States*. The act established that *de novo* was the appropriate standard of review when a sentencing court departs from the guidelines and prohibits the court from a downward departure from the guidelines with very specific exceptions.[67] The guidelines remained mandatory and would remain so until the Court held that under the Sixth Amendment they were advisory in *U.S. v. Booker* (2005) and *Kimbrough v. United States* (2007). In *Booker,* the Court held that the Sixth Amendment right to jury trial required that factors that could increase a sanction must be proved before a jury and because the guidelines allow such to be proved only before a judge, that part of the guidelines violates the Sixth Amendment. The Court held that guidelines were to be read by the courts as advisory.[68] In *Kimbrough* the Court held the 100 to 1 ratio crack-to-powder cocaine sentence is advisory and that the courts, although they must take into account the presumptive sentence, can consider the purpose of the guidelines regarding fairness and "[in] making that determination, the judge may consider the disparity between the Guidelines' treatment of crack and powder cocaine offenses."[69] The Court redeemed the sentencing Commission's position rejected by Clinton 12 years earlier.

The Bush Administration in full support of the USA PROTECT Act, under Attorney General John Ashcroft issued a memo to all Justice Department heads and U.S. attorneys on July 28, 2003, *Department Policies and Procedures Concerning Sentencing Recommendations and Sentencing Appeals*, in which he made clear that in regarding sentencing recommendations, any recommendation must include all relevant and provable facts in the case. The memo made clear that prosecutors could not "fact bargain" or agree not to provide the court with information relevant to the behavior of the defendant in exchange for a plea. Ashcroft followed up with a second memo on September 22, 2003, *Memorandum from Attorney General Ashcroft to all federal prosecutors on charging and sentencing*, which instructed federal prosecutors that under the sentencing guidelines, "It is the policy of the Department of Justice that, in all federal criminal cases, federal prosecutors must charge and pursue the most serious, readily provable offense or offenses that are supported by the facts of the case. ... The most serious offense or offenses are those that generate the most substantial sentence under the sentencing guidelines, unless a mandatory minimum sentence or count requiring a consecutive sentence would generate a longer sentence." Note the significance of this policy. The most serious offense is not the most "evil" act (criminal behavior) done, rather the most serious offense is the criminal act that carries the most stringent sentence available. Ashcroft overruled the Civiletti (1980), the Thornburgh (1989) and the Reno October 1993 policies defining how prosecutors were to determine what an appropriate sentence should be. Furthermore, the memo instructed federal prosecutors that, "The use of statutory enhancements is strongly encouraged, and federal prosecutors must therefore take affirmative steps to ensure that the increased penalties resulting from specific statutory enhancements ... are sought in all appropriate cases." The memo made clear that readily provable meant a charge the government could win in court and plea bargaining was limited to dismissing charges that could not be proven. "Once filed, the most serious readily provable charges may not be dismissed."

Two years later, the second punitive era would enjoy its last crime control model pronouncement from the Justice Department. After the Supreme Court issued its decision in *United States v. Booker* on January 12, 2005, in which it held that the federal sentencing guidelines were declared advisory, Deputy Attorney General James Comey issued a *Memo to All Federal Prosecutors on Charging and Sentencing* on January 28, 2005. He stated that Justice Department policy was clear that "we must do everything in our power to ensure that sentences carry out the fundamental purposes of sentencing. Those purposes, as articulated by Congress in the Sentencing Reform Act, are to reflect the seriousness of the offense, to promote respect for the law, to provide just punishment, to afford deterrence, to protect the public, and to offer opportunities for rehabilitation to the defendant." In that order. The role of the prosecutor and federal criminal justice was to impose punishment, to enforce deterrence, and to protect the public, and only when these have been accomplished is rehabilitation of the defendant a prosecutorial concern.

With these priorities clear, Comey instructed that even under the guidelines as advisory, "federal prosecutors must continue to charge and pursue the most serious readily provable offenses. As set forth in Attorney General Ashcroft's Memorandum ... (July 28, 2003), the 'most serious' readily provable offenses are those that would generate the most substantial sentence pursuant to (1) the guidelines, (2) one or more applicable mandatory minimums, and/or (3) a consecutive sentence required by statute. One of the fundamental principles underlying the Guidelines is that punishment should be based on the real offense conduct of the defendant. To ensure that sentences reflect real offense conduct, prosecutors must present to the district court all readily provable facts relevant to sentencing." This would be prosecution policy for seven years before a due process model would be imposed by Attorney General Eric Holder in 2010.

The USA PROTECT Act, the Ashcroft 2003 and Comey 2005 sentencing guidelines memos marked the last high-water mark of the second punitive era. By the middle of the first decade of the new century, the politics of "get tough on crime" and the policy of mass prison construction during the *second punitive era* were coming to an end. Starting in 2003, state spending on corrections began to decrease from $51.7 billion to $48.5 billion in 2010.[70] In the year 2000, the total number of people incarcerated in America was 1,945,400; by 2005, it was 2,200,400, increasing every consecutive year until 2008 with 2,310,300 incarcerated. Beginning in 2009 through 2015, each consecutive year, the number of people incarcerated decreased, resulting in 2,173,800 in 2015.[71] From 2008 through 2015, those under probation and parole also consecutively decreased from 5,093,400 to 4,650,900. "At yearend 2015, an estimated 6,741,400 persons were under the supervision of U.S. adult correctional systems, about 115,600 fewer persons than yearend 2014. This was the first time since 2002 (6,730,900) that the correctional population fell below 6.8 million."[72]

The political necessity for members of Congress to prove they were strong on drugs and violent crime was beginning to shift to other concerns. Congressional attention shifted to other criminal justice issues, including providing support for child and victim protection statutes to deal with the threat of sexual predators. These laws included the *Campus Sex Crimes Prevention Act of 2000, the Prosecutorial Remedies and Other Tools to end the Exploitation of Children Today, the Prison Rape Elimination, the Justice For All Act of 2004* (Scott Campbell, Stephanie Roper, Wendy Preston, Louarna Gillis, and Nila Lynn Crime Victims' Rights–2004), and *the Walsh Child Protection and Safety Act of 2006* (Sex Offender Registration and Notification Act).

By the end of the first decade of the new century, politics had changed, and the politics of incarceration at all costs was ending. On April 9, 2008, President Bush signed the *Second Chance Act of 2007*.[73] The **Second Chance Act** provided federal grant and research funds to support state and local pilot programs in prisons and courts with the goal of increasing the use reentry and drug court initiatives. Federal funding was also made available for nonprofit organizations specializing in providing reentry, drug treatment, and rehabilitation programs. The law also provided funding to support education programs to encourage employers to hire released offenders. Federal prison officials were required to assist prisoners in obtaining identification documents (e.g., birth certificates and social security cards) prior to release from prison. Federal prison officials were also required to provide education services to prisoners regarding health, nutrition, employment, and literacy to facilitate reentry into the community. Pilot studies on the release of elderly offenders, over 65 years old, into home detention were to receive recidivism research funds.

Two years later President Barack Obama was able to secure a more substantial change in federal law with the passage of the **Fair Sentencing Act 2010**,[74] which changed the 100 to 1 ratio under the Anti-Drug Abuse Act of 1986 to a ratio of 18 to 1 and changed the five-year minimum mandatory sentence for 5 grams of cocaine under the Anti-Drug Abuse Act of 1988 to 28 grams. These changes, along with the Supreme Court ruling in *U.S. v. Booker* (2005) and *Kimbrough v. U.S.* (2007), and his Justice Department changes to how federal drug cases would be prosecuted, discussed in Chapter 8, resulted in a reduction of black incarceration from 41 percent in 2009 to 33 percent in 2016.

The bipartisan agreement that the second punitive era was over, and rehabilitation was no longer an *in toto* abandoned concept in the second decade of the new century was affirmed under President Obama and his signing of the *Fair Sentencing Act of 2010*. In December 2018 President Trump signed the *First Step Act* of 2018 which reauthorized the *Second Chance Act* and made the crack cocaine reductions in the *Fair Sentencing Act* retroactive. Discussed in more detail in Chapter 8, the *First Step Act* expanded the *Second Chance Act* initiatives and reentry grants and while the law authorized prison officials to contract with colleges to "deliver instruction" to inmates on a "paid or volunteer basis"[75] the ban on Pell grants under the *Violent Crime and Law Enforcement Act of 1994* was retained. Subsequent to the passage of the *First Step Act*, the Trump Administration announced[76] its policy initiatives that supported private employment programs for released prisoners and allowing former inmates to have access to federal job vacancies.[77]

◆ ◆ ◆

The Congress and presidents of the 1960s–1990s were not the only sources of the modern criminal justice system. The Supreme Court was a key figure, and at first the leader, in the rise of the rehabilitation era in the 1960s. The Court issued a series of cases that came to be known as the *due process revolution*. In the due process revolution, which occurred between 1961 and 1968, the Supreme Court held that the protections of the Fourth, Fifth, Sixth, and Eighth Amendments were required and obligatory in state criminal justice trials through the Fourteenth Amendment. The reason the Philadelphia police need a warrant to search your house or the local court in New York City must provide the indigent with an attorney during criminal trials is because of the Supreme Court during the due process revolution.

The foundation of the due process revolution is rooted in the aftermath of the Civil War. After the Civil War, Southern Democrats through the police during the day and Klan riders at night murdered, raped, beat, intimidated, and imprisoned the former slaves to maintain their inferiority and white superiority in the South. The national government responded with the policy of Reconstruction. The national government also responded with the Civil War amendments. The Thirteenth Amendment was ratified on December 18, 1865, to settle a pre-Civil War question—were black people citizens of the United States. The Thirteenth Amendment settled the answer as yes. But the actions of the South made clear that simple citizenship was not enough. Congress passed the Fourteenth Amendment on June 13, 1866, which was ratified July 9, 1868, and prohibited the states from violating the due process rights and guaranteed equal protection of the law when it came to blacks. The Fifteenth Amendment, which was ratified on February 3, 1870, which on paper, guaranteed blacks the right to vote.

With the fall of Reconstruction in 1877, Southern Democrats returned to political power and Jim Crow and segregation became the social policy of the South and was adopted by the North. During the post-Reconstruction era blacks argued that the various policies of Jim Crow violated the Fourteenth Amendment. In the seminal case of *Plessy v. Ferguson* (1896) the Court held that the Fourteenth Amendment did not forbid racial segregation as along as the segregation was equal. But within constitutional jurisprudence a question remained, what was due process of law and equal protection law? What did those terms mean regarding what the states could not do? Within the realm of criminal justice jurisprudence, the question was what procedures during trials were governed by the due process and equal protection clauses? From the beginning of American constitutional history, the Supreme Court had held that criminal justice procedures were a local matter and states' rights and theories of federalism prohibited the federal courts from interfering with state criminal justice. The court had made clear that the Bill of Rights did not apply to the states in *Barron v. Baltimore* (1833).

By the middle twentieth century, the Court had adopted the jurisprudence that the Fourteenth Amendment, which only applies to the states, guaranteed that the states could not implement criminal justice practices that *shocked the conscience* of the court. In other words, the states could not implement policies that were so unfair or unjust that no civilized criminal justice system could abide by such practices. But this was a very high standard to meet. The only significant limits on state government power was that the Supreme Court ruled that the state judges could not convict a person in secret trials (*In re Oliver*, 1948) and that the police could not break into the home of man without a warrant and, by force, beat and extract evidence of a crime from his stomach and use the evidence at trial (*Rochin v. California*, 1952). The implementation of states' rights principles had required the Supreme Court to rule in 1936 that the Mississippi police, under the Fourteenth Amendment due process clause, could not tie three "defendants, all ignorant negroes" to a tree and a chair and whip confessions out of them and then use the confessions against them in court (*Brown v. Mississippi*) and to rule in 1931 that before Alabama could execute indigent defendants they had to give them a trial with competent counsel first (*Powell v. Alabama*—The Scottsboro Boys case).

In the famous *Brown v. Mississippi* case of the police believing they were free to whip confessions out of three black defendants, a police officer in open court regarding how he got the confessions out of one of the defendants was asked, "How severely was he whipped, the deputy stated, 'Not too much for a negro; not as much as I would have done if it were left to me.'"[78] Such were the limits the Court was willing to impose on the states through the Fourteenth Amendment pre-World War II—you can't beat confessions or other types of evidence out of defendants and then use it in court.

With the ending of World War II and the example of what can occur when the law does not stand against government power without check, the rehabilitation era began. It began, in part by the Supreme Court expanding the protection of the Fourteenth Amendment by abandoning the shocks the conscience (fundamental fairness) approach and adopting the *theory of incorporation* approach. The latter asserts that what the due process and equal protection clause require is what the Bill of Rights, the Fourth, Fifth, Sixth, and Eighth Amendments, requires. The Court never adopted a full application of incorporation of the Bill of Rights *in toto* into the Fourteenth Amendment, but rather it adopted a slow process of selective incorporation of key parts of the Bill of Rights on a case by case basis. Through this process of selective incorporation, the Court maintained the principles of fundamental fairness which obligated the states to protect certain fundamentals of fairness within their criminal trials. The theory of selective incorporation was first adopted by the Court in 1925 in the case of *Gitlow v. New York* in which the Court held that the right to free speech, the First Amendment, was incorporated into the due process clause of the Fourteenth Amendment and as such was obligatory on the states.

As late as 1949 in *Wolf v. Colorado* the Court made clear that the due process clause does not as a group incorporate the first eight amendments of the Bill of Rights[79] but in regard to the application of the due process clause to criminal prosecutions, the Court held that the due process clause precludes local police from entering a home of individual without a warrant. The Court wrote, "Security of one's privacy against arbitrary intrusion by the police—which is at the core of the Fourth Amendment—is basic to a free society. It is therefore implicit in 'the concept of ordered liberty' and as such enforceable against the States through the Due Process Clause. ... Accordingly, we have no hesitation in saying that were a State affirmatively to sanction such police incursion into privacy it would run counter to the guaranty of the Fourteenth Amendment."[80] The Court held that the remedy for unlawful entry by the police, exclusion of the evidence which was the rule in the federal courts under *Weeks v. United States* (1914), was not required by the due process clause of the Fourteenth Amendment.

By 1961 the Court was ready to enforce the principle that under the Fourteenth Amendment coerced evidence cannot be used in state courts. The Court held on March 20, 1961 in *Rogers v. Richmond*, affirming its decision in *Brown v. Mississippi*, that, "our decisions under that Amendment have made clear that convictions following the admission into evidence of confessions which are involuntary, i.e., the product of coercion, either physical or psychological, cannot stand."[81]

With the principle established in *Wolf* that evidence secured in violation of the Fourth Amendment is a violation of the concept of ordered liberty, the Court in *Mapp v. Ohio* on June 19, 1961 overruled the conclusion in *Wolf* that the exclusionary rule does not apply to the states.[82] The Court expanded the privacy (liberty) protection principle in *Rogers* under the theory of incorporation, rather than the concept of ordered liberty. The Court in *Mapp* held that the prohibition of the introduction in criminal trials of evidence secured without a warrant in violation of the Fourth Amendment protection of individual privacy (search of home only with a warrant) was incorporated into the Fourteenth and as such was excluded from use in state criminal proceedings.[83] With *Mapp* the due process revolution within criminal justice jurisprudence began.

The Supreme Court is significant in the history and development of American criminal justice. As shown in the following chart, the rise of the due process revolution within the rehabilitative era as well as the rise of the second punitive and post-second punitive eras were supported by the Court's interpretation and application of the criminal justice portions of the Bill of Rights. The chart (pp. 240–254) divides this development of history in four time periods, the due process revolution (1961–1968), the decline of the rehabilitation era (1968–1980), the second punitive era (1980–2000), and the post-second punitive era (2000–present).

Of course, this chart is not exclusive in listing the cases by the Court in relation to the Fourth,[84] Fifth, Sixth, and Eighth Amendments. But as shown in the chart, beginning in the 1970s the due process revolution was slowly abandoned when the Court shifted in its approach in defining the meaning and application of the amendments in reviewing law enforcement activity. The Court shifted from expanding the protections and justifications of the Fourth Amendment in the 1960s to law enforcement efficiency in crime suppression. By the middle 1980s the Court had totally abandoned the broad application of the exclusionary rule and its impact on failure to inform suspects of their rights under *Miranda*. The focus of analysis of the Fourth Amendment was no longer the need of the police to secure warrants, or the Court refusing to sanction Fourth Amendment violations by using illegally seized evidence, or limiting the power of the police to protect individual liberty from police abuse; but rather the only concern was whether the police action was reasonable.

Between the middle 1980s and 2010 the Court had made it clear that the exclusionary rule was to be applied only when the high social costs of applying it—letting the guilty go free—was outweighed by the need to deter intentional police misconduct—intentional violation of the Fourth Amendment. The word intentional being dispositive. The Court abandoned the approach that the violation of the Fourth itself is dispositive. The Court held that the Fourth Amendment only prohibits unreasonable searches and seizures, and police reasonable error (mistake) in complying with the Fourth by definition is not unreasonable.

DEVELOPMENT OF MODERN CRIMINAL JUSTICE AND SUPREME COURT JURISPRUDENCE

DUE PROCESS REVOLUTION (1961–1968)	DECLINE OF THE REHABILITATION ERA (1968–1980)	SECOND PUNITIVE ERA (1980–2000)	POST-SECOND PUNITIVE ERA (2000–PRESENT)
Elkins v. United States (1960) Federal agents cannot use illegally seized evidence secured by state or local police in violation of the Fourth Amendment	*Terry v. Ohio* (1968) Stop and frisk—lowers standard for police forcible stops from probable cause to reasonable articulable suspicion (RAS)	*U.S. v. Mendenhall* (1980) The Fourth Amendment is only implicated when the police by force prevent the movement of a person	*Kyllo v. U.S.* (2001) Reasonable expectation of privacy under *Katz* prevents warrantless police searches of a house with infrared heat detection device
Mapp v. Ohio (1961) The exclusionary rule is applied to the states	*Frazier v. Cupp* (1969) The police can use deception to secure a confession	*Rhode Island v. Innis* (1980) Police questioning that is intended, or should be known to result in, invoking incriminating statements require *Miranda* warnings	*Atwater v. City of Lago Vista* (2001) The standard of probable cause is the only standard for lawful arrest—motive of arrest by the police officer is not a factor in determining if an arrest was lawful

Whren v. U.S. (1996) Motive for a police stop is not part of Fourth Amendment analysis—a traffic violation in the presence of the officer establishes probable cause |

DEVELOPMENT OF MODERN CRIMINAL JUSTICE AND SUPREME COURT JURISPRUDENCE

DUE PROCESS REVOLUTION (1961–1968)	DECLINE OF THE REHABILITATION ERA (1968–1980)	SECOND PUNITIVE ERA (1980–2000)	POST-SECOND PUNITIVE ERA (2000–PRESENT)
Monroe v. Pape (1961) Police officers can be sued in federal court for violation of constitutional rights	*Chimel v. California* (1969) Police can search a person arrested and the immediate area where the arrest occurs without a warrant	*Rhode Island v. Innis* (1980) *Miranda* only applies in situations in which police create an environment conducive to coercion	*United States v. Ruiz* (2002) The Fifth and Sixth Amendments don't require federal prosecutors, before entering into a binding plea agreement with a criminal defendant, to disclose "impeachment information relating to any informants or other witnesses."
Robinson v. California (1962) The right against cruel and unusual punishment applied to the states	*In re Winship* (1970) All criminal convictions require beyond reasonable doubt	*Belton v. New York* (1981) The police may search the passenger side of the car when they arrest the occupant of the car and can search any container therein	*U.S. v. Patone* (2004) Failure to give a suspect *Miranda* warnings does not require suppression of the physical fruits of the suspect's unwarned but voluntary statements
Gideon v. Wainwright (1963) States must appoint counsel to indigent defendants in all felony cases	*North Carolina v. Alford* (1970) If a defendant is not subjected to coercion, a defendant can admit there is enough evidence to convict while asserting factual innocence and can refuse to admit to committing the crime as part of a plea agreement	*Berkemer v. McCarty* (1984) *Miranda* does not apply to traffic stop questioning	*Illinois v. Caballes* (2005)[85] A seizure (traffic stop), that results in the decision to issue a warning ticket to the driver, becomes unlawful when the time of the seizure is prolonged to have a police dog walk around the car to establish probable cause to search the car

(Continued)

DEVELOPMENT OF MODERN CRIMINAL JUSTICE AND SUPREME COURT JURISPRUDENCE

DUE PROCESS REVOLUTION (1961–1968)	DECLINE OF THE REHABILITATION ERA (1968–1980)	SECOND PUNITIVE ERA (1980–2000)	POST-SECOND PUNITIVE ERA (2000–PRESENT)
Downum v. United States (1963) Double jeopardy attaches when a jury is sworn	*Hill v. California* (1971) Probability, not certainty, is the touchstone of the Fourth Amendment, police reasonable but factual error makes arrest and search lawful	*New York v. Quarles* (1984) **Public Safety Exception** applies to *Miranda* warnings and incriminatory statements intentionally secured by police questioning to address a public danger are admissible and are not subject to the exclusionary rule	*U.S. v. Booker* (2005) The federal guidelines are to be treated as advisory not mandatory
Wong Sun v. U.S. (1963) Exclusionary rule does not apply to illegally seized evidence that is separated—attenuated—from the illegal act or the fruit of the illegal act	*U.S. v. White* (1971) Police don't need a warrant to place a bug on an informant to secure confession from defendant	*U.S. v. Leon* (1984) The **Good Faith Exception**—The exclusionary rule does not apply when evidence was obtained by officers acting in reasonable reliance that the search warrant established probable cause	*Hudson v. Michigan* (2006) The exclusionary rule should be used as a last resort—only when its deterrence benefits outweigh its substantial social costs; the substantial costs being letting the guilty go free and the amount of judicial time it takes to decide exclusionary cases
Escobedo v. Illinois (1964) A suspect in police custody has a right to an attorney when being questioned by the police and asked questions that could invoke an incriminatory response	*Bivens v. Six Unknown Agents* (1971) Federal law enforcement officers can be sued in federal court for violation of constitutional rights	*Massachusetts v. Sheppard* (1984) The Fourth Amendment exclusionary rule does not apply when police reasonably relay on judicial determination a warrant is valid	*Hudson v. Michigan* (2006) Exclusionary rule does not apply to evidence secured by police in violation of the knock-and-announce rule required by the Fourth Amendment

DEVELOPMENT OF MODERN CRIMINAL JUSTICE AND SUPREME COURT JURISPRUDENCE

DUE PROCESS REVOLUTION (1961–1968)	DECLINE OF THE REHABILITATION ERA (1968–1980)	SECOND PUNITIVE ERA (1980–2000)	POST-SECOND PUNITIVE ERA (2000–PRESENT)
Malloy v. Hogan (1964) Right against forced confessions applies to the states	*Adams v. Williams* (1972) Police can demand identification of individual during a Terry stop	*Nix v. Williams* (1984) Court adopts **Inevitable Discovery Exception** to the exclusionary rule and holds that if illegally seized evidence would have been found through lawful means, the exclusionary rule does not preclude use of evidence	*Kimbrough v. U.S.* (2007) The 100 to 1 ratio guidelines are to be treated as advisory not mandatory
Pointer v. Texas (1965) Right to cross-examine witnesses applies to the states	*Kirby v. Illinois* (1972) A show-up after being seized, but before the initiation of any adversary criminal proceeding (whether by way of formal charge, preliminary hearing, indictment, information, or arraignment), unlike the post-indictment confrontations involved in Gilbert (1967) and Wade (1967), is not at a "critical stage" of criminal prosecution at which the accused, as a matter of absolute right, is entitled to counsel	*U.S. v. Jacobsen* (1984) Fourth Amendment exclusion is attached to the unreasonableness of police action, not action of private individuals, thus police may use evidence secured by private invasions of individual liberty (privacy) as long as police did not orchestrate the invasion or search beyond the scope of the invasion	*Arizona v. Gant* (2009) Rejects the view that police can conduct a wholesale search of a car as a matter of right after an arrest is made of the owner of the car rather than as an exception to the warrant requirement

(Continued)

DEVELOPMENT OF MODERN CRIMINAL JUSTICE AND SUPREME COURT JURISPRUDENCE

DUE PROCESS REVOLUTION (1961–1968)	DECLINE OF THE REHABILITATION ERA (1968–1980)	SECOND PUNITIVE ERA (1980–2000)	POST-SECOND PUNITIVE ERA (2000–PRESENT)
Parker v. Gladded (1966) The right to an impartial jury applied to the states	*U.S. v. Matlock* (1973) When consent is given to the police to conduct a search any ambiguity regarding scope of the consent is given to the police	*Colorado v. Connelly* (1986) Coercive police activity is a necessary predicate to the finding that a confession is not voluntary, outside coercive factors don't invoke Fifth Amendment	*Arizona v. Gant* (2009) Search of car incident to arrest is limited to the possibility of securing evidence regarding the reason for arrest; *Arizona v. Johnson* (2009) Police may frisk passengers of stopped car if they have reasonable suspicion, they are armed
Miranda v. Arizona (1966) Police must warn the accused of the right to an attorney and to remain silent, evidence secured from him will be used in court, and if he can't afford an attorney one will be provided	*Schneckloth v. Bustamonte* (1973) Police are not required to inform a person they have a right to refuse a request to search	*Illinois v. Krull* (1987) The exclusionary rule does not apply to evidence obtained by police who acted in objectively reasonable reliance on a statute	*Herring v. U.S.* (2009) Court adopts **Mistake of Fact:** Existence of warrant—The Fourth Amendment exclusionary rule does not apply when evidence was obtained by officers acting in reasonable reliance that a warrant existed

DEVELOPMENT OF MODERN CRIMINAL JUSTICE AND SUPREME COURT JURISPRUDENCE

DUE PROCESS REVOLUTION (1961–1968)	DECLINE OF THE REHABILITATION ERA (1968–1980)	SECOND PUNITIVE ERA (1980–2000)	POST-SECOND PUNITIVE ERA (2000–PRESENT)
In Re Gault (1967) The protections of due process of law applies to juvenile court proceedings	*United States v. Robinson* (1973) Police may conduct a full search of a person arrested for weapons and/or evidence of the crime	*Maryland v. Garrison* (1987) Court adopts Good Faith Exception: **Good Faith Reasonable Mistake of Fact** and holds that exclusionary rule does not apply when the officer makes a reasonable mistake in executing a warrant in the wrong house	*District Attorney's Office v. Osborne* (2009) There is no freestanding Due Process right to a DNA test post-conviction to prove factual innocence
Berger v. New York (1967) Police must secure a warrant for wiretap	*Michigan v. Mosley* (1975) and *Oregon v. Mathiason* (1977) Police falsely telling the defendant they have evidence proving guilt does not make confession involuntary	*Arizona v. Hicks* (1987) and *Horton v. California* (1990) Court adopts **Plain View** exception to search warrant requirement	*Melendez-Diaz v. Massachusetts* (2009) Under the Sixth Amendment defendant has a right to subject lab technicians who conduct analysis on evidence presented in court to cross-examination rather than accept submission of lab results by sworn certificate
			Berghuis v. Thompkins (2010) Police can infer *Miranda* is waived when suspect is silent and for defendant to invoke *Miranda* defendant must be clear and unambiguous to force the police to stop questioning

(Continued)

DEVELOPMENT OF MODERN CRIMINAL JUSTICE AND SUPREME COURT JURISPRUDENCE

DUE PROCESS REVOLUTION (1961–1968)	DECLINE OF THE REHABILITATION ERA (1968–1980)	SECOND PUNITIVE ERA (1980–2000)	POST-SECOND PUNITIVE ERA (2000–PRESENT)
United States v. Wade (1967) Federal government cannot arrange a lineup without defense counsel being present	*Brown v. Illinois* (1975) Failure to give *Miranda* warnings do not per se make a confession involuntary; failure to give *Miranda* does not result in exclusion of physical evidence	*Murray v. U.S.* (1988) Court adopts **Independent Source Doctrine** exception to search warrant requirement and holds that unlawful evidence is admissible if an alternative legal source produces the same evidence	*Perry v. New Hampshire* (2012) When unnecessarily suggestive witness identification is not the result of improper law enforcement activity the of test reliability, the presence of counsel at post-indictment lineups, vigorous cross-examination, protective rules of evidence, and jury instructions on both the fallibility of memory in eyewitness identification and the requirement that guilt be proved beyond a reasonable doubt will suffice in meeting constitutional requirements of a fair trial
Klopfer v. North Carolina (1967) The right to a speedy trial applied to the states	*U.S. v. Miller* (1976) Reasonable expectation of privacy does not protect against warrantless searches of bank records	*California v. Greenwood* (1988) Reasonable expectation of privacy does not protect against warrantless searches of trash on public street	*Maryland v. King* (2013) Police may take a DNA sample for identification purposes after a felonious arrest

DEVELOPMENT OF MODERN CRIMINAL JUSTICE AND SUPREME COURT JURISPRUDENCE

DUE PROCESS REVOLUTION (1961–1968)	DECLINE OF THE REHABILITATION ERA (1968–1980)	SECOND PUNITIVE ERA (1980–2000)	POST-SECOND PUNITIVE ERA (2000–PRESENT)
Katz v. U.S. (1967) Fourth Amendment protection includes zone of reasonable expectation of privacy	*South Dakota v. Opperman* (1976) Police don't need a warrant to search an impounded car as long as the purpose of the search is not to secure evidence	*Illinois v. Perkins* (1990) Police officer posing as an inmate to secure confession is admissible when there is a lack of coercion	*Heien v. North Carolina* (2014) Court adopts Good Faith Exception: **Good Faith Reasonable Mistake of law:** the Fourth Amendment is not violated if a seizure occurs under officer mistaken reading of the law that authorized traffic stop
U.S. v. Wade (1967), *Gilbert v. California* (1967) and *Stovall v. Denno* (1967) The Due Process Clause of the Fourteenth Amendment and the Sixth Amendment *per se* requires a defense attorney to be present during a line-up regarding witness identification of a suspect after indictment and show-up identifications are subject to Due Process analysis. See *Kirby v. Illinois* (1972) regarding pre-critical stage right to counsel.	*Pennsylvania v. Mimms* (1977) Police can order driver out of car during a traffic stop to maintain police officer safety	*Maryland v. Buie* (1990) Police may search, without probable cause or reasonable suspicion, closets and other spaces immediately adjoining the place of arrest	*Riley v. California* (2014) Police need a warrant to search a phone seized incident to arrest

(Continued)

DEVELOPMENT OF MODERN CRIMINAL JUSTICE AND SUPREME COURT JURISPRUDENCE

DUE PROCESS REVOLUTION (1961–1968)	DECLINE OF THE REHABILITATION ERA (1968–1980)	SECOND PUNITIVE ERA (1980–2000)	POST-SECOND PUNITIVE ERA (2000–PRESENT)
Benton v. Maryland (1968) The right against double jeopardy applies to the states	*Manson v. Brathwaite* (1977) The Due Process Clause of the Fourteenth Amendment does not compel a per se rule of exclusion of witness identification evidence that is unnecessarily suggestive; but rather such cases are subjected to totality of the circumstanes and reliability to determine admissibility	*Arizona v. Fulminante* (1991) Court adopts **Harmless Error Rule** and adopts rule that a conviction with illegal evidence can be sustained if conviction would have occurred if evidence was not used	*Utah v. Strieff* (2016) Evidence secured incident to arrest based on a stop found not to be justified by RAS or probable cause is attenuated by the presence of a lawful warrant
Duncan v. Louisiana (1968) Right to a jury trial for felonies applies to the states	*U.S. v. Martin* (1977) A judgment of acquittal can not be appealed when a new trial would be the result of a successful appeal by the government; *Lee v. United States* (1977) A new trial resulting from a court ordered dismissal of an indictment at the request of the defendant is not barred by the double jeopardy	*California v. Hodari* (1991) A person has been "seized" within the meaning of the Fourth Amendment only if, in view of all the circumstances surrounding the incident, a reasonable person would have believed that he was not free to leave or walk away and complied by police command not to move	*Birchfield v. North Dakota* (2016) The search incident to arrest doctrine applies to a breath test but it does not justify the warrantless taking of a blood sample in drunk driving case

DEVELOPMENT OF MODERN CRIMINAL JUSTICE AND SUPREME COURT JURISPRUDENCE

DUE PROCESS REVOLUTION (1961–1968)	DECLINE OF THE REHABILITATION ERA (1968–1980)	SECOND PUNITIVE ERA (1980–2000)	POST-SECOND PUNITIVE ERA (2000–PRESENT)
	U.S. v. Scott (1978) A new trial after defendant secured a mistrial or termination of trial is not prohibited under double jeopardy; but a prosecution provoked mistrial does prevent a new trial (*U.S. v. Dinitz*, 1976) *Crist v. Bretz* (1978) and the double jeopardy rule attaches when a jury is sworn applies to the states through Fifth and Fourteenth Amendments	*Florida v. Bostick* (1991) The Fourth Amendment right regarding unreasonable seizure, when the person is on a bus or plane or in a train, is whether a reasonable person under the totality of the circumstances would feel free to terminate the encounter and be left alone	*Carpenter v. United States* (2018) Police need a warrant to secure cell-site location information from phone company and *Smith* and *Miller* do not cover cell phone location records
	Franks v. Delaware (1978) A defendant has right to an evidentiary hearing when false statements are knowingly and intentionally, or with reckless disregard for the truth, are included in a warrant affidavit, and the search warrant must be voided and the fruits of the search excluded if probable cause is lacking when the false evidence is excluded from the warrant application	*County of Riverside v. McLaughlin* (1991) The Fourth Amendment reasonableness requirement requires a judicial determination of probable cause of an arrest within 48 hours of arrest and the 48 hours starts from arrest and issues of case processing or weekends does not make detention longer than 48 hours reasonable	*Collins v. Virginia* (2018) Automobile exception to car searches without a warrant does not apply when car is parked in the curtilage of the house

(Continued)

DEVELOPMENT OF MODERN CRIMINAL JUSTICE AND SUPREME COURT JURISPRUDENCE

DUE PROCESS REVOLUTION (1961–1968)	DECLINE OF THE REHABILITATION ERA (1968–1980)	SECOND PUNITIVE ERA (1980–2000)	POST-SECOND PUNITIVE ERA (2000–PRESENT)
	Smith v. Maryland (1979) Reasonable expectation of privacy does not protect against warrantless searches of phone call billing records (including phone numbers dialed)	*United States v. Williams* (1992) There is no constitutional requirement that the government disclose exculpatory evidence to the grand jury	*Nieves v. Bartlett* (2018) Police who make an arrest with probable cause as a matter of law are immune from a First Amendment retaliatory arrest civil liability claim
	U.S. v. Mendenhall (1980)[86] A person is not seized when police ask permission to speak to a person or to search a person or to search a person if force is not used to establish compliance and the Fourth Amendment does not exclude evidence secured through a consensual search	*Minnesota v. Dickerson* (1993) When the protective search goes beyond what is necessary to determine if the suspect is armed, it is no longer valid under *Terry* and its fruits will be suppressed, the Court rejected application of plain view during a stop and frisk situation in which the officer conducts a search and "feels" an object, not knowing what it is, and then enters the pocket of a seized suspect to retrieve the object to inspect it	*Timbs v. Indiana* (2019) The Eighth Amendment prohibition against excessive fines, like cruel and unusual punishment and excessive bail, including asset civil forfeiture applies to the states through Fourteenth Amendment Due Process Clause

DEVELOPMENT OF MODERN CRIMINAL JUSTICE AND SUPREME COURT JURISPRUDENCE

DUE PROCESS REVOLUTION (1961–1968)	DECLINE OF THE REHABILITATION ERA (1968–1980)	SECOND PUNITIVE ERA (1980–2000)	POST-SECOND PUNITIVE ERA (2000–PRESENT)
		Thompson v. Keohone (1995) Miranda is required only when a person is in "custody" which is defined as being placed in an environment analogous to arrest or police interrogation in a police station	*Gamble v. United States* (2019) The double jeopardy right only protects against being twice put in jeopardy for the same offense by the same sovereign, and the duel sovereignty doctrine allows separate prosecutions by federal and state governments because they are *per se* two different sovereigns enforcing two different laws and prosecuting two different offenses
		Maryland v. Wilson (1997)[87] Police can order passengers out of a car during a traffic stop to preserve police safety	*Madison v. Alabama* (2019) The Eighth Amendment allows for the execution of person who because of mental illness no longer remembers the crime or suffers from psychotic delusions as long as the person has the ability to understand why he is being executed

(Continued)

DEVELOPMENT OF MODERN CRIMINAL JUSTICE AND SUPREME COURT JURISPRUDENCE

DUE PROCESS REVOLUTION (1961–1968)	DECLINE OF THE REHABILITATION ERA (1968–1980)	SECOND PUNITIVE ERA (1980–2000)	POST-SECOND PUNITIVE ERA (2000–PRESENT)
		Knowles v. Iowa (1998)[88] A Police officer may not conduct a search incident to arrest during a traffic stop for a traffic violation when the officer issues a traffic citation and declines to make an arrest for the traffic violation	*Mitchell v. Wisconsin* (2019) In DUI situations the court affirmed that a breath test, but not a blood test, can be taken incident to a DUI arrest, and held that an officer may secure blood from a driver without a warrant (1) if the facts of the specific case meet exigent circumstances or (2) if the arrested DUI driver is unconscious, a blood test can be taken under implied consent laws and generally under the rule a warrant is not needed to take blood from an unconscious suspect who can't blow into a breathalyzer[89]

DEVELOPMENT OF MODERN CRIMINAL JUSTICE AND SUPREME COURT JURISPRUDENCE

DUE PROCESS REVOLUTION (1961–1968)	DECLINE OF THE REHABILITATION ERA (1968–1980)	SECOND PUNITIVE ERA (1980–2000)	POST-SECOND PUNITIVE ERA (2000–PRESENT)
		Wyoming v. Houghton (1999) Police with probable cause to search a car may search the belongings of the passengers in the car if they are capable of concealing the object of the search and police require reasonable suspicion to frisk passengers in a car during a traffic stop—*Arizona v. Johnson* (2009)—and police require probable cause to search passengers in a car—*Knowles v. Iowa* (1998)	*Flowers v. Mississippi* (2019)[90] The court affirmed the *Batson v. Kentucky* (1986) prohibition on using peremptory strikes to remove potential black jurors and held a *Batson* claim can be established by the state's pattern of striking black prospective jurors as well as by the striking of a specific juror
		Dickerson v. United States (2000)[91] *Miranda* is a constitutional decision and the *Miranda* warnings can't be substituted by a federal statute	*Rehaif v. United States* (2019) In a prosecution under federal illegal gun possession 18 USC §922(g) and §924(a)(2), the Government must prove both that the defendant knew he possessed a firearm and that he knew he was legally barred from possessing a firearm

(Continued)

DEVELOPMENT OF MODERN CRIMINAL JUSTICE AND SUPREME COURT JURISPRUDENCE

DUE PROCESS REVOLUTION (1961–1968)	DECLINE OF THE REHABILITATION ERA (1968–1980)	SECOND PUNITIVE ERA (1980–2000)	POST-SECOND PUNITIVE ERA (2000–PRESENT)
			United States v. Davis (2019) Title 18 USC §924(c)(3)(B), which provides enhanced penalties for using a firearm during a "crime of violence," is unconstitutionally vague. See also *Johnson v. United States* (2015) 18 USC §924(e)(2)(B)—Armed Career Criminal Act of 1984—which provides enhanced penalties for three or more previous convictions for a "violent felony" is unconstitutionally vague
			United States v. Haymond (2019) The Fifth and Sixth Amendments require a defendant to be found guilty by a jury before a mandatory minimum sentence can be imposed for actions (crimes) that violate conditions for supervised release

The Court has adopted the view that motive, even racial prejudice, is not part of Fourth Amendment analysis. While the Court held in *Oyler v. Boles* (1962) that the Constitution prohibits selective enforcement based on race, the Court held in *Whren v. U.S.* (1996) that the remedy for discriminatory application of traffic laws or selective prosecution of criminal laws in general—*U.S. v. Armstrong* (1996)—is the equal protection clause of the Fifth and Fourteenth Amendments not the Fourth and the exclusionary rule. This is why the Court has rejected any application of bad faith or subjective analysis to whether police actions were reasonable. Thus, pretext stops on the basis of race is of no consequence to whether the police had conducted a lawful stop. Racial bias with objective RAS or probable cause will make the stop lawful.

In 1981 the Court held in *Steagald v. United States* that a search of home for a suspect—in which the police had an arrest warrant—but not a search warrant for the home and the owner of the home was a different person than the person wanted, was a violation of the Fourth Amendment. The Court held that "the Fourth Amendment has drawn a firm line at the entrance to the house. Absent exigent circumstances, that threshold may not reasonably be crossed without a warrant." While the Court affirmed this principle in *Florida v. Jardines* (2013) holding that the home is first among equals in protection by the Fourth Amendment and searches of a home requires a warrant and it affirmed in *Collins v. Virginia* (2018) that a search of the home, the curtilage of the home, and the property—including a car—on the curtilage without a search warrant is presumptively unreasonable; during the decline of the rehabilitative era and the rise of the second punitive era the Court made clear that the warrant clause is decoupled from probable cause for search and seizure outside of the home.

This decoupling of the warrant requirement from arrest and searches dating back to *Terry v. Ohio* (1968) was affirmed in *United States v. Robinson* (1973) (a traffic violation arrest is not rendered invalid by the fact that the initial stop was a mere pretext for a narcotics search and that a lawful post-arrest search of the person is not be rendered invalid by the fact that it was not motivated by the officer safety concern that justifies warrantless searches), *Whren v. United States* (1996) ("the decision to stop an automobile is reasonable where the police have probable cause to believe that a traffic violation has occurred. ... [I]n principle every Fourth Amendment case ... turns upon a 'reasonableness' [balancing] determination ... With rare exceptions ... the result of that balancing is not in doubt where the search or seizure is based upon probable cause ... For the run-of-the-mill case ... we think there is no realistic alternative to the traditional common-law rule that probable cause justifies a search and seizure."),[92] and *Atwater v. City of Lago Vista* (2001) ("we confirm today what our prior cases have intimated: the standard of probable cause applies to all arrests ... If an officer has probable cause to believe that an individual has committed even a very minor criminal offense in his presence, he may, without violating the Fourth Amendment, arrest the offender"). The Court summarized the decoupling of warrants from seizures in *Illinois v. McArthur* (2001) as follows:

> The Fourth Amendment says that the "right of the people to be secure in their persons, houses, papers, and effects, against unreasonable searches and seizures, shall not be violated." Its "central requirement" is one of reasonableness. See *Texas v. Brown,* 460 U. S. 730, 739 (1983). In order to enforce that requirement, this Court has interpreted the Amendment as establishing rules and presumptions designed to control conduct of law enforcement officers that may significantly intrude upon privacy interests. **Sometimes those rules require warrants.** We have said, for example, that in "the ordinary case," seizures of personal property are "unreasonable within the meaning of the Fourth Amendment," without more, "unless ... accomplished pursuant to a judicial warrant," issued by a neutral magistrate after finding probable cause. *United States v. Place,* 462 U. S. 696, 701 (1983).

We nonetheless have made it clear that there are exceptions to the warrant requirement. When faced with special law enforcement needs, diminished expectations of privacy, minimal intrusions, or the like, the Court has found that certain general, or individual, circumstances may render a warrantless search or seizure reasonable.

...

In the circumstances of the case before us [in which police officers, with probable cause believed that McArthur had hidden marijuana in his home, and as such prevented him from entering the home unaccompanied by an officer for about two hours while they obtained a search warrant and found evidence of marijuana upon entry with the warrant], we cannot say that the warrantless seizure was *per se* unreasonable. It involves a plausible claim of specially pressing or urgent law enforcement need, i.e., "exigent circumstances."[93]

While search of a home presumes the necessity of warrant, subject to exceptions, search of one's own person enjoys less protection. Search of a person is regulated by reasonableness which can be established by exigent circumstances, officer safety (*Terry* Stop and Frisk) and incident to arrest. Incident to arrest allows for a search when probable cause for arrest is established. Exigent circumstances allow the search a person without a warrant if (1) there is a compelling need and (2) there is no time to secure the warrant based on that need. The Court held in *Mitchell v. Wisconsin* (2019) that exigent circumstances occur when the facts of the case are such that, "the officer there could reasonably have believed that he was confronted with an emergency, in which the delay necessary to obtain a warrant, under the circumstances, threatened the destruction of evidence."[94] Citing *Schmerber v. California* (1966) the court held that "exigency exists when (1) BAC [Blood Alcohol Concentration] evidence is dissipating [which creates a compelling need for official action] and (2) [there is no time to secure a warrant in the face of that need because of] some other factor creates pressing health, safety, or law enforcement needs that would take priority over a warrant application."[95] The Court's jurisprudence has made clear, for example see *Terry v. Ohio* (1968), *Brigham City v. Stuart* (2006) and *Kentucky v. King* (2011), that the regulating principle of the Fourth Amendment regarding searches is not the word "warrant" or "probable cause" but the word "unreasonable" and as such the inconvenience of securing a warrant can be displaced by the need of law enforcement under emergency circumstances. The Court has been very liberal in defining what circumstances define an emergency not worthy of Fourth Amendment warrant protection.

In *Steagald* the Court held, that the police need a search warrant to enter the home of a third party regardless of having an arrest warrant for the wanted person because the purpose of the Fourth Amendment is to force the police to have their view of probable cause judged by a neutral party—a magistrate—before entering the home of person without consent. Why? Because "the [Fourth] Amendment is designed to prevent, not simply to redress, unlawful police action." The Court held, "participation of a detached magistrate in the probable-cause determination is an essential element of a reasonable search or seizure." By the middle 1980s this principle was reduced to only apply to home searches and exclusion of evidence was functionally abandoned in all cases except home searches without warrants, exigent circumstances, or consent.

The crime control model focuses on the inconveniences of securing a warrant, the time it takes to write up probable cause affidavits, the time to find a magistrate to sign off on the warrant, and the time it takes for the magistrate to read the supporting documents.[96] The inconvenience of making the police comply with securing a warrant from a neutral judge have led to the Court determination that the focus of the protection of the Fourth is not the warrant requirement but analysis of the reasonableness of police actions in the specific case. This decoupling of the warrant requirement from probable cause searches has made police pursuit of evidence for conviction much easier. Which is the point of the crime control model. It was the avoidance of this is decoupling in the 1960s that put the Court in a position of distain by social conservatives and Republicans for decades.

While social conservatives' distain for the Court dated back to its support for the FDR agenda, along with *Brown v. Board of Education* (1954), the flag and integration cases,[97] and the second red scare anti-communist cases during the cold war;[98] *Mapp v. Ohio* was the beginning of the Republican Party narrative against the Court. Distain for the exclusionary rule would be a staple of Republican election political rhetoric from Nixon through Reagan. From Goldwater to George H.W. Bush, every Republican president would secure votes, in part, by attacking the Court and Democrats as being soft on crime; in addition to using the Court as a foil for election votes in opposition to *Roe v. Wade*, integration, bussing, and affirmative action. With the elections of Nixon (four justices),[99] Ford (one justice),[100] Reagan (four justices),[101] and Bush 41 (two justices),[102] the second punitive era had secured Supreme Court justices that limited the lasting impact of the due process revolution.

Solidified in 1984 with the appointments of Nixon, Ford, and Reagan's first appointee the now crime control model Court changed the focus of criminal justice jurisprudence from protection of the individual from government power (the police) to the protection of society from crime with the police securing the benefit of legal doubt. When the Court shifted its attention to race and criminal justice, the Court made clear *McCleskey v. Kemp* (1987) that in regard to race and prosecutorial decisions and judicial imposition of the death penalty, the history of racism is not a legal factor in determining just imposition of the death penalty in a particular case. The Court held that evidence of racial disparities in the imposition of the death penalty based on the race of the victim and offender do not make criminal sentences unconstitutional.

> [A]bsent a showing that the Georgia capital punishment system operates in an arbitrary and capricious manner, McCleskey cannot prove a constitutional violation by

demonstrating that other defendants who may be similarly situated did *not* receive the death penalty.

...

There is, of course, some risk of racial prejudice influencing a jury's decision in a criminal case. There are similar risks that other kinds of prejudice will influence other criminal trials. The question is at what point that risk becomes constitutionally unacceptable ...

...

[I]t is the jury that is a criminal defendant's fundamental protection of life and liberty against race or color prejudice. ... The capital sentencing decision requires the individual jurors to focus their collective judgment on the unique characteristics of a particular criminal defendant. It is not surprising that such collective judgments often are difficult to explain. But the inherent lack of predictability of jury decisions does not justify their condemnation.

...

At most, the Baldus study indicates a discrepancy that appears to correlate with **race**. Apparent **disparities in sentencing are an inevitable part of our criminal justice system.**

...

... we hold that the Baldus study does not demonstrate a constitutionally significant risk of racial bias affecting the Georgia capital sentencing process.

...

Where the discretion that is fundamental to our criminal process is involved, we decline to assume that what is unexplained is invidious. ...

...

The Constitution does not require that a State eliminate any demonstrable disparity that correlates with a potentially irrelevant factor [race of victim or defendant]

to operate a criminal justice system that includes capital
punishment.

The Court was not moved, as the dissents by Justices Blackmun
and Brennan were, that the Baldus study showed that "within the
group of defendants who are convicted of killing white persons
and are thereby more likely to receive a death sentence, black defendants are more likely than white defendants to be sentenced to
death." The Court concluded that this anomaly did not rise to make
Georgia's death penalty process unconstitutional under the equal
protection or due process clauses of the Fourteenth Amendment.
The Court held that racial discrimination evidence in death penalty
cases only establishes a constitutional violation when it's proved in
a specific case, not when racial discrimination is proved in general
death penalty outcomes through the use of statistics.

By 2013 the Court had become more amenable to the process
of reviewing appeals from death penalty imposition by holding in
McQuiggin v. Perkins that the one year statute of limitations on the
ability to file a federal habeas petition under the *Antiterrorism and
Effective Death Penalty Act of 1996*, 28 U. S. C. §2244(d)(1), was
not a bar to appeals in which actual innocence was asserted. The
Court held that because a habeas petition is an equity pleading (a
plea seeking reprieve in the face of an outcome under the law that
is a miscarriage of justice), "actual innocence, if proved, serves as a
gateway through which a petitioner may pass whether the impedi-
ment is a procedural bar, as it was in *Schlup* [*v. Delo* (1995)] and
House [*v. Bell* (2006)], or, as in this case, expiration of the statute
of limitations." An actual innocence habeas petition asserts that
evidence submitted by the convicted defendant is significant enough
to convince the court, "that in light of the new evidence, no juror,
acting reasonably, would have voted to find him guilty beyond a reasonable doubt." But the Court held that failure to meet the statutory
delay is a factor in determining the quality of the evidence asserted
to prove actual innocence. There must be an equity justification for
failure to meet the statute of limitations. The court further limited

the impact of the case by affirming that the actual innocence, "standard is demanding. The gateway should open only when a petition presents evidence of innocence so strong that a court cannot have confidence in the outcome of the trial unless the court is also satisfied that the trial was free of non-harmless constitutional error." Harmless error is an error in the trial proceeding, the admission of evidence that shouldn't have been for example, but the error in light of the entire trial does not make a difference to the outcome. In the case of a habeas claim of actual innocence the Court held that habeas can only be granted if the evidence is such that it brings doubt to outcome of the conviction or in cases of asserted trial error, the error asserted by the petitioner must be a constitutional level error that creates doubt over the entire proceeding and result.

The second punitive era not only involved legislative federalization of crime policy in 1984 and 1994 under Reagan and Clinton, but the judicial appointments by four Republican presidents who established crime control model jurisprudence in the Fourth, Fifth, Sixth, Eighth, and Fourteenth Amendment case law regarding police use of force, police search and seizure, general trial procedures and criminal sentencing. One lesson learned from this, presidential elections matter and have consequences in the meaning and application of justice. A lesson conservatives and Republican learned in 1954 and never forgot in their political narrative. A lesson progressives and Democrats have only recently begun to consider.

chapter eight

Holder v. Sessions

A Contemporary Policy Debate on Crime and the Purpose of the Criminal Justice System

I t is a truism in the study of criminal justice, political science, and social psychology that blacks and whites perceive the criminal justice system, in general, and police interactions with blacks, specifically, differently. Ever since the question has been asked, all polling shows blacks are more suspicious and distrusting of the criminal justice system and whether it treats them fairly. In a 2019 survey conducted by the Pew Research Center, 87 percent of blacks said that blacks are treated less fairly than whites by the criminal justice system while only 61 percent of whites agreed. When asked if blacks are treated less fairly by the police, 87 percent of blacks vs. 61 percent of whites agreed.[1] Blacks in general "were much less likely than whites to say that police in their community do an excellent or good job using the right amount of force in each situation (33% vs. 75%), treating racial and ethnic groups equally (35% vs. 75%) and holding officers accountable when misconduct occurs (31% vs. 70%). Blacks were also substantially less likely than whites to say their local police do an excellent or good job at protecting people from crime (48% vs. 78%)."[2] This attitude divergence was also found among police. A recent pew survey found, "Black officers were about twice as likely as white officers (57% vs. 27%) to say that high-profile deaths of black people during encounters with police were signs of a broader problem, not isolated incidents."[3] In a recent CBS News Poll (September 21–24, 2017) when asked, "In general, do you think the criminal justice system in the United States is biased in favor of blacks, or is it biased against blacks, or does it generally give blacks fair treatment?" 84 percent of blacks said biased against blacks while only 40 percent of whites said so. While 42 percent of whites said the system was fair to blacks only 5 percent of blacks said it was fair to them.[4]

These differences are reflected in American politics. In a recent Quinnipiac University Poll (April 6–9, 2018) 84 percent of Republicans said they approved when asked, "Do you approve or disapprove of the way the police in the United States are doing their job?" while only 49 percent of Democrats approved. When asked, "Do you think the police in the United States are generally tougher on whites than on blacks, tougher on blacks than on whites, or do the police treat them both the same?" only 15 percent of Republicans said tougher on blacks than on whites, while 77 percent of Democrats said tougher on blacks than on whites. The poll found 77 percent of Republicans said the police treat them both the same while only 18 percent said the same. When it came to police use of force the divergence continued. When asked, "When faced with a possible criminal situation, do you think police in the United States are more likely to shoot someone who is black, more likely to shoot someone who is white, or do you think police are equally likely to shoot someone of either race?" 70 percent of the Democrats said the police are more likely to shoot blacks while only 10 percent of the Republicans thought so. What was interesting about this question is neither party thought whites were more likely to be shot. Republicans, 83 percent, said police are equally likely to shoot someone of either race while only 25 percent of Democrats said either. The poll found that Republicans are less afraid of the police than Democrats. When asked, "Is being the victim of police brutality something you personally worry about, or not?" only 9 percent of Republicans worried, compared to 31 percent of Democrats.[5]

Polls by ABC News/*Washington Post* Poll (December 11–14, 2014), CBS News Poll (December 6–9, 2014), NBC News/Marist Poll (December 4–5, 2014) and ABC News/Washington Post Poll (July 18–21, 2013) all showed similar results. These divergent views also influence how people view specific criminal justice cases. For example, in Pew Research Center poll (July 17–21, 2013) when asked, "As you may know, a jury found George Zimmerman not guilty in the death of Florida teen Trayvon Martin. Are you satisfied or dissatisfied with this verdict?" 49 percent of whites were satisfied while only 5 percent of blacks were. Blacks were not satisfied, 86 percent, compared to 30 percent of whites.[6] The USA Today/Gallup Poll (April 2–4, 2012) found similar results in that 72 percent of blacks said Zimmerman was guilty, and 30 percent of whites thought so. In the same poll, 85 percent of blacks thought race was a factor in the shooting while 56 percent of whites thought so.[7] In a Gallup Poll (July 16–21, 2013), when asked, "As you may know, a jury recently found George Zimmerman not guilty of second degree murder or manslaughter in the death of Trayvon Martin. From what you know about the case, do you think the verdict was right or wrong?" 54 percent of whites said the verdict was right with only 7 percent of blacks saying so. The poll showed 85 percent of blacks said the verdict was wrong with 30 percent of whites saying so. In the CNN/ORC Poll (April 13–15, 2012) 14 percent of whites thought he should not have been arrested in the first place.[8]

It is also a truism that blacks are disproportionately accounted for throughout each stage of the criminal justice system. The dispute is not whether blacks suffer bias in the system, but how and why.[9] Answers to those questions translate into policy and before that, political elections of those who make policy. The rest of this chapter engages in one aspect of the disproportionate incarceration of blacks, Justice Department policy on charging decisions. As discussed in Chapter 7 Attorney General Reno established the policy that prosecutors were to use the three-strikes law and enhanced penalties to reduce local street crime and General Ashcroft and Deputy Attorney General Comey established the policy that prosecutors were to charge the most serious offense which was defined as the charge that carried the most serious sanction available under the sentencing guidelines.

When President Obama was elected in 2008 and Eric Holder took office as Attorney General on February 3, 2009, one of the policy issues that both sought to address was the disproportionate incarceration of blacks. In 2016, Donald Trump was elected president and his appointment to the office of Attorney General, Jefferson Beauregard Sessions, was not concerned about the incarceration of blacks. The differing views of Attorneys General Holder and Sessions regarding their political narratives on the purpose of the criminal justice system, the fear of rising crime, the disproportionate incarceration of blacks, and policy initiatives to address the problem are presented in their own words. Significant quoting of op-ed and speeches made by Generals Holder and Sessions are made to let each perspective be understood in context. One of the policy determinations made by General Holder was to reverse the prosecution memos of Ashcroft and Comey replacing them with a policy reflective of the "individual assessment" in the October 1993 memo under Reno and the previous memos by Generals Civiletti and Thornburgh. The policy focus and impact of the Holder policy also sought to mitigate the impact and purpose of the Reno March 1995 memo.

As discussed earlier, Republicans and whites view the criminal justice system differently than Democrats and blacks. Voting patterns tend to follow these divergent views. Elections have consequences and the election of Obama in 2008 had consequences to how federal prosecutors made decisions regarding drug offenses. The election of Trump in 2016, as supposed to Hillary Clinton, also has had consequences to how the federal criminal justice system is now dealing with drug crimes.

Attorney General Holder and Sessions: Three Strikes and Minimum Mandatory Sentencing in Prosecutorial Charging

On February 9, 2017, Jefferson Beauregard Sessions III assumed the office of the U.S. Attorney General under President Trump. Sessions was the U.S. Senator from Alabama before being nominated by Trump. Sessions was a Reagan crime control acolyte, having served as U.S. Attorney of Alabama from 1981 to 1993 and then served as U.S. Senator from Alabama in the latter end of the golden age of the second punitive era into the post-second punitive era from 1997 to 2017. Sessions was a social conservative senator that believed in the traditional Republican use of law and order. On May 10, 2017, he reversed Justice Department policy on the use of the three-strikes and minimum mandatory sentencing in prosecutorial charging decisions that reverted to the Clinton and Bush 43 Administration policies and revoked the policy of the Obama Administration.

On August 12, 2013, Attorney General Holder, reversed the Clinton Administration policy on charging offenders under the three-strikes legislation. The *Memorandum to United States Attorneys and Assistant Attorney General Criminal Division*[10] General Holder announced the change was based on the assertion that "mandatory minimum and recidivist enhancement statutes have resulted in unduly harsh sentences and perceived or actual disparities that do not reflect our Principles of Federal Prosecution. Long sentences for low-level, non-violent drug offenses do not promote public safety, deterrence, and rehabilitation." He ordered his U.S. attorneys

> to *conduct an individualized assessment* of the extent to which charges fit the specific circumstances of the case, are consistent with the purpose of the federal criminal code, and maximize the impact of federal resources on

crime. When making these individualized assessments, *prosecutors must take into account* numerous factors, such as *the defendant's conduct and criminal history* and the circumstances relating to the commission of the offense, the needs of the communities we serve, and federal resources and priorities. Now that our charging decisions also affect when a defendant is subject to a mandatory minimum sentence, prosecutors must evaluate these factors in an equally thoughtful and reasoned manner.

It is with full consideration of these factors that we now refine our charging policy regarding mandatory minimums for certain nonviolent, low-level drug offenders. We must ensure that our most *severe mandatory minimum penalties are reserved for serious, high-level, or violent drug traffickers.*

The policy changes required prosecutors to charge and/or make recommendations for sentencing utilizing the full impact of three strikes only for certain types of offenders. The new policy sought to focus federal prosecution and sanctions on the more serious and violent offenders, not low-level nonviolent first-time offenders. This is how Holder sought to mitigate the Reno March 1995 policy. The severity of federal law was to be applied only to violent offenders, not all offenders.

> **Certain Mandatory Minimum Sentencing Statutes Based on Drug Quantity:** Prosecutors should continue to ascertain whether a defendant is eligible for any statutory mandatory minimum statute or enhancement. However, in cases involving the applicability of Title 21 mandatory minimum sentences based on drug type and quantity, *prosecutors should decline to charge the quantity necessary to trigger a mandatory minimum sentence if the defendant meets each of the following criteria*:

- The defendant's relevant *conduct does not involve the use of violence,* the credible threat of violence, the possession of a weapon, the trafficking of drugs to or with minors, or the death or serious bodily injury of any person;

- The *defendant is not an organizer, leader, manager, or supervisor* of others within a criminal organization;

- The defendant *does not have significant ties to large-scale drug trafficking* organizations, gangs, or cartels; and

- The defendant *does not have a significant criminal history.* A significant criminal history will normally be evidenced by three or more criminal history points but may involve fewer or greater depending on the nature of any prior convictions.

Timing and Plea Agreements: If information sufficient to determine that *a defendant meets the aforementioned criteria* is available at the time initial charges are filed, *prosecutors should decline to pursue charges triggering a mandatory minimum sentence.* ... If the defendant ultimately meets the criteria, prosecutors should pursue a disposition that does not require a Title 21 mandatory minimum sentence. For example, a prosecutor could ask the grand jury to supersede the indictment with charges that do not trigger the mandatory minimum, or a defendant could plead guilty to a lesser included offense, or waive indictment and plead guilty to a superseding information that does not charge the quantity necessary to trigger the mandatory minimum.

Advocacy at Sentencing: ... In cases where the properly calculated guideline range meets or exceeds the mandatory minimum, prosecutors should consider whether a below-guidelines sentence is sufficient to satisfy the purposes of sentencing as set forth in 18 U.S.C. § 3553(a). In determining the appropriate sentence to recommend to the Court, prosecutors should consider whether the defendant truthfully and in a timely way provided to the Government all information the defendant has concerning the offense or offenses that were part of the same course of conduct, common scheme, or plan.

Recidivist Enhancements: Prosecutors should decline to file information pursuant to 21 U.S.C. § 851 unless the defendant is involved in conduct that makes the case appropriate for severe sanctions. When determining whether an enhancement is appropriate, prosecutors should consider the following factors:

- Whether the defendant was an organizer, leader, manager, or supervisor of others within a criminal organization;

- Whether the defendant was involved in the use or threat of violence in connection with the offense;

- The nature of the defendant's criminal history, including any prior history of violent conduct or recent prior convictions for serious offenses;

- Whether the defendant has significant ties to large-scale drug trafficking organizations, gangs, or cartels;

- Whether the filing would create a gross sentencing disparity with equally or more culpable codefendants; and

- Other case-specific aggravating or mitigating factors.

In keeping with current policy, prosecutors are reminded that all charging decisions must be reviewed by a supervisory attorney to ensure adherence to the Principles of Federal Prosecution, the guidance provided by my May 19, 2010, memorandum, and the policy outlined in this memorandum.

The goal of the new policy was to limit the impact of sentencing that increased the federal prison population and the length of time people spent incarcerated.

Holder would later defend these policies in a *New York Times* op-ed[11] during the 2016 presidential election. After noting that America has 5 percent of the world's population but accounts for 22 percent of its known prison population and that blacks receive 20 percent longer prison sentences than their white counterparts accounting for other sentencing factors, he agreed that personal responsibility should be required of defendants but "we must also acknowledge that there is racial bias in the criminal justice system. The disparity in incarceration rates has bred distrust, alienating communities of color from those who serve valiantly in law enforcement." It was from this perspective that Holder issued policies to change prosecutions for drug cases. He wrote that he

> established the Smart on Crime initiative to reduce draconian mandatory minimum sentencing for low-level drug offenses and encourage more investment in rehabilitation programs to tackle recidivism.
>
> The preliminary results are very encouraging. Over the last two years, federal prosecutors went from seeking a mandatory minimum penalty for drug trafficking in two-thirds of cases to doing so in less than half of them—the lowest rate on record. The initiative may not be solely responsible, but 2014 saw the first consecutive drop in the federal prison population in more than three decades, coinciding with a falling crime rate.
>
> Those who argue that without the hammer of a mandatory minimum sentence defendants won't cooperate are wrong—in fact, the rate of cooperation held steady under the initiative, and the rate of guilty pleas remained constant. The system remained effective and became fairer. Reform has not made us less safe.

Holder readily admitted that the goal of criminal justice is safety, but he asserted that how it's done is equally important. Western legal tradition asserts, "A long line of cases shows that it is not merely of some importance but is of fundamental importance that justice should not only be done, but should manifestly and undoubtedly be seen to be done."[12] In the American context of crime and race, Holder wrote,

> There is still a disparity in sentencing for offenses relating to crack and powder cocaine, chemically identical substances. Given the policy's differential racial impact, which erodes confidence in the justice system, this disparity must go. In the light of recent events, we can't afford criminal justice policies that reduce the already fragile trust between minority communities and law enforcement agencies.

One of the classical principles justice asserts that, "nothing is to be done which creates even a suspicion that there has been an improper interference with the course of justice"[13] and racially disparate laws based on discrimination are such improper interferences with the course of justice.

A year after issuing the sentencing memo, Holder gave a speech at Georgetown University Law Center[14] in which he articulated the due process model of criminal justice.

> Today, we gather in recognition of the fact that, although our laws and procedures must be continually updated, our commitment to the cause of justice must remain constant. From its earliest days, our Republic has been bound together by its extraordinary legal system, and by the enduring values that define it. These values—of equality, opportunity, and justice under law—were first codified in our founding documents.
> ....
> [A] system that deters and punishes crime, keeps us safe, and ensures that those who pay their debts have the

chance to become productive citizens. Most importantly, it's about answering fundamental questions—about fairness and equality—that determine who we are, and who we aspire to be, not only as a nation, but as a people—a people resolved to move forward together, and committed to implementing criminal justice policies that work for everyone in this country.

....

Last August, I announced a new "Smart on Crime" initiative—based on the results of this review—that's already allowing the Justice Department to strengthen the federal system; to increase our emphasis on proven diversion, rehabilitation, and reentry programs; and to reduce unnecessary collateral consequences for those seeking to rejoin their communities. Among the key changes we're implementing is a modification of the Department's charging policies—to ensure that people who commit certain low-level, nonviolent federal drug crimes will face sentences appropriate to their individual conduct—rather than stringent mandatory minimums, which will now be reserved for the most serious criminals.

On the day he issued the sentencing memo, Holder defended the purpose of the memo and broader criminal justice policies the Justice Department would be pursuing. At the national American Bar Association[15] meeting, Holder found agreement with classical social conservative theory that

federal prosecutors cannot—and should not—bring every case or charge every defendant who stands accused of violating federal law. Some issues are best handled at the state or local level. And that's why I have today directed the United States Attorney community to develop specific, locally-tailored guidelines—consistent with our national priorities—for determining when federal charges should be filed, and when they should not.

Holder argued that as great as the American system is which is based on equity, equality, and justice,

> We also must confront the reality that—once they're in that system—people of color often face harsher punishments than their peers.
>
> We, as a country, must resolve to do better.
>
> We will start by fundamentally rethinking the notion of mandatory minimum sentences for drug-related crimes. Some statutes that mandate inflexible sentences—regardless of the individual conduct at issue in a particular case—reduce the discretion available to prosecutors, judges, and juries. Because they oftentimes generate unfairly long sentences, they breed disrespect for the system. When applied indiscriminately, they do not serve public safety. They—and some of the enforcement priorities we have set—have had a destabilizing effect on particular communities, largely poor and of color. And, applied inappropriately, they are ultimately counterproductive.
>
> This is why I have today mandated a modification of the Justice Department's charging policies so that certain low-level, nonviolent drug offenders who have no ties to large-scale organizations, gangs, or cartels will no longer be charged with offenses that impose draconian mandatory minimum sentences. They now will be charged with offenses for which the accompanying sentences are better suited to their individual conduct, rather than excessive prison terms more appropriate for violent criminals or drug kingpins. By reserving the most severe penalties for serious, high-level, or violent drug traffickers, we can better promote public safety, deterrence, and

rehabilitation—while making our expenditures smarter and more productive.

General Sessions was having none of this and four years later he abruptly rejected the Holder policy and the due process model underlying it.

On May 10, 2017, General Sessions issued *Memorandum for All Federal Prosecutors*,[16] which announced a new policy of charging and sentencing:

> This memorandum establishes charging and sentencing policy for the Department of Justice. Our responsibility is to fulfill our role in a way that accords with the law, advances public safety, and promotes respect for our legal system.
>
> First, it is *a core principle that prosecutors should charge and pursue the most serious, readily provable offense.* This policy affirms our responsibility to enforce the law, is moral and just, and produces consistency. This policy fully utilizes the tools Congress has given us. *By definition, the most serious offenses are those that carry the most substantial guidelines sentence, including mandatory minimum sentences.*

This policy return to those of Ashcroft and Comey in 2003 and 2005 is significant. It is now Justice Department policy that the most serious charge that can be proved, and the sanction attached to that charge, is to be pursued. The most serious charge is the one that carries the most substantial sentence. This policy returns to the Bush Administration abandonment of prior justice department policy that the most serious charge is the one that reflects the behavior of the defendant.[17] The factor of individual dangerousness and criminal culpability is no longer definitive or dispositive. The policy specifically reversed the Obama Administration policy that facts that invoke the three-strikes enhancements could be withheld in charging documents. Although Sessions allowed for the possibility that there

> will be circumstances in which good judgment would lead a prosecutor to conclude that a strict application of the above charging policy is not warranted. In that case, prosecutors should carefully consider whether an exception may be justified.
>
> Second, *prosecutors must disclose to the sentencing court all facts that impact the sentencing guidelines or mandatory minimum sentences,* and should in all cases seek a reasonable sentence under the factors in 18 U.S.C. § 3553. In most cases, recommending a sentence within the advisory guideline range will be appropriate.

The policy makes clear that it is now an exception to charge outside of the facts and to make recommendations for sentencing below the presumptive sentence under the guidelines. Any exception required U.S. attorney or assistant attorney general level approval. "Any inconsistent previous policy of the Department of Justice relating to these matters is rescinded, effective today." The policy specifically stated that the previous policies rescinded included General Holder's "Department Policy on Charging Mandatory Minimum Sentences and Recidivist Enhancements in Certain Drug Cases (August 12, 2013); and Guidance Regarding § 851 Enhancements in Plea Negotiations (September 24, 2014)."

General Sessions, in an op-ed in the *Washington Post*,[18] defended the policy change. He first rejected the proposition that a criminal engaged in the drug trade should be classified as nonviolent and that the federal prisons are filled with nonviolent drug offenders:

> Drug trafficking is an inherently violent business. If you want to collect a drug debt, you can't, and don't, file a lawsuit in court. You collect it by the barrel of a gun. For

the approximately 52,000 Americans who died of a drug
overdose in 2015, drug trafficking was a deadly business.

Reflecting and affirming the policies of Governor Rockefeller and
Presidents Nixon and then Reagan, Sessions asserted that the War
on Drugs in the 1970s and 1980s was correct and these policies
should be the policy of the second decade of the new century.
Session continued,

> Defenders of the status quo perpetuate the false story
> that federal prisons are filled with low-level, nonviolent
> drug offenders. The truth is less than 3 percent of federal
> offenders sentenced to imprisonment in 2016 were con-
> victed of simple possession, and in most of those cases the
> defendants were drug dealers who accepted plea bargains
> in return for reduced sentences.

General Sessions was correct that 3.4 percent of all state prisoners are
in prison for simple possession (15.2 percent for all drug offenses),[19]
but he neglected to note that almost half (47.5 percent) of all federal
prisoners were incarcerated for drug offenses (99 percent of drug offenses were for drug trafficking).[20] Furthermore, more than a third
(37.8 percent) of all federal prisoners for drug offenses were black and
another third were Hispanic (38.5 percent) while whites only accounted
for 21.6 percent of those incarcerated for drug offenses.[21] There is no
research that shows blacks and Hispanics are responsible for 76 percent
of all drug crime in America worthy of federal incarceration. Looking
at these disparities another way, in 2016, 56.5 percent of all Hispanics
and 48.5 percent of all blacks in federal incarceration were there for
drugs while only 37.5 percent of whites were incarcerated for federal
drug crimes.[22] Thus blacks and Hispanics are disproportionately incarcerated in federal prisons and they are disproportionately incarcerated
for drug offenses which carry more serious mandatory sentencing.

The disproportionate incarceration of blacks and Hispanics is also
reflected in state incarceration rates. In 2015, Hispanics accounted for

19.6 percent of all drug offenders, blacks accounted for 31.2 percent and whites accounted for 30.9 percent.[23] The disproportionality is amplified when incarceration for violent crimes is considered. In 2016, Hispanics accounted for 9.7 percent, blacks 50 percent, and whites 24.6 percent of violent offenders in federal prisons[24] and in 2015, Hispanics accounted 23.6 percent, blacks 35.6 percent, and whites 30.9 percent in state prisons.[25] But as discussed in chapter 1, whites account for 70 percent of all crime and 59 percent of all violent crime, while blacks account for 27 percent of all crime and 37 percent of all violent crime. Blacks commit less crime but are incarcerated more than whites.

Ignoring these disparities, Sessions implied in his op-ed that federal prisoners are not simple drug users but major drug traffickers.

> Federal drug offenders include major drug traffickers, gang members, importers, manufacturers and international drug cartel members. To be subject to a five-year mandatory sentence, a criminal would have to be arrested with 100 grams or more of heroin with the intent to distribute it—that is 1,000 doses of heroin.

But an offender does not need to be a trafficker to be subject to the five-year mandatory sentence. The five-year mandatory statute, 21 U.S.C. § 841, now, requires possession of one hundred grams (0.220462 pounds) of heroin and 500 grams (1.10231 pounds) of powder cocaine but only 28 grams (0.0617294 pounds) of crack to secure the same five-year sentence. And to secure the ten-year mandatory sentence, it requires one kilo (2.20462 pounds) of heroin and 5 kilos (11.0231 pounds) of powder cocaine but only 280 grams (0.617294 pounds) of crack.

But drug weight disparities aside, it's the disparity of sentence that General Holder sought to address. A disparity created under the *Anti-Drug Abuse Act of 1986* (one hundred to one ratio punishment crack to powder cocaine) and the *Anti-Drug Abuse Act of 1988* (five-year mandatory for 5 grams of crack cocaine) that was in effect for more than two decades before it was changed by the

Fair Sentencing Act of 2010. The result of the Holder policy was a reduction of black incarceration. Between 2013 and 2016 the number of blacks incarcerated dropped 8 percent.[26] Overall, under the Obama presidency (2009 and 2016) black incarceration decreased by 16.7 percent,[27] which was more than three times the decrease under the Bush Administration (4.8 percent).[28] In 2009, when President Obama took office, the percentage of black federal and state incarceration was 41 percent and at the end of the Obama presidency in 2016, the percentage of black federal and state incarceration had dropped to 33 percent, which was the lowest since 1964 (33 percent).[29]

Although this accomplishment is significant, the systemic incarceration of blacks remains. In 2016 there were 1,609 blacks for every 100,000 resident adults (18 and over) in federal and state prisons, while only 274 whites and 857 Hispanics for every 100,000 adult residents in federal and state prisons.[30] The total number of people incarcerated in 2016 per 100,000 adults was only 582. Between 2015 and 2016, the rate of black imprisonment decreased 4 percent (from 1,670 per 100,000 in 2015 to 1,609 per 100,000 in 2016) while the rate of white imprisonment decreased 2 percent (from 281 per 100,000 in 2015 to 274 per 100,000 in 2016) and the rate of Hispanic incarceration decreased only 1 percent (862 per 100,000 in 2015 to 857 per 100,000 in 2016). Since 2006, the imprisonment rate for Hispanics declined 20 percent (1,073 per 100,000 in 2006) and the imprisonment rate for blacks declined 29 percent since 2006 (2,261 per 100,000).[31] Although the rates of black incarceration is decreasing, "Black males ages 18 to 19 were 11.8 times more likely to be imprisoned than white males of the same age. This age group had the highest black-to-white racial disparity in 2016."[32]

The impact of this disparity on black communities provided justification for the Holder policy attempt to mitigate the disproportionate impact of the 1986 and 1988 laws was irrelevant to General Sessions. Session wrote in his op-ed that under the Holder policy, "federal drug prosecutions went down dramatically—from 2011 to 2016, federal prosecutions fell by 23 percent. Meanwhile, the average sentence length for a convicted federal drug offender decreased

18 percent from 2009 to 2016." The result being, "[w]ithin one year after the Justice Department softened its approach to drug offenders, the trend of decreasing violent crime reversed. In 2015, the United States suffered the largest single-year increase in the overall violent crime rate since 1991." He asserted that the lack of absolute federal prosecution of crime resulted in an increase in crime:

> The truth is that while the federal government softened its approach to drug enforcement, drug abuse and violent crime surged. The availability of dangerous drugs is up, the price has dropped and the purity is at dangerously high levels. Overdose deaths from opioids have nearly tripled since 2002. Overdose deaths involving synthetic opioids rose an astonishing 73 percent in 2015. My fear is that this surge in violent crime is not a "blip," but the start of a dangerous new trend—one that puts at risk the hard-won gains that have made our country a safer place.[33]

Note the conflating of violent crime with the rise of opioid addiction with the failure of the federal government to prosecute drug cases. The fact that violent crime—even drug-related violent crime—is a different dynamic than the opioid crisis (which is driven by abuse of prescription drugs) is lost on Sessions. To Sessions, in line with the crime control policies of Nixon, Reagan, Bush, and Clinton, crime is solely the result of lax and weak application of formal social control—the application of police and prosecutions in court and the utilization of prison incarceration after conviction.

Sessions concluded his op-ed by evoking the rhetoric of President Truman that the first civil right is to be free from violence and the political rhetoric of President Clinton that the first community that deserves that protection is the less affluent, which suffers the brunt of crime.

> Some skeptics prefer to sit on the sidelines and criticize federal efforts to combat crime. But it's not our privileged

communities that suffer the most from crime and violence. Minority communities are disproportionately impacted by violent drug trafficking. Poor neighborhoods are too often ignored in these conversations. Regardless of wealth or race, every American has the right to demand a safe neighborhood. Those of us who are responsible for promoting public safety cannot sit back while any American communities are ravaged by crime and violence.

There are those who are concerned about the fate of drug traffickers, but the law demands I protect the lives of victims that are ruined by drug trafficking and violent crime infecting their communities. Our new, time-tested policy empowers police and prosecutors to save lives.

On December 15, 2017, General Sessions announced a new Justice Department initiative to add an additional 40 assistant U.S. attorneys (AUSAs) specializing in violent crime and drug prosecutions.[34] He asserted that violent crime had increased over the past two years. "The overall violent crime rate is up by nearly 7% ... rape is up by nearly 11% and murder up by more than 20%" and that 25% of the increase in the murder rate is caused by increases in drug-related homicides." To address the increase in crime and to return neighborhoods to law and order, Sessions announced new funding for Project Safe Neighborhoods streets task forces. These task forces coordinate federal, state, and local law enforcement under the leadership of AUSAs that focus on prosecutions of violent crimes. Sessions asserted that the new AUSAs, funded through "shifting department resources and priorities," will "repurpose existing funds [by] reducing wasteful spending" to support the appointment of AUSAs in communities that are suffering from higher crime than the national average. He announced that over the next few months he plans on appointing an additional 260 AUSAs. He concluded, "To the communities that are suffering, hear this. Help is on the way. We are marshalling our resources and will be relentless in our pursuit of violent criminals that are victimizing your neighborhoods."

After his prepared remakes, he answered a question as to whether more AUSAs and partnerships will reduce crime by asserting that the project safe neighborhood strategy "if sustained, is somewhat akin to the New York City–proven COMSTAT model[35] where you use good intelligence, you identify what the commissioner told me the *alpha criminal,* and you make those top priority in your investigations and prosecutions. And you can see, hopefully for America, what they have seen in New York is a steady decline in homicides and violent crime. So, I believe it's a proven technique." The reduction of crime is not complicated to General Sessions, simply focus on *the alpha criminal (the super predator of the 1990s).* Clinton did not, and could not, have said it better himself.

On January 4, 2018, General Sessions continued to assert the need for a reinvigorated law and order policy to replace the policies of the Obama Administration. Sessions announced that the policy of the Obama Administration regarding federal prosecutions for marijuana prosecutions was reversed. Under the Obama Administration, *Justice Department policy announcement: Justice Department Announces Update to Marijuana Enforcement Policy August 29, 2013,* "federal marijuana enforcement policy in light of recent state ballot initiatives that legalize, under state law, the possession of small amounts of marijuana and provide for the regulation of marijuana production, processing, and sale ... the Department identifie[d] eight (8) enforcement areas that federal prosecutors should prioritize."[36] These enforcement areas included (1) selling marijuana to minors, (2) preventing sales of marijuana to drug gangs and other criminal organizations, (3) preventing sales of marijuana from states that allow such sales to states that do not, (4) preventing state-authorized marijuana activities from being co-opted by criminal organizations for illegal drug activity or money laundering, (5) preventing gun violence in the cultivation and distribution of marijuana, (6) preventing marijuana cultivation on federal lands, (7) preventing marijuana use on federal land, and (8) preventing driving while intoxicated on

marijuana. The policy left prosecution of minor marijuana possession and sale to state and local prosecution priorities and policies.[37]

Sessions reversed this policy and in the ***Memorandum to All U.S.
Attorneys Issued by Attorney General Jeffery Sessions January 4,
2018,*** he instructed his U.S. attorneys to use "well-established principles that govern all federal prosecutions" which include "federal
law enforcement priorities set by the Attorney General, the seriousness of the crime, the deterrent effect of criminal prosecution,
and the cumulative impact of particular crime on the community"
to determine whether to prosecute marijuana cases under federal
law.[38] Sessions explained in his announcement of the new policy
announced that he was "direct[ing] all U.S. Attorneys to enforce the
laws enacted by Congress and to follow well-established principles
when pursuing prosecutions related to marijuana activities. This
return to the rule of law is also a return of trust and local control
to federal prosecutors who know where and how to deploy Justice
Department resources most effectively to reduce violent crime, stem
the tide of the drug crisis, and dismantle criminal gangs."[39]

In a speech to the National Fraternal Order of Police,[40] as
Wallace did in 1968, Sessions asserted his support of police and
made clear that he was on the side of police and law and order. He
said to the assembly of officers,

> I know firsthand the important work that each of you
> do. ... to fight crime and defend the lives and liberties
> of Americans. I know that each of you has that kind of
> impact in your communities. But your work is hard, and
> in many places it's getting harder. That's because we are
> fighting a multi-front battle: an increase in violent crime,
> a rise in vicious gangs, an opioid epidemic, threats from
> terrorism, combined with a culture in which family and
> discipline seem to be eroding further and a disturbing
> disrespect for the rule of law. After decreasing for nearly
> 20 years because of the hard but necessary work our

country started in the 1980s, violent crime is back with
a vengeance. ...

....

You are the thin blue line that stands between law-
abiding people and criminals—between sanctity and
lawlessness. ...

....

Roughly translated, the FOP's motto means "Law is a
Safeguard of Freedom." I would go one step further by saying that rule of law is the safeguard of freedom. The law
secures our God-given rights, and you—the officers who
enforce it—ensure that all Americans enjoy those rights.

This is classical second punitive era rhetoric. The only institution
that protects America is law enforcement. Without the police, as
Reagan said, the jungle would take over. After which he continued
with the classical rhetoric that those who wish to control police
abuse, defame police for political purposes and that defamation is
the cause of crime and violence toward the police.

But some would undermine this support by portraying
law enforcement officers as the enemy. Instead of recog-
nizing that the Justice Department vigorously prosecutes
officers in the cases when they violate the civil rights of
our citizens, they choose to slander all of the honorable
men and women in law enforcement who serve every day
with professionalism, integrity, and selflessness.

Their divisive rhetoric treats police officers like the
problem, instead of the crucial allies that you all are. So
it can come as no surprise when we see rising levels of
violence against law enforcement.

Sessions then told his audience that under the Trump Administration
that defamation ends, and that the federal government was on their
side, the side of law and order.

Every American should appreciate—and celebrate—the work that you do and the sacrifices you make. That's why I am here today. On behalf of President Trump and the entire Department of Justice, thank you for what you do. The President is proud to stand with you. He is exceptionally proud to have run as the law and order President. I am proud to stand with you. And the Department of Justice is proud to stand with you. We have your back. We "BACK THE BLUE."

And this President stands with you—not just rhetorically—but in thought, word, and deed. President Trump sent the Department of Justice three executive orders after I was sworn in. He sent us the 'back the blue' order to support our law enforcement at all levels. The second made it our objective to "reduce crime" across the country. And the third requires us to dismantle transnational criminal organizations.

....

Helping law enforcement do their jobs, helping the police get better, and celebrating the noble, honorable, essential and challenging work of our law enforcement communities will always be a top priority of President Trump and this Department of Justice. We will always seek to affirm the critical role of police officers in our society and we will not participate in anything that would give comfort to radicals who promote agendas that preach hostility rather than respect for police.

With the obligatory praise for police completed, Sessions stated that under his watch as Attorney General prosecutions would increase the use of asset forfeiture and would provide full support of the 1033 program instituted under the Clinton Administration.

Several months ago now, we changed the charging policy for our federal prosecutors, trusting them once again and directing them to return to charging the most serious, readily provable offense.

In July, we reinstituted our equitable sharing program, ensuring that criminals will not be permitted to profit from their crimes. ... [C]ivil asset forfeiture is a key tool that helps law enforcement defund organized crime, take back ill-gotten gains, and prevent new crimes from being committed, and it weakens the criminals and the cartels. Civil asset forfeiture takes the material support of the criminals and instead makes it the material support of law enforcement. In departments across this country, funds that were once used to take lives are now being used to save lives.

....

I am here to announce that President Trump is issuing an executive order that will make it easier to protect yourselves and your communities. He is rescinding restrictions from the prior administration that limited your agencies' ability to get equipment through ... the Department of Defense's 1033 program. ...

One sheriff told me earlier this year about how, because of the prior administration's restrictions, the federal government made his department return an armored vehicle ... Those restrictions went too far. We will not put superficial concerns above public safety. ... this isn't about appearances, its about getting the job done and getting everyone to safety.

The executive order the President will sign today will ensure that you can get the lifesaving gear that you need to do your job and send a strong message that we will not allow criminal activity, violence, and lawlessness to become the new normal. And we will save taxpayer money in the meantime.

Sessions' comments on appearances were in regard to the appearance of police using military equipment to deal with social protests in Ferguson. It was during the demonstrations that most of America was introduced to the police having military training and equipment and using it on American civilians. The "appearance" of armored personal carriers that looked like tanks, use of tear gas, military weapons, and police in military looking uniforms resulted in the Obama Administration putting limits on the 1033 program.

In giving a similar speech the following year to the International Association of Chiefs of Police,[41] Sessions spoke extemporarily from his prepared remarks that the criminal justice system, when properly focusing all of its sometimes-contradictory parts, can reduce crime. He said the walls between the various parts of the system should be breached, so law enforcement can share information and save lives. That reduction occurred in the 1990s and that the recent trend of increasing crime should be opposed. "Under my tenure as Attorney General, we have already increased federal gun prosecutions to a 10-year high and violent crime prosecutions to a 25-year high." And he added to his prepared remarks that his local prosecutors are "just eager to be unleashed."

Continuing to speak off script, Sessions said, "in the last four or five years, *the federal prison population dropped from 220,000 to 180,000. That is really big. I mean this a factor I think in growing crime in this country.* We've got some space! To put some people, I've got to say to you. Also ... we've sent a message to our prosecutors that you should normally charge the most serious offense ... we say you should normally go after the criminals with the most serious offense they committed and that carries the mandatory minimum and that's why congress passed it. Why else did they put the darn thing in the law. I think that's a good step in the right direction. We need to reverse a trend that suggested that criminals won't be confronted seriously with their crime."[42]

On June 8, 2018, at the Western Conservative Summit, sponsored by the Colorado Christian University Centennial Institute,[43] Sessions actually echoed the rhetoric of President Clinton and

Attorney General Ashcroft. Ashcroft told the Senate in April 2001 that "a citizen's paramount civil right is safety. Americans have a right to be secure in their persons, homes and communities" and violent crime "deny this most fundamental right." Clinton could not and actually did not say it any better himself. At his 1996 signing ceremony for the "one strike and you're out" policy[44] regarding public housing evictions, he said,

> The only people who deserve to live in public housing are those who live responsibly there and those who honor the rule of law. ... [H]ousing authorities must work with tenants, with the police, with the courts, with our Government. ...
>
> ....
>
> [I]t's morally wrong for criminals to use up homes that could make a big difference in the lives of decent families. ... The people who are living there deserve to be protected, and the good people who want to live in public housing deserve to have a chance. ... There is no reason in the world to put the rights of a criminal before those of a child who wants to grow up safe. ...
>
> ....
>
> For too many years, the chaos in some of our public housing units has been a national blind spot and a national disgrace. Most Americans probably ... believe most people who live in public housing are lawless, are not working, are not concerned parents. All of that is wrong.
>
> Now we are going to give the good, decent, law-abiding citizens in public housing the life they deserve ...

Clinton asserted that the poor have a right to public safety and the police, along with the courts are the venue to enforce that civil right which the government is obligated to provide. As Cicero, wrote, "Salus populi suprema lex est" the *safety of the people is the supreme law*. For decades Republican rhetoric had asserted that the primary role of the national government is to support local law enforcement and to protect the first civil right in America, safety from criminals. This rhetoric, echoed by President Clinton, that the police are the thin blue line and with prosecutors are the only line between civilization and the jungle was established by the fathers of the modern Republican party, Barry Goldwater,[45] George Wallace,[46] Richard Nixon,[47] and Ronald Reagan.[48] And this rhetoric was fully endorsed by General Sessions. At the 2018 summit, Sessions said,

> The first civil right in America, and we have to know, is to be safe in our communities. And that applies to poor people and minorities who are often struggling financially. And they can't live behind in gated communities. They are entitled to public safety too. That's why we at the Department are hammering the criminal and violent groups especially MS 13, that vicious gang. ... At this Department of Justice, we are focused on the safety of the American people, not the criminals safety. ... In 2017 we brought more cases against more violent criminals in the United States than in any year in last quarter century. We charged the most federal firearms offenses, criminals with firearms, in a decade. We convicted nearly 500 traffickers, 1200 gang members, and the Trump Administration we know whose side we're on. We're on the side of police, law and order, the American people and we back the blue, not the criminals.[49]

He told his audience that Trump's first order to him was to back the police, and the first policy he implemented was the deployment of 300 additional prosecutors to rural and urban areas to address violent crime, which he said was on the rise from 2014 to 2016 after a thirty-year decline. Quoting President Trump, Session said, "If we want to bring down violent crime, we must stand up for our police." More importantly, "in this Trump era" Sessions declared that under his administration of the Justice Department, "the ACLU isn't going to be making and setting our law enforcement policies, the professionals are."

Although General Sessions and his policy changes to federal prosecutions are in alignment with the Reno and Ashcroft memos discussed in Chapter 7 and the Clinton policies instituted at the height of the golden age of crime control politics (the results being that between 1989 and 1997, blacks accounted for a majority of the total U.S. prison population—51 percent (1993–1994) and ranged between 50 percent (1989) and 46 percent (2001) of the total U.S. prison population) the second punitive era is past. In terms of both politics and governmental budgeting restraints on both the federal and state levels, the glory days of unrestrained deficit funding to build prisons and the political acceptance of the disproportionate filling of those prisons with blacks will not return. This being true, Sessions nonetheless planned on making a good faith effort to bring back those glory years. But, Sessions never had the opportunity to make his good faith effort because he was told to resign on November 7, 2018, due to Trump's disfavor with his recusal from overseeing the Russia election interference investigation by the special counsel. But Sessions did have an impact of federal criminal justice because his reversal of the policies of Holder reinstated the memos of Reno and Ashcroft regarding how the Justice Department defines "most serious, readily provable offenses" which is currently defined as offenses, "that carry the most substantial guidelines sentence, including mandatory minimum sentences."[50]

With Sessions fired, and with his intractable intransient opposition removed, the White House was able to support the passage of the **Formerly Incarcerated Reenter Society Transformed Safely Transitioning Every Person Act (First Step Act)** which Trump signed on December 21, 2018. The bill was the result of alliances between liberals and conservatives who supported changes to treatment within prison—more reentry based programing, the inclusion of faith-based organizations working with offenders both in and out of prison, better research on recidivism programs and program development, prohibiting restraints on pregnant and postpartum prisoners and requiring training of officers dealing with pregnant women, and those supporting reduction in mandatory sentencing and providing judges with more discretion in sentencing. The law also prohibited sentencing offenders to facilities too far away from their families. The law ended the Clinton era ability to make an offender disappear from family and friends by placing them in facilities outside of a family's ability to visit. In regard to sentencing, the law made the Fair Sentencing Act of 2010 reductions in disparity in sentencing between crack and powder cocaine retroactive and allowed sentencing courts to review and modify sentences to be in line with the new specifications of the Fair Sentencing Act. According to the Justice Department, four months after the passage the "Act's retroactive application of the Fair Sentencing Act of 2010 (reducing the disparity between crack cocaine and powder cocaine threshold amounts triggering mandatory minimum sentences) has resulted in 826 sentence reductions and 643 early releases."[51] The Department announced that on July 19, 2019, "Over 3,100 federal prison inmates will be released from the Bureau of Prisons' custody as a result of the increase in good conduct time under the Act. In addition, the Act's retroactive application of the Fair Sentencing Act of 2010 (reducing the disparity between crack cocaine and powder cocaine threshold amounts triggering mandatory minimum sentences) has resulted in 1,691 sentence reductions."[52]

To put the release in some perspective, in a 2017 snapshot there were 78,800 people in federal facilities for drug crimes, 46 percent of the total population. And 76 percent of those incarcerated for drugs were black and Hispanic (37 percent black and 39 percent Hispanic).[53] The release of 3,100 people for nonviolent drug offenses, 3.9 percent of the total, and 1,691 sentence reductions, 2 percent of the total, is a small *first step*. In addition, during the first four months of the law, under the "compassionate release" sentence reductions provisions 22 inmates have been released and 23 inmates are participating in the Second Chance Act home confinement pilot program.[54] The Justice Department announced in July 2019 that 51 requests for compassionate release have been approved, 2,000 inmates have been placed in home confinement and

16,000 inmates are currently enrolled in drug treatment. Attorney General William Barr said of these releases and the implementation of the First Step Act, "Our communities are safer when we do a better job of rehabilitating offenders in our custody and preparing them for a successful transition to life after incarceration" and "the Department is committed to and has been working towards full implementation of the First Step Act, which will help us effectively deploy resources to help reduce risk, recidivism, and crime."[55]

As discussed in Chapters 4 and 5, mandatory minimums were a key aspect of the second punitive era and were party supported by the desire to transfer control of sentencing from judges under indeterminate sentencing. Subsequently, under *Apprendi v. New Jersey* (2000), *Blakely v. Washington* (2004), *Alleyne v. United States* (2013) and *United States v. Haymond* (2019), the Supreme Court held that any criminal sanction or sentencing that increases a punishment given, the facts underlying the decision to impose that punishment must be made by a jury under a finding of guilt beyond a reasonable doubt. In *Haymond*, the Court not only rejected the imposition of a five year minimum mandatory sentence enhancement through a fact-finding process by the judge, the Court rejected that such fact-finding was satisfied under the preponderance of the evidence standard. In an opinion written by Trump appointee Justice Neil Gorsuch no less, the Court provided an impassioned defense of the Fifth and Sixth amendments' right of the defendant to be found guilty beyond a reasonable doubt by a jury before a mandatory minimum sentence could be imposed because of crimes committed in violation of conditions of supervised release. He wrote,

> Only a jury, acting on proof beyond a reasonable doubt, may take a person's liberty. That promise stands as one of the Constitution's most vital protections against arbitrary government. Yet in this case a congressional statute compelled a federal judge to send a man to prison for a minimum of five years without empaneling a jury of

his peers or requiring the government to prove his guilt beyond a reasonable doubt. As applied here, we do not hesitate to hold that the statute violates the Fifth and Sixth Amendments.

. . . .

Together with the right to vote, those who wrote our Constitution considered the right to trial by jury the heart and lungs, the mainspring and the center wheel of our liberties, without which the body must die; the watch must run down; the government must become arbitrary. Just as the right to vote sought to preserve the people's authority over their government's executive and legislative functions, the right to a jury trial sought to preserve the people's authority over its judicial functions.

. . . .

Consistent with these understandings, juries in our constitutional order exercise supervisory authority over the judicial function by limiting the judge's power to punish. A judge's authority to issue a sentence derives from and is limited by, the jury's factual findings of criminal conduct.

. . . .

[T]he absence of a jury's finding beyond a reasonable doubt [not] only infringe the rights of the accused; it also divested the "people at large"—the men and women who make up a jury of a defendant's peers—of their constitutional authority to set the metes and bounds of judicially administered criminal punishments.

. . . .

The Constitution seeks to safeguard the people's control over the business of judicial punishments by ensuring that any accusation triggering a new and additional punishment is proven to the satisfaction of a jury beyond a reasonable doubt.

. . . .

If the government were right, a jury's conviction on one crime would ... allow the government to evade the need for another jury trial on any other offense the defendant might commit. ... Instead of seeking a revocation of supervised release, the government could have chosen to prosecute Mr. Haymond under a statute ... for repeat child-pornography offenders. But why bother with an old-fashioned jury trial for a new crime when a quick-and-easy supervised release revocation hearing before a judge carries a penalty of five years to life?

....

In the end, the dissent is left only to echo an age-old criticism: Jury trials are inconvenient for the government. Yet like much else in our Constitution, the jury system isn't designed to promote efficiency but to protect liberty. ... [Y]et let it be again remembered, that delays, and little inconveniences in the forms of justice, are the price that all free nations must pay for their liberty in more substantial matters.

The great civil liberty and due process model Justices Thurgood Marshall and William Joseph Brennan Jr. could not have written it better themselves. As Justice Gorsuch wrote, *Apprendi, Blakely* and *Alleyne,* along with *U.S. v. Booker* (2005), *Kimbrough v. United States* (2007) and *Haymond* established that (1) the sentencing guideline system is not mandatory upon the courts and (2) the jury is primary in imposing sanctions that enhance sentences, either a minimum or a mandatory sentence, based on asserted facts by the prosecution. The government is obligated to endure the inconvenience of proving guilt before a jury beyond a reasonable doubt and can't use a sentence revocation hearing to secure a minimum mandatory sentence for the offense done while on supervised release.

With these boundaries established, it is nonetheless true that under the sentencing guidelines certain offenses that carry mandatory minimums can be enhanced based on collateral factors. For example, a drug possession charge can be enhanced at sentencing because of the possession of a gun when the possession of the drug occurred. The *First Step Act* made changes to the *enhancement* of mandatory minimums for certain violent crime and drug offenses.[56] The following discussion reviews the changes the *First Step Act* made.[57]

Conviction of the manufacture or possession of certain drugs (21 U.S.C. § 841(b)(1)(A)), one kilogram or more of heroin or 5 kilograms of cocaine or 280 grams or more of crack cocaine, the mandatory minimum sentence of 10 years could be enhanced to 20 years if there was a prior conviction for a drug felony. Under the First Step Act that enhancement was reduced to 15 years and required a serious drug felony or serious violent felony instead of any felony drug offense. In cases in which the enhancement resulted in life, the First Step Act reduced the enhancement to 25 years and required a serious drug felony or serious violent felony instead of any felony drug offense.

Conviction of manufacture or possession of certain drugs (21 U.S.C. § 841(b)(1)(B)), 100 grams or more heroin or 500 grams of cocaine or 28 grams or more of crack cocaine, the mandatory minimum sentence of 5 years could be enhanced to 10 years if there was a prior felony drug offense conviction. Under the First Step Act that enhancement was changed to require a serious drug felony or serious violent felony instead of any felony drug offense.

Conviction of transportation (trafficking) of certain drugs (21 U.S.C. § 960(b)(1)), one kilogram or more of heroin or 5 kilograms of cocaine or 280 grams or more of crack cocaine, the mandatory minimum sentence of 10 years could be enhanced to 20 years if there was a prior conviction for a drug felony. Under the First Step Act that enhancement was reduced to 15 years and required a serious drug felony or serious violent felony instead of any felony drug offense.

Conviction of transportation (trafficking) of certain drugs 21 U.S.C.§ 960(b)(2), 100 grams or more of heroin or 500 grams of cocaine or 28 grams or more of crack cocaine, the mandatory minimum sentence of 5 years could be enhanced to 10 years if there was a prior felony drug offense conviction. Under the First Step Act, that enhancement was changed to require a serious drug felony or serious violent felony instead of any felony drug offense.

The First Step Act also made changes to the application of mandatory minimum penalties for violent crimes and drug trafficking crimes involving the use of guns under 18 U.S. Code § 924(c). Before the act, when a defendant was charged with multiple crimes of violence or drug trafficking offenses the defendant would receive enhancements to the mandatory minimum terms if while committing a violent crime or drug trafficking offense the defendant, in furtherance of the said offenses, used a gun (5 years enhancement), brandished a gun (7 year enhancement), discharged a gun (10 year enhancement), or had a silencer on the gun (30 year enhancement).[58] If the defendant had prior convictions for violent crimes or drug trafficking, the enhancement could increase to 25 years to life. If the defendant had a second or subsequent gun use offense, the defendant would receive 25 years and if the gun had a silencer on the second or subsequent incident, the sentence would be life.[59]

During sentencing, what the government would do is use the various counts within a single indictment, with no prior violent crime or gun use convictions, to add or "stack" the minimum mandatory sentences. For example, a person with two drug offenses that carried a mandatory minimum of 5 years each and who possessed a gun in each drug offense incident would receive an additional mandatory 5 years for the first gun possession plus an additional mandatory 25 years for the second. The result would be 5 + 5 + 25 for a mandatory sentence of 35 years. Five years for the underlying drug offenses, five years for the first gun use and 25 years for the second gun use offense. The stacking occurs from the two gun use (possession) charges, not the two underlying drug charges. The two drug charges don't stack, and the defendant would receive one 5-year mandatory minimum for the drug charges.

The First Step Act eliminated the practice of stacking charges from the same indictment by making clear that the subsequent gun or violent crime charge resulting in the 25-year minimum mandatory enhancement can only be stacked when it is from a prior final conviction.[60] The government could no longer use a separate count in the same indictment to create the subsequent charge and gain the 25-year enhancement. Thus, in the example—two drug offenses and two gun uses (possession) in furtherance of the drug charges—the result is 5 + 5 + 5 for a sentence of 15 years. Five years for the drug offenses (not stacked) and five years each for each gun use enhancement.[61] The 25-year enhancement does not apply because the second gun offense was not a prior conviction offense. But, if in our hypothetical, we change the story to two drug offenses, one use of a gun during the drug offenses and the defendant had a prior conviction for a violent crime (25-year mandatory sentence)—the sentence would be 5 + 5 + 25 (35 years).

Thus, the First Step Act reduced a typical first offender (charges under one indictment without prior convictions) with two drug trafficking and two gun use charges from 35 years to 15 years. The First Step Act made clear that the purpose of the enhancements is limited in purpose, to target repeat drug trafficking offenders and violent crime offenders who use guns.[62]

The First Step Act also expanded the applicability of the sentencing guidelines safety valve (18 U.S.C. § 3553(f)) which allows the court not to apply minimum mandatory sentences. The act now prohibits the use of the safety valve if the defendant has more than four criminal history points, a prior three-point offense, or a prior two-point violent offense. Before the act, the guidelines prohibited the use of the safety valve if the defendant had more than 1 criminal history point. The First Step Act also amended the process known as "compassionate release" to allow an offender to apply to the court directly after, "the defendant has fully exhausted all administrative rights to appeal a failure of the Bureau of Prisons to bring a motion on the defendant's behalf ... [to] reduce the term of imprisonment [and] impose a term of probation or supervised release [if the court] finds extraordinary and compelling reasons warrant such a reduction."[63]

The significance of the First Step Act is that it provided a mechanism for people currently in federal facilities to petition for early release based on changes to the sentencing guidelines and to provide faith-based and other reentry providers more access to prisons to aid in the transition of offenders from prison to a return to civilian life. The 18 to 1 ratio of crack cocaine to powder cocaine and the use of minimal mandatory sentencing in the first place remains intact. The new law only blunted the harsher edge of minimum mandatory sentences. Like the Fair Sentencing Act of 2010 before it, the First Step Act was a limited measure to address the policies of the second punitive era. Although mitigated, the overall second punitive era policies of Reagan and Clinton and the memos of Reno, Ashcroft, and Comey prevail.

The Supreme Court has also impacted the system of federal criminal justice enhanced sentencing. In *United States v. Davis* (2019) the Supreme Court held six months before passage of the First Step Act that § 924(c)(3)(B), which provides enhanced penalties for using a firearm during a "crime of violence," was unconstitutionally vague. The Supreme Court held in *Johnson v. United States* (2015) that 18 U.S.C. § 924(e)(2)(B) (Armed Career Criminal Act of 1984) that a similar phrase—which provides for enhanced penalties for three or more previous convictions for a "violent felony"—was also unconstitutionally vague. These residual clauses allowed prosecutors to charge cases in which the facts of the case were not clearly covered by other sections of the statute. With these residual clauses being held to be unconstitutionally vague, the Court has placed limits on the ability of federal prosecutors to charge felonies with sentencing enhancements.

◆◆◆

Another narrative of the second punitive era that has returned with the election of Trump is blaming police violence on the person who the police shot. As discussed in Chapter 6, Fourth Amendment jurisprudence gives the police the benefit of the doubt when police use force. Implicit bias can lead to police use of force and the death of the person encountered by the police. When discussing police use of force, Attorney General William Barr, who replaced Sessions, made clear that the focus on police violence belongs to the citizen. At a speech at the National Association of Police Organizations' 26th Annual Top Cops Awards on May 12, 2019, General Barr lamented on how society has now moved from not condemning, if not outright approval, of people who resist the police.

> One of the factors that is increasing the danger to police officers these days is increasing toleration of the notion that it is okay to resist the police. It was once understood that resistance is a serious crime because it necessarily triggers an escalation of violence that endangers the life not only of the police office, but also the suspect.
>
> It was not too long ago that influential public voices— whether in the media, or among community and civic leaders—stressed the need to comply with police commands, even if one thinks they are unjust. "Comply first" and, if you think you have been wronged, "complain later."
>
> But we don't hear this much anymore. Instead, when an incident escalates due to a suspect's violent resistance to police that fact is almost always ignored by the commentary. The officer's every action is dissected, but the suspect's resistance, and the danger it posed, frequently goes without mention.
>
> We need to get back to basics. We need public voices, in the media and elsewhere, to underscore the needs to "Comply first, and, if warranted, complain later." This will make everyone safe—the police, suspects, and the community at large. This will save lives.

On one level, I could not agree with General Barr more. When police abuse your rights, comply, and complain later because the police on the street have the right to shoot you in the street upon aggressive resistance. General Barr is correct because there is no appeal from a police gun shot. There may be sanctions for police shooting a black man in the street, but there is no appeal or revocation from the judgment of that gun shot. This is why "the talk" is given to young black men by their parents.

It is a truism that whites are more likely to perceive American criminal justice as just and fair, while blacks are more likely to view the system with distrust and belief that it is biased against them. The difference is in the divergent historical and contemporary life experiences of both groups. For example, as discussed in Chapter 6, traffic stops, by race percentage, is more dangerous for blacks than whites. This difference is one aspect of a historical and contemporary difference in experience between blacks and whites at the hand of criminal justice. This is why whites and blacks perceive it differently. Returning to General Barr, his advice is the same as black parents, the difference is in the why and the fear behind the advice. As a historical matter,—regarding police encounters—white parents don't fear for their sons not returning home after being out with their male friends, black parents do. When considering the discretional nature of police use of traffic stops, the historical bias that has occurred in police selecting who to stop, and that traffic stops being the third-highest incident leading to police fatalities for blacks but is the ninth highest incident for whites—the fears of black parents are not irrational.

Returning to General Barr's speech, he affirmed the policies of the Clinton Administration, explaining that the Justice Department Community Oriented Policing Services office "has helped police departments hire more than 800 law enforcement officers across America since January of 2017" and "our Bureau of Justice Assistance provides funding to state and local agencies for bullet-proof vests, law enforcement officer safety and wellness training, human trafficking and firearms investigations, and for many other purposes." Barr explained to his audience of local police officers that,

> I want to assure you all that federal law enforcement is focused on helping you take criminals, illegal guns, and

dangerous drugs out of your communities and off the
streets that you patrol.

Our U.S. Attorneys have been directed to listen to officers like you about who the most dangerous criminals
are in your community—and then to focus on putting
them behind bars.

We call this program Project Safe Neighborhoods, and
it is a proven crime-reduction strategy. It is modeled after
a program I began during my previous tenure as Attorney
General, called Weed and Seed.

The role of the Justice Department is to focus on violent street
criminals and take them off the street by focusing on local gun
and drug crimes. Classical conservative theory and its rejection
of any level of federalization of local control over prosecution
of street crime that once defined the Republican party under the
1960s rhetoric of Goldwater[64] and Reagan,[65] was abandoned under
the presidency of Reagan and subsequently by Bush 41, Clinton,
Bush 43 and the abandonment found utterance and approval in
the Trump Administration under Attorney General Barr. Barr took
pride that, "over the past two years, the Department has dramatically increased the number of criminal defendants charged at the
federal level. In 2017, the Justice Department charged the greatest
number of violent crime defendants because we started to track
this category in 1992. In 2018, the Department broke the record
again—this time by a margin of almost 15 percent." Attorneys
General Thornburgh, Reno and Ashcroft would be pleased. General
Barr, again with pride, proclaimed, "our prosecutors charged more
than 15,000 defendants with federal firearms offenses, which broke
records by a margin of 17 percent." The Clinton policy has endured.

As Sessions said before him, the reduction in crime is caused
by police and prosecutors. In his presentation to the Senate
Appropriations committee in April 2019, Barr made clear, "As
prosecutions have gone up, crime has gone down. In 2017—after
two years of increases under the previous administration—violent

crime and homicide rates went down nationwide. The FBI's preliminary data for the first six months of 2018 show a 4.3 percent decline in violent crime overall, a 6.7 percent decline in murders, and a 12 percent decline in robbery and burglary compared to the first six months of 2017. To continue this momentum, President Trump has requested an additional ... $100 million for Project Safe Neighborhoods grants to state and local law enforcement [and] $5.8 million to enhance violent crime and firearms prosecutions."

On December 18, 2019 General Barr announced the implementation of Operation Relentless Pursuit in which the Justice Department would allocate 71 million dollars to seven cities along with the formation of state-local-federal task forces with the FBI, DEA, ATF and the U.S. Marshals to reduce violent drug crimes and violent street gangs. The Reagan/Bush 41/Clinton era Safe Street task forces and joint crime and drug task forces would be enhanced with extra agents and prosecutions of gun trafficking and violence. Barr explained that the seven cities selected—Albuquerque, Baltimore, Cleveland, Detroit, Kansas City, Memphis, and Milwaukee—had shown that local prosecutors and law enforcement had proven commitment to reducing crime and were suffering crime rates above the national average.

Ronald Reagan in the 1970s lamented that federal tyranny would prevail if federal law enforcement became involved in local crime prevention. Conservatives abandoned this when Reagan became president in 1980. The abandonment was agreed to by the Democrats under Clinton. As shown by Sessions and now Barr, the abandonment is complete and it is policy orthodoxy of both parties that it is the role of the federal government to reduce violent crime.

chapter nine

Conclusion on the Interaction between Justice, Racism, Rhetoric, and Policy

I n June 2019, the U.S. Commission of Civil Rights issued a report on collateral sanctions[1] and made recommendations in relieving these sanctions on the lives of released offenders, specifically the ban on the right to vote of such offenders. Collateral sanctions are the social and legal impediments that individuals endure that are not part of the official sanctions (sentence) imposed due to conviction of a crime. For example, loss of voting rights is a collateral sanction for convictions for felonies. The official sanction can be five years in prison, but the collateral sanction is loss of voting rights under separate law. Social stigmas, housing restrictions, and employment discrimination by employers are all collateral sanctions. The report had one lone dissent, the same black social conservative—appointed by Bush 43[2]—discussed in Chapter 1 who argued blacks disproportionately commit crimes and should be disproportionately incarcerated. In his dissent to the commission recommendation that,

> States should consider restoration of the right to
> vote to all people who have been released from

incarceration or are on probation/parole and are currently disenfranchised because of criminal convictions.
Denying the right to vote does not serve the public safety
or interest.

He made clear,

I disagree with this blanket recommendation and assertion. Although referred to dismissively in the body of the
report, the public does have an interest in having the laws
made by people who have managed to clear the very low
bar of avoiding incarceration.

As I noted in my statement in the Commission's report
on the use of criminal background checks in employment,
"The EEOC's Guidance states that the percentage of
Americans who have been incarcerated may reach 6.6%.
That means that 93.4% of Americans never serve time
in prison." It is not that hard to avoid going to prison if
93 percent of Americans manage to do it. There aren't
many things that 93 percent of Americans can all do,
other than breathe.

I disagree with the argument that an ex-felon has
"paid his debt to society" and therefore should automatically have all his rights restored, including the right to
vote. There are multiple purposes of justice: restoration,
deterrence—and punishment. It is often impossible to
undo the consequences of a crime, or even to know all the
consequences. A man is sent to prison for twenty years
for selling opioids or cocaine. All the law sees in imposing
the sentence is the sale itself. You don't see the mom who
lived in a drugged stupor, only half-feeding her kids and
only getting them to school half the time. No one can
know all the consequences of any action, but people who
engage in wrongful actions know that the consequences
exist. Even though a state only incarcerates a person for a

set period of time, society is within its rights to determine that the punishment for a crime is not limited to prison time. ...

Any society must be able to set boundaries. This is particularly the case in a country based on social compact theory ... The right to include necessarily encompasses the right to exclude. And excluding someone on the basis of felon status is as objective a standard as we can hope to achieve.

The report asserts that even if disfranchisement on the basis of felon status may be generally permissible, it is problematic because it has a disparate effect on blacks and Latinos. Disfranchisement has a disparate impact on blacks and Latinos because blacks and Latinos are disproportionately likely to be involved in crime. And contrary to fashionable political rhetoric, it is highly unlikely that racial discrimination is responsible for the incarceration of a significant number of blacks and Hispanics.[3]

Although he supported the concept of returning voting rights, he dissented that a reason for doing so was the unjust incarceration of blacks and that the restriction on the right to vote reduces the black vote in American politics.

Throughout this book when I used the term white social conservatives I was not speaking about individuals, but rather I use the term to explain a political social worldview. White social conservatism has nothing to do with skin color, as the Bush appointee clearly proves. Blacks can and do hold negative racist views about blacks reminiscent of Thomas Jefferson and John Calhoun and the pre-Civil War advocates of slavery. Blacks, like Bush's appointee, can as easily assert that blacks are social deficient (criminogenic) just as easily as Jefferson said blacks are biologically deficient. While I identified racism within white social conservative political rhetoric and narratives resulting in government policy and electoral results, my point is that racism can function within this worldview without distain or acknowledgment. Racism in the white social conservative worldview is implicit and subconscious while it confirms positive emotional and/or psychological preconceptions about society and negative preconceptions of subgroups in society.

Put another way, racism and dehumanization of blacks find a home in white social conservative worldview but that does not automatically mean that individual white social conservatives find a home in racism and dehumanization of blacks per se. But as discussed in Chapters 3 and 4, white social conservatives can live with racist results and can use non-explicit racist explanations to justify or otherwise excuse or deny those racist results. For example, as discussed in Chapter 4, this worldview regarding blacks is implicitly defended when white social conservatives argue that the Confederate flag and statues of Confederate generals reflect the honor of the men not of slavery. What is being discounted in this worldview is what those generals and that flag were defending in 1861 through 1865. The institution of slavery (and all of the racist assumptions that the institution of slavery were built upon) and the defense of states' rights originated for the sole purpose of providing opposition to the power of the national government to control the spread of slavery.

Another example of implicit racism in white social conservative political rhetoric is its focus on slavery, not Jim Crow. Consider this, America grew from a third-rate nation (1865) to a world superpower (1945) both economically and militarily when blacks were by law isolated from building wealth and social power intergenerationally, along with whites. Black social, economic, political, and educational achievement was systematically destroyed after Reconstruction at the hands of white mobs and their burning, killing, lynching, imprisoning, and otherwise removing blacks from land and life in America. The death of Reconstruction was not the result of peaceful elections after the second corrupt bargain of 1877. Black elected officials were physically removed from their positions by mobs of white southern Democrats when it was clear that the North had abandoned them. In the *Wilmington race riot of 1898,* the fusion government of blacks and Republicans was forcibly removed from office in Wilmington, North Carolina on November 10, 1898, and all the black males that survived the violence were rounded up and were expelled from Wilmington. Black-owned businesses that competed with white businesses were burned to the ground. The destruction sealed the complete end of Reconstruction in North Carolina and began the supremacy of white segregationist southern Democrats that would last for more than five decades into the next century. A similar event occurred in Meridian, Mississippi, in March 1871, known as the *Meridian race riot of 1871*. After starting a gunfight in the courtroom, white Democrats killed more than 30 blacks in three days of violence with no convictions. By 1875, the southern Democrats had formed red shirt brigades and had taken control of Mississippi through intimidation of voting. Reconstruction was over. Similar events occurred in Louisiana (the *Colfax Massacre*) in April 1873, and in New Orleans (the *New Orleans riot of July 1866*). The three-day riot in Memphis, Tennessee (*Memphis riot of May 1866*), and in Charleston, South Carolina (*Charleston riot of September 1876*) similarly ended reconstruction. The goal and result of post-Reconstruction violence at the hands of white Democrats was the intentional destruction of black wealth, in all its forms (economic, political, social, societal, personal), that was formed after the Civil War, and this destruction occurred under the passive and sometimes direct hand of government officials. The ability of the former slaves to create intergenerational wealth—the key to all success in a capitalist nation—was systematically taken from the former slaves.

After the fall of Reconstruction in the postbellum period, from the late 1890s through the 1940s blacks suffered subsequent destruction of black wealth through intentional government-supported white race riots. For example, the entire black city of Greenwood, Tulsa Oklahoma which was known as *the black wall street* was burned to the ground in the *Greenwood riot of 1921*. In January 1923, the entire neighborhood of Rosewood, Levy County, Florida was burned to the ground in *Rosewood massacre of 1923*.

On November 2, 1920, a similar event occurred in which the entire black neighborhood of Ocoee, Florida was burned to the ground in *Ocoee riot of November 2, 1920*. These and many other white race riots that wiped whole black neighborhoods off the face of the earth not only took black lives, but it ended black economic wealth that could be passed on to subsequent generations. It also caused displacement of black expertise and talent and dispersed it, thus avoiding its concentration and increase. Of course, none of these attacks by whites on blacks resulted in murder convictions in state courts. In a nation that is only 231 years old with a 150 years accounted for with slavery and Jim Crow, the lawful and practical inability of blacks to create and hold and transfer wealth to the following generations creates contemporary problems. Consider this, the wealth that Joseph Kennedy amassed in the early 1920s upholds the entire Kennedy family more than two generations later. The blacks that were burned out of their wealth in Greenwood and Ocoee had nothing to pass on to their children or their grandchildren or greatgrandchildren that are living today. Wealth was not passed because it was stolen, not because blacks are lazy and want an unearned handout as white social conservatives assert today.

The purpose of the white violence during early twentieth century Jim Crow was to make clear blacks were going to be kept in their place—that place being not being an economic or political (voting) threat to white economic growth. The political and social acceptance of this policy was made all the more clear with the marching of the Klan down Pennsylvania Avenue on August 8, 1925.

Culturally, the release of *Birth of Nation* on February 8, 1915, followed by its successor *Gone With The Wind* (1939), solidified the southern myth of the Confederate Lost Cause and the assertion that the South was the noble party in the war, and its loss unleased the inferior black man from his proper place.

During the *riots of the Red Summer* from February to October 1919 hundreds of blacks were killed and countless more were beaten and imprisoned.[4] Each riot was sparked by fears of blacks getting away with rape of white women or were reactions to blacks presenting economic challenges to Jim Crow as black soldiers returned from the war and rejected the imposition of second class citizenship. Socially the riots occurred as a reaction of whites to the great migration into northern cities, the release of the movie *Birth of a Nation,* the economic dislocation that occurred because of rising unemployment after World War I, the rise of organized labor unions and general fear of communism that followed. The *Elaine massacre* in Elaine, Arkansas (September 30, 1919) in which 500 soldiers fired upon and killed 200 unarmed blacks running for protection from a white mob, the *Chicago riots* (July 1919) and the *Washington, D.C., riots* (July 1919) in which an estimated 23 and 40 blacks, respectively, were killed[5] by white mobs were among the most deadly riots. The NAACP was born as a reaction and countermeasure to the lynching and destruction of black wealth as a result of *the 1919 riots.* These riots involved more than 20 cities, including Houston, Texas; East St. Louis and Chicago, Illinois; Omaha, Nebraska; Tulsa, Oklahoma and Charleston, South Carolina, in which white mobs attacked blacks and burned entire black neighborhoods and businesses to the ground.[6] This economic decimation of black wealth and social stability was made worse by the great depression and blacks being denied full access to the various new deal programs of the 1930s. This isolation did not dissipate after World War II. After the war, the benefits of the GI Bill and federal home loans were denied to blacks, and black neighborhoods were redlined to isolate them from low-interest loans and economic enhancement.

Again, the point is that while whites were allowed to create intergenerational wealth and form wealthy communities—wealthy in all its forms—blacks were as a matter of policy prevented from doing the same. The policy outcome results of a century of Jim Crow are found in urban cities and disproportionate incarceration today. Consider this, what would America as a whole and blacks in America look like if black entrepreneurs, educators, businessmen, teachers, farmers, university builders, doctors, lawyers, nurses, and simple laborers were left alone, not killed and imprisoned, and allowed to build wealth and communities after the Civil War? Consider what our cities and towns would look like. Consider what our political discourse would sound like. Consider what our politics would be like. Consider that in America it took only 40 years from the necessity of passing a law to allow blacks to move into any white neighborhood they could afford to a black man being able to move into the White House. Had Reconstruction been the norm and a permanent response to slavery, Obama would not have been the first black president and today black presidents would be no more of a novelty than apples on apple trees.

But that's not what happened. The proposition of white supremacy was written into law and then into the social fabric of America for a century. During this time black wealth was systematically decimated to enforce black inferiority to the benefit of white supremacy.

While most social conservatives generally, and especially black social conservatives that see the world through white eyes, discount all this history because they don't want to deal with its implications; some accept the history and respond rhetorically, "You are right. Had we left blacks alone and provided them with the promises of the Declaration of Independence and the legal protections of the Constitution, black presidents would be a norm. Once blacks became equal under the law, they produced a president in 40 years. Today, America is open to blacks and you are free from abuse now. What's the problem? Go build intergenerational wealth now as you would have in 1865. Besides, whites of today did not oppress the blacks of yesterday."

Addressing the second assertion first, I would answer with a question. Did you write the Declaration of Independence or the Constitution, did you fight in the Civil War, did you invent the steamboat, did you invent the light bulb, did you populate and build the states that were secured from Mexico, did you fight in World War I, did you build the wealth of America before the great depression or restore it before World War II? The answer, of course, is no. But you live in a nation that became great because of these and other events that made America great and you are enjoying the fruits of what was the American Century. Yet you did nothing to create them. Like these, you are also benefiting from the system of Jim Crow and black oppression and white superiority that also built America. You are enjoying the results of both today.

As to the first assertion, here is the problem. In 1865, America was still new and the cement of her foundations as a powerful country had not been laid yet. In 1865, there was room for all, except blacks.

In 1865, the second industrial revolution, the age of American invention and industry, the rise and design of all of the great American cities, the rise of wall street, the inventions of the telephone (1876), the electric light bulb (1879) and the automobile (1885/1886) had not yet occurred. Transportation was the horse and buggy. Domestically the full benefits of rural and industrial growth in the western expansion of America through the *Homestead Act of 1862* were yet to fully materialize. Under this act, millions of acres of land wealth were almost literally given to white settlers for free. Of course, blacks, by law or implementation, had almost no access to exploit this source of wealth. The Gilded Age (1870s–1900) followed by the Progressive Era (1900–1920), which together saw the modernization of America in all its forms also encompassed the golden age of Jim Crow.

In 1865 America had not yet taken its place on the world stage as a global power. America becoming a recognized player on the world stage after the Spanish American War (1898), the American navy taking its place among the great navies of Europe (1907–1909), America taking control of Panama (1904) and building the canal (1914), America flexing its diplomatic power in brokering a peace treaty between Japan and Russia to end the Russo-Japanese War (1905) and pushing for the International Opium Commission in Shanghai and the banning of the international opium trade in 1908, America becoming a world power after World War I was all in the future in 1865.

The point is the time between 1865 and the next 45 years was the time of America coming into its own, and there was room for all people to take a place in it. By 1968, the American economic, political, social, societal cement was laid and was hardened. The glory days of wagon trains and gold rushes and expanding states and opportunities for wealth in uncharted and unsettled lands in the Wild West are over. The days of the ignorant being able to find work in new urban areas in which he could support a family so his son could go to school and his grandson could go to Congress are gone, for the days of the living wage jobs for the ignorant is a thing of the past in modern America.

Of course, this is not intended to justify the lack of success on the individual level. As discussed previously in this book, classical traditional black social conservative thought, as opposed to black social conservatives that see the world through white eyes, asserts that racism is no excuse for failure to achieve success in America. The former acknowledges the truth of America's racial history while the latter asserts this history has no modern significance. The classical traditional black social conservative knows that this history explains the structural dynamics of present American politics and policy which have negative effects on blacks. The black social conservative that see the world through white eyes, asserts that the parts of American history that are positive and honorable should be remembered and processed in contemporary American policymaking, but rejects this use of American history when the history of slavery and Jim Crow are invoked to explain the contemporary intractable structural problems birthed, raised, and matured by the racism of the past.

Classical traditional black social conservatives totally support personal responsibility in education, but as discussed previously in this book, there are structural historical reasons why the least functional schools are in poor urban neighborhoods, just as there are structural reasons why rookie police officers are assigned to poor neighborhoods not middle-class black neighborhoods, there are structural reasons why poverty is always found to be concentrated in certain geographic areas of the city, there are structural reasons why these geographic areas are socially and politically abandoned, and there are structural reasons why young black males are more likely to be arrested, convicted, incarcerated, and shot during traffic stops than whites. As discussed in Chapter 2, these structural reasons did not occur through happenstance or by accident. The modern American urban structure of neighborhoods are the result of racial neighborhood exclusions (early 1900s), legal restrictive covenants (1920–1948), followed by racially restrictive covenants, in fact (1948–1968), and the red lining (1934–1968) of black neighborhoods through the FHA policies, the rise of segregated white suburbs, blockbusting, real estate value manipulation, and racial steering. These Jim Crow policies supplemented the impact of white flight and the rise of the suburbs in the 1950s through the early 1970s and the concentration of blacks into urban neighborhoods resulting from the second great migration. This concentration and isolation was institutionalized through the policy choices of investment in public highways over public transportation, the isolation of neighborhoods by limiting the public transportation connection between these communities and the suburbs where middle-class jobs were being placed, the use of highways and street design to break connections between communities, and the policy of public education funding being tied to property values all impacted the physical design and development of most of the modern cities and neighborhoods in America. These policies resulted in the creation of concentrated poverty (political, physical, social, and economic) in selected sections (neighborhoods) of society.

These structural social dynamics, as any freshman criminology student knows, has a personality of its own that perpetuates negative psychological behaviors that are self-perpetuating. Consider the economic structural reasons why black working-class and middle-class parents judge a neighborhood by the school district it's in and that is the sole measure of possibilities when moving or the need to move when their children grow older. Why do teachers who work in a high-preforming school district have to live outside that district because the cost of living is too high for their salaries? The answer is that its structural not racial. The point is this, black poor isolated urban neighborhoods have violence and lack of mental health services; black middle-class socially and politically integrated neighborhoods don't.

Again, as any freshman criminology student knows, the difference is in the structure, not the residents. Classical traditional black social conservatives understand this and understand how this affects people in these geographic areas, black social conservatives ignore this structural history and assert if Republicans ran these areas with low taxes and enforced school discipline without regard to political correctness concerns about disproportionate expulsions and suspensions, life would be better. As the scriptures say, let him who has an ear, let him hear. For the rest, let them only receive confusing parables.

Classical traditional black social conservative orthodoxy in the churches and in the homes make it clear to the generation of today, there is no room for an undereducated or uneducated black child in America. Classical traditional black social conservatives don't pretend racism is a thing of the past. Because it exists, we tell our children they must know two and two is four when the job only requires them to know one and one is two. Behind closed doors, we tell our children there is no room for excuses and being black and racism is not an excuse for failure. Classical traditional black social conservatives give their children "the talk" and explain why they are doing so. Black social conservatives that see the world through white eyes go on Fox News and conservative radio and say racism no longer exists, and the need for the talk is a falsity. But I digress.

Blacks have achieved great things despite the history of racism and the social injustices of Jim Crow in America. The point of this history is not that blacks can't achieve greatness now, but in the America of today, there is less growing room to do so now as compared to 1865. The former slaves walking up to the starting line of America in 1865 is different for blacks doing the same in the post-Jim Crow era of today. Today American wealth, again in all its forms, is well distributed and jealously held by those who have it. Whites rioted in the 1970s over bussing! White middle-class politics hardened against blacks in the 1980s over affirmative action. In 1865 the wealth and power that would come to define America were yet to be formed and distributed. In 1865, blacks were not structurally banned from Americas future. But by the 1890s, they were. Whites in America during this time, however, both indigenous and through immigration, intergenerationally enjoyed America's growth. While blacks were by law and practice excluded, white immigrants intergenerationally moved from ghettoes, to working-class jobs, to professional jobs, to Congress, to the Senate, to the presidency. The development of the American story that each generation in America would be better than the generation that birthed them was established by the generations of the 1860s through the 1960s. As I discuss next, and previously in this book, blacks who established economic, educational, and political independence or competition with whites between 1865 through the first four decades of the following American century were structurally met with prison, lynch mobs, and riots by whites that burned entire black towns to the ground.

As President Johnson said in 1964, you can't take a person who was chained for a century, prevented from training for the race, and then at the last minute remove the chain, place him at the starting line with those who have been trained, and then say you are free to run let the best man win.

President Johnson explained that justice does not allow the audience of the race to say, he can't run so let him lose in a fair race when the runner was prevented from gaining training for the race in the first place. Justice says, the race is unfair unless we do something about the abuse done to the runner who is now behind because of the chains that were placed on him by force.

Consider this, only when America became a great superpower and the foundations of intergenerational wealth had fully taken hold in white America and in its suburban neighborhoods and economic centers were blacks allowed to be equal under the law.

White social conservative discounting of this part of American history and what this history means structurally in America today is implicit and systemic racism. How? It's in the dehumanization and discounting of the damage done to blacks as a whole as being irrelevant. The dehumanization is manifested in regarding the history of Jim Crow as irrelevant, because, after all, we're only talking about black pain. White America did fine under Jim Crow.

The racist America of 1765, 1865, 1920, or even the 1950s has been put in the dustbin of history and that is a good thing. But the problem is that white social conservatives, and blacks who see the world through white conservative eyes, believe that because the Klan no longer walks down Pennsylvania avenue 100,000 strong in full regalia—Charlottesville notwithstanding—racism is a thing of the past. Why the racism of 1865 and 1954 is in the dustbin of history is another matter. It's dead because at one stage of its death, the federal government made it die. The federal government in all its forms, judicial, legislative, and with use of force, brought the South to heel; that is the problem for white social conservatives. As slavery was killed at the hands of the Army of the Potomac, Jim Crow was killed with federal power. It died by use of the Supreme Court (*Brown v. Board of Ed*) in 1954 to end the legality of Jim Crow under *Plessy,* and it died through the use of military troops and U.S. Marshals to bring the southern states to heel in 1957 (the Little Rock Nine), 1962 (James Meredith and integration of University of Mississippi), 1963 (integration of University of Alabama), and 1965 (protection of the second Selma Edmund Pettus Bridge march). Legal Jim Crow was buried once and for all with federal legislation, the Civil Rights Acts of 1964, 1965, and 1968. Jim Crow was not killed by adherence to states' rights and white social conservative theories of individual freedom and liberty.

Social conservatives both overlook how slavery and Jim Crow met their end and resent it at the same time. One of the underpinnings of the defeat of slavery and Jim Crow states' rights was the higher principle of racial equality and the power of the federal government to oppose the power of the states to treat blacks as second class citizens. Civil rights versus the liberty to discriminate is one of the distinctions between conservatives and liberals. Conservatives define liberty as freedom from the federal government at all costs, while liberals define liberty as freedom from abuse and injustice, with the aid of the federal government when necessary. Every election from Reagan to Trump has encompassed this distinction.

This philosophical distinction is why conservatives can live with racism or racist social outcomes, because the growth of the federal government in power to end such outcomes is worse in their eyes. This is also why white social conservatives support black social conservatives; the racist results can be accepted and even defended because the latter provides cover to the former. They can't be racists when they say blacks commit more crime than whites and are criminogenic and that's why our prisons need to be filled with blacks because black skinned conservatives say the same thing. When classical traditional black social conservatives or liberal blacks look at white social conservatism, they see the racism hiding within it. The failure of whites to see the racism and/or racist outcomes only confirms black fears and suspicions. *Aversive racism* and *dehumanization* theories have developed as explanations for the failure to see racism in policy outcomes. Aversive racism is the emotional and angry reaction that conservatives exhibit when confronted with the racist policy outcomes that they support. The reaction comes from the belief that they in fact have no racists beliefs. Aversive racism is the holding of racists ideas or support of racist outcomes while holding the aversive idea that one is not racist and is offended at the suggestion. Dehumanization is the downgrading of the outgroup and imputing onto them lower social status and being able to justify harsh treatment of them. Dehumanization is a sliding scale of negative social treatment, light discrimination or social aversion on one end of the scale and genocide on the other. An additional reason black conservative rhetoric is no answer to white social conservative racism is that racism is not skin defined, its belief defined. Blacks can support racist outcomes too. There have always been blacks that have supported the racist outcomes detrimental to blacks. When the European powers came to the African continent for slaves, they did not go into the continent to find slaves themselves. Blacks captured other blacks and brought them to the beach to be sold. But again, we digress.

Racism has many forms and the fall of overt racism in 1968 does not mean that the ideas of racism—black inferiority or blacks being biologically different than whites has been removed from the mind of America. Consider a recent article in the 2016 issue of the *Proceedings of the National Academy of Sciences* regarding attitudes of medical students. The students were asked whether they agreed with incorrect assessments of racial biological characteristics. Participants were asked objectively false concepts; for example, they were asked "is it true blacks have thicker skin," "is it true blacks have stronger immune systems than whites," "is it true black people's blood coagulates more quickly than whites," or "is it true blacks' nerve endings are less sensitive than whites." The study found that 73 percent of participants in study one (non-medical students) believed at least one of these racial statements. The study revealed that people who believed these racial biological ideas were less sensitive to the assertions of pain made by blacks.

In the second of the two study groups, the medical students were asked the same questions and were asked hypotheticals regarding measuring the pain of blacks and whites. The medical students were little better in their beliefs of racist ideas, in that 50 percent believed at least one of these biological race concepts. The study found that "participants in study 2 who endorsed false beliefs about biological differences between blacks and whites exhibited a racial bias in pain perception similar to the bias."[7] The study then determined how racial bias affected treatment determinations. The researchers found that "participants who endorsed more false beliefs about biological differences between blacks and whites showed a racial bias in the accuracy of their treatment recommendations. Participants who did not endorse such beliefs showed no bias in treatment recommendation accuracy."[8] When the researchers looked at the "relationship between racial bias in pain perception and racial bias in treatment recommendation accuracy" they determined that "a significant and sizable positive correlation, such that greater racial bias in pain ratings was associated with greater racial bias in the accuracy of treatment recommendations. As predicted, racial bias in pain perception is related to racial bias in the accuracy of treatment recommendations."[9] The researchers concluded that "the practical importance is significant: those endorsing more false beliefs rated the pain of a black (vs. white) patient half a scale point lower and were less accurate in their treatment recommendations 15% of the time."[10] The point, implicit bias is not just a social psychology concept, racist ideas can have a direct impact on how blacks receive medical treatment from medical personnel. This racial bias that discounts the physical pain of blacks in childbirth or the need for medical treatment in general is not the fault or result of black on black crime, the failure of black children to do their homework, or otherwise not taking advantage of the opportunities they are given in America as white social conservatives on Fox and conservative talk radio posit as an explanation for all disparities found with blacks in America.

As a historical and political matter, the belief that blacks are biologically different than whites and have a higher threshold of pain has been used to justify their dehumanization. "Beliefs that blacks and whites are fundamentally and biologically different have been prevalent in various forms for centuries. In the United States, scientists, physicians, and slave owners championed these beliefs alike to justify slavery and the inhumane treatment of black men and women in medical research. In the 19th century, prominent physicians sought to establish the 'physical peculiarities' of blacks that could 'serve to distinguish him from the white man'. Such 'peculiarities' included thicker skulls, less sensitive nervous systems, and diseases inherent in dark skin."[11] As a 19th scholar observed, "blacks bore a Negro disease [making them] insensible to pain when subjected to punishment."[12] Blacks did little better in the twentieth century suffering experiments at the hands of the military to test the effects of mustard gas and other chemicals of war or at the hands of the medical community during studies of the development of syphilis as exampled in the famous U.S. Public Health Service experiments at Tuskegee from 1932 to 1972.

The explicit racism that allowed for these experiments is gone but the underlying justification for them, black inferiority, has remained and is manifested in implicit or subtle racism. Implicit bias is about how a person, or a people, are perceived. White social conservative political rhetoric and narratives perceive black disproportionate incarceration as a result of individual personal failings. Thus, the impact of the disproportionate incarceration on blacks receives no sympathy. Rather than asserting blacks are biologically inferior, they assert they are socially and behaviorally inferior. Social conservatives assert that if blacks just got married and had children in wedlock instead of outside of it, all the social inequities they suffer from would disappear. It's black people's fault they are poor and arrested, not racism, and it's surely not the fault of white racism generations past.

Either perception—explicit racism, they are born that way, or implicit racism, they act that way—gets you to the same social-political narrative and policy outcome. The racism is in not acknowledging that race and ethnicity is a proxy for social constructs that explain environmental, cultural, and political outcomes. The racism is in how explicit racism defined blacks and how that negative perception (implicit racism) has remained. Assertions of black inferiority have changed in terms of their justification, not their existence. Consider the study noted earlier, black behavior has nothing to do with doctors providing poor treatment of black pain because the doctor believes that blacks biologically can suffer more pain. Black behavior has nothing to do with how doctors perceive them. Black behavior has nothing to do with poor medical treatment by the medical community on issues of disease studies, maternal birth rates, or pain medication prescription.[13]

The results of the 2016 study were not an anomaly. Similar results were found with nurses,[14] mental health providers,[15] police officers,[16] jurors,[17] managers perceptions of success,[18] voters,[19] the differential media responses to black and Hispanic children who are kidnapped or otherwise disappear[20] compared to white children,[21] and various others regarding negative bias of blacks per se or in black treatment outcomes.

These negative racial bias outcomes against blacks in 2020 America are not the result of explicit bias but are the result of implicit bias that manifests as subconscious and conscious psychological and cognitive uploads in mental processing to ambiguous or new situations. As discussed in Chapter 6, social psychology has established that individuals "upload" perceptions, descriptions, and expectations of social groups to help define the ambiguity of new situations. This process of *bidirectional stereotyping* occurs, for example, when the concept—crime—is psychologically considered, and a specific psychological category is "uploaded" into the unconscious mind—blacks, and when an individual black man is viewed, he is categorized with a concept—criminal. Crime and race are psychologically linked bidirectionally. When a police officer is confronted with a situation that does not provide enough information for cognitive level determinations, the ambiguity causes the officer to "upload" information to fill the ambiguity. This subconscious emotional/psychological thinking allows negative perceptions of blacks to color the actual situation the officer is in and then psychologically the officer acts in accordance with these negative perceptions. The actual negative stereotype does not need to reach conscious cognitive level thinking for the stereotypes to influence the behavior of the officer. The subconscious "upload" subtly colors the background of the overall situation and influences how the officer acts. When the officer sees a group of black youths on the corner the lack of facts regarding the black youths (ambiguity) is filled in with the implicit bias upload of criminal. The upload then governs how the police approach the youths until the ambiguity is solved by actual specific facts regarding them.

Are they actually kids looking for trouble, or are they kids waiting for the school bus?

Consider the November 2018 Cincinnati Ohio case[22] of a white retired police officer calling the police saying the house next door was being broken into by two black men. When the police arrive, they order the black men out of the house, handcuff, and search both, under the protests of the black men who assert they are looking at the house to buy. Even after being told, the officers search the house and then call the owner. Only when the owner confirms the house is up for sale and that the door was not broken into are the black men released from a total of nine police officers who responded to the situation and false call. When the white neighbor is questioned about the 911 call, the retired police officer admits he did not actually see the black men break into the door and he called because the black men did not belong in the neighborhood. When he was questioned about making the call when he did not see the black men break into the house, but simply enter it, the neighbor said, it's better to be safe than sorry. The white retired police officer showed no embarrassment or regret that his call got two innocent black men handcuffed and searched in the street. But why should he? They were only blacks. When the black men protested about the police use of force, the handcuffs, and search at gunpoint, when they presented the police with a realtor's card, the officer said with indignance, "Don't play the race card; we do this in all of our calls for possible break-ins, and we have to act on the information we are given."

One could ask what should they have done then. The police, trained and armed and in control of the area, did not need to escalate to handcuffs and custodial arrest. Being handcuffed and searched in the street by a gang of police officers with guns in hand is a dehumanizing and humiliating experience when you are guilty; how much more when you are innocent. The level of force used, telling the black men to come out and produce identification and remain standing while they were verifying it would have been enough to meet the needs of an ambiguous police investigation while maintaining the humanity and dignity of two black men worthy of respect as citizens of America. But the officers instead, at gunpoint, handcuffed both men when they were told the house was for sale and they protested the treatment by the police. It's the escalation of force—the handcuffs at gunpoint and the humiliation that accompanies such actions that make the police action violative of their rights. Rather than investigate the call to determine if the occupants were criminals, they approached the house guns out and handcuffed the men when they were told the men had a lawful right to be there. But because the situation was ambiguous, the police subconsciously uploaded criminal to fill in the ambiguity of a confrontation with two large black men and used force to maintain control of them. And then responded with incongruity when accused of racism. The implicit bias totally escaped the officers.

This story had a peaceful ending, but the story would have been different if the implicit bias upload also included a negative upload in the minds of the black men. What could have occurred if when they saw the police come upon them, they uploaded police harassment because they are black. In this ambiguous situation, if both parties also upload negative emotional feelings and if each had acted accordingly—police verbal and physical dominance and the black men with verbal or physical resistance—these men could have ended up face down on the street with a police knee in their backs or at worse, face down dead in the street with a bullet in their chests.

The process of uploading negative racial bias also provides a context for understanding white privilege. White privilege is not an economic concept, it's a concept of what whites don't have to worry about or think about because they are white. It's a level of foreboding or hesitation that blacks consider when acting. Consider the April 2018 incident in Rochester Hills, Michigan, a city located in northeast Oakland County in which a 14-year-old black male got lost after missing his bus for school and knocked on a white man's door for help.[23] Upon being seen by his wife, who screamed on sight of the black child, the child was met by Jeffrey Zeigler,

53 years old, with a shotgun. As he ran for his life Zeigler fired his gun at the retreating child. Zeigler testified at his trial that he was surprised that Brennan Walker was only 14—taking him as an adult[24]—but stated that he did not shoot at Brennan because he was black. Here is how white privilege works, first Zeigler truly believed that he would have shot a white child under the same circumstances. Leaving that fantasy alone, second, white privilege affects how blacks see possible reactions by whites. Because white privilege allows blacks to be seen as a physical threat an older black man at the very least would have hesitated from walking into a suburban all-white neighborhood and knocking on a strange door. He would hesitate because he would have considered the real possibility of being shot because he was black. It's the hesitation that defines white privilege. Zeigler, to his surprise, was convicted and was sentenced to two to ten years for assault with a deadly weapon, and an additional two years for illegal firearm discharge.

White privilege also manifests itself in how blacks are perceived. The privilege, of course, is in white children not being as negatively perceived as black children. Research has shown that black children are generally perceived as older, more adultlike, and sexualized than white children of the same age. This aspect of dehumanization can result in police seeing a black child with a toy gun as a threat to be shot rather than as a child to be tempered. The former being evidenced in the shooting of Tamir Rice in Columbus, Ohio, in November 2014. Tamir was 12 years old and 195 pounds, but the officers thought he was over 18 years old and 185 pounds.[25] Research has found that civilians, teachers, and police misperceive black children as older than they are, more responsible for their actions, less deserving of the presumption of childlike innocence, more likely to be treated as adults within the criminal justice system, and more likely to suffer use of force by police than white children of the same age.[26] This "adultification bias" has led to various deleterious impacts on how black boys are perceived as a threat and how black girls are stripped of their child status and seen as oversexualized and punished accordingly in school from as early as 5 years old, with a concentration of the problem when they are 10–15 years old.[27]

These negative racial bias outcomes also occur in political discourse when trying to make sense of complicated social dynamics to affirm individual self-perceptions or perceptions of others. For example, rather than consolidate complicated and nuanced historical and contemporary factors to understand concentrated poverty or disproportionate outcomes, it's easier for white social conservatives to say all negative black social dynamics are defined by their deviance from traditional family construction. Put simply, racism provides clean and simple answers to complicated policy outputs and outcomes. These negative racial outcomes can be explained by the dynamics of white privilege (superiority) versus black inferiority. White privilege is not defined by economics, it's defined by expectation and self-perceptions. As Dr. King explained at Selma, white privilege is the belief that whiteness is better and superior. White America is the standard. It's the belief that as a white man or woman, you have a right to do or say as you wish, and advocates of political correctness have no right to tell you that you can't think or say something. It's your right. In the social psychology literature, this dynamic is explained by infrahumanization. *Infrahumanization* occurs when members of a majority group perceives only positive attributes about itself and elevates itself above other groups and justifies its treatment of other groups based on its superior status. The dehumanization of blacks asserts blacks are in the lower group. They are lower by genetics, as Jefferson explained, or lower by behavior and culture as white social conservatives argue today.

This black inferiority, supplemented by white supremacy, in the modern times of today encompasses subtle enforcement of negative images of blacks as needy, and even more subtle is the rejection of images of blacks as independent and powerful without white support. This latter subtly is found in both social conservative and progressive reactions. For example, consider how both conservatives and progressives reacted to the movie *Black Panther*. The movie represented the black nation of Wakanda as not only highly advanced in science and technology, but as more advanced than the all the nations of the earth, including the first world countries of Europe and America. The movie also portrayed a debate within black culture and political discourse regarding how racism should be addressed. The plot of the movie involved T'Challa, the King of Wakanda, and his abandoned cousin, N'Jadaka ("Killmonger"), and their fight for control of Wakanda and whether its advanced military power should be used to confront the nations of the world that oppressed blacks or should Wakanda remain separated from the less developed first world. A dramatic version of the debate between King and Malcolm over racial separation. The subtle point of the movie was that the answer did not involve or require white participation. In the movie blacks were portrayed as thoughtful, intelligent, scientifically advanced, militarily powerful, and were not economically and socially dependent on whites. That was the problem. White social conservatives, and black ones who see the world through white eyes, picked up on that subtly and rejected the movie. They saw the movie as anti-white and racist. Why? Because not only were blacks positively portrayed, whites were not the center of the story, either as heroes or villains. But social progressive Hollywood, which praised the movie, also rejected the movie in the end and gave the 2019 *Oscar* for best movie to *Green Book*. *Green Book* in some peoples' eyes was a *Driving Miss Daisy* 2.0 story. Leaving that discussion aside, the point is that *Black Panther* did not reflect the subtle perception of blacks as needing white help to settle social issues, *Green Book* did.

Consider another subtle example of black inferiority and white superiority. Consider how positive versus negative images of black males are portrayed in movies in general. Consider all the positive black male roles Denzel Washington has made over his career, yet of his five Best Actor Oscar nominations his only win came from when he portrayed a psychopathic homicidal corrupt police officer in *Training Day*. Consider the 2017 movie, *Hidden Figures,* based on the true story about three black women who played significant roles in the successful orbital flight of John Glenn in 1962 as well

as designing computer programs to make various NASA computers function together despite being victims of serious overt racism.
The movie also portrayed the husband of one of the women, a
black Lt. colonel in the U.S. Army, with positive family values that
would have secured the full praise of Jerry Falwell (founder of the
"moral majority" in the 1990s) and any member of the Christian
Coalition. The movie was the epidemy of clean, Christian, pro-
American, non-nudity, non-gratuitous sex, clean language movie
and storytelling social conservatives bemoan that Hollywood does
not make. Yet it received no praise or support from this very same
constituency. Why? Could it be that it showed blacks running
whole science divisions at NASA rather than running drugs in the
street. The movie was nominated for Best Picture in 2017 but lost
to a movie, *Moonlight,* which was about the pains and sufferings
of a black man dealing with his drug-addicted mother and how
that experience led him to sell drugs when he grew up. My point
is, look at what is portrayed as the best story of the year. A story
of intergenerational drug use and crime by blacks is honored over
a true story of three family-oriented, highly educated black women
being responsible for America's first successful space flight in the
face of overt racism. The portrayal of blacks as drug dealers and
criminals had more salience than the portrayal of the true story of
blacks being at the forefront of advanced mathematics and computer science in the early 1960s. Conservatives have their racism,
but Hollywood liberals have their own.

Hollywood adoption of negative black characters or rejection of
positive ones has a long history. Consider the movie *Glory,* which
was released in 1989 and was about the great Massachusetts 54th
which was the first all-black Union regiment sent to oppose the
freedom-loving, slave-owning Confederacy. The movie portrayed
the bravery, discipline, military dominance of black men fighting
to prove their manhood and to gain their freedom. This movie
was released during the same time that local news was showing
gun-carrying black men in drug gangs running wild. At the Oscars
that year, *Glory* was not even nominated for best picture. *Driving*

Miss Daisy won. While Denzel Washington won best supporting actor for his portrayal in *Glory,* the nomination was not given to Morgan Freeman who played the master sergeant in the movie and whose character was much more upright, disciplined and focused on the significance of black men fighting for their rights and to be seen as men. Consider the subtle difference in what character was recognized.

In 1984, the movie *A Soldier's Story* was released. The movie was the adaptation of the 1981 Broadway play, *A Soldier's Play,* which won among other awards, the 1982 Pulitzer Prize for Drama. The movie centered on a proud, strong, black Army Judge Advocate General Captain, assigned to investigate the murder of a black drill sergeant. He was partnered by a white captain who pushed for the investigation, but who had never seen a black man with rank on his shoulders and acted accordingly. The movie was very black centric in that it reflected the internal debates and conflicts within black thought on how to deal with racism and both the how and why blacks should strive to maintain perfect behavior in the face of white domination through the interactions of the character of the killed black drill sergeant and his platoon. Denzel Washington played the character that killed him. Although nominated for best movie, the Oscar went to *Amadeus*, the movie celebrating the life of Wolfgang Amadeus Mozart.

Consider the subtly of black inferiority and white superiority in modern political rhetoric. When Obama "bragged" about his accomplishments or asserted his confidence, which he did not do very often, white social conservatives complained about his arrogance; but when Trump displays his narcissistic self-praise bravado twenty-four-seven, social conservatives praise him. Why? European white male dominance has existed from the ancient Greeks to the Romans to the British Empire to post-World War II America. The election of Obama represented a break in that chain of dominance. Trump's election represents its restoration. Trump's arrogant self-praise is acceptable, while any self-praise of Obama was not, because white male dominance is supposed to be seen and acknowledged and praised. Black male dominance is not. It's the latter that is an aberration and is offensive. This is why white social conservatives had such a visceral and emotional and tribal hate for Obama regardless of his accomplishments and why they support Trump regardless of his actions.

Let's compare and face facts. If Obama tweeted every day and made everything about him and said he knew more than anyone about everything, but nothing was ever his fault, would Fox News and conservative talk radio and the Republican Party praise him like they praise and support Trump? If Obama were a two-time divorcee, at least a two-time adulterer, who got caught paying off a porn star and playboy bunny he had affairs with, would white social conservative evangelical Christians have supported him without dispute or hesitation? How did the white Christian televangelist community, which hung Clinton for his adultery, turn a blind eye to Trump's behavior? What would they have said if Obama said as Trump said in an interview, "I don't like to have to ask for forgiveness. And I am good. I don't do a lot of things that are bad. ... I think if I do something wrong, I think, I just try and make it right. I don't bring God into that picture. I don't."[28] Trump's narcissism and need to be seen as right regardless of being wrong and demanding that his view of correctness be supported has no limits. After a late August 2019 poll came out that showed Trump losing to various potential democratic candidates, he said at a press gaggle that his worst polls come from Fox and that there was something going on over there and he was not happy about it.[29] When Fox interviewed the DNC Communications Director he tweeted that Fox was not serving him well anymore and that conservatives needed to find a new source for news.[30] That was too much even for Fox which released statements from their news anchors that Fox News does not work for Trump. White social conservative radio said nothing. After Trump incorrectly said that Hurricane Dorian was threatening Alabama and it was reported on Fox News and the other news outlets as false with questions regarding a storm map that Trump showed with Alabama drawn in with pen; Trump called in a Fox reporter into the White

House Office to complain about reports on Fox saying he was wrong and to argue that he was correct that the storm was heading to Alabama but had shifted by the time he tweeted—thus he was not wrong.[31] What would Fox News and white social conservative radio have said if Obama did this? To put my question into context, white social conservatives on Fox and white social conservative radio were apoplectic when Obama said "if I had a son, he would look like Travon" after the Travon Martin incident and were inconsolable in rage when he said that a group of police officers "acted stupidly" when they arrested Harvard University professor Henry Louis Gates in his own house after they received a call from a white neighbor that someone had broken into Gates' house. First consider that they responded with indignation to what Obama said, then ask why they were infuriated by what he said.

Consider this. On July 23, 2019, Trump went the Turning Point USA national conference in Washington, D.C. Turning Point is a national college campus organization that sends conservatives to make speeches to conservative student organizations at their colleges. At the speech, Trump said that he went to the Air Force Academy graduation and shook the hands of all the graduates—all 1,100 of them. He said in his Turning Point speech, "there is no way that other presidents have done that." He said he was told, "no, no, they do it, but they leave after 50 of 60 people."[32] Now consider what he said. No other president had stood on stage at U.S. military graduations and shook all the new officers' hands. Only him. The fact that Obama did it every year when he was president, and Bush before him is of no account. Only Trump did it. He lied directly to pump himself up at a national meeting of college-age white social conservatives and sent them back to colleges across the country with that lie in their heads. Leaving that aside, what would Fox News and conservative talk radio say if that Obama had pumped himself up with an outright lie at the expense of military officers at their graduation.

When trying to curry their favor, Trump went to the mecca of white social conservative evangelicals, Liberty University, and said, "we're going to protect Christianity. I can say that. I don't have to be politically correct ... I hear this is a major theme right here, but two Corinthians, right, two Corinthians 3:17, that's the whole ballgame. Where the Spirit of the Lord, right, where the Spirit of the lord is, there is liberty. And here there is Liberty College, but Liberty University. ... Is that the one, is that one you like."[33] First, it's not two Corinthians, c. Second, if Obama had shown such a lack of experience with scripture by such an incorrect citation, would they have smirked and said it's a small matter, and in Europe, some people say two Corinthians? Even worse, would they let Obama blame his Christian advisors for the mistake![34] Moreover, how could the white Christian televangelist community, four years before Trump, support a Mormon (they believe that the book of Mormon is a book equal to the Bible and that Joseph Smith was a prophet of God sent after Jesus to establish the true Christian church) over a Christian black man while asserting to their TV audience that their faith should govern who they voted for?

On September 7, 2019 Trump tweeted that a peace conference, in Camp David, that no one knew about, between the U.S. and the Taliban, was being cancelled by his order because the Taliban took credit for a car bomb that killed an American soldier. When asked about it on the following Monday, Trump explained that it was his idea, he took his own advice to get the Taliban to come to Camp David, he did not take the advice of his advisors, and that it was all his own idea. At his press gaggle on Monday, Trump said that he considered having the meeting at the White House! Consider what white social conservatives would have said if Obama even thought of inviting the Taliban—the brother terrorist group to Al Qaeda the perpetrators of the 9/11 attacks—onto U.S. soil for a diplo-matic event at Camp David, much less the White House. Consider they, along with white televangelists, accused Obama of being an anti-Semitic Israel hater for making a deal with Iran over reducing Iran's nuclear weapon capacity. But even more, the failure of the diplomatic effort did not bring a word from white social conserva-tives asserting Trump was naive and a failure for the failed event. In their eyes Obama was a failure when he achieved a deal with a

sovereign nation, but Trump showed leadership in cancelling negotiations with the benefactors of the terrorists of 9/11—negotiations
they would have cursed Obama for thinking about trying in the
first place.

When Stephanie Clifford, known as Stormy Daniels, a strip
dancer, in an interview[35] spoke about how she had an affair with
Trump when she was 27, and working as porn star, and when Trump
was 60; would white social conservatives' have smirked and would
white Christian conservatives have ignored it and said move on if
Obama had had such an affair with a porn star? Consider this, why
did members of the white televangelist community go to the White
House and publicly pray and lay hands on Trump to bless him,
because he was president they say, but they failed to offer or do the
same for Obama. Do you think he would have refused the offer of
blessing and their help? If Obama was caught on tape talking about
how he could grab women by their genitalia and could kiss women
at his pleasure because of his status as a star and billionaire,[36] would
he have won the presidency? If Obama attacked his own intelligence
community and director of the FBI in public and said the press is
fake when it challenges his statements and asserted the press is a
threat to the nation and are un-American; what would Fox News
and conservative talk radio say about his integrity, honesty, and ability to govern?

Why are white social conservatives' reactions different when
Trump does it? The answer to all these questions is that white
conservatives and Trump voters see themselves in Trump. Trump
gets away with what they want to get away with and he says what
they want to say. He represents them. They feel empowered and
dominant through him. After the 1960s and 1970s they are back on
top as they were in the 1920s and 1930s through him. Trump can
attack political icons of the civil rights era with impunity. As Trump
tweeted on July 27, 2019,

> Rep, Elijah Cummings has been a brutal bully, shouting
> and screaming at the great men & women of Border

Patrol about conditions at the Southern Border, when actually his Baltimore district is FAR WORSE and more dangerous. His district is considered the Worst in the USA. ... As proven last week during a Congressional tour, the Border is clean, efficient & well run, just very crowded. Cummings District is a disgusting, rat and rodent infested mess. If he spent more time in Baltimore, maybe he could help clean up this very dangerous & filthy place.

Why is so much money sent to the Elijah Cummings district when it is considered the worst run and most dangerous anywhere in the United States. No human being would want to live there. Where is all this money going? How much is stolen? Investigate this corrupt mess immediately!

A black district is a "disgusting, rat and rodent infested mess" that needs to be investigated for embezzlement. Trump has written, as of writing, 39,591 tweets[37] using various words to insult people and places but he only used the word "infested" when insulting places and people of color. He only used it three times. First in regard to President Obama when he sent officials to aid in the African Ebola crisis in 2014,[38] second, in regard to the district of Congressman John Lewis in 2017,[39] and lastly when describing the district of Elijah Cummings and the country of origin (Somalia) of Congresswoman Ilhan Omar.[40]

The rules of political correctness don't apply to him. Consider this, in June 2019 a woman accused Trump of outright rape, not sexual harassment, not sexual assault, but outright rape. Since the rise of the #MeToo movement in October 2017, an accusation of sexual harassment or sexual assault alone had destroyed the careers of countless men, much less white rich ones in America. So, an accusation of actual completed rape would certainly provide death to a politician. But what did Trump say regarding the accusation when asked during a White House interview while sitting in the

Oval Office, "I'll say it with great respect: Number one, she's not my type."

Consider, first he survived the accusation. But, second, leaving aside the accusation, hear his response; she too ugly for me to rape. Even more, he survived saying it! Congressmen, senators, governors, and other powerful men in entertainment, business, and national news media had said much less and were outright fired or forced to resign with their careers destroyed. But Trump prevailed. That's why his supporters provide him unconditional support—he does what they can't do and says what they can't say. He does not bow to political correctness and he prevails over those who try to enforce political correctness. Yet the same president that told Congressman Cummings to clean up his own rat-infested district, resulting in condemnation as being racist, said at the ceremony commemorating the 400th Anniversary of the Virginia Assembly,[41]

> As we mark the first representative legislature at Jamestown, our nation also reflects upon an anniversary from that same summer four centuries ago. In August 1619, the first enslaved Africans in the English colonies arrived in Virginia. It was the beginning of a barbaric trade in human lives.
>
> Today, in honor, we remember every sacred soul who suffered the horrors of slavery and the anguish of bondage. More than 150 years later, at America's founding, our Declaration of Independence recognized the immortal truth that "all men are created equal." Yet, it would ultimately take a civil war 85 years after that document was signed, to abolish the evil of slavery.
>
> It would take more than another century for our nation, in the words of Reverend Martin Luther King, Jr., to live out "the true meaning of its creed" and extend the blessings of freedom to all Americans. *In the face of grave oppression and grave injustice, African Americans have built, strengthened, inspired, uplifted, protected,*

defended, and sustained our nation from its very earliest days.

Last year, I was privileged to sign the law establishing a commission to commemorate the arrival of the first Africans to the English colonies, and the 400 years of African American history that have followed.

While admitting with no hesitation that the history of the institution of American democracy and the first elected body in the colonies was as old as the institution of slavery in the colonies and that both facts are true, Trump made clear that overall what should be said of America is positive.

As we can see today on this great anniversary ... the settlers forged what would become the timeless traits of the American character. They worked hard. ... They strived mightily to turn a profit. ... As the years passed, ships bearing supplies and settlers from England also brought a culture and a way of life that would define the New World. ... It was a heritage those patriots would fight a long war of independence to defend. And it is a heritage that countless Americans have fought and died for to secure in all of those centuries since.

....

They started the nation that settled the wilderness, won our independence, tamed the Wild West, ended slavery, secured civil rights, invented the airplane, vanquished the Nazis, brought communism to its knees, and placed our great American flag on the face of the moon. ...

But among all of America's towering achievements, none exceeds the triumph that we are here to celebrate today: our nation's priceless culture of freedom, independence, equality, justice, and self-determination under God. That culture is the source of who we are. It is our prized inheritance.

It is our proudest legacy. It is among the greatest human accomplishments in the history of the world. ...

... Above all, we must be proud of our heritage, united in our purpose, and filled with confidence in our shared, great, great, great American destiny.

For, in America, no challenge is too great, no journey is too tough, no task is too large, no dream is beyond our reach. When we set our sights on the summit, nothing can stand in our way. America always gets the job done. America always wins. That is why, after 400 years of glorious American democracy, we have returned here to this place to declare to all the world that the United States of America and the great Commonwealth of Virginia are just getting started.

Our future is bigger, bolder, better, and brighter than ever before.

As discussed in Chapter 3, white social conservatives are tired of progressive's attacks on America and Trump gives an unquestioned voice to that sentiment. This sentiment of *America First* provides a concurrent reason for Trump's unwavering political support by white social conservatives. Trump attacks progressive politics in general, and progressive enforcers of political correctness specifically, with complete abandon and defends America with equal passion.

Another aspect of Trumpism, and how he maintains support of his voters, is making himself and his voters the victims of the media and other social and political elites. They are now the victims of discrimination in society both in political and social discourse. This victimhood of Trump voters has permeated into the Republican party as the new orthodoxy of republican rhetoric. A rhetoric that was in full display on December 11, 2019 when the House Judiciary Committee debated the two articles of impeachment submitted by the democrats against Trump. In righteous indignation Representative Jim Jordan cried out at the hearing,

They're never going to stop. ... This is about one basic fact; the democrats have not accepted the will of the American people. Three weeks ago, Nancy Pelosi called the President of the United States an imposter and the attacks on the president started before the election. ... *It's not just because they don't like the president. They don't like us.* They don't like the 63 million people who voted for this president, all of us in flyover country, all of us common folk in Ohio, Wisconsin, Tennessee, and Texas, they don't like us. ... They don't like the president. They don't like the president's supporters and they dislike us so much they're willing to weaponize the government. A few years ago, it was the IRS, more recently it was the FBI, and now it's the impeachment power of congress going after 63 million people and the guy we put in the White House. ... It would be well to remember, that what can be done to a president can be done to any of us.

Leaving aside that 66 million people voted against Trump and he was elected by the math of the electoral college and not the majority of the American people and the republican rhetoric of resentment of the "common folk" by northern elites in both parties originated with the 1968 George Wallace campaign in an effort to galvanize southern and suburban northern white democrats to join the Republican party after the Democrats adopted civil rights legislation; Trump gives to his voter's annunciation regarding their victimhood at the hands of the media, academia, entertainment, and establishment politicians. Trump, reflecting them, asserts these elites do not reflect the values and policies of his voters and these elites have changed America to its detriment. Trump gives voice to voters who believe they have suffered under the cowardly leadership of the republican establishment that knuckled under to various progressive policies from the fall of Jim Crow and the rise of desegregation in the 1960s; to the policies of bussing, forced integration in the schools, quotas in higher education, and the end to all white urban and suburban neighborhoods in the 1970s; to affirmative action and the perceived imposition of anti-Christian and non-social conservative family values social policies (rise of the culture wars) in the 1980s; to the losses in the culture wars in the past ten years (LGBTQ rights, gay marriage, trans-gender rights, to name a few); to uncontrolled immigration from Mexico and Central America today.

Progressives accuse Trump of being a racist, a sexist, a rapist, and the point is not whether, in fact, he is these things, the point is that after being accused in the #MeToo movement political environment, he still stands! He stands over the carcass of political correctness enforcement. Trump's masculine approach to the presidency is reminiscent of Andrew Jackson, Abraham Lincoln, Teddy Roosevelt, and Woodrow Wilson; the role of the president is to lead and dominate the foreign and domestic politics of his day to achieve what he perceives as the will of the people. The president is the steward of the people, not a caretaker or custodian of the office of the presidency. Domestically, *Make America Great Again*. As to foreign policy, *America First*. To Christian and non-Christian white social conservatives, he is an alpha male. White social conservatives answer, regarding his tone and tweets and language, there is no perfect candidate and you take the good with the bad. He gives them conservative judges and stands up for the second amendment. To white Evangelical Christians he stands up for the faith and against anti-Christian ideals and policies and he opposes abortion. But more subtly, they see in him resistance to the progressive wing of Christianity. They see in him the rejection of social justice theology. Whether or not he actually opposes this progressive wing, they see their resistance to it in Trump. He is what they want to be, and he is what they want to see in America again. And they revere him for it. As to his social sins and style, matched against what he represents and has achieved, his supports say, "all sins forgiven." Under his leadership, opposition is paramount—Make America Great Again—and under that leadership Trump can do no wrong and no untruth from his mouth or tweet matters.

Trump's attractiveness includes his white alpha male rejection of the forces that reduced the 1950s white male dominance of the American political landscape. Under Trump social conservative populists will now confront progressive forces in political discourse at all times in all places and their enablers are to be purged from the Republican party. Trump knew instinctively and provided voice to the perception that the party that represents these voters, the Republican party, was and has been led by cowards who feared the media and accusations of racism, sexism and all other types of political correctness attacks. Under Trump and his example, that cowardice and acquiesce to political correctiveness and accusations of racism and sexism ends now.

When Trump responded to his accuser that he raped her, he gave an alpha white male answer, "she's not my type." This was not the first time Trump answered sexual harassment or assault charges by first commenting on the physical appearance or made other such comments about his female accusers. During the 2016 campaign, when a woman accused Trump of forcibly fondling her on a plane, he said to his audience at a campaign rally, "yeah, I'm going to go after you. Believe me, she would not be my first choice. That I can tell you."[42] During the campaign, Megan Kelly, a star on Fox News and no liberal, asked Trump a question during a televised debate regarding his comments on women which Trump felt was unfair to ask him. The next day Trump attacked her and said "you could see there was blood coming out of her eyes, blood coming out of her wherever."[43] The political blowback by Trump supporters was against Kelly and she was chased from her position as an anchor on Fox News.

The point is that Trump during the campaign faced down anyone who he determined did not provide him with the respect he believed he deserved, and that included white social conservative women on Fox. Trump faced down and continues to face down political correctness, which in conservative circles means stopping white people who are socially conservative from speaking by asserting they are per se racist and sexist. While there is a distinction between white people who are socially conservative and advocates of white social conservative orthodoxy, to both Trump represents and reflects the white dominance and privilege that was once without question in America a century ago.

This dominance is also reflected in Trump's view that especially under Obama but also under both Bush 41 and 43 and Clinton, the United States has been taken advantage of by the world and especially the socialist nations of Europe who are supposed to be America's allies. According to Trump, in trade, China has robbed America blind. Under Trump, this disrespect of America ends. In understanding Trump, consider his press gaggle with the White House press corp. on August 21, 2019, when Trump explained why he was cancelling a visit to Denmark to meet with the Prime Minister. A few days before, it was reported that Trump had asked his staff to look into buying Greenland, which is owned by Denmark. When the prime minister tweeted that the proposal was "absurd," Trump said to the press corp. that he canceled the meeting because the prime minister was "nasty" to him. When asked how, he said she used the word "absurd," and "she's not talking to me, she's talking to the United States of America. You don't talk to the United States that way, at least under me." He said she could have simply said she was not interested, but she showed disrespect for him and thus America by using the word "absurd." From his, and from his supporters' point of view, who does this European socialist think she is calling a policy initiative of America absurd?

To Trump, disrespect of him is disrespect of America. America First means no one disrespects America, and that is operationalized as no one disrespects him. This white alpha male persona of America—and himself, which is the same thing—has and continues to find support with Trump voters. Trump embodies the idea of *Pax Americana,* the values of Americanism, the assertion that America's best days are not behind her,[44] and America is a net positive in world history. Trump also reflects resentment of the ability of unelected international trade and policy organization bureaucrats to influence American social policy and life. This *Pax Americana*

worldview explains his rejection of transnational economic, business, c, and multinational treaties in general that limit American
power and influence in the world. But more specifically, Trump,
along with Fox News commentators, conservative radio talk show
hosts, and editors and writers like those of the online magazine
American Greatness, actively reject the idea of internationalism or
globalism, defined[45] as a world dominated by a utopian world government under a "global rule of law" rather than a world governed
by individual nations under their own laws under the leadership of
America. This is why Trump's attacks on NATO for taking advantage of the United States, for abandoning and removing America
from multinational agreements and his general disregard and hostility for the international order[46] established over the past 70 years
finds such resonance with his supporters.

Trump and his voters look at Europe and see that it is losing its
whiteness and western values. Trump-to-be voters have held this
view from the days of the presidential campaigns of Pat Buchanan
in 1992 and 1996 and his assertion that immigration from the non-
white countries of the world, as he entitled his 2002 book, would
be *The Death of the West*. Trump picked up this ancient Republican
fear and political rhetoric and said Europe was dying because of the
2015 European migrant crisis and its adoption of liberal immigration and its open borders between its nations. Trump and his voters
said the same process was working in America with immigration
from Central America, and his presidency would work to prevent
its continuance. This is why his immigration policies of ending
immigration of Central Americans has support and why he said
during the 2016 election, "Donald J. Trump is calling for a total
and complete shutdown of Muslims entering the United States until
our country's representatives can figure out what the hell is going
on." The racism is in the assumption that less white in America
means the lessening of the values that made America great. Thus,
the goal of his presidency—Make America Great Again.

Thanks to the generation of Dr. King, the America of today is
not the America of a century ago in 1920 or before that in 1820.

Although they ushered in the death of explicit racism and dehumanization of blacks, they did not usher in the death of racism and dehumanization itself. In 2020, unlike 1920, American white supremacy (privilege) is implicit, emotional, for the most part subconscious and unprocessed and unacknowledged, but it nonetheless exists and provides a subtle backdrop to how white social conservative worldview functions.

The effect of white superiority is not exclusive to the worldview of whites, consider why blacks as a whole did not support Obama until he proved white people would vote for him. It was not until after the Iowa Caucus and the New Hampshire primary that blacks only began to take Obama seriously as a candidate for president. He did not have support from black voters in toto until well after his victories on Super Tuesday. My point is this, white voters don't withhold their support for a white candidate until that candidate wins the South Carolina primary and proves black voters will support that candidate. In our electoral process, whites don't need or require black votes to be taken seriously, but black candidates do need white votes to be taken seriously. Note, I said white candidates don't need black votes to be taken seriously, not that they don't need those votes to win. Election winning is an entirely different conversation.

My point with all of these examples is that racism today is subtle, but they reflect an aversion to black accomplishments and humanness equal to whites. In the social psychology literature this dynamic is explained by dehumanization. The significance of dehumanization, within the context of criminal justice outcomes, is the lack of sympathy with black incarceration and lack of empathy to police use of force incidents in which a black youth is killed and the assertion that had the youth humbled himself and submitted to lawful authority he would not have been shot. Infrahumanization lends support to this lack of sympathy and empathy with the self-elevating assumption and assertion that racism does not exist or function within the police in the first place.[47] Remember, the police in white social conservative eyes are the protections of civilization, civilization being a reflection of them. The police are the sole protection, as Reagan said,[48] from the encroaching jungle. The jungle being social disorder, deviant behavior and those who bring it.

White social conservatives assert with passion that deviant behavior like failure in school, drug use, black men abandoning their families, and black women seeking welfare rather than getting married has nothing to do with slavery and surely nothing to do with racism. These social deviant behaviors are a choice. It is undisputed within social science literature that being in a two-parent home is better than single parenthood, completing some post-secondary education, finding gainful employment before getting married, and having children after marriage *in that order* is the best way to avoid poverty. But that has nothing to do with how a police officer sees a young black man walking down the street, how a doctor perceives the pain of a black woman in labor[49] or how a black man (or a black woman) is judged at work for leadership skills compared to white colleagues in competition for the same promotion. Nor does being from a stable middle-class home insulate a Harvard-educated black man running for president from not only being challenged with the assertion he was not a true American because he was not born in America, but is required to produce his citizenship papers as were free blacks required to produce their manumission papers on command by any white male in the antebellum period of American history. Failure to produce the papers would result in arrest and re-enslavement, as Obama was forced to produce his original birth certificate to maintain his right to run for president.

The point being racial bias to the detriment of blacks is not the result of black behavior. Implicit belief in black inferiority is independent of, not caused by, black infidelity to traditional conservative family dynamics. This dehumanization of blacks and the implicit belief in black inferiority held by white America was born in the linking blackness to slavery (whites by law could not be slaves) and the physical/visual identification of slaves to black skin under the slave laws of the early to middle 1700s. This inferiority continued with the belief that blacks were supposed to be enslaved by the middle 1800s, which continued with the belief blacks were criminogenic and lazy by the late 1800s through the middle 1900s. Today's iteration is asserted by white social conservative orthodoxy that black poverty and disproportionate incarceration are the sole result of blacks being socially deviant in rejecting traditional family values of hard work and marriage before childbirth.

◆◆◆

After the advent of the Great Society policies of Johnson, by the late 1960s, the social issue of racial discrimination in many black communities was shifting from ending segregation to addressing the needs for education, mitigating the ills of poverty, and securing medical care and political power. By the late 1960s and early 1970s, the black community suffered from the abandonment of middle-class white flight followed by black flight. Whites ran from middle-class urban neighborhoods in the city into the suburbs and blacks ran from the inner city to the middle-class urban neighborhoods. Both ran to chase better opportunities and to escape what they viewed as negative environments; whites escaping black integration and blacks escaping bad schools, concentrated poverty, and lack of middle-class employment. The social, societal, and physical environmental result was the loss of formal and informal positive social barriers to poverty and crime. The fight of middle-class barriers resulted in the concentration of chronic intractable poverty in narrowly defined communities. Upon the concentration of the loss of jobs and other informal social control mechanisms in the 1970s, crack cocaine infected these communities in the early 1980s.

In his 2016 documentary on blacks in America and criminal justice policy, social historian Henry Louis Gates observed that,

> from 1983 and 1997 the number of African Americans incarcerated for drug offense grew by over 2000 percent. That's more than six times the rate of increase for white Americans. The rise of crack cocaine birthed the new war

on crime and drugs and created the avenue that criminalized Black men and Black behavior. Crack gave birth to
significant increases in funding for police, special drug task
forces, asset forfeiture, militarization of police to deal with
drug gangs, and the rise of increased prison construction.[50]

In an interview with Sherrilyn Ifill, president, NAACP Legal
Defense Fund, she observed, "we have used the prisons essentially
as a warehouse for our race problem. We used that as the place
where we could warehouse particularly young African American
men."[51] During the 1970s the urban cities of America were abandoned for the suburbs. New York City nearly declared bankruptcy
under its abandonment by President Ford. As Cornel West observed
in the same documentary regarding many urban communities, "in
the 1950s Black communities were the most civilized communities
in America. There were ties of empathy and bonds of sympathy.
Unbelievable embrace of others who came in. Out of the seventies,
we don't have neighborhoods as much as we got hoods."[52] The Jim
Crow policies of redlining, restrictive covenants, blockbusting, and
other systems of segregation and destruction of black communities
were aggravated by the of loss industry to mechanization and trade
deals in the 1980s. Historian Lawrence D. Bobo reflected that during the 1980s and 1990s, "we have a circumstance of this persistent
and rising joblessness in urban black communities and rather than
major investment in education or training or jobs, we get a major
investment in policing and prison building and incarceration."

As any freshman student in criminology learns, social structure
has an impact on how individuals view the world and what opportunities they perceive to be available. Personal responsibility
encompasses what the individual is exposed to. Personal responsibility and social environments are not mutually exclusive, they
are coexistent and complex. As Attorney General Eric Holder
concluded, rather than deal with these complexities, in the 1980s
and 1990s, we "looked for simple solutions to complex problems
as opposed to asking ourselves what are the sociological reasons?

What are the social dysfunctions, the deficits that we see in the people who are committing these crimes? What are we going to do to deal with those? The thought was never to deal with those. The thought was always simply to get them locked up, get them away from us, and hopefully they will stay there for an extended period of time."[53]

During the second decade of the twenty-first century, black incarceration as a major political issue was supplanted by the issue of police use of force and killing of black males during police encounters. The latter was used as a reflection of modern racism. Cornel West observed, regarding the rise of the **Black Lives Matter** movement as a response to police shooting of young black men, "we know black lives matter the way all lives matter. But unfortunately, in America you got to say black lives matter because when you say all lives matter often times you don't get to the black lives."[54] The inability to secure prosecutions and convictions of police killing black males like Tamir Rice and Freddie Gray by the police, merged the issues of disproportionate incarceration and police use of force and fostered the assertion that the criminal justice system is the new Jim Crow. As Associate Professor Brittney Cooper observed, "So we know now, really clearly, whether we begin at hurricane Katrina or we begin at Travon Martin or we begin at Michael Brown that this country is having a problem affirming at the level of policy and treatment that black lives matter."[55]

Leaving police shootings aside, by the end of the second decade of the twentieth century the rhetoric of crime and explanations of it have shifted away from the second punitive era. One justification for believing this change has occurred is that in 2018 a Republican Senate with a Republican in the White House supported and signed legislation that mitigated the crime policies of the 1980s and 1990s. Under the leadership of Republicans, liberals, and progressives' concepts of rehabilitation were not only politically viable, but legislation was passed to support concepts of reentry, college-level education opportunities in prison, and providing released offenders with social support and employment. Socially, policies like banning job applications to require an offender to admit prior incarceration and criminal activity has found broad acceptance. Such policies allow applicants to reach the interview stage and thus have a chance to convince a potential employer to take a chance on hiring her. The *First Step Act* provided grants to support employers who provided employment to released offenders. In addition, white social conservatives on Fox News and on conservative talk radio notwithstanding, the political rhetoric of defining crime exclusively with a black face is no longer required for getting elected. With the rise of opioid addiction and its concentration in the white communities of America, it is no longer politically required to look at drug addiction as a black problem to be solved with prisons—as it was in the 1980s and 1990s.

While it is still orthodoxy of white social conservatives to assert that blacks commit more crime and they should be treated as such, it is no longer American political orthodoxy and police shootings of blacks now are viewed with skepticism in the modern American consciousness. The idea that black incarceration is a problem to be solved has reemerged and Republican politicians no longer need to build prisons to maintain credibility with their constituents. The rate of black incarceration did not increase under Trump, and the desired policies of General Sessions did not take dominance within criminal justice rhetoric and national policy. In the first year of his presidency, black incarceration remained at the same level it was reduced to under President Obama. The *First Step Act* should result in maintaining those reductions.

While I hold no delusions that implicit racism no longer exists in the political rhetoric of America today, it must be acknowledged that the politics of race and crime of the 1980s and 1990s are a thing of the past. White social conservatives aside, American politics and society seems to be accommodated and happy with that result.

The Secession Ordinances of the Confederate States of America

The Southern States of the Confederacy were direct and clear on the purpose, justification, and moral certitude of why they were seceding from the Union. Their official declarations of secession were based on two overarching ideas: first, the protection of slavery as an economic and social institution, along with the moral truth about the inferiority of those that were enslaved; second, the rejection of anti-slavery abolitionists' politics of the North and claims of universal failure of the federal government and the Northern states to enforce the fugitive slave clause of the Constitution and supporting legislation. Consider the major declarations and documents of the Confederate states:

The Declaration of the Immediate Causes Which Induce and Justify the Secession of South Carolina from the Federal Union (December 24, 1860)

[T]he non-slaveholding States ... have assume the right of deciding upon the propriety of our domestic institutions; and have denied the rights of property ... they have denounced as sinful the institution of slavery; they have permitted open establishment among them of societies ... They have encouraged and assisted thousands of our slaves to leave their homes; and those who remain, have been incited by emissaries, books and pictures to servile insurrection.

... A geographical line has been drawn across the Union, and all the States north of that line have united in the election of a man to the high office of President of the United States, whose opinions and purposes are hostile to slavery. He is to be entrusted with the administration of the common Government, because he has declared that that "Government cannot endure permanently half slave, half free," and that the public mind must rest in the belief that slavery is in the course of ultimate extinction.

... This sectional combination for the submersion of the Constitution, has been aided in some of the States by elevating to citizenship, persons who, by the supreme law of the land, are incapable of becoming citizens; and their votes have been used to inaugurate a new policy, hostile to the South, and destructive of its beliefs and safety.

... We, therefore, the People of South Carolina, by our delegates in Convention assembled, appealing to the Supreme Judge of the world for the rectitude of our

intentions, have solemnly declared that the Union heretofore existing between this State and the other States of
North America, is dissolved ...

Governor Isham G. Harris Speech to the General Assembly Regarding a Referendum Calling for a Tennessee Secession Convention (January 7, 1861)

The systematic, wanton, and long continued agitation
of the slavery question, with the actual and threatened
aggressions of the Northern States and a portion of their
people, upon the well-defined constitutional rights of the
Southern citizen; the rapid growth and increase, in all the
elements of power, of a purely sectional party, whose bond
of union is uncompromising hostility to the rights and
institutions of the fifteen Southern States, have produced
a crisis in the affairs of the country, unparalleled in the
history of the past, resulting already in the withdrawal
from the Confederacy of one of the sovereignties which
composed it, while others are rapidly preparing to move
in the same direction. ...

The Constitution distinctly recognizes property in
slaves—makes it the duty of the States to deliver the
fugitive to his owner, but contains no grant of power to
the Federal Government to interfere with this species of
property ... [T]he Supreme Court of the United States in
the case of Dred Scott vs. Sandford ... said:

> *"Now, as we have already said in an earlier part*
> *of this opinion upon a different point, the right of*

*property in a slave is distinctly and expressly affirmed
in the Constitution. And no word can be found in the
Constitution which gives Congress a greater power over
slave property, or which entitles property of that kind to
less protection than property of any other description.
The only power conferred, is the power coupled with the
duty, of guarding and protecting the owner in
his rights."*

This decision of the highest judicial tribunal, known
to our Government, settles the question, beyond the
possibility of doubt, that slave property rests upon the
same basis, and is entitled to the same protection, as
every other description of property; that the General
Government has no power to circumscribe or confine it
within any given boundary; to determine where it shall,
or shall not exist, or in any manner to impair its value ...
[H]ence, there is no power on earth which can rightfully
determine whether slavery shall or shall not exist within
the limits of any State, except the people thereof acting in
their highest sovereign capacity.

The attempt of the Northern people, through the
instrumentality of the Federal Government—their State
governments, and emigrant aid societies—to confine
this species of property within the limits of the present
Southern States—to impair its value by constant agitation
and refusal to deliver up the fugitive ... is justly regarded
by the people of the Southern States as a gross and pal-
pable violation of the spirit and obvious meaning of the
compact of Union. ... It claims the constitutional right to
abolish slavery in the District of Columbia ... It proposes
a prohibition of the slave trade between the States ... It
has, by the deliberate Legislative enactments of a large
majority of the Northern States, openly and flagrantly
nullified ... the fugitive slave law ... with impunity defies

the Government, tramples upon our rights, and plunders the Southern citizen. ... It has, by its John Brown and Montgomery raids, invaded sovereign States and murdered peaceable citizens. It has justified and "exalted to the highest honors of admiration, the horrid murders, arsons, and rapine of the John Brown raid, and has canonized the felons as saints and martyrs. ... It has, in the person of the President elect, asserted the equality of the black with the white race ... To evade the issue thus forced upon us at this time, without the fullest security for our rights, is, in my opinion, fatal to the institution of slavery forever. The time has arrived when the people of the South must prepare either to abandon or to fortify and maintain it.

The Ordinance of Secession of Alabama (January 11, 1861)

An Ordinance to dissolve the union. ...

Whereas, the election of Abraham Lincoln and Hannibal Hamlin to the offices of president and vice-president of the United States of America, by a sectional party, avowedly hostile to the domestic institutions and to the peace and security of the people of the State of Alabama, preceded by many and dangerous infractions of the constitution of the United States by many of the States and people of the Northern section, is a political wrong of so insulting and menacing a character as to justify the people of the State of Alabama in the adoption of prompt and decided measures for their future peace and security, therefore:

....

And as it is the desire and purpose of the people of Alabama to meet the slaveholding States of the South, who may approve such purpose, in order to frame a provisional as well as permanent Government upon the principles of the Constitution of the United States,

Be it resolved by the people of Alabama in Convention assembled, That the people of the States of Delaware, Maryland, Virginia, North Carolina, South Carolina, Florida, Georgia, Mississippi, Louisiana, Texas, Arkansas, Tennessee, Kentucky and Missouri, be and are hereby invited to meet the people of the State of Alabama, by their Delegates, in Convention, on the 4th day of February, A.D., 1861, at the city of Montgomery, in the State of Alabama, for the purpose of consulting with each other as to the most effectual mode of securing concerted and harmonious action in whatever measures may be deemed most desirable for our common peace and security.

The Declaration of Secession of Georgia (January 29, 1861)

A brief history of the rise, progress, and policy of antislavery and the political organization into whose hands the administration of the Federal Government has been committed will fully justify the pronounced verdict of the people of Georgia. The party of Lincoln, called the Republican Party, under its present name and organization, is of recent origin. It is admitted to be an anti-slavery party

... While the subordination and the political and social inequality of the African race was fully conceded by all, it was plainly apparent that slavery would soon disappear from what are now the non-slave-holding States of the original thirteen ... The material prosperity of the North was greatly dependent on the Federal Government; that of the South not at all.

In the first years of the Republic the navigating, commercial, and manufacturing interests of the North began to seek profit and aggrandizement at the expense of the agricultural interests. ... The Presidential election of 1852 resulted in the total overthrow of the advocates of restriction and their party friends. Immediately after this result the anti-slavery portion of the defeated party resolved to unite all the elements in the North opposed to slavery and to stake their future political fortunes upon their hostility to slavery everywhere. This is the party two whom the people of the North have committed the Government. They raised their standard in 1856 and were barely defeated. They entered the Presidential contest again in 1860 and succeeded.

The prohibition of slavery in the Territories, hostility to it everywhere, the equality of the black and white races, disregard of all constitutional guarantees it its favor, were boldly proclaimed by its leaders and applauded by its followers ... For twenty years past the abolitionists and their allies in the Northern States have been engaged in constant efforts to subvert our institutions and to excite insurrection and servile war among us. They have sent emissaries among us for the accomplishment of these purposes.

The Ordinance of Secession of Texas (February 1, 1861)

To dissolve the Union between the State of Texas and the other States united under the Compact styled "the Constitution of the United States of America."

WHEREAS, The Federal Government has failed to accomplish the purposes of the compact of union between these States, in giving protection either to the persons of our people upon an exposed frontier, or to the property of our citizens, and

....

WHEREAS, The recent developments in Federal affairs make it evident that the power of the Federal Government is sought to be made a weapon with which to strike down the interests and property of the people of Texas, and her sister slave-holding States, instead of permitting it to be, as was intended, our shield against outrage and aggression; THEREFORE,

... We, the People of the State of Texas, by Delegates in Convention assembled, do declare and ordain, that the Ordinance adopted by our Convention of Delegates, on the Fourth day of July, A.D. 1845, and afterwards ratified by us, under which the Republic of Texas was admitted into Union with other States and became a party to the compact styled "The Constitution of the United States of America" be, and is hereby repealed and annulled. ...

A Declaration of the Causes which Impel the State of Texas to Secede from the Federal Union (February 2, 1861)

Texas abandoned her separate national existence and consented to become one of the Confederated States ... She was received as a commonwealth holding, maintaining and protecting the institution known as negro slavery—the servitude of the African to the white race within her limits—a relation that had existed from the first settlement of her wilderness by the white race, and which her people intended should exist in all future time. Her institutions and geographical position established the strongest ties between her and other slave-holding States of the confederacy. Those ties have been strengthened by association. But what has been the course of the government of the United States, and of the people and authorities of the non-slave-holding States, since our connection with them?

The controlling majority of the Federal Government, under various pretenses and disguises, has so administered the same as to exclude the citizens of the Southern States, unless under odious and unconstitutional restrictions, from all the immense territory owned in common by all the States on the Pacific Ocean, for the avowed purpose of ... destroying the institutions of Texas and her sister slave-holding States.

By the disloyalty of the Northern States and their citizens and the imbecility of the Federal Government ... permitted in those States and ... Kansas to trample upon the ... lives and property of Southern citizens in that territory, and finally, by violence and mob law to usurp the possession of the same as exclusively the property of the Northern States.

The Federal Government, while but partially under the control of these our unnatural and sectional enemies, has for years almost entirely failed to protect the lives and property of the people of Texas against the Indian savages on our border, and more recently against the murderous forays of banditti from the neighboring territory of Mexico; and ... when our State government has expended large amounts for such ... the Federal Government has refused reimbursement ...

....

In all the non-slave-holding States, in violation of that good faith and comity which should exist between entirely distinct nations, the people have formed themselves into a great sectional party ... based upon the unnatural feeling of hostility to these Southern States and their beneficent and patriarchal system of African slavery, proclaiming the debasing doctrine of the equality of all men, irrespective of race or color—a doctrine at war with nature, in opposition to the experience of mankind, and in violation of the plainest revelations of the Divine Law. They demand the abolition of negro slavery throughout the confederacy, the recognition of political equality between the white and the negro races, and avow their determination to press on their crusade against us, so long as a negro slave remains in these States.

....

By consolidating their strength, they have placed the slave-holding States in a hopeless minority in the federal congress, and rendered representation of no avail in protecting Southern rights against their exactions and encroachments.

....

And, finally, by the combined sectional vote of the seventeen non-slave-holding States, they have elected as president and vice-president of the whole confederacy two men whose chief claims to such high positions are their approval of these long continued wrongs, and their pledges to continue them to the final consummation of these schemes for the ruin of the slave-holding States.

In view of these and many other facts, it is meet that our own views should be distinctly proclaimed.

We hold as undeniable truths that the governments of the various States, and of the confederacy itself, were established exclusively by the white race, for themselves and their posterity; that the African race had no agency in their establishment; that they were rightfully held and regarded as an inferior and dependent race, and in that condition only could their existence in this country be rendered beneficial or tolerable.

That in this free government all white men are and of right ought to be entitled to equal civil and political rights; that the servitude of the African race, as existing in these States, is mutually beneficial to both bond and free, and is abundantly authorized and justified by the experience of mankind, and the revealed will of the Almighty Creator, as recognized by all Christian nations; while the destruction of the existing relations between the two races, as advocated by our sectional enemies, would bring inevitable calamities upon both and desolation upon the fifteen slave-holding States. By the secession of six of the slave-holding States, and the certainty that others will speedily do likewise, Texas has no alternative but to remain in an isolated connection with the North, or unite her destinies with the South.

For these and other reasons, solemnly asserting that the federal constitution has been violated and virtually abrogated by the several States named, seeing that the federal government is now passing under the control of our enemies to be diverted from the exalted objects of its creation to those of oppression and wrong, and realizing that our own State can no longer look for protection, but to God and her own sons—We the delegates of the people of Texas, in Convention assembled, have passed an ordinance dissolving all political connection with the government of the United States of America and the people thereof and confidently appeal to the intelligence and patriotism of the freeman of Texas to ratify the same at the ballot box, on the 23rd day of the present month.

A Declaration of the Immediate Causes which Induce and Justify the Secession of the State of Mississippi from the Federal Union (Not Dated)

Our position is thoroughly identified with the institution of slavery—the greatest material interest of the world. Its labor supplies the product which constitutes by far the largest and most important portions of commerce of the earth. These products are peculiar to the climate verging on the tropical regions, and by an imperious law of nature, none but the black race can bear exposure to the tropical sun. These products have become necessities of the world, and a blow at slavery is a blow at commerce and civilization. That blow has been long aimed at the institution, and was at the point of reaching its consummation. There was no choice left us but submission to the mandates of abolition, or a dissolution of the Union, whose principles had been subverted to work out our ruin. [The North] advocates negro equality, socially and politically, and promotes insurrection and incendiarism in our midst. It has enlisted its press, its pulpit and its schools against us, until the whole popular mind of the North is excited and inflamed with prejudice.

The Constitution of the Confederate States Article I (March 11, 1861)

The importation of negroes of the African race from any foreign country other than the slaveholding States or Territories of the United States of America, is hereby forbidden ... Congress shall also have power to prohibit the introduction of slaves from any State not a member of, or Territory not belonging to, this Confederacy ... No ... law denying or impairing the right of property in negro slaves shall be passed.

The Constitution of the Confederate States Article IV (March 11, 1861)

The citizens of each State ... shall have the right of transit and sojourn in any State of this Confederacy, with their slaves and other property; and the right of property in said slaves shall not be thereby impaired ... No slave ... escaping shall, in consequence ... be discharged from such service or labor; but shall be delivered up on claim of the party to whom such slave belongs ... The Confederate States may acquire new territory ... In all such territory the institution of negro slavery, as it now exists in the Confederate States, shall be recognized and protected be Congress and by the Territorial government; and the inhabitants of the several Confederate States and Territories shall have the right to take to such Territory any slaves lawfully held by them in any of the States or Territories of the Confederate States.

President Jefferson Davis Message to Congress Regarding the Ratification of the Constitution of the Confederate States (April 29, 1861)

When the several States delegated certain powers to the United States Congress, a large portion of the laboring population consisted of African slaves imported into the colonies by the mother country. In twelve out of the thirteen States negro slavery existed, and the right of property in slaves was protected by law. This property was recognized in the Constitution, and provision was made against its loss by the escape of the slave. The increase in the number of slaves by further importation from Africa was also secured by a clause forbidding Congress to prohibit the slave trade anterior to a certain date, and in no clause can there be found any delegation of power to the Congress authorizing it in any manner to legislate to the prejudice, detriment, or discouragement owners of that species of property, or excluding it from the protection of the Government.

... The climate and soil of the Northern States soon proved unpropitious to the continuance of slave labor, whilst the converse was the case at the South ... [T]he constitutional provision for their rendition to their owners was first evaded, then openly denounced as a violation of conscientious obligation and religious duty; men were taught that it was a merit to elude, disobey, and violently oppose the execution of the laws enacted to secure the performance of the promise contained in the constitutional compact; owners of slaves were mobbed and even murdered in open day solely for applying to a magistrate for the arrest of a fugitive slave.

... In the meantime ... the African slaves ... In moral and social condition they had been elevated from brutal savages into docile, intelligent, and civilized agricultural laborers, and supplied not only with bodily comforts but with careful religious instruction. Under the supervision of a superior race their labor had been so directed as not only to allow a gradual and marked amelioration of their own condition" their labor undergirded "the productions of the South in cotton, rice, sugar, and tobacco, for the full development and continuance of which the labor of African slaves was and is indispensable, had swollen to an amount which formed nearly three-fourths of the exports of the whole United States and had become absolutely necessary to the wants of civilized man.

John Wilkes Booth "To Whom it May Concern" Letter (1864)

Right, or wrong, God, judge me, not man. For be my motive good or bad, of one thing I am sure, the lasting condemnation of the North.

... The very nomination of Abraham Lincoln four years ago, spoke plainly—war—war upon Southern rights and institutions, his election proved it. ... This country was formed for the white not for the black man. And looking upon African slavery from the same stand-point, held by those noble framers of our Constitution, I for one, have ever considered it, one of the greatest blessings (both for themselves and us,) that God ever bestowed upon a favored nation. Witness heretofore our wealth and power, witness their elevation in happiness and enlightenment above their race, elsewhere.

So much for the assertion that the Civil War was not a war to protect the institution of slavery.

Abraham Lincoln, Second Inaugural Address (1864)

On the occasion corresponding to this four years ago, all thoughts were anxiously directed to an impending civil-war. ... Both parties deprecated war; but one of them would make war rather than let the nation survive; and the other would accept war rather than let it perish. And the war came.

One eighth of the whole population were colored slaves, not distributed generally over the Union, but localized in the Southern half part of it. These slaves constituted a peculiar and powerful interest. All knew that this interest was, somehow, the cause of the war. To strengthen, perpetuate, and extend this interest was the object for which the insurgents would rend the Union, even by war; while the government claimed no right to do more than to restrict the territorial enlargement of it. ... If we shall suppose that American Slavery is one of those offences which, in the providence of God, must needs come. ... He gives to both North and South, this terrible war, as the woe due to those by whom the offence came. ... Yet, if God wills that it continue, until all the wealth piled by the bond-man's two hundred and fifty years of unrequited toil shall be sunk, and until every drop of blood drawn with the lash, shall be paid by another drawn with the sword, as was said f[our] three thousand years ago, so still it must be said "the judgments of the Lord, are true and righteous altogether."

James A. Garfield, Republican National Convention, Nomination of John Sherman Speech (June 5, 1880)

The Republican party offers to our brethren of the South the olive branch of Peace, and invites them to renewed brotherhood, on this supreme condition: That it shall be admitted, forever, that in the War for the Union we were right and they were wrong.

Presidential Election Confederate and Southern State Voting Patterns 1944–1992

STATE		1944	1948	1952	1956	1960	1964	1968	1972	1976	1980	1984	1988	1992
								THE SOUTHERN STRATEGY						
CONFEDERATE STATES														
ALABAMA	Republican						won		won		won	won	won	won
	Democrat	won		won	won	won				won				
	Dixiecrat (1948)		won											
	Wallace (1968)							won						
ARKANSAS	Republican								won		won	won	won	
	Democrat	won	won	won	won	won	won			won				won
	Dixiecrat (1948)													
	Wallace (1968)							won						
FLORIDA	Republican			won	won	won		won	won		won	won	won	won
	Democrat	won	won				won			won				
	Dixiecrat (1948)													
	Wallace (1968)													
GEORGIA	Republican								won			won	won	
	Democrat	won	won	won	won	won	won			won	won			won
	Dixiecrat (1948)													
	Wallace (1968)							won						

STATE		1944	1948	1952	1956	1960	1964	1968	1972	1976	1980	1984	1988	1992
								THE SOUTHERN STRATEGY						
CONFEDERATE STATES														
LOUISIANA	Republican				won		won		won		won	won	won	
	Democrat	won		won		won				won				won
	Dixiecrat (1948)		won											
	Wallace (1968)							won						
MISSISSIPPI	Republican						won		won		won	won	won	won
	Democrat	won		won	won	won				won				
	Dixiecrat (1948)		won											
	Wallace (1968)							won						
NORTH CAROLINA	Republican							won	won		won	won	won	won
	Democrat	won	won	won	won	won	won			won				
	Dixiecrat (1948)													
	Wallace (1968)													
SOUTH CAROLINA	Republican						won	won	won		won	won	won	won
	Democrat	won		won	won	won				won				
	Dixiecrat (1948)		won											
	Wallace (1968)													

(*Continued*)

THE SOUTHERN STRATEGY

STATE		1944	1948	1952	1956	1960	1964	1968	1972	1976	1980	1984	1988	1992
CONFEDERATE STATES														
TENNESSEE	Republican			won	won	won		won	won		won	won	won	
	Democrat	won	won				won			won				won
	Dixiecrat (1948)													
	Wallace (1968)													
TEXAS	Republican			won	won				won		won	won	won	won
	Democrat	won	won			won	won	won		won				
	Dixiecrat (1948)													
	Wallace (1968)													
VIRGINIA	Republican			won	won	won		won	won	won	won	won	won	won
	Democrat	won	won				won							
	Dixiecrat (1948)													
	Wallace (1968)													
SOUTHERN STATES														
DELAWARE	Republican			won	won			won	won		won	won	won	
	Democrat	won	won			won	won			won				won
	Dixiecrat (1948)													
	Wallace (1968)													

STATE		1944	1948	1952	1956	1960	1964	1968	1972	1976	1980	1984	1988	1992
								THE SOUTHERN STRATEGY						
SOUTHERN STATES														
KENTUCKY	Republican				won	won		won	won		won	won	won	
	Democrat	won	won	won			won			won				won
	Dixiecrat (1948)													
	Wallace (1968)													
MARYLAND	Republican			won	won				won			won	won	
	Democrat	won	won			won	won	won		won	won			won
	Dixiecrat (1948)													
	Wallace (1968)													
OKLAHOMA	Republican			won	won	won		won	won	won	won	won	won	won
	Democrat	won	won				won							
	Dixiecrat (1948)													
	Wallace (1968)													
WEST VIRGINIA	Republican				won				won			won		
	Democrat	won	won	won		won	won	won		won	won		won	won
	Dixiecrat (1948)													
	Wallace (1968)													

Appendix Three

Presidential Election Confederate and Southern State Voting Patterns 1996–2016

STATE		1996	2000	2004	2008	2012	2016
CONFEDERATE STATES							
ALABAMA	Republican	won	won	won	won	won	won
	Democrat						
ARKANSAS	Republican		won	won	won	won	won
	Democrat	won					
FLORIDA	Republican		won	won			won
	Democrat	won			won	won	
GEORGIA	Republican	won	won	won	won	won	won
	Democrat						
LOUISIANA	Republican		won	won	won	won	won
	Democrat	won					
MISSISSIPPI	Republican	won	won	won	won	won	won
	Democrat						
NORTH CAROLINA	Republican	won	won	won		won	won
	Democrat				won		
SOUTH CAROLINA	Republican	won	won	won	won	won	won
	Democrat						
TENNESSEE	Republican		won	won	won	won	won
	Democrat	won					
TEXAS	Republican	won	won	won	won	won	won
	Democrat						

(Continued)

STATE		1996	2000	2004	2008	2012	2016
CONFEDERATE STATES							
VIRGINIA	Republican	won	won	won			
	Democrat				won	won	won
SOUTHERN STATES							
DELAWARE	Republican						
	Democrat	won	won	won	won	won	won
KENTUCKY	Republican		won	won	won	won	won
	Democrat	won					
MARYLAND	Republican						
	Democrat	won	won	won	won	won	won
OKLAHOMA	Republican	won	won	won	won	won	won
	Democrat						
WEST VIRGINIA	Republican		won	won	won	won	won
	Democrat	won					

Notes

Preface

1 Attorney General William P. Barr Delivers Remarks at the Department of Justice's African-American History Month Observation, accessed February 26, 2019, at https://www.justice.gov/opa/speech/attorney-general-william-p-barr-delivers-remarks-department-justices-african-american

2 Kelly on Wilson dispute, monuments uproar, never Trumpers (5:29–7:30), accessed October 30, 2017 https://www.youtube.com/watch?v=RrRe4BAjffk.

3 Dennis Prager, Radio show, Archive—*Dennis Prager Show*—Full Show (1:22:51–1:25:34), accessed December 01, 2017, at https://www.youtube.com/watch?v=3NKPVvOlvpY&app=desktop.

4 Ibid.

5 *Tucker Carlson Tonight*, Fox News show - Is an immigration loophole letting MS-13 members go free? (2:27-2:37), accessed January 14, 2019, at https://www.youtube.com/watch?v=8KeIE6KuYus.

6 Alfred W. Blumrosen and Ruth G. Blumrosen, *Slave Nation: How Slavery United the Colonies & Sparked the American Revolution* (2005).

7 Cotter, W. R. (1994). "The Somerset Case and the Abolition of Slavery in England" 79 (255) *History: The Official Journal of the Historical Association* 31–56 (Feb. 1994), Rabin, Dana Y. "'In a country of liberty?': Slavery, villeinage, and the making of whiteness in the Somerset case (1772)" In *Britain and its internal others, 1750–1800*. Manchester University Press, 2017, Bradley, Patricia. "Slavery in Colonial Newspapers: The Somerset Case" 12(1) *Journalism History* 2–7 (1985), and Wiecekt, William M. "Somerset: Lord Mansfield and the legitimacy of slavery in the

Anglo-American world" 42 *The University of Chicago Law Review* 86 (1974).

8 Richard Nixon Library, Conversation 013-008 - On October 26, 1971, President Richard M. Nixon and Ronald W. Reagan talked on the telephone from 11:13 am to 11:25 am. The White House Telephone taping system captured this recording, which is known as Conversation 013-008 of the White House Tapes, accessed July 31, 2019, at https://www.nixonlibrary.gov/white-house-tapes/013/conversation-013-008.

9 Tim Naftali, "Ronald Reagan's Long-Hidden Racist Conversation With Richard Nixon: In newly unearthed audio, the then–California governor disparaged African delegates to the United Nations" *The Atlantic* (July 31, 2019), accessed July 31, 2019, at https://www.theatlantic.com/ideas/archive/2019/07/ronald-reagans-racist-conversation-richard-nixon/595102/.

10 Richard Nixon Library, Conversation 013-008.

11 Id.

Chapter 1

1 Sarah Ruiz-Grossman, "This Death Row Lawyer Says Americans Won't Be Free Until We Face Our Racist History: An HBO Documentary about Bryan Stevenson Sounds an Urgent Call to Examine the Nation's Past, from Slavery to Lynching" *HuffPost,* accessed June 23, 2019, https://www.huffpost.com/entry/bryan-stevenson-hbo-documentary-true-justice_n_5d07cff1e4b0953278382385.

2 *Timbs v. Indiana*, 586 U.S. _____ (2019), Justice Thomas concurring opinion (slip op. at 11–13) (internal citation and quotation marks omitted).

3 Brief for Amicus Curiae National African American Gun Association, Inc. in Support of Petitioners in *New York State Rifle & Pistol Association Inc. v. City of New York*, New York (May 7, 2019) at 20–21.

4 Brief of Amicus Curiae NAACP Legal Defense and Educational Fund Inc. in Support of the Petitioner in *Flowers v. Mississippi* (December 27, 2018) (internal citation and quotation marks omitted) at 6–8.

5 *Flowers v. Mississippi*, 588 U.S. ___, Slip op. at 10 (2019) (internal citation omitted). But see infra note 7.

6 Id at 1–2.

7 Id at 18, 20–22, 31.

8 In 1880, the Court addressed whether the failure of the local sheriff to establish a jury pool that excluded blacks was a violation of federal law, and the sheriff's refusal should have triggered a federal law that would allow a change of venue to a federal court. The Court concluded,

> Nor did the refusal of the court and of the counsel for the prosecution to allow a modification of the venire, by which one-third of the jury, or a portion of it, should be composed of persons of the petitioners own race, amount to any denial of a right secured to them by any law providing for the equal civil rights of citizens of the United States. The privilege for which they moved, and which they also asked from the prosecution, was not a right given or secured to them, or to any person, by the law of the State, or by any act of Congress, or by the Fourteenth Amendment of the Constitution. *It is a right to which every colored man* is entitled that, in the selection of jurors to pass upon his life, liberty, or property, *there shall be no exclusion of his race*, and no discrimination against them because of their color. *But this is a different thing from the right which it is asserted* was denied to the petitioners by the state court, *viz., a right to have the jury composed in part of colored men. A mixed jury in a particular case is not essential to the equal protection of the laws, and the right to it is not given by any law of Virginia or by any Federal statute.*

It is not, therefore, guaranteed by the Fourteenth Amendment.

Virginia v. Rives, 100 U.S. 313, 322–323 (1880) (emphasis added).

See also, *Swain v. Alabama*, 380 U. S. 202 (1965).

> Swain presented evidence that no black juror had served on a jury in Talladega County in more than a decade. See id. at 226. And in Swain's case, the prosecutor struck all six qualified black prospective jurors, ensuring that Swain was tried before an all-white jury. Swain invoked Strauder to argue that the prosecutor in his case had impermissibly discriminated on the basis of race by using peremptory challenges to strike the six black prospective jurors. The Court ruled that Swain had not established unconstitutional discrimination. Most importantly, the Court held that a defendant could not object to the state's use of peremptory strikes in an individual case. In the Court's words, "[W]e cannot hold that the striking of Negroes in a particular case is a denial of equal protection of the laws." *Id.* at 221. The Swain Court reasoned that prosecutors do not always judge prospective jurors individually when exercising peremptory strikes. Instead, prosecutors choose which prospective jurors to strike "in light of the limited knowledge counsel has of them, which may include their group affiliations, in the context of the case to be tried." Ibid. In the Court's view, the prosecutor could strike prospective jurors on the basis of their group affiliations, including race. In other words, a prosecutor could permissibly strike a prospective juror for any reason, including the assumption or belief that a black prospective juror, because of race, would be favorable to a black defendant or unfavorable to the State. *Flowers v. Mississippi*, 588 U.S. ___, Slip op. at 11–12 (2019).

The proposition that the trial court is not responsible for maintaining a fair jury pool creation and that a fair trial can occur when blacks are excluded from a jury pool or from being seated in a specific case because of their race would prevail until the Court overruled the practice in *Batson v. Kentucky* (1986).

9 "From colonial times until adoption of the Thirteenth Amendment, slaves were prohibited from keeping and bearing arms in most circumstances or altogether. Until adoption of the Fourteenth Amendment, free blacks were prohibited from possessing arms without a license, which was subject to an official's discretion. Such laws reflected that African Americans were not trusted or recognized to be among 'the people' with the rights of citizens." Brief for Amicus Curiae National African American Gun Association, Inc. in Support of Petitioners in *New York State Rifle & Pistol Association Inc. v. City of New York*, New York (May 7, 2019) at 14–15.

10 "As social science research shows, concerns that non-unanimous juries result in disenfranchisement of minority jurors and easier convictions of minority defendants are well-founded. And those concerns are all the more troubling because that is not only the effect, but also the original purpose, of the non-unanimous rule in Louisiana and Oregon—reason enough to render it constitutionally suspect. Louisiana and Oregon both initially required unanimous juries in all felony cases. The non-unanimous verdict arrived in Louisiana only after Reconstruction, as the white majority sought to perpetuate its supremacy in the State. Non-unanimous verdicts were first introduced in 1880, allowing defendants to be convicted by nine of twelve jurors. Split-verdict convictions were written into the Louisiana Constitution at the 1898 Constitutional Convention, which was deeply mired in racism." Brief for American Bar Association as Amicus Curiae supporting Petitioner in *Ramos v. Louisiana* (June 18, 2019) at 23. See also, Brief Amici Curiae of the American Civil Liberties Union and the ACLU Foundation of Louisiana in Support of petitioner in *Ramos v. Louisiana* (June 18, 2019) and Brief of Amicus Curiae NAACP Legal Defense

& Educational Fund, Inc. in support of Petitioner in *Ramos v. Louisiana* (June 18, 2019).

Interestingly, Louisiana did not dispute this history and purpose of creating nonunanimous juries. While admitting that "historical sources show that delegates at Louisiana's 1898 Constitutional Convention were impermissibly race-motivated. ... The 1898 Louisiana Constitution is long defunct [and the] most recent State Constitution was adopted in 1974 [and] Records from the constitutional convention show this considered choice was not motivated by any race animus." Brief in Opposition to Writ of Certiorari to Louisiana Court of Appeals for the Fourth Circuit (November 8, 2018) at 14–15.

11 U.S. Civil Rights Commission, Police Use of Force: An Examination of Modern Policing Practices, Dissenting Statement of Commissioner Peter Kirsanow (203–208) (2018) (internal citation and quotation marks omitted, emphasis in original).

12 Summary of Crime in the United States 2017, accessed September 24, 2018, at https://ucr.fbi.gov/crime-in-the-u.s/2017/crime-in-the-u.s.-2017/topic-pages/cius-summary.

13 See Chris Francescani, "NYPD Report Confirms Manipulation of Crime Stats," *Reuters,* March 9, 2012, https://www.reuters.com/article/us-crime-newyork-statistics/nypd-report-confirms-manipulation-of-crime-stats-idUSBRE82818620120309 and Cop Gumbo and Val Van Brocklin, "Fudge Factor: Cooking the Books on Crime Stats: What Do Police Report Writing and Fudge Have in Common?" PoliceOne. Com, June 20, 2012, https://www.policeone.com/patrol-issues/articles/5736845-Fudge-factor-Cooking-the-books-on-crime-stats/.

See also John A. Eterno, Arvind Verma & Eli B. Silverman, "Police Manipulations of Crime Reporting: Insiders' Revelations" *Justice Quarterly* 33, no. 5 (2016): 811–835. For a general review on UCR system see, Nathan James and Logan Rishard Council, "How Crime in the United States Is Measured," Congressional Research Service, January 3, 2008.

14 Id. at 201.

15 Id. at 205.

16 Id.

17 Plato, Republic, VII 514 a, 2 to 517 a, 7.

Chapter 2

1 American Enterprise Institute, "Expanding Opportunity in America: A Conversation with House Budget Committee Chairman Paul Ryan," panel discussion July 24, 2014, http://www.aei.org/files/2014/07/25/-paul-ryan-event_175426104263.pdf.

2 Racial residency laws were technically outlawed by the Supreme Court in *Buchanan v. Warley*, 245 U.S. 60 (1917).

3 Racial covenants were technically outlawed by the Supreme Court in *Shelley v. Kraemer* 334 U.S. 1 (1948). Michael Jones-Correa, "The Origins and Diffusion of Racial Restrictive Covenants," *Political Science Quarterly* 115, no. 4 (Winter, 2000–2001): 541.

4 Redlining was outlawed by the 1968 Fair Housing Act. See also, *Jones v. Alfred H. Mayer Co.*, 392 U.S. 409 (1968).

5 For a discussion on the history of blacks in American urban cities, see Douglas S. Massey, "Residential Segregation and Neighborhood Conditions in U.S. Metropolitan Areas," in *America Becoming: Racial Trends and Their Consequences,* Volume I, eds. Neil J. Smelser, William Julius Wilson, and Faith Mitchell (2001), 391–434.

6 *Floyd et al. v. City of N.Y.*, 959 F. Supp. 2d 540 (S.D.N.Y. 2013); see also Bernard E. Harcourt, "Rethinking Racial Profiling: A Critique of the Economics, Civil Liberties, and Constitutional Literature, and of Criminal Profiling More Generally," *University of Chicago Law Review* 71 (2004): 1275.

7 "Since 1965, welfare spending has increased 800 percent in real terms, while the number of major felonies per capita today is roughly three times the rate before 1960. As Senator Phil Gramm (R-TX) says, 'If social spending stopped crime we would be the safest country in the world.'" Patrick F. Fagan, "The Real Root Causes of Violent Crime: The Breakdown of Marriage, Family, and Community," *The Heritage Foundation Backgrounder* 1, no. 3 (March 17, 1995): 1026, http://thf_media.s3.amazonaws.com/1995/pdf/bg1026.pdf.

8 U.S. Census Bureau, MS-1. Marital Status of the Population 15 Years Old and Over by Sex, Race and Hispanic Origin: 1950 to Present, U.S. Census Bureau, *Historical Marital Status Tables* (November 2018), https://www.census.gov/data/tables/time-series/demo/families/marital.html.

9 U.S. Census Bureau, *Historical Marriage Trends from 1890–2010: A Focus on Race Differences* (May 2012), https://www.census.gov/library/working-papers/2012/demo/SEHSD-WP2012-12.html.

10 U.S. Census Bureau, MS-1. Marital Status of the Population 15 Years Old and Over by Sex, Race and Hispanic Origin: 1950 to Present, U.S. Census Bureau.

11 Andrew E. Taslitz, *Reconstructing the Fourth Amendment: A History of Search and Seizure, 1789–1868* (2006); see also Sally E. Hadden, *Slave Patrols: Law and Violence in Virginia and the Carolinas* (2001), C. Vann Woodward, *The Strange Career of Jim Crow* (1955).

12 See William Cohen, "Negro Involuntary Servitude in the South, 1865–1940: A Preliminary Analysis," *The Journal of Southern History* 42, no. 1 (Feb. 1976): 31–60, 34. Douglas A. Blackmon, *Slavery by Another Name: The Re-Enslavement of Black Americans from the Civil War to World War II* (2008). See also, Christopher R Adamson, "Punishment after Slavery: Southern State Penal Systems, 1865–1890," *Social Problems* 30, no. 5 (June 1983): 555; Earl Smith and Angela J. Hattery, "African American Men and the Prison Industrial Complex," *Washington Journal of Black Studies* 34, no. 4 (2010): 387; Eric Schlosser, "The Prison Industrial Complex," *Atlantic Monthly*, December 1998, at 52; Philip L. Reichel, "Southern Slave Patrols as a Transitional Police," *American Journal of Police* 7(1988): 51; Bruce P. Smith, "The Fourth Amendment, 1789–1868: A Strange History," *Ohio State Journal of Criminal Law* 5(2008): 663, Michelle Alexander, *The New Jim Crow: Mass Incarceration in the Age of Colorblindness* (2010); and Carol A Archbold, *Policing: A Text Reader* (2013).

13 *U.S. v. Booker*, 543 U.S. 220 (2005) and *Kimbrough v. U.S.*, 552 U.S. 85 (2007).

14 For example, See Stefano Luconi, "The Southern Strategy and the Post–New Deal Dynamics of the U.S. Party System," *Quarterly Journal of Ideology* 27, nos. 3 & 4 (2004): 1.

15 Gary Miller and Norman Schofield, "The Transformation of the Republican and Democratic Party Coalitions in the U.S.," *Perspectives on Politics* 6, no. 3 (2008): 433.

16 The concept of states' rights, it should be remembered, was birthed by the arguments of John Calhoun and other slave-owning southern leaders who opposed the power of the Union to place any limits on the expansion of slavery and asserted that slavery was both ordained by God and placed blacks in the natural state God intended. The fall of slavery did not eliminate the idea that the states have a right to resist the national government when it sought to enforce federal civil rights laws on the segregated South. During the 1950s, the South reintroduced interposition, the modern version of the antebellum theory of nullification.

   Both concepts have been disavowed by history and even serious conservative leaders, such as Bill Bennett, have bowed to the judgment of history. On his radio show, a caller asserted that conservatives should be more media savvy and support conservative movements. Specifically, the caller said that conservatives should support a group of "black preachers" who had an online petition to "impeach" Attorney General Holder for his support of gay marriage on "states' rights grounds" to which Bennett said that was the wrong argument because "states' rights" was the "justification of slavery" and the "states' rights" argument has been "discredited" and could not be used as an argument for the defense of marriage. He asserted that the defense of traditional marriage is moral, philosophical, and religious. He said, "States' rights was not the way to go, you have to use first principles." Bill Bennett, *Morning In America Radio Show* (March 4, 2014), http://www.billbennett. com/show-archive/.

17 Thurmond led an insurrection within the Democratic Party in 1948, after President Truman ended segregation in the military and formed a commission to study civil rights, by running for president under the States' Rights Democratic Party, the Dixiecrats. The Dixiecrats

took control of the Democratic Party in the South, and Thurmond won 39 electoral votes. He left the Democratic Party and joined the Republican Party when Johnson signed the 1964 Civil Rights Act. He was a major leader in bringing the Deep South Democrats into the Republican Party during the late 1960s–early 1970s.

18 Wallace opposed integration and famously said at his inauguration as governor in 1963, "In the name of the greatest people that have ever trod this earth, I draw the line in the dust and toss the gauntlet before the feet of tyranny, and I say segregation now, segregation tomorrow, segregation forever." He is famous for standing in the doorway of the University of Alabama to prevent the admittance of two black men to the university, forcing the Kennedy Administration to send the deputy attorney general, backed up by the nationalized Alabama National Guard, to move Wallace out of the way to allow the admittance and integration of the college.

19 Faubus opposed integration and ordered the Arkansas National Guard to prevent the integration of Little Rock Central High School in 1957, forcing President Eisenhower to nationalize the Guard and order the 101st Airborne Division to enforce the federal court order integrating the school. Faubus retaliated by closing the Little Rock high schools for the 1958–1959 school year.

20 Barnett opposed integration and had freedom riders arrested and imprisoned, and in 1962, he opposed the integration of the University of Mississippi when James Meredith was admitted. Barnett allowed a riot to occur on campus in which Meredith and a small detachment of U.S. Marshals were surrounded and attacked by an armed mob. It required the Kennedy Administration to send the U.S. Army military police from the 503rd and 716th Military Police Battalions to reinforce the marshals, and later Kennedy had to nationalize the Mississippi National Guard to protect Meredith throughout his enrollment at the university.

21 Goldwater opposed the Civil Rights Act of 1964 and established the dominance of conservative, states' rights, opposition to the Great Society politics within the Republican Party in the 1964 Republican primary election, as well as helped the facilitation of the transference of southern Democrats to the Republican Party.

22 Nixon created and implemented the southern strategy, which solidified the transference of conservative, states' rights opposition to the Great Society voters to the Republican Party.

23 Reagan became the embodiment of conservative states' rights and opposition to the Great Society politics, and he solidified the winning coalition of southern white working-class Democrats with northern Republican voters. He opposed disinvestment in South Africa to end the apartheid system, opposed the Martin Luther King Jr. holiday, opposed affirmative action programs, facilitated and provided support for the "get tough on crime" politics of the 1980s, and attacked social welfare programs by (1) supporting the assertion that they were immoral; (2) supporting the idea that the recipients of welfare support were urban, lazy black women; and (3) supported the policy assertion that they were not effective in reducing poverty.

24 David O. Sears, Carl P. Hensler, Leslie K. Speer, "Whites' Opposition to 'Busing': Self-Interest or Symbolic Politics?" *The American Political Science Review* 73, no. 2 (1979): 369.

25 David Leip's Atlas of U.S. Presidential Elections: 1968 Presidential General Election Results (2012), http://uselectionatlas.org/RESULTS/national.php?year=1968.

26 Id.

27 See Robert J. Sampson, and Janet L. Lauritsen, "Racial and Ethnic Disparities in Crime and Criminal Justice in the United States," *Crime and Justice* 21 (1997): 311; Lincoln Quillian and Devah Pager, "Black Neighbors, Higher Crime? The Role of Racial Stereotypes in Evaluations of Neighborhood Crime," *American Journal of Sociology* 107, no. 3 (2001): 717; Robert J Sampson and William Julius Wilson, "Toward a Theory of Race, Crime and Urban Inequality," in *Race, Crime, and Justice: A Reader,* eds. Shaun L. Gabbidon & Helen Taylor Greene eds. (2005): 177; and Walker Newell, "The Legacy of Nixon, Reagan, and Horton: How the Tough on Crime Movement Enabled a New Regime of Race-Influenced Employment Discrimination," *Berkeley Journal of African American Law and Policy* 15, no. 1 (2013): 3.

Chapter 3

1 Rush Limbaugh on *Fox and Friends*, Fox News Channel, July 12, 2019.

2 Transcript from *FOX News Sunday, Tara Westover on her journey from a survivalist family to the heights of academia,* July 21, 2019, https://www.foxnews.com/transcript/tara-westover-on-her-journey-from-a-survivalist-family-to-the-heights-of-academia.

3 Miller asserted regarding the four congresswomen,

> There's a fundamental distinction between people who think that we need to lean into and strengthen America's core values, whether it'd be our constitutional values, the rule of law, the principles of Western Civilization, or people who think it would basically need to turn America into Venezuela.
>
> ....
>
> WALLACE: But here's what Alexandria Ocasio-Cortez [said]
>
> All of these things could sound radical compared to where we are, but where we are is not a good thing. And this idea of 10 percent better from garbage shouldn't be what we settle for.
>
> She didn't say the country was garbage. She said some of the policies she opposes are garbage.
> MILLER: It's impossible to read the quote that way. The quote—what she's trying to say is—
>
> ....
>
> MILLER: She's saying that America in her view right now is garbage.
>
> ....
>
> MILLER: Throughout this interview, Chris, you're continuing to conflate Donald Trump's criticisms of President Obama versus AOC's deep and systemic criticisms of the country itself.

And so, let me just cut to the heart of the issue. These four congresswomen detest America as it exists, as it is currently constructed. They want to tear down the structure of our country. They want it to be a socialist, open borders country.

If you, as Donald Trump says, want to destroy America with open borders, you cannot say you love your country. If you attack border agents the way that Ocasio-Cortez has, it means you have a deep-seated hatred of the nation as it exists. That's why you want to erase its borders, fundamentally transform the country and in the process, it doesn't matter if American citizens lose their jobs, lose their homes, lose their livelihoods, lose their health coverage, and lose their very lives.

There's a gigantic, enormous distinction between Donald Trump saying I'm going to get on the world stage and put America first in every single thing we do, versus a view that says America should never come first and American citizens should never come first, which is their view, and that's what we're going to take to the ballot box.

4 Brian Taylor, "'They Are Free To Leave': Trump Accuses Congress women of Hating America," NPR, accessed July 15, 2019, https://www.npr.org/2019/07/15/741771445/trump-continues-twitter-assault-on-4-minority-congresswomen.

5 President Obama interview with Marc Maron, June 22, 2015, http://qz.com/433923/obama-used-the-n-word-in-a-podcast-interview-to-nail-a-complicated-truth-about-racism. See also Chapter 1.

6 History of Jamestown web page, http://www.historyisfun.org/jamestown-settlement/history-jamestown/.

7 James Oliver Horton and Lois E. Horton, *Slave and the Making of America* (2005), 29.

8 Smithsonian National Museum of African History and Culture.

9 James Oliver Horton and Lois E. Horton, *Slave and the Making of America*, 27 (2005).

10 John Rolfe, National Park Service web page, https://www.nps.gov/ jame/learn/historyculture/john-rolfe.htm.

11 James Oliver Horton and Lois E. Horton, *Slave and the Making of America*, 29.

12 James Oliver Horton and Lois E. Horton, *Slave and the Making of America* (2005), 30.

13 U.S. Constitution Article IV, Section 2, Clause 3 (1789). "No person held to service or labour in one state, under the laws thereof, escaping into another, shall, in consequence of any law or regulation therein, be discharged from such service or labour, but shall be delivered up on claim of the party to whom such service or labour may be due."

14 Tamar R. Birckhead, "The New Peonage," *Washington and Lee Law Review* 72, no. 4 (2015): 1595.

15 Douglas A. Blackmon, *Slavery by Another Name: The Re-Enslavement of Black Americans from the Civil War to World War II* (2008). See also, Christopher R Adamson, "Punishment after Slavery: Southern State Penal Systems, 1865–1890"; *Social Problems* 30, no. 5 (June 1983): 555; Earl Smith and Angela J. Hattery, "African American Men and the Prison Industrial Complex," *Washington Journal of Black Studies* 34, no.4 (2010): 387; Eric Schlosser, "The Prison Industrial Complex," *Atlantic Monthly*, December 1998, 52; Philip L. Reichel, "Southern Slave Patrols as a Transitional Police," *American Journal of Police* 7(1988): 51; Bruce P. Smith, "The Fourth Amendment, 1789–1868: A Strange History," *Ohio State Journal of Criminal Law* 5(2008): 663; Michelle Alexander, *The New Jim Crow: Mass Incarceration in the Age of Colorblindness* (2010); and Carol A Archbold, *Policing: A Text Reader* (2013).

16 Jonathan A. Klusmeyer, *Slavery Continued: Peonage in Missouri*.

17 Michael J. Klarman, *From Jim Crow to Civil Rights: The Supreme Court and the Struggle for Racial Equality* (2004), 71.

18 Michael J. Klarman, *From Jim Crow to Civil Rights* (emphasis added).

19 Michael J. Klarman, *From Jim Crow to Civil Rights*, 72.

20 Michael J. Klarman, *From Jim Crow to Civil Rights*.

21 Douglas A. Blackmon, *Slavery by Another Name: The Re-Enslavement of Black Americans from the Civil War to World War II* (2008). See also Christopher R Adamson, "Punishment after Slavery: Southern State Penal Systems, 1865–1890"; *Social Problems* 30, no. 5 (June 1983): 555, Earl Smith and Angela J. Hattery, "African American Men and the Prison Industrial Complex," *Washington Journal of Black Studies* 34, no. 4 (2010): 387; Eric Schlosser, "The Prison Industrial Complex," *Atlantic Monthly*, December 1998, 52; Philip L. Reichel, "Southern Slave Patrols as a Transitional Police," *American Journal of Police* 7(1988): 51; Bruce P. Smith, "The Fourth Amendment, 1789–1868: A Strange History," *Ohio State Journal of Criminal Law* 5(2008): 663; Michelle Alexander, *The New Jim Crow: Mass Incarceration in the Age of Colorblindness* (2010); and Carol A Archbold, *Policing: A Text Reader* (2013).

22 Harold D. Woodman, "Post–Civil War Southern Agriculture and the Law," *Agricultural History* 53, no. 1 (January 1979): 319, 337, 335.

23 Jonathan A. Klusmeyer, *Slavery Continued: Peonage in Missouri* (Master's Thesis, University of Central Missouri, November 2013), 7–8.

24 United States Statutes at Large, 39th Cong., Sess. II., Chp. 187, p. 546 (March 2, 1867). *The Peonage Act* was amended in 1909 (60th Cong., Sess. II., Chp. 321, section 269 p. 1142, March 4, 1909) and amended into its modern form on June 25, 1948 (18 U.S.C. § 1581). See, generally, 18 U.S.C. Chapter 77 (18 U.S.C. §§ 1851–1897) for modern federal laws prohibiting various types of slavery, involuntary servitude, slave trafficking, and sex trafficking. The modern federal law prohibiting slavery is 18 U.S.C. 1589.

25 Pete Daniel, *The Shadow of Slavery: Peonage in the South 1901–1969*, 10–11 (University of Illinois Press, 1972). See also David M. Oshinsky, *Worse than Slavery: Parchman Farm and the Ordeal of Jim Crow Justice* (Prentice Hall, 1997) and Alex Lichtenstein, *Twice the Work of Free Labor: The Political Economy of Convict Labor in the New South* (Verso, 1996).

26 Harold Woodman, "Sequel to Slavery: The New History Views the Postbellum South," *The Journal of Southern History* 43, no. 4 (1977): 523, 551–53.

27 Jonathan A. Klusmeyer, *Slavery Continued: Peonage in Missouri,* 54 (Internal citations omitted). See also, Tamar R. Birckhead, "The New Peonage," *Washington and Lee Law Review* 72, no. 4 (2015): 1595, 1610.

28 See Pete Daniel (ed.) *The Peonage Files of the Department of Justice, 1901–1945* (1989). "This microfilm publication contains fresh material on the first federal prosecution under the peonage statute, *U.S. v. Eberhart,* in 1898. The first Supreme Court case dealing with peonage, *Clyatt v. United States,* began in 1901 in Florida." Id. at v.

29 *United States v. Clyatt*, 197 U.S. 201 (1905).

30 *United States v. Reynolds*, 235 U.S. 133 (1914). For further discussion see, William Wirt Howe, "The Peonage Cases," *Columbia Law Review* 4, no. 4 (April 1904): 279–86; Pete Daniel, "Up from Slavery and Down to Peonage: The Alonzo Bailey Case," *The Journal of American History* 57, no. 3 (December 1970): 654–70; Aziz H. Huq "Peonage and Contractual Liberty," *Columbia Law Review* 101, no. 2 (March 2001): 351–91; Aviam Soifer, "Federal Protection, Paternalism, and the Virtually Forgotten Prohibition of Voluntary Peonage," *Columbia Law Review* 112, no. 7 (November 2012): 1607–39; and Benno C. Schmidt Jr., "Principle and Prejudice: The Supreme Court and Race in the Progressive Era. Part 2: The 'Peonage Cases,'" *Columbia Law Review* 82, no. 4 (May 1982): 646–718.

31 William Cohen, "Negro Involuntary Servitude in the South," 55.

32 Michael J. Klarman, *From Jim Crow to Civil Rights: The Supreme Court and the Struggle for Racial Equality* (Oxford University Press, 2004), 74. See also Douglas A. Blackmon, *Slavery by another Name* (2008), 53–57.

33 William Cohen, "Negro Involuntary Servitude in the South," 35.

34 William Cohen, "Negro Involuntary Servitude in the South," 36.

35 Pete Daniel, *The Shadow of Slavery: Peonage in the South 1901–1969* (1972), 3.

36 William Cohen, "Negro Involuntary Servitude in the South, 1865–1940: A Preliminary Analysis," *The Journal of Southern History* 42, no. 1: 39.

37 William Cohen, "Negro Involuntary Servitude in the South," 42.

38 William Cohen, "Negro Involuntary Servitude in the South."

39 *Bailey v. Alabama*, 219 U.S. 219 (1911).

40 William Cohen, "Negro Involuntary Servitude in the South, 1865–1940: A Preliminary Analysis," *The Journal of Southern History* 42, no. 1: 43.

41 William Cohen, "Negro Involuntary Servitude in the South," 47.

42 William Cohen, "Negro Involuntary Servitude in the South," 50, 51.

43 William Cohen, "Negro Involuntary Servitude in the South," 55.

44 The compromise of 1877 resulted from the election of 1876 between Rutherford B. Hayes (R) and Samuel Tilden (D), which the House of Representatives decided in spring 1877. Southern Democrats agreed to support the election of Hayes (R) with his promise to remove federal troops from the South. The result of the bargain was the establishment of home rule in the South, the complete decimation of the economic and political gains made by former slaves during the first Reconstruction, the rise of Jim Crow, and the criminalization of blacks as a means of social control. This bargain also resulted in the death of the Republican Party political influence in the South until the rise of Strom Thurmond, Barry Goldwater, and George Wallace nine decades later.

45 The first great corrupt bargain being the election of 1824 when the House of Representatives voted for John Quincy Adams over Andrew Jackson, who had won the popular vote. Henry Clay, who did not have enough electoral votes to be considered by the House, is believed to have supported Adams in return for a cabinet position, which, in fact, he received—the position of secretary of state. Neither Adams nor Clay ever lived down accusations of a stolen election, and Jackson defeated Adams in the 1828 election, ushering in the age of Jackson and Jacksonian Democracy.

46 For example, see Jeff Forret "Before Angola: Enslaved Prisoners in the Louisiana State Penitentiary," *Louisiana History* 54, no. 2 (2013): 133–71.

47 Jonathan A. Klusmeyer, *Slavery Continued: Peonage in Missouri,* 63 (internal citation omitted) and Douglas A. Blackmon, *Slavery By Another Name* (2008), 100–102.

48 See United States Department of Justice Civil Rights Division, *Investigation of the Ferguson Police Department* (March 4, 2015), 2 ("The City budgets for sizeable increases in municipal fines and fees each year, exhorts police and court staff to deliver those revenue increases, and closely monitors whether those increases are achieved. City officials routinely urge Chief Jackson to generate more revenue through enforcement. ... Ferguson police officers from all ranks told us that revenue generation is stressed heavily within the police department, and that the message comes from City leadership.")

The Ferguson judiciary was also found to be complicit in the revenue generating process. ("Ferguson has allowed its focus on revenue generation to fundamentally compromise the role of Ferguson's municipal court. The municipal court does not act as a neutral arbiter of the law or a check on unlawful police conduct. Instead, the court primarily uses its judicial authority as the means to compel the payment of fines and fees that advance the City's financial interests. This has led to court practices that violate the Fourteenth Amendment's due process and equal protection requirements. The court's practices also impose unnecessary harm, overwhelmingly on African-American individuals, and run counter to public safety.") Id. at 3.

See also, "Ferguson's Conspiracy Against Black Citizens: How the City's Leadership Harassed and Brutalized Their Way to Multiple Civil-Rights Violations," accessed March 5, 2015, https://www.theatlantic.com/national/archive/2015/03/ferguson-as-a-criminal-conspiracy-against-its-black-residents-michael-brown-department-of-justice-report/386887/ and NPR, "In Ferguson, Court Fines And Fees Fuel Anger," accessed August 25, 2014, https://www.npr.org/2014/08/25/343143937/in-ferguson-court-fines-and-fees-fuel-anger.

49 Gordon N. Carper, "Slavery Revisited: Peonage in the South," *Phylon* 37, no. 1: 86. ("Of all the Black Codes ... vagrancy was applied most often to freed Negroes. And few convicted of vagrancy

were able to pay their fines and court costs. As a result they took the second alternative, one to six months as a county convict. At this point they were usually leased to the highest bidder and privileged to participate in another peculiarly Southern institution, the convict-lease system. Frequently, the convicts were detained beyond the term of sentence. When this happened a condition of peonage existed. Throughout the South the convict-lease system directly led to and brought about peonage [and] there was a positive relationship between peonage and convict leasing [in which] convicts were leased and subleased and not allowed to depart upon the expiration of their sentences.")

50 Jonathan A. Klusmeyer, *Slavery Continued: Peonage in Missouri*, 67 (internal citation omitted).

51 Gordon N. Carper, "Slavery Revisited: Peonage in the South," *Phylon* 37, no. 1: 86, 93–94.

52 Douglas A. Blackmon, *Slavery by Another Name* (2008), 95–96, 109–110.

53 William Cohen, "Negro Involuntary Servitude in the South, 1865–1940: A Preliminary Analysis," *The Journal of Southern History* 42, no. 1 (February 1976): 31–60, 56–57.

54 *Belle,* directed by Amma Asante (2013; Released 2014), Film.

55 *Gregson v. Gilbert* (1783) (3 Doug. KB 232).

56 James Walvin, *The Zong: A Massacre, The Law and the End of Slavery,* 153.

57 James Walvin, *The Zong: A Massacre, The Law and the End of Slavery* (2011) and Jeremy Krikler, Jeremy, "A Chain of Murder in the Slave Trade: A Wider Context of the *Zong* Massacre" *International Review of Social History* 57, no. 3 (2012): 393.

58 See, Genesis 9:18–27, 10:2, 5:11:26.

59 For additional scholarship on Christian justification of slavery, see Larry R. Morrison, "The Religious Defense of American Slavery Before 1830," *Journal of Religious Thought* 37 (1980): 16; Larry E. Tise, *Proslavery: A History of the Defense of Slavery in America, 1701–1840* (University of Georgia Press, 1990); Stephen R. Haynes, *Noah's Curse: The Biblical Justification of American Slavery* (2002), David M. Goldenberg, *The Curse of Ham: Race*

and Slavery in Early Judaism, Christianity, and Islam (2009); John Coffey, "Evangelicals, Slavery & the Slave Trade: From Whitefield to Wilberforce," *Anvil-Bristol* 24, no. 2 (2007): 97; David Meager, "Why Did Christians Justify African Slavery," *Cross Way* 104 (Spring 2007); and Ibram X. Kendi, *Stamped from the Beginning: The Definitive History of Racist Ideas in America* (2016).

60 Deuteronomy 20:17 and Numbers 31:9–11 (NIV). See also Numbers 31:17–18, 32–35 (NIV), respectively, regarding the war with the Midianites ("Now kill all the boys. And kill every woman who has slept with a man, but save for yourselves every girl who has never slept with a man." "The plunder remaining from the spoils that the soldiers took was 675,000 sheep, (33) 72,000 cattle, (34) 61,000 donkeys (35) and 32,000 women who had never slept with a man.")

In defense of the law allowing the taking of young women by the children of Israel authorized in the Bible, God commanded that the Midianites and Moabites and others be destroyed because they practiced various types of abominations and idol worship and human sacrifices. God wanted those practices wiped off the face of the earth. As for the young women, because they were too young to have participated in the abominations, they could not be punished with death. Furthermore, upon capture by the soldiers of Israel, the young girls were not to be mistreated; they were not to be raped and sold into slavery but rather married to the soldiers as wives, and if not married they were to be freed unharmed as required by the command of God in Deuteronomy 21:10–14 (NIV). Historically, at the time, such a command was without equal.

61 See Colossians 3:22, Ephesians 6:5–9, 1 Peter 2:18–20, and Philemon 8–21(NKJV).

62 Galatians 3:28 (NIV).

63 For additional scholarship on Christian justification of slavery, see Larry R. Morrison, "The Religious Defense of American Slavery Before 1830," *Journal of Religious Thought* 37 (1980): 16; Larry E. Tise, *Proslavery: A History of the Defense of Slavery in America, 1701–1840* (University of Georgia Press, 1990); Stephen R. Haynes, *Noah's Curse: The Biblical Justification of American Slavery* (2002); David M. Goldenberg, *The Curse of Ham: Race*

and Slavery in Early Judaism, Christianity, and Islam (2009); John Coffey, "Evangelicals, Slavery & the Slave Trade: From Whitefield to Wilberforce," *Anvil-Bristol* 24, no. 2 (2007): 97; David Meager, "Why Did Christians Justify African Slavery," *Cross Way* 104 (Spring 2007); and Ibram X. Kendi, *Stamped from the Beginning: The Definitive History of Racist Ideas in America* (2016).

64 *The Ten Commandments* directed by Cecil B. DeMille (1956), Film.

65 Genesis 6:5 (AMP).

66 Moses acknowledged that the Jews had taken slaves but limited the practice.

> As for your male and female slaves whom you may have—you may acquire male and female slaves from the pagan nations that are around you [and] from them you may buy *slaves* and from their families who are with you, whom they have produced in your land; they may become your possession. You may even bequeath them as an inheritance to your children after you, to receive as a possession; you can use them as permanent slaves. But in respect to your fellow countrymen, the children of Israel, you shall not rule over one another with harshness (severity, oppression).

Leviticus 25:44–46 (AMP).

Moses commanded that in the eyes of God, since the Jews had slaves and were prone to be cruel and would enslave their fellow Jews as well as those who were not, it was commanded that they could only enslave non-Jews. Moses commanded,

> If your fellow countryman becomes so poor ... that he sells himself ... you shall not let him do the work of a slave ... he is to be with you as a hired man, as if he were a temporary resident. ... For the Israelites are My servants whom I brought out of the land of Egypt; they shall not be sold in a slave sale. You shall not rule over him with harshness (severity, oppression), but you are to fear your God [with profound reverence].

Leviticus 25:39–43 (AMP).

67 Matthew 19:8 (AMP).

68 Exodus 21:16 (NKJ). See also Arthur H. Garrison, "Defining the Meaning and Purpose of Justice, Law, and Criminal Justice" *Journal of Catholic Legal* Studies 55, no. 1 (2016): 1.

69 For an example of the application of the science of hermeneutics to the Bible, see Arthur H. Garrison, "A Hermeneutical Judeo-Christian Biblical Perspective" *Journal of Grace Theology* 5, no. 1 (2018): 3.

70 For example, see, Senator Jefferson Davis's, the future president of the Confederacy, March 2, 1859, speech on the floor of the U.S. Senate regarding the status of slaves in the south and the biblical justification for that treatment.

> It is the presence of a lower caste, those lower by their mental and physical organization, controlled by the higher intellect of the white man, that gives this superiority to the white laborer. Menial services are not there performed by the white man. We have none of our brethren sunk to the degradation of being menials. That belongs to the lower race—the descendants of Ham, who, under the judgment of God speaking to the prophet Noah, were condemned to be servants.

Jefferson Davis, "Speech in U.S. Senate," in *The Essential Writings of Jefferson Davis* (New York: Modern Library, 2004), 159–160. See Chapter 4 for further discussion of Davis and this speech regarding the inferiority of blacks and the significance of this belief in the rise of the Civil War and conservative political rhetoric.

71 See 1 John 2:2, Ephesians 1:7 (NKJV).

72 See 1 John 2:2, Ephesians 1:7 (NKJV).

73 Ephesians 6:5–9 (NKJV). See also Colossians 3:22 and 1 Peter 2:18 (NKJV) in which the instruction of slaves obey your masters is written within the context of how Christian homes can maintain order, peace, and love between members. It was not written within a context of domination.

74 See, generally, the Book of Philemon (NKJV).

75 Galatians 5:1 (AMP).

Chapter 4

1 Thomas Jefferson, "Notes on the State of Virginia, Query XIV: The Administration of Justice and Description of the Laws?" (1781).

2 Thomas Jefferson, "Notes on the State of Virginia, Query XVIII: Manners, The particular customs and manners that may happen to be received in that state?" (1781).

3 John Calhoun, "On the Importance of Domestic Slavery," Speech in the U.S. Senate on January 10, 1838.

4 Eduardo Bonilla-Silva, *Racism Without Racists*, Second Edition (Rowman & Littlefield, 2006).

5 Jefferson Davis, "Speech in U.S. Senate," in *The Essential Writings of Jefferson Davis*, ed. William Cooper (New York: Modern Library, 2004), 159.

6 Dr. Martin Luther King, Address at the Conclusion of the Selma to Montgomery March, Montgomery, Alabama, March 25, 1965.

7 Lyndon Johnson, "Message to Congress: Johnson on Crime and Law Enforcement." In CQ Almanac 1966, 22nd ed., 1268–72. Washington, D.C.: Congressional Quarterly, 1967, http://library.cqpress.com/cqalmanac/cqal66-1299805.

8 Andrew E. Busch, 1966 Foreshadows Republican Era (2006), http://ashbrook.org/publications/oped-busch-06-1966/.

9 Eddie Glaude, MSNBC "Deadline: White House," July 15, 2019.

10 Quoted by Tim Alberta, author of American Carnage: On the Front Lines of the Republican Civil War and the Rise of President Trump (2019) MSNBC "Deadline: White House," July 15, 2019.

11 Ian Haney Lopez, Dog Whistle Politics: How Coded Racial Appeals have Reinvented Racism and Wrecked the Middle Class (2014) at 26–34. See also, Kevin Phillips, The Emerging Republican Majority, 1st ed. (1969), Dan T. Carter, The Politics of Rage: George Wallace, The Origins of the New Conservatism and the Transformation of American Politics, second ed. (LSU Press, 2000) and Dan T. Carter, From George Wallace to Newt Gingrich: Race in the Conservative Counterrevolution 1963–1994 (LSU Press, 1996).

12 For further discussion on the origin of the silent center and silent majority rhetoric, see interview with Nixon speech writer Richard Whalen at http://weekendamerica.publicradio.org/display/web/2008/05/16/silent_center.html

Chapter 5

1 For broader discussion on the history of Christianity in defining American and Western traditions on the meaning of law and justice, see Arthur H. Garrison, A. "Defining the Meaning and Purpose of Justice, Law, and Criminal Justice: A Hermeneutical Judeo-Christian Biblical Perspective," Journal of Catholic Legal Studies 55, no. 1(2016): 1–82.
2 Id. See also, Arthur H. Garrison, "The Traditions and History of the Meaning of the Rule of Law," *Georgetown Journal of Law & Public Policy* 12, no. 2 (2014): 565–619.
3 Radley Balko, *Rise of the Warrior Cop*, 58–59.
4 Radley Balko, *Rise of the Warrior Cop*, 76–80.
5 Radley Balko, *Rise of the Warrior Cop*, 77.
6 Radley Balko, *Rise of the Warrior Cop*, 78–80.
7 Radley Balko, *Rise of the Warrior Cop*, 126–37.

Chapter 6

1 For detailed discussion see, Arthur H. Garrison, "Criminal Culpability, Civil Liability, and Police Created Danger: Why and How the Fourth Amendment Provides Very Limited Protection from Police Use of Deadly Force," *George Mason University Civil Rights Law Journal* 28, no. 3 (2018), 241–339 (2018).
2 Arthur H. Garrison, "NYPD Stop and Frisk, Perceptions of Criminals, Race and the Meaning of *Terry v. Ohio*: A Content Analysis of *Floyd, et al. v. City of New York*," *Rutgers Race and the Law Review* 15 (2014): 65–156 (2014).

3 *Manuel v. Illinois*, 580 U. S. ____ (2017), Slip. Op. at 11 nt 8 ("[T]
he nature of the legal proceeding establishing probable cause
makes a difference for purposes of the Fourth Amendment ... if
the proceeding is tainted—as here, by fabricated evidence—and the
result is that probable cause is lacking, then the ensuing pretrial
detention violates the confined person's Fourth Amendment rights,
for all the reasons we have stated. By contrast ... once a trial has
occurred, the Fourth Amendment drops out: A person challenging
the sufficiency of the evidence to support both a conviction and any
ensuing incarceration does so under the Due Process Clause of the
Fourteenth Amendment. [There is a] constitutional division of labor. ... [T]he Framers drafted the Fourth Amendment to address the
matter of *pretrial* deprivations of liberty and the Amendment thus
provides "standards and procedures" for "the detention of suspects
pending trial.") (Internal citation and quotation marks omitted).

4 *Manuel v. Illinois*, 580 U. S. ____ (2017), Slip. Op. at 7–8, 9 ("The
Fourth Amendment, we began, establishes the minimum constitutional standards and procedures not just for arrest but also for
ensuing detention. ... The Fourth Amendment [is] tailored explicitly
for the criminal justice system, and it always has been thought to
define the appropriate process for seizures of persons ... in criminal cases, including the detention of suspects pending trial. That
Amendment, standing alone, guaranteed a fair and reliable determination of probable cause as a condition for any significant pretrial
restraint. Accordingly, those detained prior to trial without such a
finding could appeal to the Fourth Amendment's protection against
unfounded invasions of liberty. ... [A] pretrial deprivation of liberty
may invoke the Fourth Amendment when (as here) that deprivation
occurs after legal process commences. ... If the complaint is that a
form of legal process resulted in pretrial detention unsupported by
probable cause, then the right allegedly infringed lies in the Fourth
Amendment.") (Internal citation and quotation marks omitted).

5 *Kingsley v. Hendrickson*, 576 U. S. ____ (2015), Slip. Op. at 5–6,
9 ("As to ... whether ... the defendant's physical acts ... was
"excessive," ... We conclude with respect to that question that the
relevant standard is objective not subjective. Thus, the defendant's

state of mind is not a matter that a plaintiff is required to prove ... [A] pretrial detainee must show only that the force purposely or knowingly used against him was objectively unreasonable ... Our standard is also consistent with our use of an objective "excessive force" standard where officers apply force to a person who ... has been accused but not convicted of a crime, but who ... is free on bail."). The Court held that the objective reasonableness test must be applied in like manner to claims of excessive force made against police. Id. at 7, 9–10.

6 *Kingsley v. Hendrickson*, 576 U. S. ___ (2015), Slip. Op. at 7–8 ("Several considerations have led us to conclude that the appropriate standard for a pretrial detainee's excessive force claim is solely an objective one. For one thing, it is consistent with our precedent. We have said that the Due Process Clause protects a pretrial detainee from the use of excessive force that amounts to punishment ... [W]e explained that such "punishment" can consist of actions taken with an expressed intent to punish. But ... in the absence of an expressed intent to punish, a pretrial detainee can nevertheless prevail by showing that the actions are not rationally related to a legitimate nonpunitive governmental purpose or that the actions appear excessive in relation to that purpose. ... [A] pretrial detainee can prevail by providing only objective evidence that the challenged governmental action is not rationally related to a legitimate governmental objective or that it is excessive in relation to that purpose.") (Internal citation and quotation marks omitted).

7 For example, see *Bucklew v. Precythe*, 587 U. S. ___ (2019) within the context of death penalty implementation.

8 Arthur H. Garrison, "Enhanced Washington Post Shooting Data: A Descriptive Analysis," Presented at the 2019 Annual ACJS Conference, Baltimore, Maryland (March 2019).

9 Id.

10 General population and violent crime are shown because these are the most common benchmarks used when discussing police use of force and race. As discussed in Chapter 1, I fully acknowledge research literature that has demonstrated the inadequacy of these

two measures and the need for more nuanced benchmarks. See Samuel Walker, "Searching for the Denominator: Problems with Police Traffic Stop Data and an Early Warning System Solution." *Justice Research and Policy* 3, no. 1 (2001): 63–95; James E. Lange, Mark B. Johnson, and Robert B. Voas. "Testing the Racial Profiling Hypothesis for Seemingly Disparate Traffic Stops on the New Jersey Turnpike." *Justice Quarterly* 22, no. 2 (2005): 193–223; and Joseph Cesario, David J. Johnson, and William Terrill. "Is There Evidence of Racial Disparity in Police Use of Deadly Force? Analyses of Officer-Involved Fatal Shootings in 2015–2016." *Social Psychological and Personality Science* (2018): 1948550618775108 (Online advanced publication).

11 Social science, social psychology, and critical race theory suggests that police are more likely to shoot blacks than whites when under emotional stress or ambiguous situation threat pressure. Literature on police training suggests the level of training (tactical and cultural) and experience (working memory) can influence police use of force and shoot decisions. For additional research see, Correll, J., Park, B., Judd, C. M., Wittenbrink, B., Sadler, M. S., & Keesee, T., "Across the Thin Blue Line: Police Officers and Racial Bias in the Decision to Shoot," *Journal of Personality and Social Psychology*, 92, no. 6: (2007) 1006; Joshua Correll, Bernadette Park, Charles M. Judd, and Bernd Wittenbrink. The Police Officer's Dilemma: Using Ethnicity to Disambiguate Potentially Threatening Individuals." *Journal of Personality and Social Psychology* 83, no. 6 (2002): 1314; Kleider, H. M., Parrott, D. J., & King, T. Z., "Shooting Behaviour: How Working Memory and Negative Emotionality Influence Police Officer Shoot Decisions," *Applied Cognitive Psychology* 24, no. 5 (2010): 707–17; Heather M. Kleider-Offutt, Amanda M. Clevinger, and Alesha D. Bond. "Working Memory and Cognitive Load in the Legal System: Influences on Police Shooting Decisions, Interrogation and Jury Decisions," *Journal of Applied Research in Memory and Cognition* 5, no. 4 (2016): 426–33; Fleming, Kevin K., Carole L. Bandy, and Matthew O. Kimble, "Decisions to Shoot in a Weapon Identification Task: The Influence of Cultural Stereotypes and Perceived Threat on False Positive Errors," *Social Neuroscience* 5,

no. 2 (2010): 201–20; Melody S. Sadler, Joshua Correll, Bernadette Park, and Charles M. Judd, "The World Is Not Black and White: Racial Bias in the Decision to Shoot in a Multiethnic Context" *Journal of Social Issues* 68, no. 2 (2012): 286–313; Ravindra S. Goonetilleke, Errol R. Hoffmann, and Wing Chung Lau, "Pistol Shooting Accuracy as Dependent on Experience, Eyes Being Opened and Available Viewing Time" *Applied Ergonomics* 40, no. 3 (2009): 500–508; Ljubica Damjanovic, Amy E. Pinkham, Philip Clarke, and Jeremy Phillips, "Enhanced Threat Detection in Experienced Riot Police Officers: Cognitive Evidence from the Face-in-the-Crowd Effect," *The Quarterly Journal of Experimental Psychology* 67, no. 5 (2014): 1004–18; Anthony J. Pinizzotto, Edward F. Davis, Shannon B. Bohrer, and Benjamin J. Infanti, "Law Enforcement Restraint in the Use Of Deadly Force Within the Context of 'the Deadly Mix'", *International Journal of Police Science & Management* 14, no. 4 (2012): 285–98; Heather M. Kleider, Dominic J. Parrott, and Tricia Z. King, "Shooting Bhaviour: How Working Memory and Negative Emotionality Influence Police Officer Shoot Decisions," *Applied Cognitive Psychology* 24, no. 5 (2010): 707–17; and Heather M. Kleider and Dominic J. Parrott, "Aggressive Shooting Behavior: How Working Memory and Threat Influence Shoot Decisions," *Journal of Research in Personality* 43, no. 3 (2009): 494–97.

12 Newer neurological research suggests that police decision making under stress and ambiguity resulting in the use force or shoot is influenced by biochemical brain functions resulting from anxiety and stress or involuntary extreme focus on possible threats. See Lorraine Hope, "Evaluating the Effects of Stress and Fatigue on Police Officer Response and Recall: A Challenge for Research, Training, Practice And Policy," *Journal of Applied Research in Memory and Cognition* 5, no. 3 (2016): 239–45; Michael D. White and David Klinger. "Contagious Fire?" *Journal of Research in Crime and Delinquency/Crime Delinquency Online First*, June 24 (2008); and Arne Nieuwenhuys, Geert JP Savelsbergh, and Raôul RD Oudejans, "Shoot or Don't Shoot? Why Police Officers Are More Inclined to Shoot When They Are Anxious," *Emotion* 12, no. 4 (2012): 827.

"When performing under anxiety, police officers showed a response bias towards shooting, implying that they accidentally shot more often at suspects that surrendered. Furthermore, shot accuracy was lower under anxiety and officers responded faster when suspects had a gun. Finally, since gaze behavior appeared to be unaffected by anxiety, it is concluded that when they were anxious, officers were more inclined to respond on the basis of threat-related inferences and expectations rather than objective, task-relevant visual information."

This neurological research also suggests that police under pressure are more accurate in judging whether blacks are or are not armed.

Modupe Akinola and Wendy Berry Mendes, "Stress-Induced Cortisol Facilitates Threat-Related Decision Making among Police Officers," *Behavioral Neuroscience* 126, no. 1 (2012): 167.

"As cortisol levels increased, officers were better able to discriminate between armed and unarmed targets when targets were Black. This relationship between cortisol reactivity and discriminability was not seen for White targets."

"This study was designed to examine the relationship between stress-induced cortisol increases and threat-related decision making. Our data show that police officers who had larger cortisol increases to the stress task subsequently made fewer errors in the decision-making task. ... the relationship between increased cortisol reactivity and fewer error rates in the decision making task was stronger when the targets were armed and Black than when the targets were armed and White. That is, the greater the cortisol response the fewer the shooting errors, but only when responding to armed Black targets."

13 Equal Justice Initiative, *Lynching in America: Confronting the Legacy of Racial Terror*, Third Edition (2017), 22.

14 Equal Justice Initiative, the National Memorial for Peace and Justice, Lynching in America web page, https://museumandmemorial.eji.org/memorial.

15 Equal Justice Initiative, *Lynching in America: Confronting the Legacy of Racial Terror*, Third Edition (2017), 30.

16 National Institutes of Health, National Institute of Drug Abuse, *Opioid Overdose Crisis* (January 2019), https://www.drugabuse.gov/drugs-abuse/opioids/opioid-overdose-crisis.

17 Thomas famously said at his Senate confirmation hearing, "This is a circus. It is a national disgrace. And from my standpoint, as a black American, as far as I am concerned, it is a high-tech lynching for uppity-blacks who in any way deign to think for themselves, to do for themselves, to have different ideas, and it is a message that, unless you kowtow to an old order, this is what will happen to you, you will be lynched, destroyed, caricatured by a committee of the U.S. Senate, rather than hung from a tree."

18 For discussion see Andrew J. Costello, "A Closer look at the Eric Garner Incident: The New York Police Department Should Review Its Policy Instead of Trying Its Police Officer," *Journal of Criminal Justice and Law: Official Journal of the Law and Public Policy Section of the Academy of Criminal Justice Sciences* 122 (2018) and Joe D. Mazza, "The Eric Garner Incident: Sentinel Calls for Greater Scholarly Support in Policymaking" *Journal of Criminal Justice and Law: Official Journal of the Law and Public Policy Section of the Academy of Criminal Justice Sciences* 136 (2018).

19 Statement by U.S. Attorney Richard P. Donoghue, Department of Justice, U.S. Attorney's Office, Eastern District of New York (July 16, 2019), https://www.justice.gov/usao-edny/pr/statement-united-states-attorney-richard-p-donoghue.

20 See opinion *In the Matter of the Charges and Specifications Against Police Officer Daniel Pantaleo* by Rosemarie Maldonado, NYPD Deputy Commissioner of Trials (August 2, 2019) at https://int.nyt.com/data/documenthelper/1645-read-the-judges-opinion/1ab51bece4671aa10d11/optimized/full.pdf.

21 Police Commissioner James P. O'Neill Announces Decision in Disciplinary Case of Officer Daniel Pantaleo (August 19, 2019) at

https://www1.nyc.gov/site/nypd/news/s0819/police-commissioner-
james-p-o-neill-decision-disciplinary-case-officer-daniel#/0. See full
press conference at https://www.youtube.com/watch?v=ie3oJrgV9Mo.

22 Nick Wing, "911 Caller Will Not Be Charged For Giving Cops Bad
Info Before Fatal Police Shooting: John Crawford III Was Holding
a Toy Gun When Police Killed Him. The Caller Said He Was
Pointing A Rifle at Children," *HuffPost,* April 18, 2016, https://
www.huffpost.com/entry/ronald-ritchie-john-crawford_n_57065a
21e4b0b90ac2714e86.

23 Madison Park, "Police Shootings: Trials, Convictions Are Rare for
Officers" *CNN* October 3, 2018, https://www.cnn.com/2017/05/18/
us/police-involved-shooting-cases/index.html and Ralph Ellis,
Christopher Lett and Sara Sidner, "Ex-Oklahoma Deputy Robert
Bates Guilty of Killing Unarmed Suspect," *CNN* April 28, 2016,
https://www.cnn.com/2016/04/27/us/tulsa-deputy-manslaughter-
trial/index.html.

24 See, generally, Thomas Tracy, Christina Carrega-Woodby, John
Marzulli, Denis Slattery, Stephen Rex Brown, "NYPD Officer
Peter Liang Found Guilty of Manslaughter in Fatal Shooting of
Akai Gurley in Brooklyn Housing Development," *New York Times*
(February 12, 2016), http://www.nydailynews.com/new-york/
nyc-crime/nypd-peter-liang-guilty-fatal-shooting-akai-gurley-arti-
cle-1.2528827. See also Emily Saul, "DA Recommends Ex-NYPD
Cop Peter Liang Not Serve Jail Time in Fatal Shooting," *New York
Post* (March 23, 2016), http://nypost.com/2016/03/23/brooklyn-
da-to-recommend-liang-not-serve-jail-time-for-stairwell-shooting/.
See also Emily Saul, Kevin Fasick, and Kate Sheehy "NYPD Cop
Peter Liang Dodges Prison for Killing Akai Gurley," *New York Post*
(April 19, 2016), http://nypost.com/2016/04/19/nypd-cop-peter-
liang-gets-community-service-for-killing-akai-gurley/.

25 Christoph Koettl, "What We Learned From the Videos of Stephon
Clark Being Killed by Police," June 7, 2018, https://www.nytimes.
com/2018/06/07/us/police-shooting-stephon-clark.html.

26 Mark Osborne, "Minneapolis Police Shooting: No Charges to Be
Filed against Officers in Death of Thurman Blevins," July 30, 2018,

https://abcnews.go.com/US/minneapolis-police-release-video-fatal-shooting-black-man/story?id=56907450.

27 Report of the Hennepin County Attorney's Office Regarding the Shooting Death of Thurman Blevins on June 23, 2018, July 29, 2018, 3.

28 Antonia Farzan and Mark Berman, "Minneapolis Police Officers Won't Be Charged for Fatally Shooting Thurman Blevins," July 30, 2018, https://www.washingtonpost.com/news/morning-mix/wp/2018/07/30/thurman-blevins-shooting-graphic-body-cam-footage-shows-fleeing-black-man-killed-by-minneapolis-police-who-say-he-was-armed/?utm_term=.7b1f8ebbd594.

29 Report of the Hennepin County Attorney's Office, 18–20.

30 Enjoli Francis, "Police Fatally Shoot Bronze Star Recipient after He Shot Home Intruder," July 31, 2018, https://abcnews.go.com/US/police-fatally-shoot-resident-shot-home-intruder/story?id=56945256.

31 Aurora Police Chief Nick Metz Press Conference regarding Aurora Police Shooting of Homeowner, August 2, 2018, https://www.youtube.com/watch?v=XMDdG3Svk3I.

32 Id. (37: 29–37: 42).

33 Id. (20: 17–24: 45).

34 Id. (38: 46–39: 52).

35 Lehigh Valley District Attorney Jim Martin Press Conference Announcing Charges against Jonathan Roselle, August 7, 2018, https://www.youtube.com/watch?v=IkIIMUx7op0.

36 Id. See also "South Whitehall Officer Charged in Shooting Said He Thought He 'F---Ed Up,' 'Didn't Know What To Do,' Court Docs Say," *The Morning Call*, http://www.mcall.com/news/breaking/mc-nws-jonathan-roselle-statements-court-docs-20180807-story.html and Manuel Gamiz Jr., Sarah M. Wojcik, Laurie Mason Schroeder and Carol Thompson, "South Whitehall Rookie Officer Charged with Manslaughter in Unjustified Shooting of Unarmed Latino Man, DA Rules" *The Morning Call*, August 7, 2018, http://www.mcall.com/news/breaking/mc-pol-south-whitehall-police-shooting-district-attorney-announcement-20180807-story.html#.

37 Id.

38 For a detailed discussion on self-defense law, see Arthur H. Garrison, "Criminal Culpability, Civil Liability, and Police Created Danger: Why and How the Fourth Amendment Provides Very Limited Protection from Police Use of Deadly Force" *GMU Civil Rights Law Journal* 28, no. 3 (2018), 241.

39 Dominic Barone, "Trial Date Set For Former Policeman Jonathan Roselle," January 26, 2019, https://www.brctv13.com/news/local-news/23312-trial-date-set-for-former-policeman-jonathan-roselle.

40 Lauren del Valle and Ralph Ellis, "Former East Pittsburgh officer found not guilty in fatal shooting of unarmed teenager," *CNN*, March 23, 2019, at https://www.cnn.com/2019/03/22/us/officer-michael-rosfeld-antwon-rose-pittsburgh-testimony/index.html.

41 Id.

42 Ramesh Santanam, "Michael Rosfeld Says He Thought Gun Was Pointed At Him," Associated Press, March 21, 2019, https://www.wesa.fm/post/michael-rosfeld-says-he-thought-gun-was-pointed-him.

43 Jennifer Emily Tasha Tsiaperas, "Fired Cop Who Killed 15-Year-Old Jordan Edwards Indicted on Murder Charge," *Dallas Morning News,* July 17, 2017, https://www.dallasnews.com/news/crime/2017/07/17/fired-cop-killed-15-year-old-jordan-edwards-indicted-murder and Sara Hoye, "Fired Officer Gives Detailed Account of Shooting Teen Jordan Edwards," *WFAA,* July 19, 2017, http://www.wfaa.com/news/local/fired-officer-gives-detailed-account-of-shooting-teen-jordan-edwards/457774294.

44 Eva Ruth Moravec, "Former Police Officer Convicted of Murder for Shooting Unarmed Black Teen," *The Washington Post,* August 28, 2018, https://www.washingtonpost.com/national/former-police-officer-convicted-of-murder-for-shooting-unarmed-black-teen/2018/08/28/e5488fe6-aaf8-11e8-a8d7-0f63ab8b1370_story.html?noredirect=on&utm_term=.192643371344.

45 Eva Ruth Moravec, "Former Texas police officer sentenced to 15 years in prison for fatally shooting teen" *The Washington Post* (August 30, 2018) at https://www.washingtonpost.com/news/post-nation/wp/2018/08/29/

former-texas-police-officer-sentenced-to-15-years-in-prison-for-fatally-shooting-teen/?noredirect=on&utm_term=.13d46fbde25f.

46 Reis Thebault, "Minnesota police officer convicted of murder in fatal shooting of Australian woman who called 911" *Washington Post* (April 30, 2019) at https://www.washingtonpost.com/nation/2019/04/30/minnesota-police-officer-convicted-murder-fatal-shooting-australian-woman-who-called/?utm_term=.c99ad1c16796.

47 Judge Kathryn Quaintance Delivers Sentence to Mohamed Noor, June 7, 2019, https://www.youtube.com/watch?v=LmxOfmeNEeU.

48 Id. at (0:37–1:25).

49 Mohamed Noor Delivers Statement in Court Before Sentencing, June 7, 2019, 3:04–3:24, https://www.youtube.com/watch?v=UnMjTp5580c.

50 Judge Kathryn Quaintance Delivers Sentence to Mohamed Noor, June 7, 2019, (4:18–5:23).

51 Mohamed Noor Delivers Statement In Court before Sentencing, June 7, 2019, (4:38–4:47).

52 Mel Reeves, a civil rights activist, quoted in Reis Thebault, "Minnesota police officer convicted of murder in fatal shooting of Australian woman who called 911," *Washington Post*, April 30, 2019.

53 Melissa Gray, "Memorial Held for Minneapolis Police Shooting Victim Justine Ruszczyk," CNN, August 11, 2017, http://www.cnn.com/2017/08/11/us/justine-ruszczyk-memorial-minneapolis-police-shooting/index.html.

54 Reis Thebault, "Minnesota Police Officer Convicted of Murder in Fatal Shooting of Australian Woman Who called 911," *Washington Post*, April 30, 2019.

55 *United States of America v. Michael Slager*, United States District Court for the District of South Carolina Criminal No: 2:16–378 Global Plea Agreement, May 2, 2017, 1–3. In agreement to the plea, the two remaining federal charges and state murder charges were dropped.

56 Monica Davey and Mitch Smith, "3 Chicago Officers Charged With Conspiracy in Laquan McDonald Case," *New York Times,* June 27, 2017, https://www.nytimes.com/2017/06/27/us/chicago-officers-indicted-laquan-mcdonald-shooting.html.

57 Mark Guarino and Mark Berman, "Chicago Police Officer Jason Van Dyke Convicted of Second-Degree Murder for Killing Laquan McDonald," October 5, 2018, https://www.washingtonpost.com/news/post-nation/wp/2018/10/05/chicago-police-officer-jason-van-dyke-convicted-of-second-degree-murder-for-killing-laquan-mcdonald/?noredirect=on&utm_term=.3e5b0d9fee60.

58 Grand Jury, Cook County, Ill. Indictment of David Marsh, Joseph Walsh, and Thomas Gaffney 2, June 27, 2017, https://assets.documentcloud.org/documents/3878758/Indictment-of-3-Chicago-cops-in-Laquan-McDonald.pdf.

59 Nicole Chavez, Dakin And one, and Marlena Baldacci, "Former Chicago Officer Jason Van Dyke Sentenced to 81 Months for Fatally Shooting Laquan McDonald," *CNN*, January 19, 2019, https://www.cnn.com/2019/01/18/us/jason-van-dyke-chicago-police-sentencing/index.html.

60 *People of the State of Illinois v. David March*, Joseph Walsh and Officer Thomas Gaffney Order of Acquittal, https://www.documentcloud.org/documents/5688671-Cover-up-case-ruling.html.

61 Matt Ferner and Nick Wing, "Here's How Many Cops Got Convicted of Murder Last Year for On-Duty Shootings," *HuffPost,* January 13, 2016, https://www.huffingtonpost.com/entry/police-shooting-convictions_us_5695968ce4b086bc1cd5d0da citing Criminologist Philip Stinson.

62 Philip M. Stinson, "Op-Ed: Cops Shoot and Kill Someone about 1,000 Times a Year: Few Are Prosecuted: What Can Be Done?" *Los Angeles Times*, December 15, 2016, http://scholarworks.bgsu.edu/cgi/viewcontent.cgi?article=1072&context=crim_just_pub.

63 Philip M. Stinson, "Charging a Police Officer in Fatal Shooting Case Is Rare, and a Conviction Is Even Rarer," *New York Daily News*, May 31, 2017, http://scholarworks.bgsu.edu/cgi/viewcontent.cgi?article=1079&context=crim_just_pub.

64 See Kimberly Kindy and Elliot Kennedy data page, "Police Officers Prosecuted for Use of Deadly Force," https://www.wsj.com/articles/police-rarely-criminally-charged-for-on-duty-shootings-1416874955 linked to *Washington Post* article by Kimberly Kindy and Elliot Kennedy "Thousands Dead, Few Prosecuted," *The*

Washington Post, April 11, 2015, http://www.washingtonpost.com/
sf/investigative/2015/04/11/thousands-dead-few-prosecuted/?utm_
term=.a0b55c6c0293.

65 On December 20, 2011, Anthony Smith was shot and killed by
Officer Jason Stockley of the St. Louis Missouri Police Department
after a high-speed chase. Stockley was charged with first-degree
murder in August 2016, and on September 15, 2017, he was acquitted after a bench trial conducted by Judge Timothy Wilson.

66 On January 16, 2016, Daniel Shaver was shot while crawling on
his knees by Officer Philip "Mitch" Brailsford of the Mesa Police
Department after the officer told Shaver not to move his hands
but to crawl to him. When Shaver moved his hands to pull up
his pants as he crawled, begging not to be shot, he was shot by
Brailsford. The incident involved a suspected active shooter, and
the police had ordered Shaver to crawl over to them under threat
of being shot. The encounter was filed by body cameras (see at
https://www.youtube.com/watch?v=VBUUx0jUKxc).   The   jury
found the officer not guilty of second-degree murder. Uriel J.
Garcia, "Ex-Mesa Officer Philip Brailsford Found Not Guilty of
Murder in Shooting of Unarmed Man," December 8, 2017, https://
www.azcentral.com/story/news/local/mesa-breaking/2017/12/07/
philip-brailsford-verdict-daniel-shaver-killing/927052001/.

67 Officer Jason Stockley of the St. Louis Missouri police killed
Anthony Lamar Smith. Stockley was charged with murder in which
the prosecution asserted that Stockley planted a gun on Smith's
dead body. He was acquitted on September 15, 2017. See "Some
Recent Cases in Which Police Officers Were Charged in Shootings,"
NBC News, October 5, 2018, https://www.nbcchicago.com/news/
national-international/Cases-in-Which-Police-Officers-Were-
Charged-in-Shootings-495302741.html.

68 Brian T. Encinia Criminal Indictment, https://assets.document-
cloud.org/documents/2678589/Trooper-Brian-Encinia.pdf.

69 *Birchfield v. North Dakota* 579 U. S. ___, Slip op at (35–36) (2016).

70 See Nurse Alex Wubbels Arrested for Doing Her Job, https://
www.youtube.com/watch?v=JFxe86QQKF8   and   Mayor,   Police

Chief Respond to Cop Arresting *Nurse,* https://www.youtube.com/watch?v=cITA9HcX77I.

71 Id. See, also, Melissa Gray, "'I've Done Nothing Wrong': Utah Nurse's Arrest Prompts Police Apology," *CNN,* September 2, 2017, http://www.cnn.com/2017/09/01/health/utah-nurse-arrest-police-video/.

72 Derek Hawkins, "Utah Police Officer Fired after Manhandling, Arresting Nurse Who Was Doing Her Job," *Washington Post,* October 11, 2017, https://www.washingtonpost.com/news/morning-mix/wp/2017/10/10/utah-police-officer-fired-after-manhandling-arresting-nurse-who-was-doing-her-job/?utm_term=.0e9a00242d33.

73 Jessica Miller, "Salt Lake City police lieutenant demoted after nurse's arrest loses his appeal" *The Salt Lake Examiner* (April 19, 2019), https://www.sltrib.com/news/2019/04/19/salt-lake-city-police-2/.

74 The officer was subsequently fired from the police department on August 31, 2017. See "We Only Shoot Black People"—Georgia Police Officer, https://www.youtube.com/watch?v=YBRIHNn78dc.

75 *60 Minutes*, CBS, April 4, 2017.

76 Nicole Chavez, "The Fort Worth officer who shot Atatiana Jefferson wasn't actually asked to do a wellness check" (October 17, 2019) *CNN* at https://www.cnn.com/2019/10/16/us/police-response-fort-worth-shooting/index.html.

Chapter 7

1 U.S. Department of Justice, Bureau of Justice Statistics, *Prisoners in 1981 Bulletin* (May 1982).

2 Id. at 1.

3 Id.

4 U.S. Department of Justice, Bureau of Justice Statistics, *Prisoners in 1990* Bulletin (May 1991), 1.

5 Id.

6 U.S. Department of Justice, Bureau of Justice Statistics, *Prisoners in 1992 Bulletin* (May 1993), 1.

7 U.S. Department of Justice, Bureau of Justice Statistics, *Prison and Jail Inmates, 1995* (August 1996).

8 U.S. Department of Justice, Bureau of Justice Statistics, *Prisoners in 2007 Bulletin* (December 2008).

9 U.S. Department of Justice, Bureau of Justice Statistics, *Correctional Populations in the United States, 2011* (November 2012), 3.

10 U.S. Department of Justice, Bureau of Justice Statistics, *Prisoners in 2001 Bulletin* (July 2002).

11 U.S. Department of Justice, Bureau of Justice Statistics, *Prisoners in 2008 Bulletin* (December 2009).

12 U.S. Department of Justice, Bureau of Justice Statistics, *Prisoners in 2016 Bulletin* (January 2018), 1.

13 Id. at 3.

14 Id. (emphasis added).

15 Id. at 1.

16 U.S. Department of Justice, Bureau of Justice Statistics, *Prisoners in 2017 Bulletin* (April 2019).

17 Id.

18 Id.

19 Id at 1.

20 U.S. Department of Justice, Bureau of Justice Statistics, *Correctional Populations in the United States, 2016* (April 2018) at 2.

21 U.S. Department of Justice, Bureau of Justice Statistics, *Prisoners in 1980 Bulletin* (May 1981), 1.

22 "Presidential Veto Message: Reagan Vetoes Anti-Crime Bill," *CQ Almanac* (January 14, 1983), 1982 https://library.cqpress.com/cqalmanac/document.php?id=cqal82-858-25803-1162811.

23 See Comprehensive Crime Control Act of 1984 Title II of the H.J.Res.648—A Joint Resolution Making Continuing Appropriations for the Fiscal Year 1985, and For Other Purposes Signed by President Reagan on October 12, 1994, https://www.congress.gov/bill/98th-congress/house-joint-resolution/648.

24 See 18 U.S. Code § 3553 (a)(2)(A-D)(6)(7) Factors To Be Considered in Imposing a Sentence.

25 See generally, Criminal forfeitures, Warrant of seizure 21 U.S. Code § 853(f). Under federal law asset forfeiture can be used to seize property before charging a defendant to protect possible property

or funds that can be seized upon charging and/or conviction. 21 U.S. Code § 853(e) and (f).

26 See, Comprehensive Drug Abuse Prevention and Control Act of 1970 (codified at 21 U.S.C. §§ 853 and 881).

27 See, Psychotropic Substances Act of 1978 (codified at 21 U.S.C. § 881(a)(6)).

28 See, Comprehensive Crime Control Act of 1984 (codified at 21 U.S.C. § 881(a)(7), 28 U.S.C. § 524 and 21 U.S.C. § 881(e)(1)(A), 19 U.S.C. § 1616a(c), 18 U.S.C. § 981(e)(2).

29 See, Anti-Drug Abuse Act of 1986 codified at 21 U.S.C. § 853(p). See also, *Civil Asset Forfeiture* at https://www.drugpolicy.org/sites/default/files/Drug_Policy_Alliance_Fact_Sheet_Civil_Asset_Forfeiture.pdf.

30 See U.S. Attorney Manual 9-131.000—The Hobbs Act—18 U.S.C. § 1951, https://www.justice.gov/jm/jm-9-131000-hobbs-act-18-usc-1951.

31 See Racketeer Influenced and Corrupt Organization Act (RICO), *U.S. Attorney Manual* 109. RICO Charges at https://www.justice.gov/jm/criminal-resource-manual-109-rico-charges.

32 For example, see *Taylor v. United States* (2016) (the prosecution in a Hobbs Act robbery case satisfies the Act's commerce element if it shows that the defendant robbed or attempted to rob a drug dealer of drugs or drug proceeds), *Boyle v. United States* (2009) (RICO applies to a gang of bank robbers—the enterprise was the operation and organization of the gang itself (an "association-in-fact enterprise") for the purpose of committing the bank robberies), *Combating Street Gangs*, U.S. Department of Justice, Juvenile Justice Delinquency Prevention (1994–1996), https://www.ojjdp.gov/pubs/reform/ch2_e.html; Justice Department Press Release *Six Individuals with Ties to National Gang Charged with Hobbs Act Conspiracy, Narcotics and Firearms Offenses* (June 5, 2019), https://www.justice.gov/usao-ma/pr/six-individuals-ties-national-gang-charged-hobbs-act-conspiracy-narcotics-and-firearms, Justice Department Press Release, *North Carolina Bloods Gang Member Sentenced to Prison for Racketeering Conspiracy* (March 22, 2019), https://www.justice.gov/opa/pr/north-carolina-bloods-gang-member-sentenced-prison-racketeering-conspiracy.

33 See, generally, Gun Control Act of 1968 18 U.S.C. § 922 (unlawful possession, manufacture, purchase, selling, transportation of a
gun or ammunition), 18 U.S.C. § 922(g) (unlawful for a convicted
person "to ship or transport in interstate or foreign commerce,
or possess in or affecting commerce, any firearm or ammunition;
or to receive any firearm or ammunition which has been shipped or
transported in interstate or foreign commerce") and § 924 (c)(1)(A)
("any person who, during and in relation to any crime of violence
or drug trafficking crime ... uses or carries a firearm, or who, in
furtherance of any such crime"). For history on passage and judicial interpretation of Gun Control Act of 1968 See also George
P. Apostolides, "18 U.S.C. 924(c)(1)—The Court's Construction
of Use and Second or Subsequent Conviction", 84(4) *Journal of
Criminal Law and Criminology* 1006 (Winter 1994).

34 Dan Baum, "Legalize It All How to Win the War on Drugs,"
Harper's Magazine (April 2016), 22. For commentary on why
the statement can be believed, see Erik Sherman, "Nixon's Drug
War, An Excuse to Lock Up Blacks and Protesters, Continues,"
Forbes Magazine (March 23, 2016), https://www.forbes.com/sites/
eriksherman/2016/03/23/nixons-drug-war-an-excuse-to-lock-up-
blacks-and-protesters-continues/#5333aaec42c8.

35 See Jason E. Glenn, "The Birth of the Crack Baby and the History
that "Myths" Make" (2006), https://biblio.csusm.edu/sites/default/
files/reserves/birth_of_the_crack_baby_and_the_history_that_
myths_make.pdf.

36 George H.W. Bush Address to the Nation on the National Drug
Control Strategy, September 5, 1989, at http://www.presidency.
ucsb.edu/ws/?pid=17472.

37 See National Drug Policy 1989, https://www.ncjrs.gov/pdffiles1/
ondcp/119466.pdf.

38 George H.W. Bush, Address to Students on Drug Abuse,
September 12, 1989, http://www.presidency.ucsb.edu/ws/index.
php?pid=17509&st=students&st1.

39 42 U.S. Code § 13703(a)—Violent Offender Incarceration Grants.

40 BJA, *Report to Congress: Violent Offender Incarceration and Truth-
In-Sentencing Incentive Formula Grant Program* (February 2012), 3.

41 BJA, *Report to Congress: Violent Offender Incarceration and Truth-In-Sentencing Incentive Formula Grant Program* (February 2012), 2.

42 Thornburgh Blue Sheet: Plea Policy for Federal Prosecutors: Plea Bargaining Under the Sentencing Reform Act, 6(6) Federal Sentencing Reporter 347, 347 (May/June 1994).

43 U.S. Department of Justice—Principles of Federal Prosecution—July 1980, 6(6) Federal Sentencing Reporter 317 (May/June 1994): 323.

44 Jo Ann Harris Assistant Attorney General, *Memorandum for All Unites States Attorneys Subject: Three Strikes,* March 13, 1995, https://www.justice.gov/usam/criminal-resource-manual-1032-sentencing-enhancement-three-strikes-law.

45 Walter J. Dickey and Pam Hollenhorst, "Three-Strikes Laws: Five Years Later," *Corrections Management* 3, no. 3 (1999): 1, 3.

46 U.S. Sentencing Commission, *Special Report to the Congress: Cocaine and Federal Sentencing Policy* (Feb 1995) at vi–xi.

47 U.S. Sentencing Commission, *Special Report to the Congress: Cocaine and Federal Sentencing Policy* (Feb 1995) at xiv–xv.

48 U.S. Sentencing Commission, *Special Report to the Congress: Cocaine and Federal Sentencing Policy* (Feb 1995).

49 William J. Clinton, Statement on Signing Legislation Rejecting U.S. Sentencing Commission Recommendations October 30, 1995, at http://www.presidency.ucsb.edu/ws/?pid=50716.

50 Ronald Reagan, Remarks on Signing the Anti–Drug Abuse Act of 1986, October 27, 1986 at http://www.presidency.ucsb.edu/ws/?pid=36654.

51 42 U.S.C. § § 13661 *Screening of applicants for federally assisted housing (a) Ineligibility because of eviction for drug crimes (b) Ineligibility of illegal drug users and alcohol abusers* and § 13662 *Termination of tenancy and assistance for illegal drug users and alcohol abusers in federally assisted housing.*

52 U.S. Department of Housing and Urban Development Officer of Public and Indian Housing, "Subject: 'One Strike and You're Out' Screening and Eviction Guidelines for Public Housing Authorities (HAs)" March 1996 at 1.

53 42 U. S. C. § 1437d (l)(6) *Leases; terms and conditions; maintenance; termination.*

54 U.S. Department of Housing and Urban Development Officer of Public and Indian Housing, "Subject: 'One Strike and You're Out' Screening and Eviction Guidelines for Public Housing Authorities (HAs)," March 1996 at 7–8. See also, Barclay Thomas Johnson, "The 'One Strike' Policy in Public Housing" 35(3–4) *Journal of Poverty Law and Policy* 159 (July/August 2001).

55 William J. Clinton, Remarks Announcing the "One Strike and You're Out" Initiative in Public Housing, March 28, 1996 at http://www.presidency.ucsb.edu/ws/?pid=52598 (emphasis added).

56 *Department of Housing and Urban Development v. Rucker*, 535 U. S. 125 (2002).

57 Justice Policy Institute, *Too Little Too Late: President Clinton's Prison Legacy* (2001), 3.

58 Justice Policy Institute, *Too Little Too Late: President Clinton's Prison Legacy* (2001).

59 Justice Policy Institute, *Too Little Too Late: President Clinton's Prison Legacy* (2001), 4.

60 Justice Policy Institute, *Too Little Too Late: President Clinton's Prison Legacy* (2001), 8.

61 Andrew Lang Golub and Bruce D. Johnson, *Crack's Decline: Some Surprises Across U.S. Cities*, National Institute of Justice (July 1997) at https://www.ncjrs.gov/pdffiles/165707.pdf.

62 Bureau of Justice Statistics, *State Corrections Expenditures, 1982–2010* (December 2012), 10. https://www.bjs.gov/content/pub/pdf/scefy8210.pdf.

63 Department of Justice Press Release, Attorney General Testimony Before the Senate Committee on Appropriations, April 26, 2001, https://www.justice.gov/archive/opa/pr/2001/April/189ag.htm.

64 *Koon v. United States*, 518 U.S. (1996), 81, 89.

65 *Koon v. United States*, 518 U.S., 89–90.

66 *Koon v. United States*, 518 U.S., 90.

67 U.S. Sentencing Commission, *Report to the Congress: Downward Departures from the Federal Sentencing Guidelines* (2003) at ii–iii, https://www.ussc.gov/sites/default/files/pdf/news/

congressional-testimony-and-reports/departures/200310-rtc-downward-departures/departrpt03.pdf.

68 *U.S. v. Booker*, 543 U.S. _____, Slip opinion by Justice Stevens speaking for the Court at 2 (2005). The Court concluded, any fact (other than a prior conviction) which is necessary to support a sentence exceeding the maximum authorized by the facts established by a plea of guilty or a jury verdict must be admitted by the defendant or proved to a jury beyond a reasonable doubt.

See, also, U.S. Sentencing Commission, *Report to the Congress: Downward Departures from the Federal Sentencing Guidelines* (2003) at 20.

> As to the status of the Sentencing Guidelines, the Court held the provision of the federal sentencing statute that makes the Guidelines mandatory [is] incompatible with today's constitutional holding. We conclude that this provision must be severed and excised ... So modified, the Federal Sentencing Act makes the Guidelines effectively advisory. It requires a sentencing court to consider Guidelines ranges, but it permits the court to tailor the sentence in light of other statutory concerns as well.

Slip opinion by Justice Breyer speaking for the Court at 2 (2005) (internal citations omitted).

69 *Kimbrough v. United States*, 552 U.S. _____, Slip opinion at 2 (2007).

> Under the statute criminalizing the manufacture and distribution of crack cocaine and the relevant Guidelines prescription a drug trafficker dealing in crack cocaine is subject to the same sentence as one dealing in 100 times more powder cocaine. The question here presented is whether, as the Court of Appeals held in this case, "a sentence ... outside the guidelines range is *per se* unreasonable when it is based on a disagreement with the sentencing disparity for crack and powder cocaine offenses." We hold that, under *Booker*, the cocaine Guidelines, like all other Guidelines, are advisory only, and that the

Court of Appeals erred in holding the crack/powder disparity effectively mandatory. A district judge must include the Guidelines range in the array of factors warranting consideration. The judge may determine, however, that, in the particular case, a within-Guidelines sentence is "greater than necessary" to serve the objectives of sentencing. In making that determination, the judge may consider the disparity between the Guidelines' treatment of crack and powder cocaine offenses.

U.S. v. Booker at 1–2 (internal citations omitted).

70 Bureau of Justice Statistics, *State Corrections Expenditures, 1982–2010* (December 2012), 10.

71 Bureau of Justice Statistics, *Correctional Populations in the United States, 2015* (December 2016), 2. https://www.bjs.gov/content/pub/pdf/cpus15.pdf.

72 Bureau of Justice Statistics, *Correctional Populations in the United States, 2015,* 1.

73 See *H.R.1593 – Second Chance Act of 2007* at https://www.congress.gov/bill/110th-congress/house-bill/1593.

74 See *S.1789 – Fair Sentencing Act of 2010* at https://www.congress.gov/bill/111th-congress/senate-bill/1789/text.

75 See *S.756 – First Step Act of 2018* at https://www.congress.gov/bill/115th-congress/senate-bill/756/actions.

76 See *Transcript of White House event – Remarks by President Trump on Second Chance Hiring* (June 13, 2019), https://www.whitehouse.gov/briefings-statements/remarks-president-trump-second-chance-hiring/.

77 See *Policy Fact Sheet – President Donald J. Trump Is Helping Americans Gain a Second Chance to Build a Brighter Future* (June 13, 2019), https://www.whitehouse.gov/briefings-statements/president-donald-j-trump-helping-americans-gain-second-chance-build-brighter-future/.

78 *Brown v. Mississippi*, 297 U.S. 278, 284–86 (1936).

79 *Wolf v. Colorado*, 338 U.S. 25, 26 (1949).

80 Id at 26–27.

81 *Rogers v. Richmond*, 365 U.S. 534, 540 (1961).

82 *Mapp v. Ohio*, 367 U.S. 643, 655 (1961).

83 Id at 657. The Court held, "Our holding that the exclusionary rule is an essential part of both the Fourth and Fourteenth Amendments ... makes very good sense. ... Presently, a federal prosecutor may make no use of evidence illegally seized, but a State's attorney across the street may. ... Thus, the State, by admitting evidence unlawfully seized, serves to encourage disobedience to the Federal Constitution which it is bound to uphold." The Court concluded that such a result was not acceptable.

> The ignoble shortcut to conviction left open to the State tends to destroy the entire system of constitutional restraints on which the liberties of the people rest. Having once recognized that the right to privacy embodied in the Fourth Amendment is enforceable against the States, and that the right to be secure against rude invasions of privacy by state officers is, therefore, constitutional in origin, we can no longer permit that right to remain an empty promise. Because it is enforceable in the same manner and to like effect as other basic rights secured by the Due Process Clause, we can no longer permit it to be revocable at the whim of any police officer who, in the name of law enforcement itself, chooses to suspend its enjoyment. Our decision, founded on reason and truth, gives to the individual no more than that which the Constitution guarantees him, to the police officer no less than that to which honest law enforcement is entitled, and, to the courts, that judicial integrity so necessary in the true administration of justice.

Id at 660.

84 For additional research and presentation of Supreme Court Fourth Amendment jurisprudence, Arthur H. Garrison, "Criminal Culpability, Civil Liability, and Police Created Danger: Why and How the Fourth Amendment Provides Very Limited Protection

from Police Use of Deadly Force" *George Mason University Civil Rights Law Journal* 28:3 241–339 (2018) Arthur H. Garrison, "NYPD Stop and Frisk, Perceptions of Criminals, Race and the Meaning of *Terry v. Ohio*: A Content Analysis of *Floyd, et al. v. City of New York*" *Rutgers Race and the Law Review* 15: 65–156 (2014).

85 A police dog alert can establish probable cause to search. See *Florida v. Harris* (2012) in which the court held that at a suppression hearing regarding whether probable cause is established by the dog alert, the court should determine whether under the totality of the circumstances was probable cause established. The court held that if the state can establish the credentials of the dog and reasonable reliance on the dog's ability to sense drugs and alters accordingly and if the officer has no reason to doubt the dog's ability and the plaintiff can not disprove the dog's ability—probable cause for the search is established.

86 When it comes to the scope of consent to search the court held in *Florida v. Jimeno* (1991), the focus is what a reasonable police officer, under the totality of the circumstances of the request to search and the nature of the thing searched for, would have thought the consent authorized. The reviewing court will ask what would a "reasonable observer have interpreted the consent under the circumstances." *U.S. v. Rodney* (CADC 1992). In other words, "What a reasonable person would have understood from the exchange between the officer and the suspect under the totality of the circumstances." *Reppert v. City of Allentown* (CA 3rd Cir, 2007). The focus is not on what the person searched actually thought the scope of search would be upon giving consent. The courts have held that withdrawal of consent must be unequivocal, and silence or irritation does not constitute withdrawal of consent to search. The same unequivocal language is required for refusal to give consent. See Supreme Court holdings in *Georgia v. Randolph* (2006) and *Fernandez v. California* (2013).

87 Although police may order passengers out of car, police may not prolong the seizure of car during a traffic stop. The Court held in *Rodriguez v. United States* (2014), "We hold that a police stop exceeding the time needed to handle the matter for which the stop

was made violates the Constitution's shield against unreasonable seizures." The Court similarly held in *Muehler v. Mena*, 2005 that the police cannot delay a seizure by asking questions unrelated to the lawful stop. See, generally, "the initial seizure of respondent when he was stopped on the highway was based on probable cause and was concededly lawful. It is nevertheless clear that a seizure that is lawful at its inception can violate the Fourth Amendment if its manner of execution unreasonably infringes interests protected by the Constitution. *United States v. Jacobsen*, 466 U. S. 109, 124 (1984)." *Illinois v. Caballes*, 543 U.S. 405 (2005).

88 The Court held, "While the concern for officer safety in this context may justify the 'minimal' additional intrusion of ordering a driver and passengers out of the car, it does not by itself justify the often considerably greater intrusion attending a full field type search." The Court summarized the authority of the police during a traffic stop as follows:

> The police may order out of a vehicle both the driver, *Pennsylvania v. Mimms*, 434 U. S. 106, 111 (1977) and any passengers, *Maryland v. Wilson,* 519 U. S. 408, 414 (1997); perform a "patdown" of a driver and any passengers upon reasonable suspicion that they may be armed and dangerous, *Terry v. Ohio,* 392 U. S. 1 (1968); conduct a "*Terry* pat down" of the passenger compartment of a vehicle upon reasonable suspicion that an occupant is dangerous and may gain immediate control of a weapon, *Michigan v. Long,* 463 U. S. 1032, 1049 (1983); and even conduct a full search of the passenger compartment, including any containers therein, pursuant to a custodial arrest, *New York v. Belton*, 453 U. S. 454, 460 (1981).

But,

> once Knowles was stopped for speeding and issued a citation, all the evidence necessary to prosecute that offense had been obtained. No further evidence of excessive speed was going to be found either on the person

of the offender or in the passenger compartment of the car. *Knowles v. Iowa,* 525 U.S. 113, 117–118 (1998).

89 The Court concluded,

> When police have probable cause to believe a person has committed a drunk-driving offense and the driver's unconsciousness or stupor requires him to be taken to the hospital or similar facility before police have a reasonable opportunity to administer a standard evidentiary breath test, they may almost always order a warrantless blood test to measure the driver's BAC without offending the Fourth Amendment.

But the Court vacated the conviction of Mitchell and remanded the case to the Wisconsin Supreme Court because the Court's decision was limited based on the question presented to it.

> We do not rule out the possibility that in an unusual case a defendant would be able to show that his blood would not have been drawn if police had not been seeking BAC information, and that police could not have reasonably judged that a warrant application would interfere with other pressing needs or duties. Because Mitchell did not have a chance to attempt to make that showing, a remand for that purpose is necessary.

Mitchell v. Wisconsin, 588 U. S.___, slip op. at 16–17 (2019).

90 In a 7-2 opinion written by Justice Kavanaugh, the Court held,

> In sum, the State's pattern of striking black prospective jurors persisted from Flowers' first trial through Flowers' sixth trial. In the six trials combined, the State struck 41 of the 42 black prospective jurors it could have struck. At the sixth trial, the State struck five of six. At the sixth trial, moreover, the State engaged in dramatically disparate questioning of black and white prospective jurors. And it engaged in disparate treatment of black and white prospective jurors, in particular by striking black prospective juror Carolyn Wright.

To reiterate, we need not and do not decide that any one of those four facts alone would require reversal. All that we need to decide, and all that we do decide, is that all of the relevant facts and circumstances taken together establish that the trial court at Flowers' sixth trial committed clear error in concluding that the State's peremptory strike of black prospective juror Carolyn Wright was not motivated in substantial part by discriminatory intent. In reaching that conclusion, we break no new legal ground. We simply enforce and reinforce *Batson* by applying it to the extraordinary facts of this case.

Flowers v. Mississippi, 588 U. S. ____, Slip opinion at 31 (2019).

91 For discussion see, Arthur H. Garrison, "Rehnquist vs. Scalia— The *Dickerson* and *Miranda* cases: A debate on what makes a decision a constitutional decision" *American Journal of Trial Advocacy Law Review* 25(1): 91–133 (2001).

92 The Court held, "Where probable cause has existed, the only cases in which we have found it necessary actually to perform the "balancing" analysis involved searches or seizures conducted in an extraordinary manner, unusually harmful to an individual's privacy or even physical interests-such as, for example, seizure by means of deadly force, see Tennessee *v.* Garner, 471 U. S. 1 (1985), unannounced entry into a home, see *Wilson v. Arkansas*, 514 U. S. 927 (1995), entry into a home without a warrant, see *Welsh v. Wisconsin*, 466 U. S. 740 (1984), or physical penetration of the body, see *Winston v. Lee*, 470 U. S. 753 (1985). The making of a traffic stop out of uniform does not remotely qualify as such an extreme practice, and so is governed by the usual rule that probable cause to believe the law has been broken "outbalances" private interest in avoiding police contact. *Whren v. United States*, 517 U.S. 806, 818 (1996).

93 *Illinois v. McArthur*, 531 U.S. 326, 330–331 (2001) (Emphasis added).

94 *Mitchell v. Wisconsin*, 588 U. S. ____, slip op. at 12–13 (2019).

95 Id. at 13.

96 Id. at 16 quoting *Missouri v. McNeely*, 569 U. S. 141, 155 (2013).

97 See *West Virginia State Board of Education v. Barnette*, 319 U.S. 624 (1943) (salute the flag and pledge of allegiance), *Engle v. Vitale*, 370 U.S. 421 (1962)(prayer in school), *Abington School District v. Schempp*, 374 U.S. 203 (1963) (required Bible recitation), State of Illinois ex rel *McCollum v. Board of Education*, 333 U.S. 203 (1948) (mandatory religious instruction), *Holmes v. City of Atlanta*, 350 U.S. 877 (1955) (desegregation of golf courses), *Mayor of Baltimore v. Dawson*, 350 U.S. 877 (1955) (desegregation of beaches and bathhouses), *Gayle v. Bowder*, 352 U.S. 903 (1956) (the Montgomery boycott case), *New Orleans City Park Improvement Association v. Detiege*, 358 U.S. 54 (1958) (desegregation of public parks), and *State Athletic Commission v. Dorsey*, 359 U.S. 533 (1959) (desegregation of school athletic competitions).

98 The Court held at the height of the second red scare and during the cold war that membership in the communist party, standing alone, was not enough to allow the firing of government employees and that the government could not use secret evidence of communist activity in a criminal trial while not allowing the defendant to see the evidence. See Arthur H. Garrison, *Supreme Court Jurisprudence in Times of National Crisis, Terrorism, and War* (2011) at 159–87.

99 Nixon appointed Chief Justice Warren Burger (1969), Justices Harry Blackmun (1970), Lewis Powel (1971), and William Rehnquist (1971).

100 Ford appointed John Paul Stevens (1975).

101 Reagan appointed Sandra Day O'Connor (1981), William Rehnquist to Chief Justice (1986), Antonin Scalia (1986), and Anthony Kennedy (1988).

102 Bush appointed David Souter (1990) and Clarence Thomas (1991).

Chapter 8

1 Pew Research Center, *Race in America 2019* (April 9, 2019), https://www.pewsocialtrends.org/2019/04/09/race-in-america-2019/#majorities-of-black-and-white-adults-say-blacks-are-

treated-less-fairly-than-whites-in-dealing-with-police-and-by-the-criminal-justice-system.

2 Pew Research Center, *From Police to Parole, Black and White Americans Differ Widely in Their Views of Criminal Justice System* (May 21, 2019), https://www.pewresearch.org/fact-tank/2019/05/21/ from-police-to-parole-black-and-white-americans-differ-widely-in-their-views-of-criminal-justice-system/.

3 Id. See also Pew Research Center, *Black and White Officers See Many Key Aspects of Policing Differently* (January 12, 2017), https://www.pewresearch.org/fact-tank/2017/01/12/black-and-white-officers-see-many-key-aspects-of-policing-differently/.

4 PollingReport.com, *Crime/Law Enforcement/Criminal Justice,* https://www.pollingreport.com/crime.htm.

5 Id.

6 Id.

7 Id.

8 Id.

9 For commentary and list of research, see Radley Balko, "There's Overwhelming Evidence That The Criminal-Justice System Is Racist. Here's the Proof." *Washington Post,* September 18, 2018, https://www.washingtonpost.com/news/opinions/wp/2018/09/18/ theres-overwhelming-evidence-that-the-criminal-justice-system-is-racist-heres-the-proof/?utm_term=.e2572e3e3333 and "21 More Studies Showing Racial Disparities in the Criminal Justice System," *Washington Post,* April 9, 2019, https://www.washing-tonpost.com/opinions/2019/04/09/more-studies-showing-racial-disparities-criminal-justice-system/?noredirect=on&utm_term=. c00af4d299af.

10 *Memorandum to United States Attorneys and Assistant Attorney General Criminal Division* (August 12, 2013) (emphasis added), https://www.justice.gov/sites/default/files/oip/legacy/2014/07/23/ ag-memo-department-policypon-charging-mandatory-minimum-sentences-recidivist-enhancements-in-certain-drugcases.pdf.

11 Eric Holder, "Eric Holder: We Can Have Shorter Sentences and Less Crime," *New York Times,* August 11, 2016, https://www.

nytimes.com/2016/08/14/opinion/sunday/eric-h-holder-mandatory-minimum-sentences-full-of-errors.html.

12 Lord Chief Justice Gordon Hewart, *R v. Sussex Justices, ex parte McCarthy* ([1924] 1 KB 256, [1923]).

13 Id.

14 Eric Holder, *Remarks on Criminal Justice Reform Delivered at Georgetown University Law Center* (February 11, 2014), https://www.justice.gov/opa/speech/attorney-general-eric-holder-delivers-remarkson-criminal-justice-reform-georgetown.

15 Eric Holder, *Attorney General Eric Holder Delivers Remarks at the Annual Meeting of the American Bar Association's House of Delegates* (August 12, 2013), https://www.justice.gov/opa/speech/attorney-general-eric-holder-delivers-remarks-annual-meeting-american-bar-associations.

16 *Memorandum for All Federal Prosecutors* (May 10, 2017), https://www.justice.gov/sites/default/files/oip/legacy/2014/07/23/ag-memo-department-policypon-charging-mandatory-minimum-sentences-recidivist-enhancements-in-certain-drugcases.pdf.

17 See Memorandum from Attorney General Thornburgh: March 13, 1989 ("A federal prosecutor should initially charge the most serious, readily provable offense or offenses consistent with the defendant's conduct. ... Once prosecutors have indicted, they should find themselves bargaining about charges which they have determined are readily provable and reflect the seriousness of the defendant's conduct.")

18 Jeff Sessions, "Being Soft on Sentencing Means More Violent Crime. It's Time to Get Tough Again," *Washington Post,* June 19, 2017, https://www.washingtonpost.com/opinions/jeff-sessions-being-soft-on-sentencing-means-more-violent-crime-its-time-to-get-tough-again/2017/06/16/618ef1fe-4a19-11e7-9669-250d0b15f83b_story.html?utm_term=.c16553a2540b.

19 U.S. Department of Justice, Bureau of Justice Statistics, *Prisoners in 2016* (January 2018), 18.

20 U.S. Department of Justice, Bureau of Justice Statistics, *Prisoners in 2016* (January 2018), 20.

21 U.S. Department of Justice, Bureau of Justice Statistics, *Prisoners in 2016* (January 2018), 20.

22 U.S. Department of Justice, Bureau of Justice Statistics, *Prisoners in 2016* (January 2018).

23 U.S. Department of Justice, Bureau of Justice Statistics, *Prisoners in 2016* (January 2018), 19.

24 U.S. Department of Justice, Bureau of Justice Statistics, *Prisoners in 2016* (January 2018), 20.

25 U.S. Department of Justice, Bureau of Justice Statistics, *Prisoners in 2016* (January 2018), 19.

26 U.S. Department of Justice, Bureau of Justice Statistics, *Prisoners in 2016* (January 2018), 5.

27 U.S. Department of Justice, Bureau of Justice Statistics, *Prisoners in 2016* (January 2018).

28 Under President Bush 2002 (622,700) and 2008 (592,800) and under President Obama 2009 (584,800) and 2016 (486,900). U.S. Department of Justice, Bureau of Justice Statistics, *Prisoners 2002,* (July 2003—revised August 2003) at 9 and U.S. Department of Justice, Bureau of Justice Statistics, *Prisoners in 2016* (January 2018), 5.

29 See Chapter 1 and U.S. Department of Justice, Bureau of Justice Statistics, *Prisoners in 2016* (January 2018), 5.

30 U.S. Department of Justice, Bureau of Justice Statistics, *Prisoners in 2016* (January 2018), 8.

31 U.S. Department of Justice, Bureau of Justice Statistics, *Prisoners in 2016* (January 2018), 10.

32 U.S. Department of Justice, Bureau of Justice Statistics, *Prisoners in 2016* (January 2018) at 13.

33 Jeff Sessions, "Being Soft on Sentencing Means More Violent Crime. It's Time to Get Tough Again," *Washington Post,* June 19, 2017, https://www.washingtonpost.com/opinions/jeff-sessions-being-soft-on-sentencing-means-more-violent-crime-its-time-to-get-tough-again/2017/06/16/618ef1fe-4a19-11e7-9669-250d0b15f83b_story.html?utm_term=.c16553a2540b.

For rebuttal to General Sessions op-ed see David Cole and Marc Mauer, "Jeff Sessions Wants a New War on Drugs. It Won't

Work" Op-ed, *Washington Post,* June 22, 2017, https://www.washingtonpost.com/opinions/the-new-war-on-drugs-wont-be-any-more-effective-than-the-old-one/2017/06/22/669260ee-56c3-11e7-a204-ad706461fa4f_story.html?utm_term=.3ccfb75cb818 and op-ed by former Acting Attorney General Jessica Yates, "Making America Scared Again Won't Make Us Safer" Op-ed, *Washington Post,* June 23, 2017, https://www.washingtonpost.com/opinions/making-america-scared-again-wont-make-us-safer/2017/06/23/f53d238e-578a-11e7-ba90-f5875b7d1876_story.html?utm_term=.aea9b6a119ab.

34 See General Jeff Session Press Conference, December 15, 2017, https://www.c-span.org/video/?438603-1/attorney-general-jeff-sessions-holds-news-conference.

35 COMSTAT is short for COMPare STATistics. COMSTAT is a law enforcement strategy pioneered by the New York Police Department in the 1990s to reduce crime by creating computer generated maps to analyze crime patterns in geographic areas, COMSTAT utilized police reports, intelligence, crime report and arrest statistics to focus police resources to reduce both nuisance and serious crime in specific geographic areas.

36 Justice Department policy announcement: Justice Department Announces Update to Marijuana Enforcement Policy, August 29, 2013, https://www.justice.gov/opa/pr/justice-department-announces-update-marijuana-enforcement-policy.

37 Memorandum to All U.S. Attorneys Issued by Deputy Attorney General James M. Cole, August 29, 2013, https://www.justice.gov/iso/opa/resources/3052013829132756857467.pdf.

38 Memorandum to All U.S. Attorneys Issued by Attorney General Jeffery Sessions, January 4, 2018, https://www.justice.gov/opa/press-release/file/1022196/download.

39 Justice Department policy announcement: Justice Department Issues Memo on Marijuana Enforcement, January 4, 2018, https://www.justice.gov/opa/pr/justice-department-issues-memo-marijuana-enforcement.

40 Prepared remarks by Attorney General Sessions at the 63rd Biennial Conference of the National Fraternal Order of Police Nashville, TN Monday, August 28, 2017, https://www.justice.gov/opa/

speech/attorney-general-sessions-delivers-remarks-63rd-biennial-conference-national-fraternal.

41 Attorney General Sessions Delivers Remarks to the International Association of Chiefs of Police Nashville, TN, on March 15, 2018, https://www.justice.gov/opa/speech/attorney-general-sessions-delivers-remarks-international-association-chiefs-police-0.

42 Attorney General Sessions Delivers Remarks to the International Association of Chiefs of Police Nashville, TN on March 15, 2018 (15:40–17:26) https://www.youtube.com/watch?v=8kt10eIT1O4.

43 The Centennial Institute, a think tank for the Colorado Christian University, asserts that its goal is to "impact our culture in support of traditional family values, sanctity of life, compassion for the poor, Biblical view of human nature, limited government, personal freedom, free markets, natural law, original intent of the Constitution and Western civilization." "To be a magnet for outstanding students and prepare them for positions of significant leadership in the church, business, government, and professions by offering an excellent education in strategic disciplines." Centennial Institute welcome to our think tank at http://www.ccu.edu/centennial/about-us/.

44 See Chapter 4.

45 "Security from domestic violence, no less than from foreign aggression, is the most elementary and fundamental purpose of any government. … History shows us—demonstrates that nothing—nothing prepares the way for tyranny more than the failure of public officials to keep the streets from bullies and marauders." Barry Goldwater acceptance speech at the Republican Convention on July 16, 1964.

46 "If the police of this country, could just run it for about two years, then we could walk in the parks and on the streets in safety. And you are doing a magnificent job. Thank you very much." George Wallace campaign speech at the 1968 Fraternal Order of Police National Convention in Chicago. CNN Documentary *1968: The Year That Changed America part 1* (aired May 27, 2018).

47 "But let them also recognize that the first civil right of every American is to be free from domestic violence, and that right must

be guaranteed in this country." Richard Nixon acceptance speech for the Republican nomination for president on August 8, 1968.

48 "[T]here are those who've done everything but tie your hands and take your guns. It is time for society to give to those on the firing line the weapons needed in this fight against crime. ... [T]he jungle still is waiting to take over. The man with the badge holds it back." Ronald Reagan 1967 speech to the National Sheriffs Association (June 19, 1967).

49 Attorney General Jeff Sessions delivers remarks at the 2018 Western Conservative Summit (12:08–14:45), https://www.youtube.com/watch?v=60iY7lBYYX0.

50 U.S. Attorney Manual, Principles of Federal Prosecution 9–27.300—Selecting Charges—Charging Most Serious Offenses [updated February 2018].

51 U.S. Department of Justice Announces First Step Act Implementation Progress (April 8, 2019), https://www.justice.gov/opa/pr/department-justice-announces-first-step-act-implementation-progress.

52 U.S. Department Of Justice Announces the Release of 3,100 Inmates Under First Step Act, Publishes Risk And Needs Assessment System, July 19, 2019, https://www.justice.gov/opa/pr/department-justice-announces-release-3100-inmates-under-first-step-act-publishes-risk-and.

53 U.S. Department of Justice, Bureau of Justice Statistics, *Prisoners in 2017* (April 2019), 24.

54 U.S. Department of Justice Announces First Step Act Implementation Progress (April 8, 2019).

55 U.S. Department Of Justice Announces the Release of 3,100 Inmates Under First Step Act, Publishes Risk and Needs Assessment System (July 19, 2019).

56 United States Sentencing Commission, Office of Education & Sentencing Practice newsletter, *The First Step Act* (February 2019), https://www.ussc.gov/sites/default/files/pdf/training/newsletters/2019-special_FIRST-STEP-Act.pdf.

57 Id.

58 See, 18 U.S.C. § 924(c)(1)(A)(i)–(iii), (B)(ii). Examples are not exclusive. Use of explosives, machine guns, other types of automatic weapons also have mandatory minimum enhancements.

59 See, 18 U.S.C. § 924(c)(1)(C)(i)–(ii).

60 See U.S.C. § 924(c)(1)(C)—"In the case of a violation of this sub-section that occurs after a prior conviction under this subsection has become final."

See, also United States Sentencing Commission, Office of Education & Sentencing Practice newsletter, *The First Step Act* (February 2019), https://www.ussc.gov/sites/default/files/pdf/training/newsletters/2019-special_FIRST-STEP-Act.pdf; U.S. Senate Judiciary Committee *The First Step Act Section by Section Analysis*, https://www.judiciary.senate.gov/imo/media/doc/S.%203649%20-%20First%20Step%20Act%20Section-by-Section.pdf; Brandon Sample, *First Step Act: A Comprehensive Analysis* (December 19, 2018), https://sentencing.net/legislation/first-step-act; Alan Ellis and Mark H. Allenbaugh, INSIGHT: *The First Step Act of 2018—A Significant First Step in Sentencing Reform*, https://news.bloomberglaw.com/white-collar-and-criminal-law/insight-the-first-step-act-of-2018-a-significant-first-step-in-sentencing-reform.

61 United States Sentencing Commission, Office of Education & Sentencing Practice newsletter *The First Step Act* (February 2019) at https://www.ussc.gov/sites/default/files/pdf/training/newsletters/2019-special_FIRST-STEP-Act.pdf.

62 U.S. Senate Judiciary Committee *The First Step Act Section by Section Analysis*, https://www.judiciary.senate.gov/imo/media/doc/S.%203649%20-%20First%20Step%20Act%20Section-by-Section.pdf.

63 See Modification of an Imposed Term of Imprisonment, 18 U.S.C. 3582(c)(1)(A)(i).

64 Barry Goldwater, *The Conscience of a Conservative* (1960): 28–30; Barry Goldwater's acceptance speech at the Republican Convention on July 16, 1964. ("We Republicans seek a government. ... Our towns and our cities, then our counties, then our states, then our regional contacts—and only then, the national government.")

65 Ronald Reagan, Speech by the Governor to the National Sheriffs' Association—Riviera Hotel—Las Vegas, Nevada, June 19, 1967.

Chapter 9

1 U.S. Sentencing Commission, Collateral Consequences: The Crossroads of Punishment, Redemption, and the Effects on Communities, https://www.usccr.gov/pubs/2019/06-13-Collateral-Consequences.pdf.

2 He was appointed in December 2001 and took his seat in May 2002 and then was reappointed in January 2006 and reappointed for a third term by Speaker of the House Paul Ryan in 2013, which will end in December 2019.

3 U.S. Sentencing Commission, Collateral Consequences at 146–47 (emphasis in original).

4 See, EJI, Red Summer of 1919, https://eji.org/reports/online/lynching-in-america-targeting-black-veterans/red-summer and Christina Maxouris, "100 Years Ago, White Mobs across the Country Attacked Black People. And They Fought Back," *CNN*, July 27, 2019, https://www.cnn.com/2019/07/27/us/red-summer-1919-racial-violence/index.html.

5 Abigail Higgins, "Red Summer of 1919: How Black WWI Vets Fought Back Against Racist Mobs: When Dozens of Brutal Race Riots Erupted across the United States in the Wake of World War I and the Great Migration, Black Veterans Stepped Up to Defend Their Communities Against White Violence," History Channel, July 26, 2019, https://www.history.com/news/red-summer-1919-riots-chicago-dc-great-migration.

6 Supra note 4. See also, David F. Krugler, 1919, The Year of Racial Violence: How African Americans Fought Back (2014).

7 Kelly M. Hoffman, Sophie Trawalter, Jordan R. Axt, and M. Norman Oliver. "Racial Bias in Pain Assessment and Treatment Recommendations, and False Beliefs about Biological Differences between Blacks And Whites," *Proceedings of the National Academy of Sciences* 113, no. 16 (2016): 4296–301, 4299.

8 Id. at 4299.

9 Id.

10 Id. at 4300.

11 Id. at 4297.

12 Id.

13 See Racial and Ethnic Disparities in Obstetrics and Gnecology. Committee Opinion No. 649. American College of Obstetricians and Gynecologists. *Journal of American College of Obstetricians and Gynecologists* (December 2015): 126:e130–4; William A. Grobman, Jennifer L. Bailit, Madeline Murguia Rice, Ronald J. Wapner, Uma M. Reddy, Michael W. Varner, John M. Thorp Jr et al., "Racial and Ethnic Disparities in Maternal Morbidity and Obstetric Care," *Obstetrics and Gynecology* 125, no. 6 (2015): 1460; Allison S. Bryant, Ayaba Worjoloh, Aaron B. Caughey, and A. Eugene Washington. "Racial/Ethnic Disparities in Obstetric Outcomes and Care: Prevalence and Determinants," *American Journal of Obstetrics and Gynecology* 202, no. 4 (2010): 335–43; Andreea A. Creanga, Brian T. Bateman, Elena V. Kuklina, and William M. Callaghan, "Racial and Ethnic Disparities in Severe Maternal Morbidity: A Multistate Analysis, 2008–2010," American Journal of Obstetrics and Gynecology 210, no. 5 (2014): 435-e1; Carmen R. Green, Karen O. Anderson, Tamara A. Baker, Lisa C. Campbell, Sheila Decker, Roger B. Fillingim, Donna A. Kaloukalani, et al., "The Unequal Burden of Pain: Confronting Racial and Ethnic Disparities in Pain," *Pain Medicine* 4, no. 3 (2003): 277–94; Alan Nelson, "Unequal Treatment: Confronting Racial and Ethnic Disparities in Health Care," *Journal of the National Medical Association* 94, no. 8 (2002): 666; Vickie L. Shavers and Martin L. Brown, "Racial and Ethnic Disparities in the Receipt of Cancer Treatment," *Journal of the National Cancer Institute* 94, no. 5 (2002): 334–57; Kevin Fiscella, Peter Franks, Marthe R. Gold, and Carolyn M. Clancy, "Inequality in Quality: Addressing Socioeconomic, Racial, and Ethnic Disparities in Health Care," *Jama* 283, no. 19 (2000): 2579–84.

14 Sophie Trawalter, Kelly M. Hoffman, and Adam Waytz, "Racial Bias in Perceptions of Others' Pain," *PloS ONE* 7, no. 11 e48546 (2012): 1–8.

15 Joseph A. Flaherty and Robert Meagher, "Measuring Racial Bias in Inpatient Treatment," *The American Journal of Psychiatry* (1980):

679–82. See also endnote 65. For a counter result finding no implicit racial bias, see Adam T. Hirsh, Nicole A. Hollingshead, Leslie Ashburn-Nardo, and Kurt Kroenke, "The Interaction of Patient Race, Provider Bias, and Clinical Ambiguity on Pain Management Decisions," *The Journal of Pain,* 16: 6 (June 2015): 558–68.

16 Arthur H. Garrison, "Disproportionate Incarceration of African Americans: What History and the First Decade of Twenty-First Century Have Brought," *Journal Institute of Justice & International Studies* 11 (2011): 87; John Knowles, Nicola Persico, and Petra Todd, "Racial Bias in Motor Vehicle Searches: Theory and Evidence, *Journal of Political Economy* 109, no. 1 (2001): 203–29; Joshua Correll, Bernadette Park, Charles M. Judd, Bernd Wittenbrink, Melody S. Sadler, and Tracie Keesee," Across the Thin Blue Line: Police Officers and Racial Bias in the Decision to Shoot," *Journal of Personality and Social Psychology* 92, no. 6 (2007): 1006; Shamena Anwar and Hanming Fang, "An Alternative Test of Racial Prejudice in Motor Vehicle Searches: Theory and Evidence," *American Economic Review* 96, no. 1 (2006): 127–51; Kate Antonovics and Brian G. Knight, "A New Look at Racial Profiling: Evidence from the Boston Police Department," *The Review of Economics and Statistics* 91, no. 1 (2009): 163–77; Arthur Garrison, "Disproportionate Minority Arrests, the Police and Juveniles: A Note on What Has Been Said and How It Fits Together," *New England Journal on Criminal and Civil Confinement Law Review* 23(1): (1997) 29–61.

17 Tara L. Mitchell, Ryann M. Haw, Jeffrey E. Pfeifer, and Christian A. Meissner. "Racial Bias in Mock Juror Decision-Making: A Meta-Analytic Review of Defendant Treatment," *Law and Human Behavior* 29, no. 6 (2005): 621–37; Samuel R. Sommers and Phoebe C. Ellsworth, "White Juror Bias: An Investigation of Prejudice against Black Defendants in the American Courtroom," *Psychology, Public Policy, and Law* 7, no. 1 (2001): 201; Samuel R. Sommers and Phoebe C. Ellsworth, "Race in the Courtroom: Perceptions of Guilt and Dispositional Attributions," *Personality and Social Psychology Bulletin* 26, no. 11 (2000): 1367–79; Christopher S. Jones and Martin F. Kaplan, "The Effects of Racially Stereotypical

Crimes on Juror Decision-Making and Information-Processing Strategies," *Basic and Applied Social Psychology* 25, no. 1 (2003): 1–13.

18 Ashleigh Shelby Rosette, Geoffrey J. Leonardelli, and Katherine W. Phillips, "The White Standard: Racial Bias in Leader Categorization," *Journal of Applied Psychology* 93, no. 4 (2008): 758; Beth G. Chung-Herrera and Melenie J. Lankau, "Are We There Yet? An Assessment of Fit between Stereotypes of Minority Managers and the Successful-Manager Prototype," *Journal of Applied Social Psychology* 35, no. 10 (2005): 2029–56; Thomas Sy, Lynn M. Shore, Judy Strauss, Ted H. Shore, Susanna Tram, Paul Whiteley, and Kristine Ikeda-Muromachi, "Leadership Perceptions as a Function of Race–Occupation Fit: The Case of Asian Americans," *Journal of Applied Psychology* 95, no. 5 (2010): 902; Andrew M. Carton and Ashleigh Shelby Rosette, "Explaining Bias against Black Leaders: Integrating Theory on Information Processing and Goal-Based Stereotyping," *Academy of Management Journal* 54, no. 6 (2011): 1141–58.

19 Carol K. Sigelman, Lee Sigelman, Barbara J. Walkosz, and Michael Nitz, "Black Candidates, White Voters: Understanding Racial Bias in Political Perceptions," *American Journal of Political Science* (1995): 243–65; Candidates, When White Voters Evaluate Black. "Color, Prejudice, and Self-Monitoring," *American Journal of Political Science* 37, no. 4 (1993): 1032–53; Jack Citrin, Donald Philip Green, and David O. Sears, "White Reactions to Black Candidates: When Does Race Matter?" Public opinion quarterly 54, no. 1 (1990): 74–96; Benjamin Highton, "White Voters and African American Candidates for Congress," *Political Behavior* 26, no. 1 (2004): 1–25; Monika L. McDermott, "Race and Gender Cues in Low-Information Elections," *Political Research Quarterly* 51, no. 4 (1998): 895–918; Tasha S. Philpot and Hanes Walton Jr. "One of our Own: Black Female Candidates and the Voters who Support Them, *American Journal of Political Science* 51, no. 1 (2007): 49–62.

20 In 2018 the FBI reported that 37% of missing and kidnapped children are Black but black children are more likely to be declared

as runaways by police. Black families are more likely not to report missing children to the police due to fear and distrust of police agencies and have less financial ability to mount and maintain media coverage of their missing children. See, Harmeet Kaur, "Black kids go missing at a higher rate than white kids. Here's why we don't hear about them" *CNN* (November 3, 2019) at https://www.cnn.com/2019/11/03/us/missing-children-of-color-trnd/index.html.

21 See, Min, Seong-Jae, and John C. Feaster. "Missing children in national news coverage: Racial and gender representations of missing children cases." *Communication Research Reports* 27 (3) (2010): 207–216 and Moss, Jada L. "The Forgotten Victims of Missing White Woman Syndrome: An Examination of Legal Measures That Contribute to the Lack of Search and Recovery of Missing Black Girls and Women." *William and Mary Journal of Race Gender and Social Justice.* 25(3) (2018): 737.

22 See *Inside Edition*, "Cop Tells Black Realtor and Prospective Buyer to 'Quit Playing the Race Card' as They're Detained," July 18, 2019, https://www.insideedition.com/cop-tells-black-realtor-and-prospective-buyer-quit-playing-race-card-theyre-detained-54562 and *Black Real Estate Agent and Client Handcuffed at Gunpoint After White Retired Cop Calls 911 to Report an Alleged Break-In*, Video, https://atlantablackstar.com/2019/07/17/video-black-real-estate-agent-and-client-handcuffed-at-gunpoint-after-white-retired-cop-calls-911-to-report-an-alleged-break-in/.

23 Mihir Zaveri, "Man Who Fired at a Black Teenager Asking for Directions Is Convicted," *New York Times,* October 13, 2018, https://www.nytimes.com/2018/10/13/us/jeffrey-zeigler-brennan-walker-trial.html and Aileen Wingblad, "Jeffrey Zeigler Sentenced to at Least 4 Years for Firing at Rochester Hills Teen," *The Oakland Press,* November 13, 2018, https://www.theoaklandpress.com/news/copscourts/jeffrey-zeigler-sentenced-to-at-least-years-for-firing-at/article_911fc15e-e767-11e8-80c0-2f8c93f06f6f.html.

24 See, Phillip Atiba Goff, Matthew Christian Jackson, Brooke Allison Lewis Di Leone, Carmen Marie Culotta and Natalie Ann DiTomasso, "The Essence of Innocence; Consequences of Dehumanizing Black

Children," *Journal of Personality and Social Psychology* 106, no. 4 (2014): 526.

25 Kimberly Crawford, "Review of Deadly Force Incident: Tamir Rice" at http://prosecutor.cuyahogacounty.us/pdf_prosecutor/en-US/Tamir%20Rice%20Investigation/Crawford-Review%20of%20Deadly%20Force-Tamir%20Rice.pdf, Timothy J. McGinty *Cuyahoga County Prosecutor's Final Report* at http://prosecutor.cuyahogacounty.us/pdf_prosecutor/en-US/Rice%20Case%20Report%20FINAL%20FINAL%2012-28a.pdf and sworn incident statements by Officer Tmothy Loehmann and officer Frank Garback at http://i2.cdn.turner.com/cnn/2015/images/12/01/officer.garmback.statement.pdf and https://i2.cdn.turner.com/cnn/2015/images/12/01/officer.loehmann.statement.pdf. See also,

26 Id. See also, John Wilson, Hugenberg, Kurt, and Rule, Nicholas, "Racial Bias in Judgments of Physical Size and Formidability: From Size to Threat," *Journal of Personality and Social Psychology* 113, no 7 2017: 59. See also, Anti-Defamation League, "Race, Perception and Implicit Bias: Table Talk: Family Conversations About Current Events" (n.d.) at https://www.adl.org/education/resources/tools-and-strategies/table-talk/race-perception-and-implicit-bias and AJ Willingham, "Study: We think black men are bigger than white men (even when they're not)" *CNN* (March 14, 2017) at https://www.cnn.com/2017/03/13/health/black-men-larger-study-trnd/index.html.

27 See, Jamilia J. Blacke and Rebecca Epstein, *Listening to Black Women and Girls: Lived Experiences of Adultification Bias*, Georgetown Law Center on Poverty and Inequity: Initiative on Gender Justice and Opportunity (2017). See also, P.R. Lockhart, "A new report shows how racism and bias deny black girls their childhoods 'Black girls are not getting the benefits of being viewed as innocent.'" *VOX* (May 16, 2019) at https://www.vox.com/identities/2019/5/16/18624683/black-girls-racism-bias-adultification-discipline-georgetown.

28 Maxwell Tani, "Trump on God: 'I Don't Like to Have to Ask for Forgiveness,'" *Business Insider*, January 17, 2016, https://www.businessinsider.com/trump-on-god-i-dont-like-to-have-to-ask-for-forgiveness-2016-1.

29 Chris Cillizza, Donald Trump's latest conspiracy theory target? Fox News, *CNN* (August 19, 2019) at https://www.cnn.com/2019/08/19/politics/donald-trump-fox-news/index.html.

30 Caitlin O'Kane, "'Fox isn't working for us anymore': President Trump promises to find a new outlet" *CBS News* (August 29, 2019) at https://www.cbsnews.com/news/fox-news-donald-trump-tweet-fox-isnt-working-for-us-anymore-2019-08-28/.

31 Jake Tapper, "Trump called Fox News correspondent into Oval Office to argue he wasn't wrong about Alabama" *CNN* (September 5, 2019) at https://www.cnn.com/2019/09/05/politics/donald-trump-alabama-fox-news-white-house/index.html.

32 President Trump Marathon Speech at Turning Point USA—Full Speech, July 23, 2019 (2:30–3:35), https://www.youtube.com/watch?v=1E8IpeWoYCc.

33 Donald Trump: "Two Corinthians ... ," C-SPAN, https://www.youtube.com/watch?v=8EIgHsGZAmk.

34 Eric Bradner, "Trump Blames Tony Perkins for '2 Corinthians,'" *CNN*, January 21, 2016, https://www.cnn.com/2016/01/20/politics/donald-trump-tony-perkins-sarah-palin/index.html.

35 See transcript of *60 Minutes* Interview of Stormy Daniels with Anderson Cooper, March 25, 2018, https://www.usatoday.com/story/news/politics/2018/03/25/transcript-stormy-daniels-60-minutes-interview/457437002/.

36 "You know, I'm automatically attracted to beautiful—I just start kissing them. It's like a magnet. Just kiss. I don't even wait. And when you're a star, they let you do it. You can do anything. Grab 'em by the pussy. You can do anything." Transcript of the *Access Hollywood* tape, https://www.nytimes.com/2016/10/08/us/donald-trump-tape-transcript.html.

37 Trump Twitter Archive, http://www.trumptwitterarchive.com/.

38 Id. ("Why are we sending thousands of ill-trained soldiers into Ebola infested areas of Africa! Bring the plague back to the United States? Obama is so stupid.") (September 19, 2014).

39 Id. ("Congressman John Lewis should spend more time fixing and helping his district, which is in horrible shape and falling apart (not

to mention crime infested) rather than falsely complaining about election results.") (January 14, 2017).

40 See Chapter 3.

41 Donald Trump Speaks at the 400th Anniversary of the Jamestown Assembly, July 30, 2019, https://www.youtube.com/watch?v=BUTGUIdKFfk.

42 Trump on accuser: "She would not be my first choice," https://www.youtube.com/watch?v=CAEh2GH6c9E.

43 Donald Trump, Megyn Kelly Feud HIGHLIGHTS, https://www.youtube.com/watch?v=CAEh2GH6c9E.

44 For an example of the progressive theory that America's best days are behind her see, Christopher Layne, "The End of Pax Americana: How Western Decline Became Inevitable: The Euro-Atlantic World Had a Long Run of Global Dominance, but It Is Coming to an End." *The Atlantic,* April 26, 2012, https://www.theatlantic.com/international/archive/2012/04/the-end-of-pax-americana-how-western-decline-became-inevitable/256388/.

45 For example, see, John Fonte, "Who Makes the 'Rules' in a 'Rules-Based' Liberal Global Order?" American Greatness, August 12, 2019, https://amgreatness.com/2019/08/12/who-makes-the-rules-in-a-rules-based-liberal-global-order/.

46 For example, bemoanment of "the end of Pax Americana; the end of a generally benign U.S. hegemony; the end of U.S. support for a global system created by America and her allies after the Second World War." See "America First and the End of Pax Americana," *Europe Now,* November 7, 2018, https://www.europenowjournal.org/2018/11/07/america-first-and-the-end-of-pax-americana/ written by Stuart P.M. Mackintosh the executive director of the Group of Thirty, which is an international financial think tank, the very type of organization Trump and his voters despise.

47 For example, see Frank Gale, National Second vice president, Grand Lodge, Fraternal Order of Police, Denver Colorado, opening statement opposing Senate Bill 1670—Ending Racial Profiling Act of 2011 (April 17, 2012), https://www.govinfo.gov/content/pkg/CHRG-112shrg20969/html/CHRG-112shrg20969.htm. ("This bill provides a solution to a problem that does not exist unless one

believes that the problem to be solved is that our Nation's law enforcement officers are patently racist and that their universal training is based in practicing racism. This notion makes no sense, especially to anyone who truly understands the challenges we face protecting the communities we serve. ... There is the mistaken perception on the part of some that the ugliness of racism is part of the culture of law enforcement. I am here today not only to challenge this perception, but to refute it entirely.") For written statement, see https://fop.net/CmsDocument/Doc/tst_20120417.pdf. The bill died in committee in both the House and Senate.

48 Ronald Reagan, Speech by the Governor to the National Sheriffs' Association—Riviera Hotel—Las Vegas, Nevada June 19, 1967; Ronald Reagan, Remarks in New Orleans, Louisiana, at the Annual Meeting of the International Association of Chiefs of Police, September 28, 1981.

49 Elizabeth Chuck, "How Training Doctors in Implicit Bias Could Save the Lives of Black Mothers: Black Women Are Three to Four Times More Likely than White Women to Die of Pregnancy-Related Causes. Doctors Are Taking a New Approach to the Crisis," *NBC News*, May 11, 2018, https://www.nbcnews.com/news/us-news/how-training-doctors-implicit-bias-could-save-lives-black-mothers-n873036; Erika Stallings, "This Is How the American Healthcare System Is Failing Black Women: Racial Bias in Medical Care Is Real—and It Put These Women's Lives at Risk," *O, the Oprah Magazine*, August 1, 2018, https://www.oprahmag.com/life/health/a23100351/racial-bias-in-healthcare-black-women/; Michael O. Schroeder, "Racial Bias in Medicine Leads to Worse Care for Minorities: Mounting Research Finds That Facing Discrimination, in General, Is a Risk Factor for Poor Health," *U.S. News and World Reports*, February 11, 2016, https://health.usnews.com/health-news/patient-advice/articles/2016-02-11/racial-bias-in-medicine-leads-to-worse care-for-minorities; Looking for the Roots of Racial Bias in Delivery of Health Care, September 6, 2011, https://www.hopkinsmedicine.org/news/media/releases/looking_for_the_roots_of_racial_bias_in_delivery_of_healhcare.

50 Henry Louis Gates, *Black America Since MLK and Still We Rise,* PBS documentary, 2016.

51 Id.

52 Id.

53 Id.

54 Id.

55 Id.

Index

www.ingramcontent.com/pod-product-compliance
Lightning Source LLC
Chambersburg PA
CBHW020652270326

41928CB00005B/82